International City Management Association

D0066599

The International City Management Association is the professional and educational organization for chief appointed management executives in local government. The purposes of ICMA are to strengthen the quality of local government through professional management and to develop and disseminate new approaches to management through training programs, information services, and publications.

Managers, carrying a wide range of titles, serve cities, towns, counties, and councils of governments in all parts of the United States and Canada. These managers serve at the direction of elected councils and governing boards. ICMA serves these managers and local governments through many programs that aim at improving the manager's professional competence and strengthening the quality of all local governments.

The International City Management Association was founded in 1914; adopted its City Management Code of Ethics in 1924; and established its Institute for Training in Municipal Administration in 1934. The Institute, in turn, provided the basis for the Municipal Management Series, generally termed the "ICMA Green Books." ICMA's interests and activities include public management education; standards of ethics for members; *The Municipal Year Book* and other data services; urban research; and newsletters, a monthly magazine, *Public Management*, and other publications. ICMA's efforts for the improvement of local government management—as represented by this book—are offered for all local governments and for educational institutions.

Municipal Management Series

Management of Local Planning

Municipal Management Series

Management of Local Planning

Published by the
International
City
Management
Association

David C. Slater
Vice President
Hammer, Siler,
George Associates

In cooperation
with the
ICMA
Training Institute

Municipal Management Series

Library of Congress Cataloging in Publication Data

Slater, David C.
  Management of local planning.
  (Municipal management series)
  Bibliography: p
  Includes index.
  1. Municipal government—Planning.   2. Local govern-
ment—Planning.   I. Title.   II. Series.
JS145.S53   1984   352.9'6   84–6577
ISBN 0–87326–031–7
ISBN 0–87326–032–5 (pbk.)

Printed in the United States of America.
1 2 3 4 5 90 89 88 87 86 85 84

Management of
Local Planning

is dedicated to the planners and managers
who have struggled—often at great odds or
at personal sacrifice—to bring long-range
perspectives, the interrelatedness of issues,
and equity to local government decision making.

Foreword

Part of my graduate education in urban planning at the University of Illinois included a hefty dose of the third edition of the ICMA planning bible, *Local Planning Administration*, and some review work on the fourth edition, *Principles and Practice of Urban Planning*, then being edited by two of my professors, William Goodman and Eric Freund. When the fifth edition, *The Practice of Local Government Planning*, was published in 1979, it was evident that local planning had become very diverse and functionally specialized. In the five years since publication of that book, a new set of professional challenges has altered the nature of planning as it penetrates the center of local government management and policy.

Having previewed David Slater's *Management of Local Planning*, I can assure the reader that these issues have been effectively treated in the context of planning principles which have remained amazingly consistent over time. The substance of this excellent work reveals a planning practice in lively transition to a more influential and effective future.

The central thrust of this book is recognition of the now stronger role of planning in relation to both management and public policy decision making within city and county governments. This exciting development demands that planners acquire new professional skills, especially in management and administration, financial and strategic planning, written and oral communication, computer utilization, negotiation, and conflict management. *Management of Local Planning* deals responsibly with these issues and broadens the conceptual reach of planning as an integral factor in the daily practice of local government management.

While *The Practice of Local Government Planning* focused on the wide range of subjects within the purview of planning, *Management of Local Planning* turns attention to the central relationships between planning and management, has a stronger focus on necessary skills for planners, and deals with the importance of the linkages required for planning to be *effective* at the local level (i.e., a better understanding of the political process, information sharing, networking, and consensus building).

Planning *is* management and management is the *effective implementation* of planning. Let us divest ourselves of jurisdictional barriers artificially circumscribing inviolate "territories" to each of these critical functions. The essential diffusion of conceptual and philosophical limitations between managers and planners is now. We need each other.

"The last shall be first . . . and the first shall be last." In my judgment, the final chapter on values and ethics should be the framework within which this book delivers its important message. All technical, professional, and operational achievements will ultimately be judged within the parameters of an understood set of relatively well-defined ethical standards and values. The professional challenge is to plan and manage competently, with a sense of fairness and equity, in the public interest.

The acquisition of more sophisticated technical skills through continuing education and on-the-job training is vital to the competitive livelihood of planners and planning. Elected county executives, mayors, appointed county administrators, and city managers understand the importance of good planning to the process of effective decision making. Professional planners must experience, understand, and appreciate the atmospheric and practical complexities of decision making in order to become valued and credible participants in the process.

The art of making responsible, competent, and ethically proper public decisions emanates from the crucible of a good education, a solid core of ethical standards, continuing professional development, hard work, dedication, loyalty, a strong sense of the public good, prudent judgment, and sufficient experience in the "school of hard knocks." Only with these ingredients can we expect to wrestle successfully with the incredibly complicated public policy dilemmas inherent in those issues requiring a balanced judgment among the competing interests of long vs. short range planning, comprehensive vs. project planning, neighborhood vs. downtown emphasis, physical vs. social/economic considerations, public vs. private interests, and political vs. technical and administrative concerns.

A "revival of the spirit" is in order for managers and planners. A renewed sense of enthusiasm is central to a positive attitude and approach concerning job performance, goal achievement, and relations with family, friends, peers, employees, and the community at large. Excitement is infectious, and a sustained sense of perseverance will produce positive results on a regular basis. Professionals should consider courses in executive management leadership, occasional periods of mental revitalization (meditation, retreats, and vacations), mentor exchanges, and other methods of staying at the cutting edge of one's potential.

Reading *Management of Local Planning* will provide a strong intellectual foundation for a greater understanding of the significant integration of two highly related professional disciplines. Its lessons will help us all become better professionals, improve the quality of public decisions, and ultimately have a long-term positive impact on the quality of life in our communities.

Michael A. Carroll, AICP
Director of Community Development

Lilly Endowment, Inc.
Indianapolis, Indiana

Preface

This is a book on the interrelatedness of planning and management in local government, on how local government planners can be more effective in solving problems through the governmental process.

Management of Local Planning describes ways that the planning process is being redefined as it moves into the mainstream of city and county government. It was not a great many years ago that the perception of planning was limited to land use and to zoning and subdivision controls. In recent years, however, many planning directors and planning staff members have become indispensable advisors to mayors, elected council and board members, city and county managers, and others in highly responsible positions in city and county government. Planning is now a built-in part of both operating and capital budgets as well as the implementation of projects.

As planning is brought closer to governmental decisions, planning leadership has enlarged its contributions from technical skills to a mix of technical and political contributions to the resolution of problems. Both elected officials and city and county managers will benefit because planners now can bring their unique perspective—the interrelatedness of issues, and long-range values—to a larger setting.

As local government gets more complicated, those of us in local government management need the skills of planners to support streamlined decision making, equity in policies and services, and long-term solutions to vital issues.

One of the major contributions of this book is to show how planning is a process that builds on the contributions from many people in striving for consensus. It is a sign of maturity in both planning and management that we no longer expect planners to provide prescriptive, ultimate solutions or precise, irrefutable forecasts.

Management of Local Planning takes its place in the Municipal Management Series, the Green Books published since 1935 by the International City Management Association. This book bridges *The Practice of Local Government Planning*, which covers a wide range of planning principles and methods, and *The Effective Local Government Manager*, which places local government management in the setting of internal effectiveness and external sensitivity.

The author of *Management of Local Planning*, David C. Slater, brings a rich background in consulting, planning, and teaching to his authoritative coverage of planning and management. He has observed and worked with city, county, regional, and state planning agencies in more than 100 jurisdictions in the United States and Canada. As part of his work for this book he interviewed planners and managers in many cities and counties across the country to develop case histories. We are grateful for the enthusiasm and skill David Slater has brought to writing this book.

The Municipal Management Series is the responsibility of Barbara H. Moore,

Senior Editor, ICMA. Other ICMA staff members who worked on this book were David S. Arnold, who had primary editorial responsibility; Cecilia Claire Blankinship, who assisted in the preparation of many of the figures; and Christine Ulrich, who assisted in the final checking of manuscript, figures, and sidebars. We are grateful also to the many other persons who have helped in developing the book. These persons are shown in the Acknowledgments.

William H. Hansell, Jr.
Executive Director

International City
Management Association

Contents

Figures

Tables

The context of public planning

This book is about the ways that planners and managers in city and county governments:

Apply the skills of comprehensive and project planning, budgeting, negotiation, personnel management, and communication.

Bring public, quasi-public, and private interests together.

Transform policies and proposals into completed work.

Planners bring to these institutions and processes their expertise in interrelating public issues, in providing long-range perspectives, and in allocating capital resources. Managers bring to the same setting their expertise in serving the needs of officials while balancing resources and facilitating the delivery of public services. The qualities brought to the job by planners and managers are thus the sum of their education and experience, both of which help to shape their values, opinions, and work habits.

With the growing number of planning and management clients, however, both professions have had to redefine and expand their roles. As a result, the two have become more and more interrelated. As it is, planners already engage in management when they are involved in local government decision making, and managers engage in planning when they strive to balance needs and resources against local demands as well as the forces outside local control.

Many planners believe that in addition managers should bring a longer-range perspective to their work by spending more time analyzing the possible outcomes of their recommendations. Meanwhile, many managers expect planners to spend more time on managing their responsibilities effectively.

A primary goal of all planners and managers in local government today is to improve the quality of public policy outcomes. That means further changes can be expected. In other words, to achieve this goal, planners will have to engage in more management and managers in more planning than has traditionally been the case.

The purposes of this book

This book is intended to help planners become better managers in the thousands of cities and counties in the United States and Canada that provide roads, streets, water supply, education, social services, police and fire protection, and other first-line services to people. Implicit in these services is a panoply of investment decisions for economic development; capital facility development; social service expansion, contraction, and change; and physical land use change affecting the lives, and livelihood, of millions of people.

Planners know they must be good managers to be effective, that is, to see their recommendations realized and their objectives achieved. But it is not easy for most planners to change or augment their beliefs and values when their professional backgrounds stress long-range goals, social equity, design and esthetics, and analytical processes. Management is much more concerned with work programs that are short-range, immediate, action oriented, and results oriented. The central theme of this book is that each needs the other and that the points of common interest and gain substantially outnumber the differences. The theme is developed through the discussion of three broad topics:

1. Institutions and people involved in planning and management, including the local government chief administrator (mayor, city manager, county manager); elected officials; other government officials such as planning board members, local government managers, and employees; citizen groups and associations; and individual citizens.
2. Methods for improving planning and management, including new approaches to long-term and short-term planning; financial planning; community relations; and the management of personnel, information, and communication.
3. Processes at the heart of planning and management, such as working with elected officials, negotiating large-scale developments, establishing financial policies, measuring citizen input, formulating information policies, and working with consultants.

Subsequent sections of this chapter outline the interactive elements of planning and management, including characteristics of planning for the 1980s, changes in education and skills in planning and public administration, political influence, managers' perceptions of planners, planners' perceptions of managers, and ways of improving public policy.

From definitions to characteristics

In the early twentieth century when the planning and management professions were in their infancy and had just evolved from issues of urban development and municipal government reform, the practitioners by and large were the ones to define their professions. People trained in the principles and practices of engineering, architecture, landscape architecture, and accounting found that they had some of the answers to problems of planning and management. That is to say, they had the knowledge needed to deal with traffic, housing, water quality, and open space issues. As they worked on these problems, the practitioners of these professions were led to seek out others with common experiences. This need for networking—no less important seventy years ago than it is today—led them to develop a body of information on problem definition, analytical methods, alternative solutions, and successful implementation.

Planning and management were easy to define when the big issues were zoning, subdivisions, and economy and efficiency, but this situation changed rapidly after the late 1930s, when the federal government came into the picture. In addition suburbanization after the Second World War increased the need for effective planning and management in many more local governments. Since the end of World War II, planning concepts and definitions have evolved (and once or twice changed abruptly) through the growth of planning law and education in the 1950s, the citizen participation movement that came to fruition in the 1960s, the tax limitation and cutback movement of the 1970s, and the economic development movement of the 1980s.

Planning became a controversial issue in the 1960s when, for complex sociological and political reasons, citizen participation increased greatly. In particular, citizens became interested in public programs, many of which they considered detrimental to neighborhoods, housing, and the quality of life. With this response came a shift in the definitions of planning and management, as the professionals listened more and more to the consumers of their work. The consumers said, "Wait a minute; we are not satisfied with the results." Of course, the citizens were right. Many of the massive highway, housing, and other public

Figure 1–1   Scottsdale, Arizona—a village of just a few thousand people
in 1950—has coped well with the complexities of rapid growth that
brought its population to almost ninety thousand people in 1980. This
aerial photograph shows the Indian Bend Wash Greenbelt Flood Control
Project in Scottsdale. The mixed land uses include commercial,
residential, and recreational.

programs had disrupted, even destroyed, their way of live. What they asked in
response was that greater emphasis be placed on neighborhood planning and
on sensitivity to citizen needs.

Planning and management were greatly affected by this turn of events. For
one thing, single-issue neighborhood groups and local candidates for public office
introduced greater caution into planning and management. At the same time,
when the "movers and shakers" of the community could get together and chart
the direction of a policy, it was felt that the decisions could be implemented and
the job could be done. Although opening up this process did release more
information on the breadth of citizen concerns, it actually slowed the decision-
making process and impeded implementation. The effect, nonetheless, was to
put more planning and management into the hands of local government than it
had ever experienced before.

In the 1970s, however, people grew critical of increased planning and management. Tax revolts and resistance to expanding bureaucracies led to proposals
for cutting back staffs and programs. From one end of the country to the other,
ballot initiatives and political campaigns were waged on reducing the breadth
and depth of government. In addition, sharp reductions in federal funding for

local planning programs made hard choices inevitable, one outcome of which was reduced citizen control. As a result, planning shifted back to the domain of elected officials.

Local governments soon found themselves engaged in preparing two lists: essential and nonessential services. Planning often turned up on the nonessential list because it lacked the political constituency and the short-term payoff promised by other programs.

A time of austerity Localities are learning to live with tax and expenditure limitations, but the current efforts of the federal government to transfer certain program responsibilities to state and local governments make it likely that the greatest change affecting local governments will be de facto transfers of programs in social services, especially education, training, employment, and income security.

For the short term, most state and local governments face austerity, service reductions, revenue declines, and the unappetizing prospect of raising taxes, service charges, and other revenue sources. It is possible, however, to end this report on a more hopeful note. . . . Thirty-five states, along with a large number of cities, are encouraging citizen efforts to get ready for growth or decline—and to take steps to control

these processes. State government actions have been particularly noteworthy in providing preferential tax relief for open space, coastal zone management, and other aspects of land use and growth management. The time is propitious for a change in the adversary relationship that has hitherto characterized state-local relationships in many states. It is possible that both the states and local governments can revivify themselves in the 1980s if they develop a better understanding of the profound changes taking place in the economic and social structures that underpin government actions.

Source: David S. Arnold, "Significant State Actions Affecting Municipal Governments," *The Municipal Year Book, 1982* (Washington, D.C.: International City Management Association, 1983), 56, 59.

The 1980s have seen a new emphasis on local determination of local planning programs, perhaps the greatest such emphasis since federal support of these programs began in 1954. Local determination of planning programs means, in general, reducing programs, focusing on current local issues, and shortening the time horizon of recommendations.

Not only have local budget constraints played an important role in the definition of planning and management in the 1980s, but widespread unemployment has increased the importance of economic development. In spite of the fact that local elected officials have only marginal influence on the creation of additional jobs, many constituents think that action in this direction should be their top priority. In response to these pressures, elected officials have created economic development agencies (which now number about 4,500) and many business investment incentives. Public policies have been debated, passed, and implemented at all levels of government to promote job growth. Many of these programs have been keyed to public-private partnerships for development. As a result, local planning and management now has a new central role: to define *the required return on investment prior to planning for the level of service or type of land use to be accommodated*. The definitions of planning and management are no longer dominated by professional standards or by citizen preferences. They are dominated by local political support expressed in budget allocations, and by the likely return on the public investment.

Education and skills

Planning and management are relatively new disciplines in the academic community, having first appeared in the 1920s. Since that time, they have evolved in somewhat similar directions. That is, both planning and public administration programs teach theory, methods, techniques, and skills; both draw from the same fields: most notably, mathematics, communication, sociology, management, engineering, and law. Yet, many institutions of higher learning with both planning and management programs do not require students in one field to take courses in the other.

Accommodation planning

Many planning schools teach that reform is at the heart of the discipline. Others, however, teach that political accommodation is the ultimate purpose of the planning process.

The reformists say that there are technical solutions to society's ills and that in order to cure them institutions must be changed. Improving the quality of life can lead to fundamental changes in political institutions. Once these changes are accomplished, reformists say, communities will be better places in which to live.

Although a sound argument can be made for this view, the question remains: How can planners influence public policy when, in many communities, property owners, elected officials, and even some managers are highly resistant to planning? There is great pressure to balance the ledger, accomplish what you can in the short term, and accommodate investors' interests, even if it means compromising community development standards. So many of the current financial and political objectives are inconsistent with long-range, public-interest-oriented, high-quality communities that it is not surprising to find that tension exists between planners who advocate reforming the system and those who say that accommodation is the best way.

The accommodation approach to planning education places high value on identifying policy issues, working within the system to identify achievable targets, and doing whatever can be done to realize better rather than superior communities. Accommodation planners place high priority on the management of scarce resources and low priority on fundamentally changing institutions. If you place high value on working within the political system, focusing your energies on what others define as high-priority issues, reducing the number of targets of change to a manageable few, and being satisfied with piecemeal results, you may be an accommodation-oriented planner.[1]

Public administration values

To many, public administration education seems to be a more pragmatic discipline than planning education. If your primary purpose is to manage implementation rather than make public policy, your professional role is prescribed differently. Public administration education is less likely to emphasize institutional reform than is planning education. Rather, public administration education tends to emphasize different institutional settings as a framework for determining what the public administrator does. That is to say, institutions prescribe programs rather than the other way around.

Two especially important tenets of public administration are at odds with traditional planning education. First, the public administrator believes that top-down facilitation is the primary means of achieving organizational objectives.

Planners, on the other hand, believe that bottom-up identification of issues is the best way. Whereas the public administrator accepts the political definition of issues, the planner neither trusts this definition nor feels that it is sufficiently sensitive to the public interest.

The second point is that administrators believe the budget should be the guiding light in making and executing public policy. One of the reasons planning has not had more influence on public policy is that public administrators are reluctant to include planners in the process of allocating resources and setting priorities known as budget making. Some managers believe that if they share the responsibility for allocating resources with planners, it will be distorted by the planner's long-range and bottom-up values. Although this could happen, planners argue that nonetheless ways must be found to accommodate these values or community development will suffer.

Elements in common

Changing interests and values have not been the only problems to confront the academic community. The drop in graduate enrollments, the shrinking job market, and the budget cutbacks in graduate programs in planning and public administration have all taken their toll—limiting the number of institutions offering programs, prohibiting expansion of faculty and courses, and reducing research. Academic programs have also been affected by the accelerating changes in communications technology, and by the continuing search for the right "turf" to distinguish one academic program from another.

In view of these common problems, not to mention the interdisciplinary nature of both professions, it is surprising that relatively little effort has been made to promote cross-disciplinary teaching. Few students in either discipline are required to take courses in the other. Now and then, students who are aware of courses in the other area may select them when core curriculum requirements are out of the way. Only a small number of graduate schools have integrated the two disciplines in the same department and required courses be taken in each.

The "shelf life" of the planner and manager is shorter now than it has ever been. One of the reasons is that academic courses cannot keep up with all of the changes on the job. Another problem is that planning schools do not offer courses on how to manage planning offices; yet this is one of the first stumbling blocks to greet the first-time planning director. Although public administration programs typically offer little in the way of planning theory, local government managers, like the chief executives of any corporation, constantly face future-oriented issues. Technical change also contributes to the relatively short shelf-life of professionals. The new technology for acquiring, analyzing, and producing information cannot be utilized by planners or managers who are apprehensive about or unfamiliar with data, computers, and telecommunications.

Professors teach what they know. Therefore, if the profession changes and the professor doesn't, changes in the field may not become part of the curriculum. Like practitioners, professors have difficulty in keeping up with changes in the field. In addition, programs may suffer because tenured faculty usually have a lock on the limited number of faculty positions available, especially when the department is not growing or is being reduced in size. Without the opportunity for faculty expansion and turnover, programs are liable to experience perpetual sameness. This occurs at the expense of students who wish to begin their careers at least with a knowledge of the field as it exists upon their entrance into it. Many institutions of higher learning have resolved this problem by employing practitioners as part-time teachers. In this way, current information on evolving practices is shared with students.

Figure 1–2   The office professional, then and now. The top photo shows a
typical office at the turn of the century for a managerial/professional
employee. Note the telephone and the pen. The bottom photo, taken in
1984, shows an integrated work station for the office professional, with
a microcomputer, keyboard, and screen for data and graphics.
Multiple tasks can be displayed and simultaneously manipulated
through on-screen windows.

8 *Management of Local Planning*

Political influence

Planners are committed, because of their beliefs and professional values, to an out-front position on the future of the community: that is, to the long-range outlook, including both the good news and the bad news, and the interrelatedness of conditions that make political consensus so difficult to achieve. Public assertiveness about these kinds of questions can create political hazards for planners. Even so, many a planner has gone out on a limb to advocate policies and proposals among citizens, elected officials, and other staff.

Planners and politicans are at odds in some cases because "each believes he is best fitted—through training, experience, and institutional expectations—to serve the public as broker-mediator, coordinator, and goal-maker."[2] At times, their conflicting interests spawn irreconcilable differences of opinion. With experience, however, planners learn that not everyone can be satisfied on any given issue, and in settings like these they begin to hone their negotiating and reconciliating skills. Because they have had to develop these skills in this way, planners today are better able to serve the needs of elected and appointed officials. In fact, the planner is turning more and more to the political process to get the job done. He or she recognizes the limitations of the independent planning commission and knows that the elected official votes on questions that matter to the planner. Budget, staffing, development permission, plan adoption, and capital facility financing votes go a long way toward determining the relevance of the planner and politician to each other's interests.

Perhaps the area in which the planner can be of the greatest utility to the politician is in broadening the latter's perspective. Many have complained about the short-term horizon of the politician (which may be the result of the politician's personal interests as much as the necessity to return to the ballot box every two to four years). To the extent that the planner can translate long-term and interrelated perspectives into short-term benefits, the interests of the planner and politician will merge. As they do, the politician's self-image may change. The tentative may become assertive, the journeymen experts. And persons filled with questions may become persons filled with answers.

Managers look at planners

In the view of city and county managers, the principal problems of planners lie in the areas of communication and interpersonal relations. According to the interviews conducted for this book on the opinions of managers and planners about one another, some planners are thought to have the following problems:

1. The information they present is convoluted and obtuse.
2. Their work is too theoretical.
3. Research and reports arrive too late to be useful.
4. They are insensitive to the views and wishes of others.
5. They are dogmatic.

Managers complain primarily about the way planners communicate information. They are said to be verbose and methodologically mysterious. They use too many words to describe issues, analyses, and recommendations. Some of what they say is unclear, particularly analytical methods.

In addition, managers find the work of planners too theoretical, and their written and oral communication inapplicable in many cases to the situational dynamics that managers are especially sensitive to. Theory clearly has its place as a foundation for analysis, managers argue, but if the analysis does not include a full discussion of political issues, the planner can be criticized for not serving the needs of elected officials.

The third major criticism of planners is that their recommendations are usually based on research that is out of date by the time it is finished. At the community level, some planning staffs have taken years to prepare plans that are eventually put forth for the review of elected and appointed officials long after the issues have been moved to the archives. Some planning staffs are criticized for preparing memoranda with recommendations a day too late. Others are said to organize their work so poorly that too little time is available for writing and for the review of products.

Waiting until the last minute to prepare written materials may increase the time available for collecting information and thinking through it, but less time will be available between the arrival of the final product and the moment it will be acted on; this time squeeze minimizes the time available for review and maximizes the reviewer's irritation. It also increases the likelihood that proposals will be tabled rather than acted on.

As for the question of sensitivity, planners are sometimes found to be hostile toward developers or other applicants for development permission. This attitude may be caused by budget cutbacks and pressures to complete work within tight deadlines.

Finally, managers have been heard to say that planners are overzealous in applying their values and standards: "Planners frequently have a strong zeal to advocate their distinctive views on problems, but public administrators are more sensitive to compromise and are more willing to settle for 'half a loaf' in pursuing objectives."[3] Managers are not talking about ethical values here. They are referring to the application of development standards and principles, often learned in planning school, without adequate thought to compromises that may mean the difference between project implementation and the loss of the project to another community. No rules of thumb can be used to achieve the proper balance. Each situation is left up to the individual planner, who must know when to defend standards and when to compromise. Managers feel they are much more practiced at this than planners are.

Planners look at managers

When planners look at managers, they see a lack of understanding and commitment to planning that is coupled with needless compromises and a lack of planning authority commensurate with responsibility. According to planners, managers have the following types of problems:

1. They do not bring planners into budget preparation, the heart of the decision-making process in local government.
2. They have a narrow definition of planning.
3. They do not work at planning, especially strategic planning.
4. They are too willing to compromise over their proposals.
5. They do not give planners access to the internal information needed for analysis and reports.

The central concern of planners is that managers are unwilling to share with them the responsibility of allocating resources. Unless a city or county charter or ordinance requires it, or the planners possess unique information essential to budget making, planners generally are not asked to contribute to the process. In some cities, however, it has been acknowledged that the types of data planners work with and their intellectual perspectives are needed to prepare the budget. Although some managers recognize that employment, population, housing, income, and land use forecasts are essential inputs, most of them, it is said, believe that if planners are included, the influence of other persons already participating in the process will be reduced.

Another complaint is that some managers still believe that urban design, land

The bridge to tomorrow   A city manager cannot give proper consideration to all facets of community problems which we face in our urban environments without professional planning advice. Most professional people involved with delegated responsibilities for advising the manager and citizens concerning city management and policy making are operational people who historically concern themselves with the limited range of their responsibilities and tend, as a rule, to think on a short range basis. It must be true that the profession of city planner developed to fill the gap between everyday reality and long range planning.

Source: Paul D. Noland, "What Is the Importance of the Planner to City Management?" *Public Management* 51 (December 1969): 4.

use, and development permission are the only interests of planning. Regardless of the public policy, capital improvement programming, or the responsibilities many planners have in negotiating projects, some managers continue to equate planning with zoning. (Experienced planners of course know better.) The manager's narrow definition of planning also applies to the planner's responsibility, which thereby becomes less of a threat to the manager's authority.

A third criticism of the manager is that he or she spends far too little time in anticipating problems and selecting strategies to solve them. Many managers admit to this failing but are not sure how to correct it. The problem seems to stem from two factors. One is that the manager has neither education nor experience in planning and is unsure about how to establish a strategic planning system. Another problem, and one that should be emphasized, is the extraordinary number and frequency of nonpolicy tasks heaped on the manager by elected officials. It takes time not only to execute but also to anticipate them.

A further problem is that many planners think managers are too willing to compromise in order to get something achieved. The balance between drawing a line in the sand and maintaining one's standards will forever be debated, and there are neither prescriptions nor easy solutions to the continuing question of whether to hold out for a whole loaf or be willing to accept something less. Because planners have very little authority over spending decisions, their role remains one of competing in the arena of ideas and convincing others to follow suit.

Planning depends on information that is drawn from a wide variety of sources. Persuading individual city, county, and state departments to relinquish data they have gathered and analyzed can be a herculean task. Representatives of those departments frequently are suspicious about the use that might be made of the information. At other times, they are concerned that what they consider proprietary information will be shared with the wrong parties.

Without a sound data base or access to experts in other departments who have information, however, planners are forced into making unsubstantiated recommendations. Many planners think that managers should play a greater role in prying this information loose from other departments. Many managers, on the other hand, are reluctant to do so because they do not want to make their department heads unhappy, or they do not understand why the information is needed in the first place.

Working together

The perceptions of planners and managers set forth in the preceding sections of this chapter are significant because they affect the way in which the work of the local government gets done. It is not just a question of being nice, but rather of being empathetic and having a common commitment. In addition, planners and managers can take five specific steps to improve both planning and management.

1. Do not surprise elected officials.
2. Be prepared for elected officials.
3. Stay out of the technical closet.
4. Exploit the analytical skills of planners.
5. Program planning time and tasks for results.

Neither planners nor managers should ever surprise elected officials. The reason is that elected officials do not like to be embarrassed with questions about issues or recommendations they know nothing about. Therefore, all communication with elected officials should alert them to the issues, to the possible outcomes of alternative actions, and to the reasons that one action is preferred over another.

The importance of formal communication between staff members and elected officials cannot be overemphasized. If the staff is doing an inadequate job here, it is important to determine its shortcomings and work toward improvement. One effective way of improving communication is to rehearse council or board presentations. Without rehearsal, it is impossible to have flawless presentations.

Persons responsible for explaining and justifying planning department positions should not place themselves in a technical closet. It is extremely important for planners and managers to establish and maintain communication networks outside the office. Information received from these contacts can be used to define programs, responses to issues, and reasons for and against recommendations.

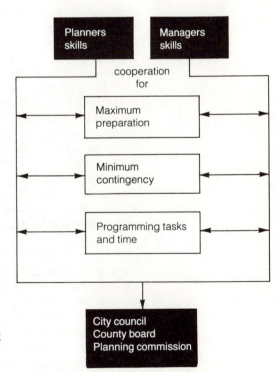

Figure 1–3 Working together for planning and management. If planners stay out of the technical closet, and managers exploit planners' skills, then both can work effectively with elected and appointed officials.

Managers should exploit the analytical and forecasting skills of planners for bottom-line resource allocations. As allocation decisions evolve by placing more and more emphasis on long-range implications, the data base, perspectives, and analytical methods used by planners will become increasingly useful tools for the manager.

One of the central lessons of cutback management is that time and analytical energies should be focused on the most important planning tasks of the day. Because less staff time is generally available for planning and managing, that time must be used effectively. The budget-making process is an excellent framework for anticipating important issues and programming staff time to help resolve them.

The role of the chief executive is important here. If the chief executive is to be responsible for the future of the organization, this task, of course, involves planning. The manager can improve public policy by planning for ways to do so, and planners can contribute to the management practices that buttress better policy. Managers can help elected officials by providing information on the possible outcomes of alternative decisions. Planners are in a position to provide this information and thus aid the manager.

An important point to clear up at this juncture is that planning and management, in this book, refer to professions that are unlike most other professions. They are *public* in their commitments and values. As has been noted elsewhere, city and county managers, for example, "have demonstrated that professional public service ethics and ideals, oriented to democratic values and processes, are not only eminently practical but of the essence of public administration in the United States."[4] Planners have worked toward the same context of public service, which could well be termed the essence of planning administration in the United States.

Planners can also be useful in helping anticipate outside or exogenous variables. Some communities are using information on interest rates, energy prices, inflation indexes, and federal legislation to aid in anticipating financial and community development problems. The planner's typical eclecticism and curiosity can serve the community and manager well in the investigation of these variables and in the determination of their effects on local issues.

The objectives of planners and managers are essentially the same: to improve public policy and the delivery of services. Although planners and managers still have their differences, they are in the same boat and will sail or sink together. Managers are finding that it is important to assume more planning responsibility if for no other reason than to avoid embarrassment in serving public policy makers. Planners, meanwhile, are finding that it is important to husband their limited resources and try to manage the outputs of the planning process more effectively. In the chapters that follow, ideas and techniques for these pursuits will be explored and examples of planning for management and the management of planning will be discussed.

To provide the setting, Chapter 2 reviews the historical development and changing nature of planning and management and the ways in which they are coming together in strategic planning. Chapters 3 and 4 cover organization for long- and short-term planning with particular reference to policy development, project negotiation, and the development permission process. Chapter 5 examines both budgeting and financial policies, while Chapter 6 describes community relations programs and ways of working with elected officials and citizens.

Chapter 7 turns to the internal management of the planning agency and reviews personnel management, the recruitment of employees, continuing education, and working with consultants. Chapters 8 and 9 deal with information and communication. The topics of interest here are objectives, performance measurement, information management, citizen feedback, written and oral communication, telecommunications, and other forms of communication.

The last chapter—which is concerned with values and ethics—suggests a way for the planner to look at himself or herself within the framework of both planning and management in an arena where the financial and political stakes are high.

1 Interview with Robert C. Einsweiler, 13 October 1983.
2 Norman Beckman, "The Planner as Bureaucrat," *Journal of the American Institute of Planners* 30 (November 1964): 3–4.
3 James M. Mayo, "Sources of Job Dissatisfaction: Ideals Versus Realities in Planning," *Journal of the* *American Planning Association* 48 (Autumn 1982): 490.
4 Chester A. Newland, "Professional Public Executives and Public Administration Agendas," in *Professional Public Executives*, ed. Chester A. Newland (Washington, D.C.: American Society for Public Administration, 1980), 26.

2 The blending of planning and management

In many cities and counties, especially the smaller ones, planning and management have been moving closer together for some time. Particularly since the early 1970s, more and more city managers, county managers, planners, budget officers, attorneys, finance directors, public works directors, and others have worked in teams in the search for solutions to local problems. One obvious sign of this change has been the move to bring departments of community development or planning into the office of the city or county manager. This is but one of the ways in which planning and management have been blended. That blending is the subject of this chapter.

The product of the blending is termed "strategic planning" here. Although some might argue that this is merely a new label for ancient work methods, there is more to it than that. As this chapter will show, the change has not just been a matter of introducing a systematic approach to problems, or a particular organization design, or specific goals. Rather, a fundamental change has come about in the philosophy and work methods of these disciplines, the repercussions of which have been political, intergovernmental, pluralistic, and public-private sector oriented.

Because the blending cannot be fully understood unless it is seen in its historical context, this chapter begins with an account of the development of planning and local government management since the early 1900s. The next two sections focus on the changing nature of planning and of local government management. They are followed by a description of strategic planning. The chapter concludes with a discussion of the management of planning.

Historical development

Both planning and management owe much of their early development in the United States to two civic reform movements, one emphasizing esthetic improvement, or *the city beautiful*, and the other emphasizing governmental efficiency, or *the city efficient*. Both were founded on ideals that led small, devoted bands of followers to see in civic reform the remaking of life in the twentieth century. These people—whether they were in planning, local government management, or other fields such as social welfare, housing, and recreation—expected to change urban life in the United States for the better.

Planning

City planning as a profession dates back to 1917 and the formation of the American City Planning Institute with fifty-two charter members. The United States was rapidly becoming an urbanized nation at that time, and its burgeoning communities recognized that planning was a useful tool in developing large city parks, controlling the worst kinds of housing, developing suburbs, and locating utilities, highways, and commuter railroads.

The first signs of the planning profession appeared somewhat earlier, however. Between 1900 and 1920 pioneers such as John Nolen, Benjamin C. Marsh,

Edward M. Bennett, and Alfred Bettman were already using planning to deal with issues of the day such as congestion, sanitary housing, population density, building codes, and zoning. Their efforts led to the formation of the first official citizen planning commissions and the development of civic centers and long-range plans.[1]

A new development during the 1920s as a result of some major legal decisions was the introduction of controls on private development in the United States, particularly through zoning ordinances and subdivision regulations. That decade also saw the start of pioneering housing developments, of which Radburn, New Jersey, is the best known example. On the academic side, formal training in planning became available with the establishment in 1929 of the first school of city planning at Harvard University.

The 1930s, meanwhile, brought increasing federal action in the form of extensive studies of natural resources, the creation of the Tennessee Valley Authority, the establishment of federal public housing programs, and the construction of extensive public works such as the Bonneville and the Hoover dams.

Table 2–1   Indicators of change in the United States, 1900 to 1980.

Indicator	1900	1920	1940	1960	1980
Population (in millions)	76.0	105.7	131.7	150.7	226.5
Median age	22.9	25.3	29.0	29.6	30.0
Life expectancy at birth	47.3	54.1	62.9	69.7	73.7[1]
Motor vehicle registrations (in thousands)[2]	8.0	9,239.0	32,453.0	73,869.0	155,796.0
Consumer Price Index (1967 = 100)	25.0	60.0	42.0	88.7	246.8
Percent of homes owner occupied	64.4	58.1	53.2	65.7	64.4
Index of manufacturing production (1967 = 100)[3]	. . .	15.0	25.0	65.0	147.0

Source: Data for 1900 through 1960 from: U.S. Bureau of the Census, *Historical Statistics of the United States, Colonial Times to 1970*, Bicentennial edition, parts 1 and 2 (Washington, D.C.: Government Printing Office, 1975), A–2, A–143, B–107, Q–152, E–135, N–243, and P–13. Data for 1980 from: U.S. Bureau of the Census, *Statistical Abstract of the United States, 1982–83*, 103d edition (Washington, D.C: Government Printing Office, 1982), tables 1, 32, 105, 1059, 757, 1355, and 1379.
[1] Data are for 1979.
[2] Includes automobiles, buses, and trucks.
[3] Federal Reserve Board Index.

Throughout this early period, both the professional training of planners and their field of practice gradually expanded as the problems at hand multiplied and grew more complicated. During the 1940s, however, planners turned their attention to the war effort, as did most people, and it wasn't until after World War II that planning further evolved, with the great expansion of federal programs. One highlight of the decade was the passage of the Housing Act of 1949, which added significantly to the public housing legislation of the previous decade by requiring that urban renewal be based on a "workable program." This was the federal government's first legislative definition of planning. (No such definition has yet been established for management.) That definition still holds for local planning. The components of the workable program are:

1. Comprehensive plan
2. Neighborhood analysis
3. Codes and ordinances
4. Code enforcement
5. Relocation of persons displaced by urban renewal
6. Citizen participation
7. Administration and implementation.

Figure 2–1   The wholesale market in the preautomobile age (top) provides
an instructive contrast with the acres of free parking provided at
Woodfield Mall, northwest of Chicago, seen below.

Subsequently the Housing Act of 1954 extended urban renewal to deteriorating
neighborhoods and established the Section 701 Comprehensive Planning Program to help pay for community planning. The 701 planning money was to
support local and intergovernmental planning and management and thus to
protect federal investment in urban renewal, highways, defense installations,
and federal buildings. Once planning and management were in place, the local
government was to be responsible for the financial support of these activities.

Planning was given a further boost in the 1962 Highway Act—enacted six
years after the interstate highway program was established—which required
planning for all federally funded highways. This was the first functional planning
requirement for local governments to be passed by Congress.

Intergovernmental service transfers Governments embracing large areas, including states, counties, and metropolitan special services districts, have been assuming functions and delivery of services formerly performed by local governments. Under the new arrangement, the local governments still retain their political identity but with fewer responsibilities and smaller budgets.

The significance of what is happening, according to a range of authorities, goes beyond an academic concern with functions of government. It suggests that the states and suburbs, long accused of ignoring the needs of the central cities with their concentrations of the poor and the elderly, are beginning to share more of the responsibilities for public services there. And this tends to reduce the pressures for more federal aid to cities, pressures that increased steadily over the 1960s and 1970s.

Officials like Governor Richard A. Snelling of Vermont predict that the trend will continue.

"Few if any domestic problems—human services, resources, conservation, transportation, what have you—can be solved by the solitary efforts of any one sphere," Governor Snelling said in a recent address to the Council of State Governments. And he said the movement was beginning to spill over state boundaries.

"As I see things in my crystal ball for the year 2000, more regional bodies will be moving beyond planning and coordination into outright service delivery, for example, in such areas as water supply, waste disposal, recreation and public health."

Source: John Herbers, "Larger Governments Assuming Services from Cities." Copyright © 1984 by The New York Times Company. Reprinted by permission.

As the 1960s unfolded, local planning and management moved into its heyday. In 1965 Congress created the Department of Housing and Urban Development—the first cabinet-level department to represent urban interests. Then in 1966 the Demonstration Cities and Metropolitan Development Act established model cities programs through which people in neighborhoods could influence planning and capital investments in their areas. Neighborhood groups learned quickly about the political world and the federal money that was available, and before long "citizen participation" was added to the vocabulary of planners and managers. The model cities programs helped identify neighborhood spokespersons, gave them platforms to deal with important issues, and realigned the political power base among elected officials, appointed officials, technicians, and citizens.

A significant development in 1969 was the passage of the National Environmental Policy Act, which required functional impact assessments of federally funded projects and alternatives to them. As a result, the "environmental impact statement" became a politically potent force in resource allocation disputes.

That same year the U.S. Office of Management and Budget issued Circular A-95 (authorized by the Intergovernmental Cooperation Act of 1968), which soon changed the local government planning map. Circular A-95 provided the opportunity for areawide cooperative review of applications for federal funding prior to their approval. Councils of governments and regional planning agencies were thus able to compare areawide development objectives with individual project proposals and to comment on any discrepancies between the two. Because these areawide agencies also were eligible for Section 701 planning money, their political visibility and influence were substantially enlarged.

In the 1970s, however, the national mood toward government shifted from a proactive to a conservative one that sparked a number of fundamental changes in federal community development programs and federal-local relationships. In providing for community development block grant funds, for example, the landmark Housing Act of 1974 introduced categorical grants and increased local responsibility for setting community development funding priorities. Proposition 13 and other tax limitation measures were further symptoms of the national desire to reduce the size, cost, and pervasiveness of government. The end result was that A-95 was changed from mandatory to voluntary review, and its administration was shifted to state governments (by Executive Order 12372 in 1982). With that, the U.S. Office of Management and Budget abandoned its role—such as it was—as a coordinator of domestic capital programs. These various developments were the precursors of extensive changes in professional planning.

For one thing, the sheer scope and variety of problems and issues to be dealt with expanded tremendously. During the 1920s, the federal presence was known only through the standard planning and zoning acts issued by the U.S. Department of Commerce. During the 1930s, the federal presence was known marginally through the Tennessee Valley Authority and other large projects for public works and conservation. By the 1940s and 1950s, federal participation had increased sharply in housing, urban renewal, and other activities related to the development and redevelopment of cities. By the 1960s and 1970s, local activities involving federal money were extended to citizen participation, environmental protection, and intergovernmental management—areas in which planning and management were irrevocably joined.

At the same time, planners had to move out from the protective technical shelters of the independent planning commission and turn their attention from the design and development of civic centers and residential areas to controversial issues involving the pursuit of grants and a regulatory environment. That, in turn, forced them to interact more and more with elected officials, advocates for neighborhoods and special interest groups, and the state government.

Physical, social, and economic planning—the long idealized triad—at last began to come together as did planning for the management of strategic planning. Planning now encompassed a wide range of management activities that formerly were detached from the planning mainstream.

Management

The history of local government management is slightly more complicated in that two streams of development are involved here: the civic reform movement, which began with the founding of the National Municipal League in 1894, and the management movement, which is said to have originated in Frederick Winslow Taylor's *The Principles of Scientific Management* published in 1913.

Civic reform   The first model city charter was drafted under the auspices of the National Municipal League in 1897. The major provisions included centralization of executive powers in the office of the mayor, centralization of legislative powers in a unicameral city council, a short electoral ballot, and the elimination of elected officials for city offices except the city council.

The commission form of city government was born in Galveston, Texas, in 1900, and thereafter the league quickly endorsed the concept for national application. The commission form of government reached its peak in 1917, at which time it was in effect in about five hundred communities across the country. By then, however, the league had already begun to favor the emerging council-manager plan, as was evident at its annual convention in Dayton, Ohio, in 1915, where it adopted a new model city charter providing for the council-manager plan.

Two elements of the 1915 model city charter continue to be key components of the council-manager plan to this day: (1) powers are unified in the governing body, the city council or the county board; and (2) authority and responsibility are concentrated in the office of the city or county manager. The civic reform movement and the model city charter contained other features that have had a bearing on local government but that are not fundamental to the points of concentrated legislative and management authority. The other features—their importance is being debated by political scientists to this day—include nonpartisan elections, elections at large, the direct election of the mayor, and the short ballot.

The council-manager plan of local government usually is dated to the appointment of a "general manager" in Staunton, Virginia, in 1908. By early 1983 the plan had spread to 2,500 cities and counties in the United States. If to that number are added the general managers and directors of councils of governments (for places meeting criteria established by the International City Management Association), the grand total in 1983 was 3,212. Perhaps the most telling statistic is that 59 percent of the municipalities between 10,000 and 500,000 population have either the council-manager or general management plan. In either case, professional management is provided. (The ratio is much lower for counties and councils of governments.)

The civic reform movement was the setting for the council-manager plan that produced the city manager, one of the earliest full-time appointed professionals in local government. (Other such appointees of that time would have been school superintendents, municipal engineers, and public health officers.) Although the early city managers certainly crusaded for better government, and thus were caught up in the civic reform movement, they were managers first. To the extent that they theorized about management, they were followers of Frederick Winslow Taylor.

Trends in management   Management, like planning, is constantly changing—growing, maturing, aging, being reborn, and growing. The concept appears to have originated in three theories of organization that management relies on to this day: (1) the rational theories of organization, which by and large have their roots in Frederick Winslow Taylor's formulation of scientific management and Max Weber's formulation of bureaucracy; (2) humanistic or human relations management, which grew out of the Hawthorne studies in the 1920s and early 1930s at a plant operated by the Western Electric Company; and (3) the integration of management, which stems from the work of Douglas McGregor and others.

Taylor's ideas about scientific management were first set forth in 1903 in a paper entitled "Shop Management." Scientific management, according to Taylor, centers on factors such as analysis of work, standardization of the purchase and storage of materials, job analysis, time study, matching the employee to the job, job training, and incentive pay. When we talk about economy, efficiency, and productivity, we are actually talking about elements of Taylorism.

The human relations movement is usually associated with the work done between 1923 and the early 1930s by Elton Mayo and Fritz Roethlisberger at the Hawthorne Works of the Western Electric Company, just outside Chicago. During this period small work groups were studied under strictly controlled conditions. At first the researchers examined the effects of environmental factors such as light, temperature, and noise. Then their experiments were extended to rest periods, refreshments, and hours and days of work. Productivity was measured at every stage of the experiments. From these and other experiments (including 21,000 interviews with employees!), the researchers concluded that productivity is governed both by "rational" considerations and by group codes that regulate human behavior. Perhaps their most important finding was that

Civic reform, the Progressive Movement, and local government professionalism The corruption and blatant political partisanship of municipal government in the latter half of the 19th century have been fully documented in the writings of historians, political scientists, and journalists. Not as fully documented were the changes that took place when the work of the reformers began to coalesce in the 1890s. The National Conference for Good City Government, held in 1894, was a turning point that led to the formation of the National Municipal League. In 1897 the League started to draft a "municipal program." After reviews and revisions in 1898 and 1899, the program was adopted in 1900 with thoroughgoing provisions for municipal powers, a strong mayor, civil service, debt limitations, financial responsibility, state-municipal relations, utility franchises, and nonpartisan elections.

A correlative development was the nascent professionalism in municipal services. Municipal engineers already were experts in sewerage, water supply, water purification, and street paving. Public health was attracting widespread attention with its programs of environmental sanitation. Accounting was a recognized field. School superin- tendents were recognized professionals, among the earliest to move from city to city as job opportunities opened. By 1900, when civic reformers looked at the shoddy condition of L'Enfant's plan for Washington, D.C., the time was propitious for city planning to achieve correlative recognition and professionalism.

Several organizations were formed for civic advancement in the early 1900s, including the American Civic Association (1904), the National Conference on City Planning (1909), and the National Housing Association (1911). An outgrowth of the National Conference was the formation in 1917 of the American City Planning Institute with fifty-two charter members who met the membership requirement of "at least two years of experience in responsible charge of some major phase of city planning." From the Institute evolved the American Institute of Planners (1939). The American Society of Planning Officials was separately organized in 1934, and the two organizations merged to form the American Planning Association in 1978.

Two of the earliest council-manager cities were Staunton, Virginia (1908), and Sumter, South Carolina (1912). By

persons within a work group tend to develop specific types of relations with each other, with their supervisors, with their work, and with the policies of the organization. Later research would refer to these and other similar phenomena as "group dynamics."

The third theory of organization derives from Douglas McGregor's postulation that there are two fundamental approaches to management. One is based on a negative view of human nature, and assumes that people have to be bribed, coerced, or goaded into doing their work properly. The other takes a much more positive view of people with a much broader and more positive view of motivation, incentives, the capacity to learn, and the willingness to accept responsibility. Another important factor here, according to researchers, is the desire of people for self-fulfillment and self-development, which Abraham Maslow called self-actualization (and which he ranked at the top of the hierarchy of human needs).

Management today attempts to balance all these elements—the rational approach to jobs, the needs and interests of people especially in groups, and the potential for self-development—in a favorable organizational environment. In addition, it takes into account the outside forces that cannot be controlled by the local government (inflation and tax limitation measures are examples), and

1914, when fourteen cities had adopted the plan, eight of the city managers in those cities met in Springfield, Ohio, and organized the International City Managers' Association. The name was changed to the International City Management Association in 1969 when membership eligibility was broadened.

As the council-manager plan spread, Richard S. Childs preached the "gospel" of structural reform (nonpartisan elections, a small city council, elections at large, etc.) and an appointed city manager. It was logical, therefore, with the awakening civic consciousness, for the three organizations to take on separate missions and responsibilities. The National Municipal League (now the Citizens' Forum for Self-Government— The National Municipal League) helped promote the council-manager plan and provided many kinds of practical help through research, legislative compilations, and publications. Today the League's mission is more broadly defined to stimulate effective citizen participation in all phases of state and local government.

The American Planning Association is primarily an association of teachers, students, and practitioners in planning at all levels of government. Professional planning is represented through an affiliated group, the American Institute of Certified Planners, which has strict eligibility requirements involving both education and experience in planning plus passing a certifying examination.

The two major purposes of the International City Management Association have been the same since the ICMA constitution was originally adopted in 1914: ". . . to increase the proficiency of city managers, county managers, and other urban administrators and to strengthen the quality of urban government through professional management."

Sources: Based on Russell VanNest Black, *Planning and the Planning Profession: The Past Fifty Years 1917– 1967* (Washington, D.C.: American Institute of Planners, 1967), 19–24; Ernest S. Griffith, *A History of American City Government: The Conspicuous Failure, 1870–1900* (New York: Praeger Publishers, 1974), 258–59, 271–72; Richard J. Stillman, II, *The Rise of the City Manager: A Public Professional in Local Government* (Albuquerque: University of New Mexico Press, 1974), 12–19.

the changing expectations of workers today compared with their counterparts of a generation ago.

One way to illustrate the magnitude of these management changes is to compare the first public administration training offered in 1916 with the typical graduate curriculum in public administration today. In 1916, the Training School for Public Service, affiliated with the New York Bureau of Municipal Research, offered courses in law; legislative drafting; municipal highway engineering; politics and administration; accounting; engineering administration; charities, schools, and health administration; police and fire administration; and budgeting and accounting. Although most of these courses are still available in graduate programs in public administration, the curricula today emphasize organization and management, human behavior, organization theory, political economy, economic analysis, political environment, policy formation, policy analysis, and, in almost every program, statistics and quantitative methods. Thus the procedural perspective of the past has given way to a broad environmental perspective. The new approach is hinted at in a chapter title in a recent publication: "On being an effective local government manager."[2] The key word here is *being*, which implies growth, process, and change.

13

STATEMENT OF PRESCRIBED COURSES IN THE SCHOOL OF CITY PLANNING*

To attain the degree of Master in City Planning a student must satisfy the School as to his preparation, pass each of the following courses with a grade of B— or better, complete a satisfactory thesis, acquire facility of expression in freehand drawing, and show satisfactory attainment in design. Students entering the School who believe that they have already mastered the material covered in any of the required courses may take advance credit examinations at the time of their entrance. Those who pass an advance credit examination in any course with a grade of B— or better will be excused from taking that course.

FIRST YEAR

CITY PLANNING 2d†. — Theory of Design, with special reference to landscape architecture and city planning. Lectures, collateral reading, and tests. *Wed., Fri., 2–3, and at least three additional hours.* Professor HUBBARD.

The course is intended to prepare the student for the problems of the second year. It aims to develop the student's ability to organize his own thinking in attacking actual problems.

CITY PLANNING 4d‡. — Principles of Construction (introductory course). Lectures, collateral reading, problems, and criticisms. *Mon., Wed., Fri., 12–1, Mon., Tu., 2–5, and four additional hours.* Asst. Professor WILLIAMS, Mr. LANGHORNE, and Mr. WEBEL.

The course deals with the use of contours, the preparation of grading plans, the calculation of cut and fill by means of cross-sections and by the prismoidal method, and the calculation of costs of road construction and grading.

* For more complete statements of courses required in the School of City Planning which are given in other Departments of the University, see the pamphlets of those Departments.

† In the title of all City Planning courses, the digit serves only to identify the course, the letter indicates the year in the curriculum in which the course is normally taken ("a" indicates first year, "b," second year, and "c," third year), while the index figure indicates the half of the year in which the course is given. Absence of an index figure indicates a whole year's course.

14

CITY PLANNING 10d. — Principles of City and Regional Planning (introductory course). Lectures, conferences, collateral reading, and tests. *Mon., Wed., Fri., 11–12, and three additional hours.* Professor HUBBARD and Asst. Professor COMEY, Mr. NOLES and Mr. SHURTLEFF, assisted by Mr. MENHINICK.

The course aims to supply a comprehensive view of the subject of city planning in a series of lectures by persons experienced in the field of city planning, each treating some special part of the subject. The continuity and completeness of the course are maintained by lectures given and readings supervised by Asst. Professor COMEY. Lectures for the year 1929–30 included:

Arthur C. Comey	Henry V. Hubbard	Alfred Bettman
Thomas Adams	L. H. Weir	Richmond D. Moot
John Nolen	Edward M. Bassett	Warren H. Manning
Robert Whitten	James Ford	Charles W. Eliot, 2d
Miller McClintock	George B. Ford	Jay Downer
Gordon M. Fair	Jacob L. Crane, Jr.	Theodore K. Hubbard
Arthur A. Shurtleff	Frank B. Williams	Lawson Purdy

CITY PLANNING 11d. — Elementary Drafting. Lectures and problems. *Tu., Th., 3–5, and five additional hours.* Mr. LANGHORNE.

The course consists of exercises to familiarize the student with the use of instruments and to give him a preliminary training in the types of graphic presentation commonly used in professional offices. It affords practice in the careful delineation of curves, in simple perspective, lettering and the composition of titles, and in the rendering of simple plans.

CITY PLANNING 12d. — Topographic Surveying. Lectures, field work, and problems. *Tu., 9–1.* Asst. Professor WILLIAMS.

The course consists of instruction in simple topographic methods introducing the use of common surveying instruments and equipment and giving practice in making simple topographic maps, chiefly by the stadia method with transit and plane table.

CITY PLANNING 13a. — Elementary Architectural Drawing and Design. Problems, measured drawings, lectures, collateral reading, and criticisms. First half-year: *Mon., Wed., Fri., 2–5, and fourteen additional hours.* Second half-year: *Wed., Fri., 3–5, and eleven additional hours.* Mr. BOGNER, assisted by Mr. LANGHORNE.

The course includes a short study of the orders and such measured drawings and simple problems as will introduce the student to the wide range of architectural form and detail.

Figure 2–2   Education for planning and administration, then and now. Shown above is a page from the "Statement of Prescribed Courses" for the first graduate program in city planning in the United States, the School of City Planning formed at Harvard University in 1929. The above reproduction shows two pages (in reduced size) from the 1930 catalog. The four-year Harvard program stressed design, architecture, and landscape architecture.

Today planning at Harvard is offered within the John F. Kennedy School of Government program in public policy leading to the degree of master of city and regional planning. Students enrolled in the MCRP program must take a core curriculum in public policy, which emphasizes institutional analysis, empirical analysis, economics, public management, and decision making. They then can concentrate on work in professional planning and urban management.

On the facing page is shown the first curriculum for the master's degree in public administration at the Maxwell School of

SCHOOL OF CITIZENSHIP AND PUBLIC AFFAIRS

Public Administration
PROFESSORS MOSHER, BENNETT, BERRY, BRYANT, MITCHELL, SARASON,
TILFORD, WILSON;
INSTRUCTOR MYERS;
LECTURERS BASSETT, BUCK, CORNICK, GREER, GULICK, McCOMBS
RINGUEBERG, SMITH, WATSON

300. PUBLIC ADMINISTRATION. *12.* The purpose of this course is to prepare students for work in the field of municipal research, public administration and especially of city management. The following subjects will be considered:

I. GENERAL ORGANIZATION AND MANAGEMENT.

Types of Municipal Organizations.
Charters and Municipal Corporations.
Zoning and City Planning.
Business Methods.

II. PERSONNEL AND SUPPLIES.

Civil Service and Personnel Management.
Purchasing and Storing of Supplies.

III. FINANCES—ADMINISTRATION AND CONTROL.

Budgets and Budget Making.
Taxation and Assessments.
Accounting.
Collection and Management of Funds.
Debt Administration.

IV. PUBLIC SAFETY AND WELFARE.

Police.
Fire.
Health and Welfare.

V. PUBLIC WORKS.

Streets—Construction and Maintenance.
Street Cleaning.
Traffic Problems.
Sewers—Construction and Maintenance.
Waste Collection and Disposal.
Water Supply and Distribution.

Citizenship and Public Affairs, Syracuse University. Offering one of the earliest degrees in public administration, the Maxwell program first opened for the 1924–25 academic year and was built around the immediate concerns of cities in the 1920s: public works, public safety, finance, personnel, welfare, and general management. A three- to six-month internship was part of the degree requirements.

According to the 1982–84 Maxwell catalog, modern course work with a concentration in public administration includes 32 courses in subjects such as national planning, communication skills, public administration history, ethics, law, organization theory, policy analysis, state and local financial management, state government and administration, personnel, budgeting, and intergovernmental relations. The six required core areas for the public administration degree are economics, quantitative methods, organization theory, organization development, management, and political context.

Synthesis

It has been said that "Planning is the basic function of management."[3] Indeed, in many cities, particularly smaller ones, planning is becoming more and more integrated into management: "The old fashioned turf issues between city managers and city planners are seldom heard these days. Managers, planners, budget officers, public works directors, and others are increasingly working together as teams, planning for development and cooperatively solving city problems."[4]

In the early days, however, the interdependency of planning and management was not so obvious. Thus, when graduate training in planning and public administration began in the 1920s and 1930s, there were no books on the "principles" of planning and management for local government. Things began to change in the following decade with the publication of *The Technique of Municipal Administration* (1940) and *Local Planning Administration* (1941), by the International City Managers' Association (now the International City Management Association). These two books laid the foundation for the blending.

These books not only represented the first thorough effort to demonstrate the relationship between planning and management, but they established the first lines of communication among practitioners in the days when professional peers were rarely available for consultation and when local government newsletters and periodicals were scarce. Moreover, they provided the first reliable information when there was no money for individuals to collect data.

From that time on—as graduate programs in planning and public administration grew to more than two hundred, and as the books and journals multiplied—the two professions became increasingly aware of each other and slowly began to move toward each other. In the 1970s this process picked up steam as a result of several developments (sketched out in earlier sections of this chapter). The blending of planning and management can be expected to continue accelerating for a number of reasons:

Planners, like managers, are becoming facilitators and negotiators among diverse and often competing interests in the public sector, the private sector, and the nonprofit sector.

City and county managers, like planners, are learning about land use policy, real estate economics, and the consequences of development decisions.

Both planners and managers are concerned with regulatory powers, and are working with consultants, conducting meetings and hearings, working with developers, managing information, negotiating real estate developments, and linking budgeting with planning.

Both professions are concerned with the local political economy and with policy analysis, social expectations, and economic development.

Changing nature of planning

Planning, as we have just seen, has changed both in substance and in professional outlook. Its early concerns with the design of public spaces and buildings and with reserving transportation rights-of-way have blossomed into a wide range of interests, from playgrounds and buildings to large regional parks, housing developments of many kinds, commercial developments, industrial parks, historic preservation, planning for the arts, and planning for public schools. Many of its activities now involve regulation and depend on analysis, timing, and political decisions. Furthermore, in addition to the original tools of engineering, architecture, and law, it now relies on systems analysis, computer modeling, community organization, financial analysis, social program needs, and housing.

Important changes have occurred in other areas as well—namely, the planning process, the governmental process, and the skills needed for the practice of local government planning. The changing nature of planning cannot be fully understood without some knowledge of these additional factors.

Planning process

The planning process now encompasses both technical and political work. What this means can be illustrated by an example of planning activities in the area of transportation, where analytically derived measures of land use and transportation modes can be used to forecast transportation demand for a new bus system. At the same time, impressionistic and intuitive forecasts can be made on the basis of the likelihood of political support in the form of funding and of local approval. Part of the process may involve recommending to the city council or county board that only one part of the project be financed so as to "get a foot in the door." If all goes well, the system can be expanded later.

This division between the technical and political sides of planning offers a means of classifying its practitioners. That is, planners who emphasize the quantitative analysis of scientifically derived data and the conclusions drawn from those data can be said to be technicians and theoreticians (*analysts*). Planners who emphasize bargaining to achieve implementation can be said to be technicians and politicians (*infighters*). The mixture of analyst and infighter varies from planner to planner. Most planners are likely to emphasize their role as analysts in part because of their professional training and their value system. Therefore, the reputation planners have gained as analysts is warranted.

Many planners, however, have gone through career changes in this respect. Some trained but inexperienced planners have started out with technical assignments, but have quickly learned that it is the managerial and political environment that helps or hinders implementation. In the absence of local political awareness, peer acceptance by local elected officials, and control of the bargaining chips, the planner has virtually no infighter role. With experience, however, the planner may advance to managerial responsibility, and in so doing may gain political awareness, be able to exploit competitive ideas, and take some control over funding sources. At that point the infighter can emerge.

In actuality, the work done by planners is not quite that clear-cut. Even the most cloistered researcher knows that his or her findings and recommendations will be reviewed in some type of public arena.

Governmental process

During the 1940s and 1950s the governmental process and the practices of public administration were examined intensively by means of theoretical analysis and empirical research. Political scientists, sociologists, psychologists, and social psychologists all began to ask how government *really* works. As a result of their inquiries, the concept of "pluralism" was redefined to show how legislatures, courts, and elected executives are influenced by and interact with myriad groups and associations in society—veterans' groups, farm groups, civic associations, professional associations, and thousands of others. Pluralism was deemed to be a significant component of the governmental process even though it was not formally recognized in the trichotomy of the executive, the legislature, and the courts.

Although the governmental process sometimes goes under different names, in every instance it is recognized to be a complex process wherein a wide range of interests and influences interact with institutions and formal authorities so that decisions can be made and programs carried out. The budgeting process

[*Text continued on page 33*]

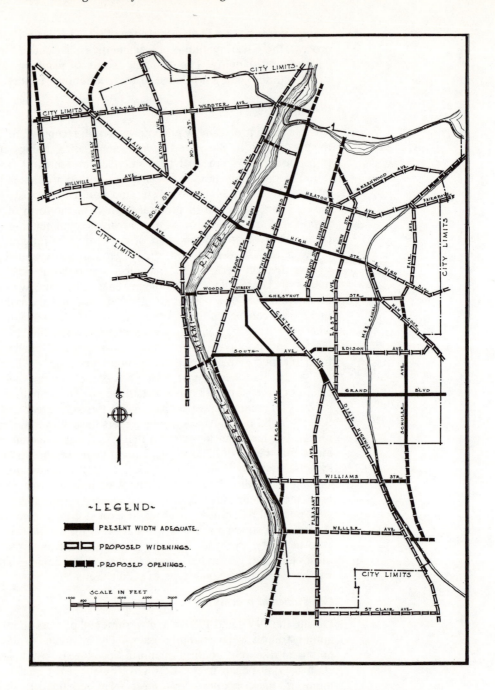

Figure 2–3 Problems and solutions in city planning in 1920–21, 1947, and 1978–84.
This page and the following six pages show approaches to planning over sixty-four
years in four cities. All of these line drawings are from the files of Harland
Bartholomew & Associates. The first four pages are from Hamilton, Ohio, and show
the emphasis on land use and population distribution and density. The last three
pages are from Wyoming, Ohio; Williamsburg, Virginia; and Rock Springs, Wyoming, and
illustrate the additional planning coverage of policy framework, urban design,
and plan details. This page shows the proposals for the major street system in
Hamilton, Ohio, in 1920–21. Note the extensive mileage with broken lines indicating
proposed street widenings, which often were adequate in those days
for improving automobile traffic flow.

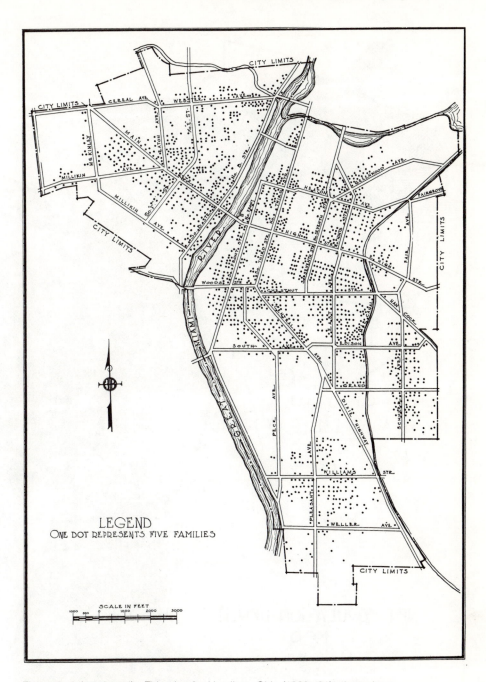

LEGEND
ONE DOT REPRESENTS FIVE FAMILIES

Figure 2–3 (continued)   This plan for Hamilton, Ohio (1920–21), shows how the proposed major street system would serve the distribution and density of population at that time.

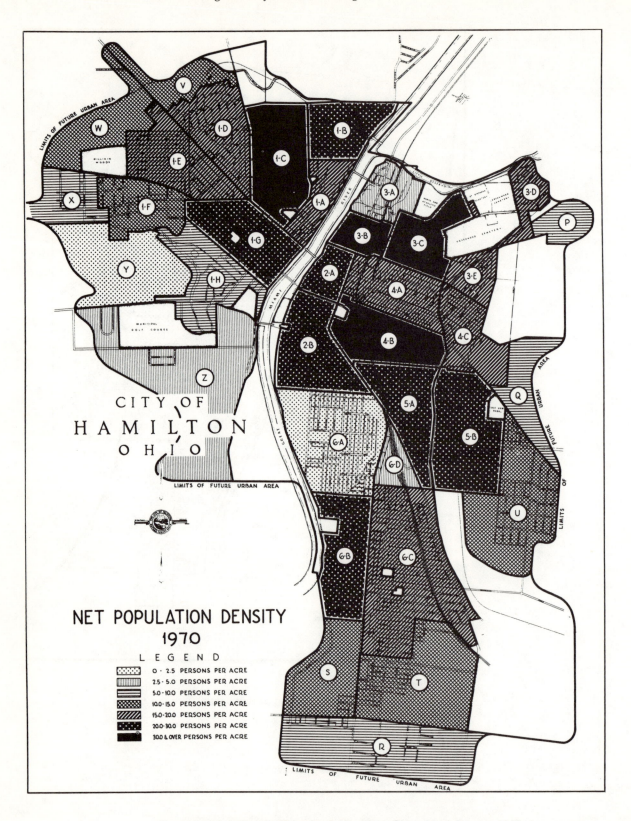

Figure 2–3 (continued)   This plan for Hamilton, Ohio, dated January, 1947, shows population density projections for 1970. Note the high densities projected in contrast to the even spread of population shown on the preceding page for 1920–21.

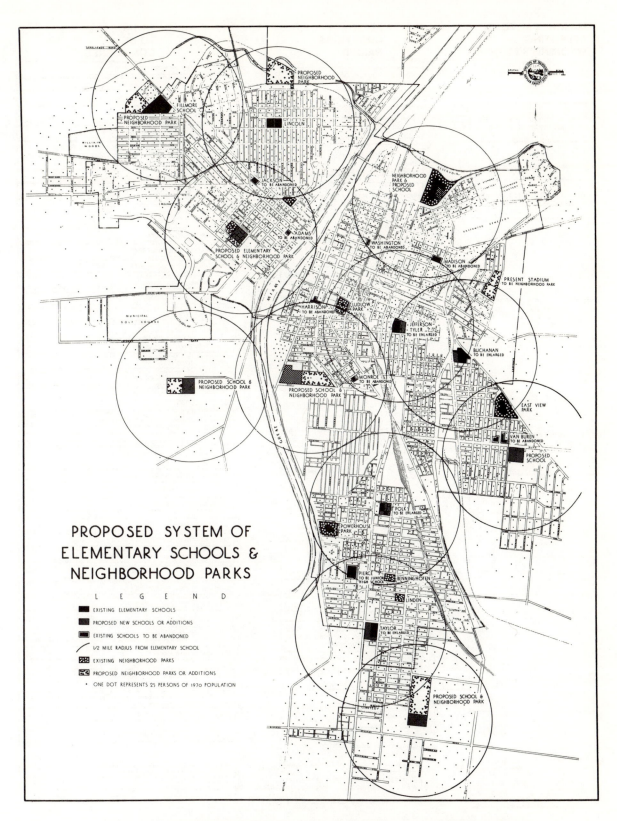

PROPOSED SYSTEM OF
ELEMENTARY SCHOOLS &
NEIGHBORHOOD PARKS

L E G E N D

■ EXISTING ELEMENTARY SCHOOLS

◆ PROPOSED NEW SCHOOLS OR ADDITIONS

▣ EXISTING SCHOOLS TO BE ABANDONED

⟋ 1/2 MILE RADIUS FROM ELEMENTARY SCHOOL

▓ EXISTING NEIGHBORHOOD PARKS

▒ PROPOSED NEIGHBORHOOD PARKS OR ADDITIONS

• ONE DOT REPRESENTS 25 PERSONS OF 1970 POPULATION

Figure 2–3 (continued)   This system of neighborhood elementary schools and
parks proposed for Hamilton, Ohio, is dated February, 1947. Most of the proposals
combine the school and park in one location.

MAJOR FACTORS AFFECTING WYOMING'S FUTURE

POLICY QUESTIONS RAISED

PROPOSALS TO BE CONSIDERED

Changes in family size, life styles and number of children
- What measures should we undertake to make the city more attractive to families with children?
  - Establish day care center
  - Establish after-school program
- How can we maintain the high quality of public education?
  - Complete school rehab program
  - Improve school and park grounds
  - Undertake Wyoming publicity program
- How can we enhance the city's image?
  - Establish and plant Wyoming tree, bush and flower
  - Improve entrance to city and major facilities

Adaptation of the built-up city to these changes
- How can we bring a better relation between facilities and needs?
  - Establish retirement center
  - Provide housing assistance

Aging of buildings and facilities
- Should we provide inducements for renovation and rehabilitation?
  - Give awards and prizes
  - Get houses on National Register
- Should we strengthen zoning and building ordinances and better enforce them?
  - Improve building plan review procedures
  - Streamline zoning districts
  - Provide systematic inspections
- How shall we maintain, replace, and rebuild public facilities to keep them at a high standard?
  - Carry out street plan
  - Carry out street tree plan
  - Consolidate overhead wires
  - Improve Springfield Pike
  - Improve Fleming and Compton
  - Continue water distribution improvements
  - Establish joint committee regarding use of public facilities
  - Develop and carry out a public building plan

A changing metropolitan environment
- Should we participate in organizations and movements promoting the metro area?
  - Encourage early construction of Cross County Highway

Insufficient public open space
- How can we keep the open space that we have?
  - Continue Green Areas program
- Should we fund the acquisition of more public open space?
  - Enlarge school and park sites

Inadequate recreational opportunities
- Should we build and operate more public recreation facilities?
  - Carry out recreation survey
  - Make landfill into park
  - Consider year-round swimming pool
  - Add sidewalks and walkways
  - Develop bikeway system
- How can we assist and encourage provision of recreation by private and semi-public agencies?
  - Enhance viability of Civic Center

The weak tax base
- How can we provide a high standard of public services to a small population at a reasonable cost?
  - Continue professional creative cost-effective management
  - Acquire private streets
- Should we annex land to increase size of city?
  - Consider annexation of adjacent areas
- How can we keep existing commercial areas viable?
  - Carry out commercial area improvement program
  - Carry out K-Mart area renewal program
- Can we enlarge any existing commercial areas?
  - Enlarge central commercial area

Informed participation in local government
- How can we obtain the maximum in public understanding, participation and support.
  - Enhance communication program
  - Establish community corporation

Figure 2–3 (continued)   Summary of the 1984 city plan for Wyoming, Ohio. Note the policy framework of questions and proposals.

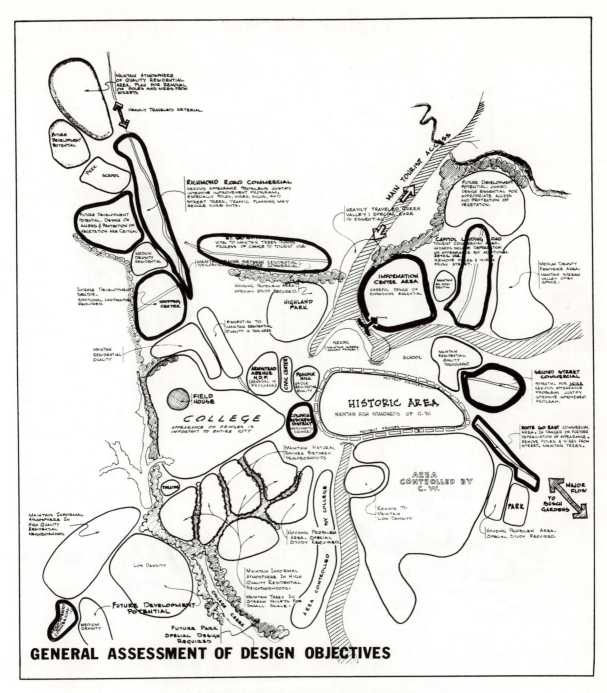

Figure 2–3 (continued)   General design objectives, Williamsburg, Virginia
(1981). Many natural elements of community life that were taken for granted
in the 1920s are given specific attention here, including stream valleys,
tree preservation, and open space.

Typical Sidewalk Improvements

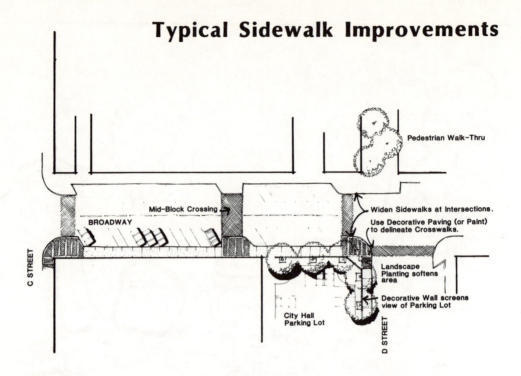

Pedestrian Walk-Thru

Mid-Block Crossing

BROADWAY

C STREET

Widen Sidewalks at Intersections.

Use Decorative Paving (or Paint) to delineate Crosswalks.

Landscape Planting softens area

Decorative Wall screens view of Parking Lot

City Hall Parking Lot

D STREET

New Light Feature / Electric Lines to be put Underground

Rehab. Buildings / Front & Rear. Use Flush Signs.

Wall Mural

Develop Pedestrian Walk-Thrus.

Decorative Walls around Parking Lots

Widen Sidewalks at Intersections – Use Decorative Pavement to add Interest. Crosswalks could be Delineated with Similar Materials or Paint.

Figure 2–3 (continued)   Central business district improvement proposals, Rock Springs, Wyoming (1980). Since the turn of the century, planning has been concerned with details such as street planter boxes, planting and maintenance of street trees, and street lights. Today this concern has been broadened (as shown here) to include art in public places, pedestrian ways, decorative pavement and walls, and sidewalk improvements.

for the federal government, for example, involves just such a broad range of interests. For local governments, these interests are also wide ranging and diverse, and may include unions, schools, veterans' organizations, social clubs, social service organizations, health organizations, neighborhood groups, ethnic societies, and many others. It is into this maelstrom that planners are being thrust as planning and management grow closer together.

Local control

The availability of state and federal planning money, especially federal funds beginning in 1954, encouraged local governments to gear their activities toward specific federal programs. Although matching local funds were required, many planners and managers convinced elected officials to apply for outside funding because it was like getting something for almost nothing. The something was funding that would not have been available otherwise—"seed money" without which a local planning program would remain a dream. As the local planning programs and federal and state requirements proliferated, the competition for nonlocal funding increased. Some of these requirements, like water quality planning under Section 208 of the National Water Quality Act of 1972, ran their course. Others, like the continuing, coordinated, cooperative planning program required of the 1962 Highway Act, took on lesser importance as the number of new federally assisted highways declined.

Since the time that federal planning dollars first became available, they expanded from around $150 million (in constant 1980 dollars) in 1954 to around $825 million in 1980, but they dropped sharply thereafter. Consequently, local government planning in the mid-1980s is supported by a greater proportion of locally derived revenue than at any time since the mid-1950s. The responsibility for *prescribing* planning programs rests with the government that pays the bills. This responsibility has thus moved from federal to local, or from top-down to bottom-up planning. In assuming greater responsibility, local officials found themselves faced with hard choices by the early 1980s: reduce the planning staff, find more local money, or a combination of the two. Most of these decisions had a twofold purpose: to reduce the planning staff, and to increase the local government portion of the planning budget. With more local money going into planning, the councils (or boards), managers, and planning directors all exerted more power and influence on the substance of the planning programs.

Although federal and state planning grants had restricted planning in significant ways, the top-down approach could be used by local governments to their advantage. Where planning was politically weak, for example, grant requirements could be a godsend in the form of technical justification for recalcitrant councils. If councils were reluctant to authorize specific studies with conclusions they did not want to hear, such as cost-revenue analyses, the planning staff could say this type of assignment was an integral part of a broader planning program. If the staff and council did not want to be identified with a politically sensitive development issue, or the staff did not know how to do the work, outside funding could be used to hire a consultant.

On the other hand, bottom-up prescriptions of planning work differently. Local prescriptions are more (1) sensitive to the priorities of elected officials, (2) concerned with the consequences of specific development activities, (3) involved with short- rather than long-term consequences, (4) limited in their attention to the intergovernmental effects of recommendations, and (5) directly influenced by managers and chief administrative officers to whom or through whom planners report.

Less common than in earlier years is the separation of "current" and "long-range" planning or the development permission and research functions. In general, the long-range perspective or research function is directly related to what-

Local initiative and local solutions
It is the smaller political units—cities, counties, and individual communities—that are claiming local authority over, and taking responsibility for, social issues that hit hard at the local level. What is surprising is their success rate. Local communities are tackling difficult problems and achieving solutions where the federal government with its vast but clumsy resources has failed: in energy, transportation, waste disposal, even in the controversial area of genetic research.

In policy making, we are giving up the grand top-down strategies imposed from above and substituting bottom-up approaches, that is, limited, individual solutions that grow naturally out of a particular set of circumstances.

For example, we have no national urban policy because the old top-down, master-plan approach is completely out of tune with the times. It is inappropriate to ask: "Are we going to save our cities?" We are going to save some of our cities and we are not going to save others. We are going to save parts of some of our cities and allow other parts to decline. And the whole process is all going to turn on local initiative. The only "national urban policy" that is in tune with the times is one that is responsive to, and rewarding of, local initiative. The same can be said for energy, national health, and scores of other considerations.

Source: John Naisbitt, *Megatrends: Ten New Directions Transforming Our Lives* (New York: Warner Books, 1982), 102.

ever the local government's highest priorities are at a given time. Often they are connected to the development permission process. The exigencies of contemporary local government management—the cost-revenue squeeze, staff cutbacks, the identification of prospective consequences of development decisions before they are made, and public-private funding partnerships—have thus strengthened the linkages between planners and managers.

It is interesting to note that planning has acquired greater local responsibility at the same time that planning expenditures have been reduced. In addition, elected officials and managers are defining planning in ways that can more directly serve their needs than was often the case in the past. They are also placing greater emphasis on measuring the performance of the planning process and on monitoring output. Overall, planning in many communities is being brought closer to management to serve both elected and appointed officials.

Communication/information skills

One development that has greatly affected planning and management has been the growing interest in improving communication/information skills. Rising educational levels, the pervasiveness of television, and the surge of interest (sometimes mandated by law) in citizen participation in the governmental process have all convinced planners of the need to improve their communication/information skills. Planners who lack such skills must try to acquire them because those who have the skills to successfully carry out planning programs are the most likely practitioners to stay on board.

An informal survey of local government managers has suggested that the skills of planners are enhanced by:

Communication

Information from other departments

Quality and timeliness of data for decision making

Negotiating skills

Figure 2–4   The disaggregation of the comprehensive plan.
Bottom-up planning is different—more sensitive, more specific,
more concerned with the short term, more managerial.

Citizen participation

Telecommunications technology.[5]

Communication   Many local government managers believe that the most important improvement that can be made to the local planning process is to communicate ideas and information more clearly. They note that sometimes significant information can become lost in the interval between the technical plan and the policy makers' decisions; or that planners, planning, and plans can be too complicated and unintelligible, verbose and obfuscatory, and technical and theoretical. As a result, many nonplanners tend to see plans as declarations handed down from an ivory tower and divorced from political reality.

Information from other departments   Comprehensive planning, strategic planning for the issues of highest priority, and departmental planning, programming, and budgeting require a great deal of information. In addition, some local planning agencies are responsible for capital improvement programming and other activities that involve automatic interdepartmental transfer of information. Planners who can establish and maintain a flow of useful information here are better able to achieve their technical objectives and to assist other departments with their planning.

Quality and timeliness of information   Some planners are criticized for letting complexity overtake a document via verbosity or for letting the technical methods gain the upper hand via redundancy. The quality of communication is an important criterion that the elected official can use to evaluate the planning department's performance. Because the subject of many of these communications is controversial, complex, and spontaneous, or all three, it is more difficult to prepare them than might be expected.

Timely communication is just as important. In fact, timely communication with inadequate information is more important than completely documented communication that is too late. Documents should be prepared ahead of time so that last-minute changes can be reviewed by the manager or some other supervisor. Information that is not reviewed in advance may cause needless embarrassment.

Negotiating skills   A number of useful practices have evolved from local government experience in negotiations for land development. First, it has been found that one person should be given the responsibility for representing the local government's interests. The greater authority this person has to speak on behalf of the local government, the better it is from the perspective of both the applicant and the local government. Second, the major issues should be defined during the negotiation so that subsequent agendas can be prioritized to allow the greatest amount of time to be spent on the most important issues.

Citizen participation   The reasons for public involvement in the planning process should be documented in order to encourage the planning staff to think through and write out its objectives here. Such objectives might be

1. To satisfy the requirements of legislation or governmental regulation
2. To define next year's planning program to enhance political support
3. To honor planning department promises made last year to include certain citizen groups in planning for certain development issues
4. To obtain feedback on neighborhood group concerns to be shared with other department heads
5. To coopt a group that has been nettlesome and obstructive in a technically sound neighborhood planning process
6. To obtain critiques of technical work to make it more relevant to citizens.

Telecommunications technology   Of all the services and responsibilities of local government, planning is tailor-made for televised presentation since the public development policy issues with which planners are concerned include a spatial component that is generally easier to describe visually than verbally. Already planners have found cable television (CATV) useful for

1. Presenting information on development permission applications
2. Showing spatial relations with the aid of maps
3. Relaying discussions of development issues by planning commissioners and city council members
4. Videotaping existing land use to show special relationships and to promote economic development
5. Teleconferencing information exchange between remote sites
6. Holding question-and-answer sessions with citizen groups at neighborhood community centers and with individuals at their homes.

Owing to the pluralistic definitions of the planning process and of its functions, planners have become more responsive to the needs of local elected and appointed officials. The challenge now is to establish and maintain the technical and political proficiency required to meet these needs. Up to this point, the skills and interests of planners have centered on analyst and infighter responsibilities and various admixtures of them, but emphasis is being placed on the six communication/information skills described above that are considered to be especially useful by local government managers. Management of the local planning process has changed in some jurisdictions and is changing in others, with the result that more emphasis is being placed on (1) comprehensive planning for only the really important issues, and (2) planning for local government delivery of services. Thus, the principles and practices of public comprehensive planning and of corporate planning are merging into a new entity, local government strategic planning.

Changing nature of management

Over the years public administration in general and management in particular have moved from a narrow and prescriptive emphasis on economy and efficiency to a much broader emphasis on making organizations effective. As a result, the work of the local government manager today is concerned with many facets of community affairs, which (as suggested by the major topics covered in the ICMA book, *The Effective Local Government Manager*) include the nature of the community; the governing body; effectiveness, efficiency, and economy; conditions for excellence; the future of the community; and the community and other governments. Basically, however, this work consists of four principal managerial functions: policy and program innovation, policy and program implementation, organization development and change, and organization leadership.

The following paragraphs summarize these roles and then describe the new skills that local government managers will have to develop if they are to keep up with changing times.[6]

Policy and program innovation

Local government management today puts more emphasis on new ideas for proposed policies and programs. Even in the smallest and quietest of organizations, the traditional ways of doing things do not remain traditional for very long. Innovations can range from a proposal for a drastic change in employment and educational opportunities to a modest change, say, in police patrol shifts or the number of persons on duty at fire stations. It is management's responsibility to be on top of the policy and program innovations that are needed to keep communities, organizations, and people "viable."

Policy and program implementation

Management used to be concerned primarily with efficiency and economy—that is, with keeping the machinery of the organization running right. Obviously, that is still a basic concern because the organization will not last long if it overspends its budget or provides such poor delivery of services that political repercussions ensue. Today, however, management is also oriented toward performance and results; goals and objectives are emphasized together with the measurement and evaluation of results. Here are several examples.

Prescriptive management—the one best way—is avoided.

Management balances the needs of elected officials, the city or county manager, department heads, and rank-and-file employees.

Policy formulation is based on an open process of consultation, negotiation, and compromise. Information is much more widely solicited and disseminated before decisions are made.

Effective use is made of tools, including the computer, word processor, computer software, quantitative methods, telecommunications, and measurement standards.

Work measurements are developed for both the hard (public works and fire, for example) and the soft (social services, library services) kinds of services.

Results are evaluated by input and output indicators, efficiency comparisons, quality measures, numerical scores, financial return, and other measures.

Other examples could be cited, especially in the area of productivity and evaluation, but they too would show that policy and program implementation has become a complex and viable aspect of management.

Organization development and change

In promoting organization development and change, management must recognize that the work of the organization is a process. The key variables are people, organizational structure, and organizational purpose. These three variables provide the framework within which motivational concepts for employees are formulated. According to *The Effective Local Government Manager*, five such concepts are particularly important: (1) contingency/expectancy, which refers to the differences in people and the complexity of motivation; (2) goals achievements/responsibility, which refers to goal setting and individual responsibility for effective performance that will help to achieve those goals; (3) needs hierarchy, which refers to Maslow's five levels of need (physiological needs; safety; belonging, love; esteem; and self-actualization);[7] (4) motivational factors broadly placed in two groups: dissatisfiers and motivators; and (5) reward/punishment, which refers to motivational theories dealing with rewards and punishments as reinforcers of behavior.

It has been suggested that motivation can be improved, and thus performance made more effective, in several ways: (1) results-oriented management; (2) performance appraisal or evaluation; (3) training and development of employees; (4) work design/redesign; and (5) reward systems. These motivational concepts can be applied in all types of situations in an organization, from routine problems to major reorganizations. They can also be used to effect major changes in organizational behavior. In a word, they are the means by which change takes place in an organization.

It is beyond the scope of this book to discuss these methods further, except to say they contribute significantly to the changing nature of management because they are appropriate to the cultural setting of local government employment; provide practical means of enhancing organizational effectiveness; protect and enlarge the skills and self-esteem of workers; and build on solid research findings in sociology, psychology, social psychology, and anthropology.

Organization leadership

Many books have been written about leadership, and the term has been defined in so many ways that it would be impossible to provide a thorough or systematic analysis of it here. There is little doubt, however, that leadership plays a major part, perhaps the major part, in the change being experienced by management. Leadership is exercised wherever human beings come together to perform a task, whether it be in small work groups or entire organizations. Various leadership styles have been identified and described, and many leadership variables have been isolated and analyzed. The qualities emphasized today are a long way from the authority, command, and charisma emphasized a generation ago. What leadership means at the present time can be summarized as follows:

1. Leadership is a set of skills involving persuasion and negotiation, teaching and coaching, learning and development, interaction with people, and decision making.
2. Leaders have certain styles and traits. Employee-centered managers, for example, are adept at communicating objectives and then setting high standards. At the same time, their employees are allowed reasonable

autonomy in getting their work done. Production-centered managers, on the other hand, tend to give detailed directions and to set up rigid rules and procedures.

To this list should be added two other distinctive characteristics: (1) leadership sets up and sets apart the manager from employees, and (2) effective leadership, more than any other factor, makes an organization responsive.

New skills

The skills that now reflect the changing nature of management are orchestration, articulation, empathy, and interpretation. This is flowery language for skills in negotiation, communication, work with elected officials, citizen participation, and telecommunications.

Brokerage/negotiation   One of the major findings of the ICMA Committee on Future Horizons of the Profession, organized in 1978, was that the major role of the manager in the future will be that of a broker or negotiator.[8] In other words, it is expected that the manager will be called upon more and more to negotiate agreements among the competing interests of community groups and elected officials.

Communication   Communication obviously is a means of exchanging and sharing information, but it can also be considered a social function that has value for any organized group. Because of its importance, two chapters in this book are devoted to communication, one to the technical side of information and information management, and the other to its social functions—that is, the ways in which it facilitates the work of organizations.

Empathy with elected officials   Managers (and planners!) will not be able to perform effectively unless they understand the interests, values, and needs of members of city councils and county boards. Elected officials often are extroverts who enjoy the limelight, whereas managers by and large prefer to avoid the limelight. Elected officials frequently have personal and family ties that go back for generations in the community. Managers (and planners) tend to be strangers the first day on the job; and in general are more concerned with professional standards and obligations than the hurly-burly of life in a specific place. These and other differences underscore the need for empathy with elected officials.

Citizen participation   Since this topic is discussed at several points in the book, all that needs to be said here is that citizen participation has greater influence on community decision making than it used to and that it is much more complicated in structure than the service clubs and miscellaneous associations of earlier years. To be tuned in to citizen participation is now considered an important characteristic of management.

Telecommunications   In the context of local government, telecommunications refers not only to cable television, but also to telephone systems, automated office equipment, word processors, and the computer. It is likely to become a major tool of planning, productivity measurement, and program evaluation.

Strategic planning

Any definition of planning that refers to a specific sphere of activity will obviously be of limited usefulness; only conceptual descriptions can cover the diverse political, social, economic, visual, and geographical settings in which local planning takes place. These settings have a bearing on the way in which the planning process will be organized and staffed and on the methods that will be used to carry it out. Most conceptual definitions of planning equate it with a process that consists of at least the following steps:

1. Determining goals to be achieved within a given time
2. Describing measurable objectives to be achieved
3. Describing standards to be used or products to be manufactured in accordance with the standards
4. Drawing on a body of knowledge embracing methodologies and techniques for conducting the activities of the government
5. Monitoring activities on a predetermined schedule to evaluate progress toward objectives
6. Maintaining retrievable records so that the process can be replicated or altered and tried again.

More specific definitions of planning generally apply only to selected political, economic, functional, or geographic areas. For example, if the housing planning process were described in sufficient detail for someone to prepare a housing plan, the methodology would include an analysis of housing units authorized by the building code for an area. Meanwhile, the highway planning process would include a detailed analysis of soil conditions that would not be included in the housing plan. The conceptual definition of planning, then, is based on the many functions of a government or a private enterprise, but the specific definition is based on the needs of the organization. Thus, the recreation planning process described in detail in recreation planning texts and the body of knowledge known to professional recreation staffs both refer to recreation planning at any given time. Similarly, public safety planning is a generic term for a process that may take place in various settings, for example, the criminal justice system or the fire prevention and control system. The comprehensive planning process draws on the standards, methodologies, techniques, and body of knowledge of many professions and disciplines to balance functional plans within an integrated comprehensive plan. Then, for purposes of implementation, the plan is disaggregated into a series of budget allocations, personnel decisions, equipment purchases, and day-to-day operational decisions that cumulatively may make it possible to achieve the objectives described in the comprehensive plan.

In a relatively stable economic, regulatory, and consumer environment, the emphasis of the planning process is on day-to-day operations. Delivery of a product or a service to a well-defined market in this environment does not require as much top-down (strategic) planning by a private or municipal corporation. As the economic, regulatory, or consumer environment becomes more competitive, however, managers at the top of the organization assess strategic plans, frequently in the light of new information and changed conditions.

Many of these conditions are outside the span of direct local government control; these might be interest rates, energy pricing, construction costs, state and federal grant regulations, consumer preferences, and a host of other factors that influence the provision of public services and private goods. Technically they are exogenous, or outside, variables that many local governments do not even observe, much less control. An important part of top management's strategic planning, then, is to consider the effects of these exogenous variables on management and planning decisions. *The more unstable these variables are, the greater the emphasis must be on top management strategic planning.*

Fourteen management processes have been identified to help define strategic planning. Those listed below have been adapted for local government use:

1. Setting objectives: Deciding on the services government should handle and the fundamentals to guide and characterize government policy. An objective is typically enduring and timeless.

2. Planning the strategy: Developing concepts, ideas, and plans for achieving objectives successfully, and for meeting and beating competition. Strategic planning is part of the total planning process that includes management and operational planning.

3. Establishing goals: Deciding on achievement targets that are shorter in time range or narrower in scope than the objectives, but designed as specific subobjectives in making operational plans.

4. Developing a government philosophy: Establishing the beliefs, values, attitudes, and unwritten guidelines that add up to "the way we do things around here."

5. Establishing policies: Deciding on plans of action to guide the performance of all major activities in carrying out strategy in accordance with the government's philosophy.

What is strategic planning?

Strategic planners often use a variety of techniques of group dynamics to arrive at consensus. Thus, the government strategic planner may have to shift his role slightly from being a proposer of policies and plans (which he then tries to sell) to being a facilitator of a strategic planning process.

The strategic planner must also be incisive, never using a lack of data as an excuse for inaction. In other words, the planner must get to the point of the problem, the solution, or the policy.

A corollary point is that strategic planners stress the use of intuition. Business planners started out trying to get business leaders, who often relied on intuitive solutions, to act on more rational grounds. Recent experience indicates that intuition is extremely important. Public planners, too, need to get away from the fear of acting intuitively.

Another key element of strategic planning is a shift of emphasis away from long-range end states to the decisions that need to be made today. The literature calls this "emphasizing the futurity of present decisions." While forecasting plays a role, choosing a specific course of action is seen as even more important.

Strategic planning, especially through the situation analysis, sorts out those things about which you can do something and those things about which you can't do much of anything at all. Strategic planning, for example, may require that local government weed out unnecessary programs, activities, or units. This sorting out requires a degree of realism that may be very difficult to achieve in a political environment.

Private strategic planners pay a great deal of attention to money, and, if public planners are to follow their lead, they will have to do the same. Effectively administered, strategic planning can in fact provide a better framework for public service programming and budgeting.

Strategic planning also can play an important role in involving elected officials. The process demands interaction between technicians and administrators and policy makers. Further, a good strategic plan states its missions and objectives in clearly understandable language.

Strategic planning in government can provide a vehicle for improving managerial effectiveness. Forcing top administrators to concentrate on key strategic issues means that a better sense of mission and purpose can be achieved. Strategic planning can be a mind-stretching exercise for top managers, a way of promoting creativity and innovative thinking and of forcing department heads to ask and answer questions of the highest importance to government.

Source: Frank S. So, "Strategic Planning: Reinventing the Wheel?" *Planning* 50 (February 1984): 20–21. Copyright © 1984 by the American Planning Association.

6. Planning the organization structure: Developing the plan of organization—the "harness" that helps people pull together in performing activities in accordance with strategy, philosophy, and policies.
7. Providing personnel: Recruiting, selecting, and developing people—including an adequate proportion of high-caliber talent—to fill the positions provided for in the organization plan.
8. Establishing procedures: Determining and prescribing how all important and recurrent activities shall be carried out.
9. Providing facilities: Providing the plant, equipment, and other physical facilities required to carry on services and the administration of government.
10. Providing capital: Making sure the government has the money and credit needed for physical facilities and working capital.
11. Setting standards: Establishing measures of performance that will best enable the government to achieve its long-term objectives.
12. Establishing management programs and operational plans: Developing programs and plans governing activities and the use of resources which—when carried out in accordance with established strategy, policies, procedures, and standards—will enable people to achieve particular goals.
13. Providing control of information: Supplying facts and figures to help people follow the strategy, policies, procedures, and programs; watching for forces at work inside and outside the business; and measuring performance against established plans and standards.
14. Activating people: Commanding and motivating people up and down the line to act in accordance with philosophy, policies, procedures, and standards in carrying out the plans of the government.[9]

The significance of these fourteen processes has been demonstrated by the experience gained since the 1950s; by the strategic planning done by many private corporations to prioritize the allocation of resources and the assignment of personnel; by the widespread use of 701 planning grants, adopted in 1954, to enlarge the horizons of local government officials; and by the Workable Program for Community Improvement, adopted in 1949, which set up a seven-part methodological framework for planning.

How the components of strategic planning have been derived can perhaps be illustrated in terms of the functional or departmental planning that takes place in recreation. (It could just as well be housing, transportation, or some other area.) Figure 2–5 shows elements that are typical of recreation planning. Note that many of these elements match or are similar to the fourteen processes in strategic planning.

A corporate example

In the 1960s the General Electric Company (GE) had a highly decentralized profit-center structure with the number of profit centers determined by sales volume.[10] This decentralized structure was adopted to stimulate growth and diversity and to motivate general managers. As the company's return on investment declined, however, it became apparent that there was some duplication in the competitive use of company resources and that new business opportunities were not adequately appraised. The response was to define a planning structure, introduce a planning process, and impose a planning discipline in the 1970s. Strategic Business Units (SBUs) were defined with the following characteristics:

1. A unique business mission within the company
2. Identifiable competitors outside the company
3. An external market focus
4. All major business functions present, to wit: manufacturing, engineering, finance, and marketing.

The forty-three designated SBUs were "inserted" into the existing organiza-

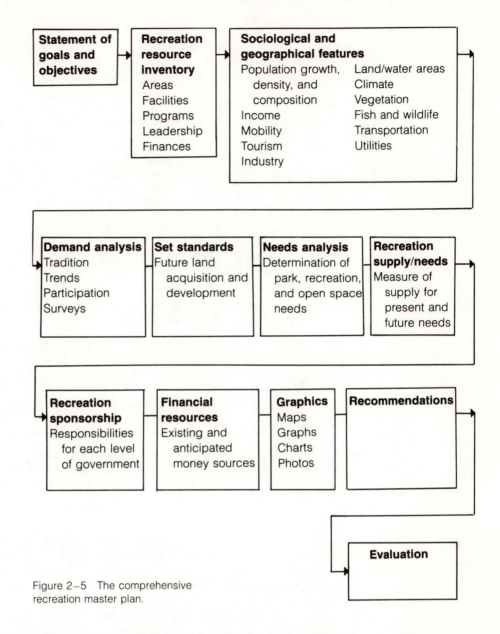

Figure 2–5   The comprehensive recreation master plan.

tional hierarchy at the most appropriate of three levels: the group, the division, or the department. The emphasis was on the strategic planning process rather than on the written plan. The process includes the six elements shown in Figure 2–6.

The strategic planning process used by General Electric is built on analyses of factors in the external environment (exogenous variables) such as those shown in Figure 2–7. City and county governments can also build their strategic planning

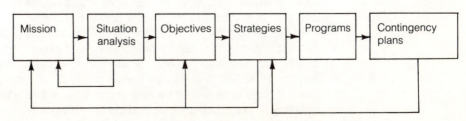

Figure 2–6   A corporate strategic planning process.

Factor	General Electric	City or county
Social	Population, income, education	Population, housing
Political and economic	National tax policy, international trade, defense contracts	Real property taxes, industrial revenue bonds
Financial	Union wage scales, setting prices, supplier contracts	Employee salaries and wages, pension liabilities
Bottom line	Stock dividends, net earnings per share, corporate debt	Balanced budget, acceptable postaudit, debt position
Technology	Laser research	Microcomputers
Markets	National and regional markets, special markets, defense contracts	Local service delivery, service to special groups
Customers	National, regional, special governmental, contractual	City or county residents
Competitors	Other manufacturers in U.S. and abroad	Other local governments
Accountability	Board of directors, stockholders, state and federal regulatory agencies	Citizens, governing body, state government, federal agencies, bondholders

Figure 2–7 Comparisons and contrasts between a large corporation and a typical city or county government. Note that both deal with the external environment but on a totally different scale. Note also the public accountability of city and county government.

on the external environment, as suggested in Figure 2–7. Note, however, the differences between the two—for example, compare the national and international scope of GE's activities with the local scale for cities and counties; or the *public accountability* of local governments (legal, electoral, and financial) with that of GE.

Because GE products and services may be consumed by a given city, its technological awareness of products and services would have to be years ahead of the city's awareness. The same could be said of services that the city provides to local industries; the city should be ahead of the industry in anticipating service demands.

The first step in introducing GE's strategic planning process was a four-day orientation for 320 top executives, which was followed by a two-week workshop for 428 persons who were to do the planning. Subsequently 10,000 managers received one day of awareness training. A planning calendar was established to review strategic plans and review budgets. Competitiveness of each SBU was to be analyzed annually. Measures of effectiveness were to be changed from one year to the next as more data became available.

In the 1980s, groups of SBUs with similar strategic plans were to be organized into six sectors immediately below the chief executive office in the hierarchy. Unlike the planning discipline for the 1970s, strategic plans were to be prepared for the six sectors and for the entire company. Economies of scale and coordination were to be sought through corporatewide functional planning and through planning of the company's worldwide activities.

A public example

More and more communities in the United States and Canada are redefining their planning processes as strategic planning. The strategy of taking the long-standing principles from comprehensive local government planning and applying them to contemporary issues of the highest priority distinguishes public strategic planning from corporate planning.

The following example from Canada illustrates how the strategic planning process operates in one community, the Regional Municipality of Halton (hereafter referred to as Halton Region). Located in the province of Ontario about twenty miles west of Toronto, Halton Region used a process that is similar to other strategic planning in both public and private sectors in that it was built on the following steps:

1. Identifying and forecasting pertinent factors
2. Evaluating the community's resources
3. Setting objectives
4. Formulating strategies to achieve objectives
5. Implementing strategies.[11]

Originally a county in Ontario, Halton became a regional municipality in 1974 under the province's municipal planning act. The city of Burlington and the towns of Oakville, Central Halton, and North Halton gave up responsibilities for certain services at that time and these services were assumed by the new regional municipality. Roads, health, welfare, police, water, sewage, and planning services are now performed by what amounts to an urban county form of government. Unlike the municipality's earlier planning, which had been oriented to land use, the new "corporate plan" was a strategic planning process.

Work on the corporate plan began in 1980 with a meeting of the chief administrative officer, ten department heads, and the corporate planning coordinator.[12] Each department head was asked for views on the following topics:

1. Responsibilities
2. Current tasks
3. Major new tasks or expansion of existing tasks to be undertaken in the next five years
4. Major new tasks or expanded tasks that the department would ideally like to undertake
5. Changes, particularly by the provincial government, affecting the department
6. Changes in the direction of the department perceived by the department head.

The tasks to be performed in the future became the basis for the Halton Region corporate plan. The aim was to set task priorities within departments, merge these priorities into an overall set of task priorities, and rerank them as a group. Once this was done, the tasks were costed for review by the standing committees of the Halton Region Council (the elected governing body for the region). The CAO and planning staff agenda for these committees was to: reiterate regional aims; prepare draft departmental work programs; describe key assumptions about the future; analyze and review draft departmental work programs; establish corporate directions and priorities; prepare and review the draft corporate plan; estimate costs and revenues; and prepare, review, and adopt the final corporate plan.

Together with department heads, the sixteen elected officials held a one-day workshop and developed these priorities:

1. Seek alternatives to the solid waste landfill
2. Create jobs

3. Improve communication with and service delivery to citizens
4. Improve financial accountability
5. Seek better intergovernmental coordination
6. Increase cost effectiveness
7. Strengthen management staff and practices
8. Return utilities and road responsibilities to city and town governments (this priority was later rescinded by the regional council)
9. Improve interaction with provincial policies and funds (intergovernmental relations)
10. Concentrate on tasks that draw the region together
11. Continuously examine levels of service
12. Reduce debenturing
13. Get rid of the sewer surcharge system.

Next, the CAO and department heads reviewed and edited tasks, thereby reducing them from 225 to 116. This process acquainted department heads with what the other departments intended to do during the next five years.

The CAO and department heads then used the paired comparison method to rank the 116 tasks. They took two tasks at a time and determined their ranking, then introduced a third task to obtain its relative ranking in comparison with the tasks already ranked, and so forth. This was done for four groups of tasks: previous, essential, desirable, and beneficial. When this work was completed, it represented the essence of the draft corporate plan: key directions (as identified by council), and tasks in priority order (as identified by the CAO and department heads).

However, it was decided to redo the exercise for setting priorities. To increase the council's involvement, four task forces were established, and the staff prepared a list of 46 basic responsibilities and/or functions of the government. This list was sent to each councillor, who was asked to score the responsibilities or functions on a scale of 1 to 5—1 signifying that the responsibility or function was "needed, but not so important" and 5 indicating that the responsibility was "crucial, vital, urgent." The ranking of these functions appeared in the final version of the corporate plan.

The final step was to rank the 116 tasks within the 46 basic responsibilities and/or functions of the government. The four councillor task forces simply listed tasks in order of priority within each responsibility or function, and this became the basic plan.

In this example the Halton Region used the planning process to identify objectives, determine priorities among tasks, and estimate costs of those tasks for a five-year period. Any local government can apply the process by following the steps described above.

Corporate and public differences

The GE example cited earlier shows the organizational commitment required for strategic planning. In this instance it involved a philosophical commitment of top management, the midcareer training of thousands of employees, organizational and reporting changes, and monitoring and refinement over a period of fifteen years.

Because their purposes differ, corporate planning experiences are not directly or wholly transferable to the public sector. Local government is a more complex organization than a corporation because, as Jacob B. Ukeles has pointed out, "Government performs two basic missions—service delivery and development—whereas the typical private company provides only a product or service."[13] In addition the types of services delivered by government are more varied than those offered by private companies. Another striking difference is that even corporate conglomerates with diverse markets have sharply distinguished profit centers. According to Ukeles, "This complexity of mission and activity makes the job of improving public management harder and more time-consuming than comparable improvements in industry."[14] The highly diverse and changing political constituencies, all of which have a voice in public affairs, further complicate the management of planning in the public sector.

Donald P. Crane and William A. Jones, Jr., have identified four differences between public and private managers' jobs.[15] First, government managers are expected to be loyal to the authority represented by the sovereignty of government as the "law of the land." Second, except when they are political appointees, career public managers are expected to refrain from partisan politics. Those who do not are often removed, or their responsibilities are reduced. Third, despite this neutrality, the job requires political responsiveness. Because the public manager interacts with elected officials and is responsible for implementing policy, his or her roles often cannot be sharply distinguished from the political process, except that the manager has no vote. Fourth, public managers must strive to represent the interests of the entire population of a given jurisdiction and take into account its concerns on all issues. The interests that managers represent in private corporations are confined to those of owners and stockholders; therefore, changing public opinion does not concern or affect these managers quite as much.

Benefits of strategic planning

The need for the General Electric Company to improve its return on investment, use company resources more efficiently, and better appraise business opportunities justified its decision to define and use a strategic planning process. Halton Region turned to strategic planning because it needed to reorganize governmental functions, initiate new tasks, and streamline administrative activities. Other communities have similar needs to revise, expand, or embark on a strategic planning process to achieve community objectives. George A. Steiner has identified some of the reasons for considering strategic planning, many of which apply to city and county governments:

1. Strategic planning is indispensable to top management's effectively discharging its responsibilities.
2. Strategic planning forces managers to ask and answer questions that are of the highest importance and that skilled managers should address.
3. Planning can simulate the future on paper, a practice that not only is comparatively inexpensive but also permits managers to make better decisions about what to do now about future opportunities and threats than waiting until events just happen.
4. Strategic planning is an effective way to look at a business as a system and thereby prevent suboptimization of the parts of the system at the expense of the whole organization.
5. Planning stimulates the development of appropriate aims, which in turn are powerful motivators of people.
6. Planning provides a framework for decision making throughout the entire organization and thereby makes it more likely that lower level managers will make decisions in conformance with top management's desires.
7. Planning is necessary for the better exercise of most other managerial functions.
8. Planning provides a basis for measuring the performance of the entire organization and its major parts.
9. Strategic planning flushes up to top management key issues and helps to establish appropriate priorities for dealing with them.
10. Strategic planning systems are superb channels of communication by means of which people throughout an organization converse in a common language about problems of central importance to them and to the organization.

11. Strategic planning helps train managers and helps build a managerial and staff capability that facilitates quick and proper response to new events.
12. Strategic planning systems provide an opportunity for people in organizations to contribute their talents to the decision-making process.
13. It is quite possible for an organization to be successful without formal planning, but for most organizations, success is more likely with formal strategic planning than without it.
14. Strategic planning is not without limitations. Forecasts on which it is based may not occur; internal resistance may thwart its effectiveness; it is expensive and difficult; it requires a certain type of talent that may not exist in an organization; it cannot get an organization out of a current crisis; and there are pitfalls that it must avoid.[16]

Strategic planning stimulates greater public dialogue and more political inputs into community development decisions; often this escalates the traditional planning process from the departmental level to the top manager and elected official level. When policy choices are made to undergird technical recommendations, management must take a more active part in planning. This means that the chief administrator of the city or county government should join the planning director and others by establishing the climate for inquiry, designating the people for specific assignments, and facilitating interdepartmental discussions that bring a variety of ideas to bear on common issues. The benefits to the organization and to the chief administrator will be evident in preparing operating and capital budgets, in reviewing programs and activities, and in evaluating operations.

Contingency planning

A contingency plan is a set of actions to be taken in the event that conditions planned for do not take place—a fallback, as it were. Contingency plans may be thought of as scenarios depicting the future and alternative responses to forecasted events. For example, if interest rates pass a preselected figure, the contingency plan may call for delaying a capital improvement bond sale. If the contingency plan were not implemented, the bonds would be sold and the interest drawdown would deplete funds to a point where insufficient principal would remain to construct the improvement.

Contingency planning means analyzing events that are not highly probable or that are not simply extensions of trends into the future; it introduces new information and ways of thinking into community policy making. This discipline will broaden the staff's understanding of the actual workings of processes that affect the community's ability to deliver services. A better understanding of the real estate market's behavior, construction material costs, energy pricing elasticity, and other factors influencing development permits local governments to incorporate this information into their decision-making processes and thus enables them to minimize costs, maximize revenues, or both.

A word of caution is in order, however. Planning for unanticipated events may connote pessimistic forecasting or generally negative thinking. Cultivating a doomsayer mentality is not the purpose of contingency planning; rather, it is to provide information that will guide decision makers in times of extraordinary economic, social, or climatological conditions. Public acceptance of such plans may not be widespread; witness the apathy surrounding civil defense preparedness planning. Nevertheless, they have proved their worth, as can be seen in the case of Wichita Falls, Texas, which happened to plan its response to natural disasters shortly before a 1980 tornado devastated a portion of the city. This plan saved lives and facilitated the orderly return of municipal services.

Contingency planning begins with determining what to measure and temporarily ends with a written document; then the process resumes and new variables are used to prescribe other scenarios. If the manager decided to measure interest rates by tracking Treasury Bill yields, local financial institution yields, and the published prime rate, flows of this information would be established. A "trigger" rate would be set, above which consideration would be given to altering municipal decisions. The probability of this rate being reached at selected points in time would be estimated. The estimated probability simply allows the staff to begin preparing decision makers and themselves for subsequent actions that may have to be taken.

The management of planning

Although this book has been written primarily for the professional planner in local government, the discussion would be incomplete without some mention of the local government manager. It is the local government manager who stands between professional/technical planning and the city council or county board (where the most important policy decisions are made). It is the local government manager who has a decisive influence on decisions concerning the planning agency budget—ranging from the major decisions about new computer hardware and software to the authorization for expansion of staff. It is the local government manager who, apart from the governing body, can most ably defend the planning director and staff from public attack. It is the local government manager who can best mesh planning agency work with the work of police, fire, parks, public works, and other departments. In the ideal community, it is the local government manager who can, perhaps better than anyone else, sit down with the planning director and think, anticipate, evaluate, schedule, classify, and forecast—in other words, plan the community's future.

The manager as planner

Four factors in particular determine the extent to which the local government manager is also the key local government planner. That is to say, these factors govern whether more than one-half of his or her time will be spent on the future of the community.

To begin with, the roles that elected officials and the manager have "carved out" for the manager will have a bearing on the time spent on planning. More than a job description is involved here. These roles include initiatives the manager takes and initiatives elected officials expect him or her to take.

Also important are the managerial performance criteria established formally and informally by elected officials. If the elected officials expect the manager to be on top of detailed daily departmental activities and to be prepared to report on them at any time, the manager will have precious little time to devote to the future.

A third factor is the manager's training and interest in planning. Managers who come from a professional planning background may take special pride in applying planning methods to their management of local affairs. Other managers may develop a strong interest in planning and use it successfully for the same purposes.

Finally, the manager may be in a position to fill a planning vacuum. This may involve describing and prioritizing contemporary issues or working with the planning commission and council in the absence of an in-house staff.

The amount of time local government managers spend in planning and promoting their community's future is often less than they would like to devote to this activity. It is said that Armand Hammer, chairman of the board, Occidental Petroleum Corporation, spends all of his working time in planning because it is the single most important activity for the corporation's future.[17] Some local government managers have a similar ideal, but few of them have been able to convince local elected officials that they can make the best use of their time in planning. The managers interviewed for this book estimated that the highest proportion of time they spent on planning was 75 percent. When the four factors described above were taken into account, however, this proportion dwindled to less than 20 percent in most cases, and less than 10 percent in some.

The work of the manager

What kind of planning do managers typically engage in? What can managers do who want to spend more time on planning? What can the planning staff do to aid the manager who cannot spend more time planning? Interviews conducted for this book and for ICMA's *The Effective Local Government Manager* highlight three planning functions of the local government manager.

The most general type of planning that managers engage in is the goal-setting process informally undertaken by almost all communities and formally undertaken by many. In this process, the manager is cast in the role of community leader and technical coordinator. At times, this role amounts to little more than shifting the focus of elected officials from administrative details to development issues. On the whole, however, managers and local elected officials alike are expected to articulate and reestablish community goals as a prerequisite to policy making and budgeting.

The second planning function of the manager is to prepare and monitor the operating and capital budgets. The annual budget—which some consider to be the community plan—clearly has an important effect on development plan implementation. However, in any given year, the manager probably does not influence more than 5 to 10 percent of expenditures.[18] This is due to locked-in legal, policy, and administrative parameters typically committing more than 90 percent of revenues. Therefore, the expenditure leverage available to the manager is relatively small.

The third planning role of the manager is to monitor and evaluate citizen participation. The manager must keep his "ear to the ground" to assist the council in making politically acceptable decisions and to refocus staff services to assure responsiveness to council demands.

The manager's role in fostering planning has been described as follows:

1. Set aside periodic time to meet with your senior staff to brainstorm the future of the city and its government. Encourage senior staff members to participate in professional activities and to subscribe to and read professional journals.
2. Identify emerging issues about which the council should be thinking, and expose them by meetings, retreats, field trips, and other contacts with officials of jurisdictions which have dealt with these problems and can speak about them from experience.
3. Do as much reading as you can about impending developments and all aspects of society, and especially about technology which may be of value to your city government.
4. Encourage citizen and civic associations to sponsor programs and to think and talk about what they want for the future of their city.[19]

Because the manager is the intermediary between the planning staff and elected officials in the planning process, the quality of that process is especially important for the manager who does not have the time or technical background to manage it. It has been pointed out that "by helping provide a technically competent plan and a supporting planning process that is open and consistent, the manager can assist the mayor and council to spot the community problems ahead, and develop acceptable assurances, modifications or alternatives which will, at the minimum, maintain crisis at a manageable level."[20]

The manager also can facilitate community planning by having in place:

a well conceived plan and action program and an organization that is goals oriented. We should think more in terms of what can be done, and how we are going to measure our progress in doing it; then we should assign responsibility for accomplishing goals to the right unit or individual within our organization. . . . We [Walnut Creek, California] have long since established the traditional general planning process to which we have added a financial plan—both short-term and long-term—necessary to implement objectives reflected in the general plan. We continue to assess the public's attitude toward its community . . . and to the extent possible move forward accordingly. The manager in this situation must be a planner and a facilitator, not the judge and jury. He can bring his experience and expertise to the process, however, deferring assessment of public needs and wants to the elected officials, leaving final judgments on key issues affecting the future of the community in their hands rather than assuming that responsibility.[21]

The work of the planner

Once the scope of planning has been determined, it is the responsibility of the planning staff to meet their job responsibilities accordingly. At this point the planning process takes on a unique prescription oriented to community needs. Planning directors sensitive to these needs play a great supporting role in community management.

Because organizational interrelations are built around people rather than abstract and generalized titles and job descriptions, roles of the planner in assisting the manager will vary with the manager's definition of his or her planning role and with the skills the planner brings to his or her assignment.

In some communities, the planner is responsible for preparing the land use plan and for overseeing development permission ordinances. In other communities, planners have, in addition to those responsibilities, the job of preparing capital improvement programs and revenue and expenditure forecasts for the operating budget. In still other communities, planners engage in all of these activities and also act as policy advisers to appointed and elected officials.

In the first instance, the planner's role is constrained by the classical definition of physical planning. In the last role, the planner's work blends technical, administrative, and political skills. This role must be earned; it is not given to the planner. It is earned by demonstrating political competence and earning the confidence of the elected and appointed officials responsible for development decisions.

Plans, policies, and power　More and more city planners are integrating policy advice with their technical recommendations. But they still do not wish to actively "sell" their proposals.

Convinced of the validity of the pluralistic model of decision making, many political scientists have concluded that comprehensive planning is impossible.

The bulk of resources for power is held by the chief executive. Opposition to the executive would doom the planner to failure, since, more than anyone else in the system, it is the executive who directs development.

Only if the profession's image includes the picture of the planner as rightfully a political actor will planners obtain both professional rewards and the completion of concrete programs.

Source: Francine F. Rabinovitz, *City Politics and Planning* (New York: Atherton Press, 1969), 12, 77, 82, and 132.

The mix of technicians with political advisory roles changes with the interests and competence of the technician, and with the technician's influence over funding. For example, it has been reported that the three most influential persons in the inner circle of political advisers in one community are the traffic engineer, housing program director, and wastewater facilities administrator.[22]

This is not to suggest that the wholly technical or a technical-political mix of skills is preferred. Both are needed. The distinguishing feature is that persons with the technical-political mix of skills are more likely to participate in development decisions earlier and to have greater influence on the final decision. In the eyes of most people, this is a more effective role for the planner than the narrower one of preparing land use plans and administering the development permission process.

Conclusion

"Comprehensive planning," a term in use for many years, has been redefined to cover the full range of consequences of specific development decisions as well as analyses and alternative forecasts of long-range growth. As a result, comprehensive planning has become much more operational—that is, it is now built into planning and management processes of local government that produce community development decisions and local government services. This new definition assumes that change is a constant, and it includes the worst-case scenario (if something can go wrong, it will).

Local planning had its roots in the efforts to correct the physical degradation of cities that accelerated in the late nineteenth and early twentieth centuries owing to immigration and rapid growth. In those days planning began with improving physical design and was accompanied by the Civic Reform Movement, which brought in the short ballot, fewer elective offices, nonpartisan elections, the commission plan, and then the council-manager plan of city government. The movement was not known as a management movement, but that was one of its results.

After World War II, local planning and management began to converge, in part because of the stimulus of federal grants for urban renewal and related programs. As planning and management moved closer together, often goaded by necessity, it became harder to distinguish between planning, management, and political decisions, and social, economic, and land use consequences. Proposals for a new shopping center, housing for the elderly, and the ubiquitous convention center are examples of decisions that involve technical planning, neighborhood fears and aspirations, the city or county credit rating, and the tax rate. Today the roles of planners and managers are continuing to merge, and together the practitioners are aiming to achieve locally determined objectives for community development.

The names may vary—comprehensive planning, the Workable Program for Community Improvement, corporate planning, strategic planning, and so on—but the process is basically the same. Drawing on both public sector and private sector practices, this kind of planning adds a new dimension to local governments and to the roles of their chief administrative officers.

1   For a series of essays on the work of pioneers in planning, see: Donald A. Krueckeberg, ed., *The American Planner: Biographies and Recollections* (New York: Methuen, 1983).

2   This is the title of Chapter 1 in: Wayne F. Anderson et al., *The Effective Local Government Manager* (Washington, D.C.: International City Management Association, 1983).

3   Joseph M. Heikoff, *Planning and Budgeting in Municipal Management* (Chicago: International City Managers' Association, 1965), 37.

4   Frank S. So, untitled paper presented at the national planning conference of the American Planning Association, Cincinnati, 27 October 1980.

5   This informal survey was conducted by the author as part of the research for this book.

6   Much of this section is based on: Anderson et al., *Effective Local Government Manager*, 109–11, 123–25.

7   The key work is Abraham Maslow, *Motivation and Personality*, 2d ed. (New York: Harper & Row, 1970).

8   Laurence Rutter, *The Essential Community: Local Government in the Year 2000* (Washington, D.C.: International City Management Association, 1980), 133–37.

9   Marvin Bower, *The Will to Manage: Corporate Success through Programmed Management* (New York: McGraw-Hill, 1966), 17–18.

10   Stanley H. Hoch, "Strategic Management in GE," in *Proceedings of the White House Conference on Strategic Planning*, ed. Susan M. Walter (Washing-

ton, D.C.: Council of State Planning Agencies, 1980), 12–26.

11   Adapted from: William R. Dodge, Jr., and Douglas Eadie, *Strategic Planning: An Approach to Launching New Initiatives in an Era of Retrenchment*, Management Information Service Reports, vol. 14, no. 9 (Washington, D.C.: International City Management Association, 1982): 3.

12   Information for this process was provided by C. E. Babb, former Halton Region Corporate Planning Coordinator.

13   Jacob B. Ukeles, *Doing More with Less: Turning Public Management Around* (New York: AMACOM, 1982), 14.

14   Ibid., 141.

15   Donald P. Crane and William A. Jones, Jr., *The Public Manager's Guide* (Washington, D.C.: Bureau of National Affairs, 1982), 12–13.

16   George A. Steiner, *Strategic Planning: What Every Manager Must Know* (New York: The Free Press, a Division of Macmillan, Inc., 1979), 47–49.

17   Interview with Frank B. Friedman, Vice President, Health and Environment, Occidental Petroleum Corporation, 20 August 1982.

18   Interview with Thomas W. Fletcher, Vice President, SRI International, 19 August 1982.

19   Quoted in: Wayne F. Anderson et al., *Effective Local Government Manager*, 154.

20   Communication from Elisha C. Freedman, Commissioner of Administrative Services, State of Connecticut.

21   Communication from Thomas G. Dunne, City Manager, Walnut Creek, California.

22   Interview with Kyle C. Testerman, Knoxville, Tennessee, 9 July 1982.

3 Organizing for comprehensive planning

Most city councils, county boards, and other legislative bodies fear the decisions that bring unintended consequences. The shopping center that generates traffic jams for the next thirty years, the downtown parking garage that is used at 60 percent of capacity, and the highway bypass that almost shuts down some central business district stores are but a few examples of the mistakes that can be seen in many parts of the country. Comprehensive planning helps to anticipate and plan for these unintended consequences.

Elected officials and appointed administrators depend on planners to help prevent bad political decisions and reduce the effects of past mistakes. Planners, partly because of the social and economic complexity and long-term ramifications of development issues, are now in positions of influence in decision making. Their specialized skills—especially their ability to obtain, interrelate, and analyze information—have moved planning and planners into the mainstream of local government.

Local government budgets, for example, are highly related to land use decisions. Political careers have been launched and terminated by votes on development decisions. And, as growth has slowed in communities across the country, high technology decisions on issues such as cable television have taken on nearly equal significance to local politicians.

The degree to which planning influences decisions is said to depend on three factors: organizational, technical, and political conditions.[1] The local government reform movement of the early twentieth century recognized the importance of all three of these conditions. Reform interests centered not only on improving city life, but also on civil service, the short ballot, the commission plan, the council-manager plan, and nonpartisan elections. The city planning movement— generally thought to have originated with the publication of the McMillan Committee Plan for Washington, D.C. in 1902—was to be nonpolitical with an independent planning commission, composed of appointed community leaders, that would recommend and influence decisions affecting community development. Some people thought this was a necessary arrangement but that it could be done away with as soon as the technical quality of local government improved, presumably within a few years. This organizational set-up allowed the planning process to become more directly tied to elected officials with constituencies and budget-making powers. Those who thought the planner should be an adviser to the mayor were seeking to increase the planner's influence over land use decisions. They failed to recognize, however, that in communities with the weak mayor form of government, the planner would be able to influence only one member (the mayor) of the city council.

Others advocated that planning should be a function of the city council.[2] This approach could have been of great service to the city council, but it did not provide the strong mayor or the city manager with the technical depth required to carry out policy.

Achieving objectives

Many factors contribute to achieving an organization's objectives, but, according to recent evidence, personal and organizational interrelationships are particularly critical to the success of a local planning process. It follows that great amounts of time should be spent only on the most important factors that determine effectiveness of the planning agency. But what are these factors?

In a 1980 survey of planning executives in central cities, organization for planning ranked only sixth among the factors influencing the effectiveness of planning. Those interviewed assigned higher priorities to legal powers, expectations of the chief administrator, the local economy, and other factors. They ranked the factors in this order:

1. The legal powers of planners (whether planning is advisory, mandatory, or binding)
2. Expectations of the boss (chief elected or appointed official)
3. The abilities, biases, and motivations of the planning agency
4. The agency's resources, budget, and manpower
5. Structure of the local economy and the city's fiscal capability
6. The organization chart—that is, how the planning director relates to decision makers
7. The abilities, biases, and motivations of other agency heads
8. Conflicts between federal and state planning requirements and conflicts with local goals
9. Public expectations about the future of the city
10. The community's perception of the usefulness of planning
11. Environmental and other constraints, including the degree of existing development
12. The centralization or decentralization of the local power structure
13. The community's social fabric.[3]

In a 1982 survey, about ninety planning officials working in the fifty-three largest U.S. city planning agencies and about ninety faculty members working in forty graduate schools of planning were asked to comment on similar factors, but in this case the results were different.[4] The practicing planners ranked the seven factors listed as follows: (1) personalities and power structure, 19.8%; (2) economic and environmental conditions, 17.8%; (3) local governmental structure, 16.7%; (4) community and social fabric, 15.2%; (5) local planning agency, 12.9%; (6) legal powers of planners, 10.2%; (7) and intergovernmental relations, 7.4%.

The planning faculty members ranked the seven factors in the following order: (1) personalities and power structure, 21.8%; (2) economic and environmental conditions, 17.4%; (3) community and social fabric, 15.9%; (4) local planning agency, 12.9%; (5) local governmental structure, 12.8%; (6) legal powers of planners, 10.1%; and (7) intergovernmental relations, 9.1%.

For both groups, the highest ranking factors were: personalities and power structure, economic and environmental conditions, and community and social fabric.

In addition, local government structure was ranked third by the planning practitioners. Both the ranks and the ratios of these factors strongly attest to the interwoven *context* of planning. If that is the case, what is the most appropriate way to organize the local planning function? A number of possibilities exist. Conceptually, the planning function could be organized around its goals, technical specialties, clientele, or geographic area. In a given community, other factors may be equally important, including personality traits, tenure, statutory constraints, or the availability of funding.

Making comprehensive plans

As the focal point for determining alternative courses of action, the plan's time horizon depends on outside forces and the intensity of community needs and desires. Issues have different relative significance to elected officials and their constituents. Some issues, as has been pointed out elsewhere,

have major, long-term economic and social impacts that directly affect a large segment of a community, typically involve intense debate or conflict over a prolonged period of time, have major fiscal implications for a city, involve irreversible investment decisions, are a significant factor in determining the nature of the city's physical development, and are unique issues which do not recur on a frequent basis.[5]

Other issues have a much more limited impact, are of concern to fewer people, have less effect on the budget, and are given lower priority by elected officials. Whatever the case, the technical response to these factors makes it possible to classify a given issue as strategic or nonstrategic.

Strategic issues are those that greatly affect a public or private organization but that the organization can deal with. Examples of strategic issues might include highway construction, extension of trunk sewerage lines, acquisition of region-serving parkland, and location of a sanitary landfill.

Nonstrategic issues are those that, at a given time, include exogenous variables over which local officials have little or no control. For example, the price of oil is outside the community's control; therefore, trying to influence that price would not be part of the community's strategic planning. An example closer to home for many communities would be a developer's decision to build a new shopping center in an unincorporated area just outside the city limits. Other examples of nonstrategic issues might be the location of an elementary school, replacement of a waterline, or installation of playground equipment.

The point to remember is that a project or decision that is nonstrategic in one community might be strategic in another. The classification may depend on the community's size, citizen awareness, amount of regulation that is politically acceptable, or other factors peculiar to that community.

The next question is, who determines whether an issue is strategic or non-strategic? The answer lies in the setting in which planning takes place. That is to say, long-term planning takes place in both functional (intradepartmental) and comprehensive (interdepartmental) settings. Functional areas include public safety planning, water quality planning, social services planning, health planning, and others. The comprehensive planning process consists of interrelating and reconciling differences among these functional area plans. Its locus of staff involvement moves up the pyramid of responsibilities to the office of the chief administrator as greater coordination among departments and greater interpretation of policy are required (see Figure 3–2). It is at the level of the chief administrator that issues are determined to be strategic or nonstrategic. More political and technical resources should be devoted to strategic issues because, by definition, they are of greater consequence to the community.

Comprehensive planning objectives

Like strategic planning, comprehensive planning is defined differently from community to community. In older communities where the physical plant is declining, infrastructure and neighborhood maintenance and conservation may require immediate attention. Because these facilities are already in place, the time period for planning may be relatively short if the capital improvement budget covers only a five- or six-year period. In growing communities that anticipate conversion of unimproved land to urban uses, the time period may be longer since growth accommodation will be the highest priority there. Perhaps a ten- to twenty-year planning period would be most appropriate in a case like this because of the need to extend facilities and to reserve portions of the land.

What is comprehensive planning?
The term comprehensive planning refers to the process of developing the overall plan for a city or county government and placing and keeping the plan in effect.

The comprehensive plan may also be known as the master plan (although that term has fallen into disfavor because it promises more than it can deliver), the development plan, the general plan, or simply the city (or county) plan.

The subject of this chapter, comprehensive planning, is characterized by emphasis on physical development, a long span of time (hence, long-range planning), and comprehensiveness (covering all major aspects of the community's future).

The comprehensive plan is first a statement of community goals. These goals,

which usually are quite broad, are identified more specifically by statements of policy for the city or county government. The comprehensive plan in many places also serves as a legal document that is the base for a variety of land use controls. Finally, the comprehensive plan is a guide to decision making, including operating and capital budgets, land use measures that encourage (or discourage) growth, economic development measures, and other steps in directing community growth and change.

Source: Based in part on Frank Beal and Elizabeth Hollander, "City Development Plans," in *The Practice of Local Government Planning*, ed. Frank S. So et al. (Washington, D.C.: International City Management Association, 1979), 163–72.

Regardless of the time selected, the primary purpose of comprehensive planning is to help managers and elected officials define objectives, set their priorities, and seek solutions to long-term issues. The plan may call for an immediate response to pressing issues or a more complicated assessment of the consequences of investment and other decisions.

There is no pretense that the land use plan contains a complete set of solutions for issues relating to physical development. . . . The plan acknowledges the existence of uncertainty: the fact that policies are in transition and offer no final prescription for the future.[6]

Thus, the quality of a comprehensive plan is determined by its relevance to locally defined issues and its usefulness to its clients—citizens, elected officials, appointed officials, and others. "A good comprehensive plan," it has been said, "helps to keep big ideas in perspective, to prevent short-term expedient development decisions from foreclosing preferable options in the future, and to direct

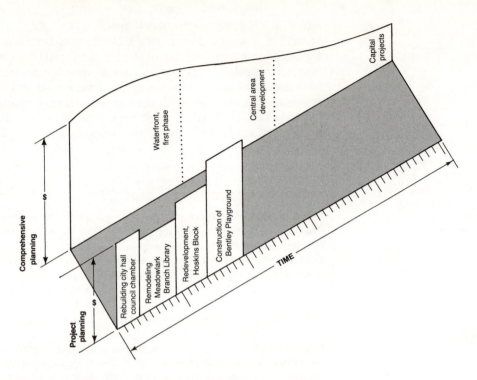

Figure 3–1   Comprehensive and project planning by money, time, and geographic area. The differences in size, cost, and time usually separate comprehensive and project planning.

scarce capital funds from year to year. It also helps people directly by providing some visible official basis for predicting what will happen to their neighborhoods."[7]

Recap

Both planners and managers, in working toward city and county government objectives, need to set up a scorecard or tally sheet with which to evaluate factors that are likely to control their communities. A 1982 survey of planners and planning teachers showed that people and power, economics and environment, and community and social fabric were the most important factors in most of the places surveyed. These would be the factors to look at first in your community.

It would be useful now to look at two paired elements that help define comprehensive planning: strategic/nonstrategic and functional/comprehensive. This approach will yield different definitions of the comprehensive planning process in each community.

First, strategic planning involves issues that are important, expensive, controversial, and lasting. The decisions that will be made are likely to affect many people for a long time, and the mistakes will be visible and costly. Nonstrategic planning, on the other hand, involves decisions that are less urgent, less drastic, less expensive, and less controversial.

Second, functional planning means taking on and thinking through one issue at a time, whereas comprehensive planning includes interdepartmental questions for which the planning and management solutions may be closely integrated. (Figure 3–2 shows this process as a pyramid.)

Comprehensive planning is the subject of this chapter; project planning is covered in Chapter 4.

Planning for policy development

Many types of problems compete for the attention and resources of local governments. Some problems beg for immediate attention. Concluding a deal with a developer, for example, must be taken care of immediately.

Other problems permit a more contemplative approach. Problems concerning appropriate land use patterns, water supply sources, and the purchasing of fire equipment are the type that can be anticipated and planned for over the long term (which is generally taken to mean more than two years).

Administrators and elected officials can develop policies to meet problems before they occur. When contentious issues arise because of competing demands on governments, policies are needed to guide decisions. Figure 3–3 shows an orderly way to think about problems generically, excluding personalities and events that will be built in later. Look at the problem as a continuum from perception and definition to "legitimation" in the budget. Once a problem has been recognized by looking at demands and priorities, it is possible to develop proposals for meeting the problem. And once it has been decided that the government should act, programs and budgets can be prepared and put into effect.

The process of identifying problems and establishing the limits of demand for their solution has both a technical and a political dimension. At times technical persons will be the first to identify a problem, as in the case of acid rain. At other times the political pulse of the community will be the harbinger of a deeply rooted problem such as minority unemployment. Because of their emphasis on the future and on the interrelatedness of problems, planners continually refine definitions of and prospective solutions to problems.

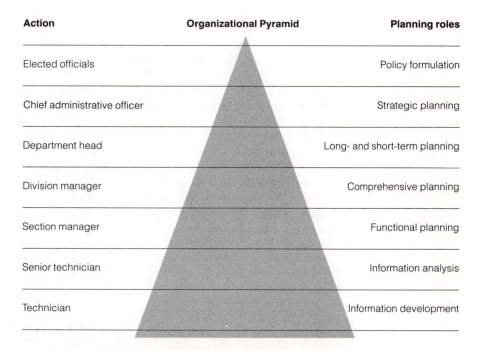

Action	Organizational Pyramid	Planning roles
Elected officials		Policy formulation
Chief administrative officer		Strategic planning
Department head		Long- and short-term planning
Division manager		Comprehensive planning
Section manager		Functional planning
Senior technician		Information analysis
Technician		Information development

Figure 3–2 Actors and their planning roles in the planning pyramid.

Phase	Activities	Initial product
Problem to government	Perception Definition	Problem
	Aggregation Organization Representation	Demand
	Agenda setting	Priorities

	Formation
	  Research
	  Review
	  Projection
	  Selection
		Proposal

Action in government	Legitimation
	  Identification of interests
	  Communication
	  Bargaining
	  Compromise
		Program

	Appropriation
	  Formation
	  Legitimation
		Budget

Figure 3–3   Policy
formation activities.

Setting the agenda

Planners frequently have assisted local officials to set public agendas, often by a goals articulation process. These goal-setting programs have generated dialogue between citizens, elected officials, and staff members on important contemporary problems and solutions. Since the demands for action on the whole have far exceeded local government finances and political will, however, the proposed solutions usually have been stretched into the future. Since the problems usually have been highly interrelated with local issues and local revenue sources, planning agencies across the country have become deeply involved in these community goal-setting programs.

These programs have all been patterned after local needs. Some have emphasized community development funding, whereas others have emphasized general growth patterns, economic changes, or the environment. An interesting case is that of Long Beach, California. Acknowledging the change in development priorities from serving growth to managing the conservation of existing facilities, the city decided in 1979 to change its approach to community development. The city council agreed that the growth phase had all but ended and that the physical plant was aging while the population was changing. The council therefore adopted a community development strategy that called for three new approaches:

First, the city must view its role not only as a regulator of private development but also as a stimulator of private investment. In many areas of our city the level of private investment is not sufficiently high to guarantee continued viability. In fact, there are clear signs of deterioration which must be overcome. City actions can help direct and stimulate a renewed high investment level in these areas. These actions might include land assembly programs to encourage developer investment in new commercial, industrial, and residential construction; incentive zoning to attract investment capital to high quality developments in areas of the city where new

Goals for Americans, 1960 *First*, we must recognize that the physical environment is indivisible. Houses, pipes, roads, schools, factories, offices, wilderness parks and dams are all part of the same organic system.

Second, a creative partnership between public agencies and private enterprise is essential. The old battle between "private" and "public," fortunately disappearing at many points, has no meaning in relation to the physical environment, which is shaped by both.

Third, over-all goals and guidance are needed for the metropolitan community, since public decisions are so important in determining the development pattern which affects the whole economic and social structure.

Fourth, we must be prepared to devote a bigger share of our total income to the physical improvements that growth and obsolescence demand.

Fifth, federal and state aids must be flexibly coordinated to serve locally determined ends, and to stimulate responsible local action.

Source: Catherine Bauer Wurster, "Framework for an Urban Society," in *Goals for Americans* (Englewood Cliffs, N.J.: Prentice-Hall, 1960), 245–46.

investment is desperately needed; or code enforcement and low interest loans to encourage consumer reinvestment in aging homes.

Second, the city must begin to view its service delivery on a geographic as well as functional basis. In addition to defining its mission in terms of miles of streets to be repaired, tons of trash to be collected, and numbers of crimes to be solved, the city must also view its service delivery in terms of neighborhoods to be maintained and improved. This is the basic thrust of this community development strategy. All neighborhoods are not the same in their needs. While many are strong and self-maintaining, others are declining and in need of immediate attention to arrest deterioration. A coordinated approach to service delivery in these neighborhoods is required together with direct city actions to stimulate reinvestment.

Third, the city must relate its economic development in job training efforts to the needs of the changing population. The city is not and cannot become a provider of basic social services. But it can utilize the economic development and job training resources available to it to provide opportunities for many of our dependent population to become self-supporting. By matching people to job training programs which are, in turn, matched to jobs being created through economic development efforts, large numbers of our underemployed work force can find productive jobs to support themselves and their families. With increased income, they can afford to rent or own decent housing and can participate positively in the economy of the city.[8]

This strategy has a number of distinctive features:

1. It is a departure from past efforts to encourage and service growth and is part of a process of managing community development.
2. It recognizes how development occurs while prioritizing only those programs that the city can control and that complement the efforts of the private sector and of other levels of government.
3. It is built up from the neighborhood level to achieve communitywide goals.
4. It seeks to leverage public investment to stimulate private investment since the two go hand-in-hand in the community-building effort.
5. It acknowledges that limited financial resources are available to implement the strategy and concentrates on only three priorities for reinvestment rather than stretching those resources even thinner by taking on additional activities.

6. It integrates the physical, social, and economic responses necessary to deal with the highest priority issues. This approach crosses program and service delivery lines and seeks to coordinate them to achieve community development goals.
7. The strategy is to be revised annually as the staff obtains a better understanding of the problems of the city and the impact of various programs, and becomes more successful in meeting the city's most pressing needs.
8. The strategy is related to allocation of the federal community development block grant as funds are allocated to projects over successive twelve-month periods.

Protecting public investment

Since many communities make no effort to quantify the long-term investment in public land, facilities, buildings, and equipment, the importance of protecting that investment is often not appreciated by elected officials and citizens. It has been estimated that approximately one-third of the value of these properties in urban areas is owned by the public, and the remaining two-thirds is owned by the private sector.[9]

Public ownership includes streets, sewage systems, parks, schools, and other investments that have been made during the life of the city. For example, the real property tax base of Evansville, Indiana, was more than $2.8 billion in 1983. If the estimated ratio of the value of public investment is reasonable, Evansville and other levels of government invested about $1.4 billion in plant and equipment.

One objective of comprehensive planning is to protect that investment from deteriorating and to make additional investments that will yield a real (constant dollar) increase. Public investment is a city or county's net worth, and it can be stabilized, increased, or decreased largely by means of local policy. If the local government neglects its investment—through failure to maintain the sewer system, for example—its net worth will fall, at first slowly, then at an accelerated pace. Indeed, preservation and enhancement of local government net worth has been one of the major objectives of the urban renewal and community development programs administered by the federal government since 1949.

Increasing the tax base

The problem of raising local revenue is a central one for all local elected officials. Revenue shortfalls, statutory and political constraints on raising capital funds, state and federal mandates, and pressure to reduce taxes have sharply increased the importance of forecasting and managing revenues to meet these obligations. Comprehensive planning goals often include revenue enhancement, either explicitly or implicitly. An early lesson in political reality for many a planner has been to observe the close relations elected officials see between land use planning and protecting and enhancing the revenue base. Generation of revenue is an important criterion for selecting and advocating development projects in many communities.

Many municipal planning department plans include goals which, if implemented, would increase revenues or reduce expenditures. The *Phoenix Concept Plan 2000: A Program for Planning* includes the following goals for the city's economy:

A. *Stability*
Maximize the stability of employment and income generation in Phoenix through diversification of employment opportunities.

1. Facilitate the continued growth of tourism through protecting the natural and man-made attractions which draw people to the valley.
2. Facilitate the development of manufacturing enterprises by providing for a wide choice of sites with good access to labor markets, suppliers and buyers.
3. Protect and encourage agricultural industries.

B. *Taxes*
1. Minimize the local tax burden by providing public services and facilities in the most efficient manner possible.
2. Revise the local property tax system to encourage rather than penalize maintenance and rehabilitation of older units.

C. *Employment*
1. Provide opportunities for diversification of basic employment.
2. Create conditions conducive to attracting and retaining a labor force.
3. Revitalize business and industrial enterprises which provide meaningful employment opportunities to low-income people and increase the tax base in low-income areas.

D. *Development Costs and Incentives*
1. Encourage partnership of public and private sectors in providing for both development and redevelopment.
2. Emphasize the use of incentives over the use of restrictions to achieve appropriate development.[10]

These goals establish a policy-making framework that elected officials and staff members can use as a guide in their program activities. The goals of the Phoenix plan are relatively explicit in comparison with goals of other comprehensive plans. Consider, for example, those adopted by the council of the Lexington-Fayette urban county government:

1. Encourage balanced distribution of employment opportunities at locations near residential concentrations and major transportation systems.
2. Maintain an appropriate balance between economic development activities and natural and human resources.
3. Provide full and equal employment opportunities for all citizens in order to maintain a low unemployment rate.[11]

Other comprehensive plans, meanwhile, are less explicit about the economy or about raising revenue. For example, the West Vancouver, British Columbia, Community Plan was based on two goals:

1. Retain the parklike, neighborhood-oriented character of West Vancouver.
2. Plan the community in the framework of the above, within a policy of fiscal responsibility.[12]

In still other communities contemporary development goals have not yet been defined and adopted. A case in point is Prince William County, Virginia. In 1980 the county administration began preparing a management plan for the county.[13] The first issue to be identified was finance, which raised three sets of questions: (1) how revenues would be raised, (2) how capital projects would be financed, and (3) how funds would be managed. Financial and planning data were analyzed to set the stage for defining management goals. An analysis of these and other questions facing the county appeared in a 1981 report that identified the three most crucial issues as: (1) management, (2) finance, and (3) the development permission process.[14] These issues established the framework for a strategic planning process that linked planning, management, and budgeting.

The central reality for Prince William County's government in the 1980s, according to the plan, is that citizen expectations and the cost of service delivery are increasing at a more rapid rate than revenues. As a result three objectives have been identified: (1) improve management and productivity; (2) increase revenues; and (3) improve management of funds.

This strategic plan identified the most important issues that the county government could control and recommended changes in management processes that would improve the delivery of local government services. The plan did not distinguish the need for departmental management improvements as anything more than delivering better local government to citizens.

Emphasizing economic development

As Chapter 2 has pointed out, a number of events have greatly influenced the evolution of planning at the local level, among them the passage of the federal Economic Development Act of 1974. This act emphasized economic development strategies, urban economic development, and the coordination of economic development programs as a means of expanding job opportunities and the tax base. Because employment in manufacturing was declining at the time, the number and variety of federal, state, and local programs and staffs devoted to competing for new or relocated jobs increased. As the competition for growth became more sophisticated, the arsenal of programs to attract development became more varied. Local economic development strategies were reoriented toward specific projects, often known as public-private partnerships. From communitywide or overall neighborhood investment strategies, the emphasis turned toward joint financing and public assistance in working out development issues.

More often than not, organizations responded to federally supported economic development by establishing a new city or county government staff. Compared with planning staffs, the economic development staffs were expected to be proficient in development economics, negotiation, and urban revitalization. In addition, some economic development agencies were established independently of governments to promote job growth.

With the increased interest in planning for economic development there has naturally been a greater emphasis on data and indexes. Land use data, for instance, can be tied into computer-assisted assessment records to determine the real and personal property tax base and changes in it over time. Retail square footage and sales data can be used to estimate sales tax yields under future development scenarios. Average household income data can be used to forecast income tax yields on an at-place (location of job) or residence-of-employed-persons basis. Development permission and business license fee forecasts can be based on data commonly collected and analyzed by local planning departments. Similarly, user fees associated with parks, solid waste collection and disposal, water service, and other services can be estimated from employment, population, and building size data that are typically collected by planning staffs.

This approach is taken in Modesto, California, where the city's finance and community development departments collaborate annually on a four-year operating budget with revenue and expenditure forecasts. The budget includes comparative estimates of the current fiscal year and each of the following three years. As a city report has explained, "The primary purpose of the multiyear forecast is to offer a preview of the city's future financial position and, in doing so, to extend the reaction time for addressing issues that come into sharper focus during the process."[15]

Revenue forecasts are made for ten separate funds and for twenty-two sources of revenue for the general fund. Expenditure forecasts are made for thirty-seven separate accounts, and anticipated changes in service levels in staffing are discussed for each account. This approach successfully ties the planning data base to programming and budgeting.

Recap

Planning has become enmeshed in management and policy matters because the boundaries between technical, managerial, and political issues are now blurred.

This is a new development in local government. In the past, the planner proposed, the manager reviewed, and the council disposed. Now the planner must develop proposals that are technically sound and that are based on current strategies and on factors that are controllable.

This trend is evident in Long Beach, California, for example, where the planning strategy is built on neighborhoods, complements the private sector, and recognizes factors outside city government control. This kind of comprehensive planning protects the large public investment in streets, sewers, parks, public buildings, and other facilities by building on the public investment through measures that will encourage private investment.

Another major part of this process is developing long-term goals for city or county revenues and expenditures. The linkage with taxes and the employment base shows again the extent to which planning and management are interrelated.

Organizational alternatives

There is no model organization for long-term planning. Experience tells us that a well-organized local government can fail to deliver services in a socially responsible and cost effective manner if, for example, productivity is low, funding is inadequate, equipment is poorly maintained, community dissension exists, or policy-making and operational roles are not clearly defined. Conversely, poorly organized local governments may be able to deliver services in spite of organizational barriers. As one researcher has pointed out,

It is likely that the utility of organization as the sole key to effective planning is at least questionable. The persistence of the belief in the advantageous effect of organization may be more a result of the fact that proponents, having oversold reorganization as a panacea in the reformist era, feel a need to keep proving that promised improvements will materialize rather than of evidence that organization has actually been fundamental to effectiveness.[16]

Theoretically, organizational choices are many if you are starting fresh with a new local government. In practice, this is almost never the case. Statutory requirements, past practices, interpersonal relations, functional relations, budget constraints, and other factors narrow the range of organizational arrangements available to the planner and the manager.

A convenient way to categorize organizational structures is to label them according to whether they provide line or staff services. Line agencies directly provide a service or produce a product. Staff agencies provide general services within the organization. For example, the responsibilities of most public works departments fall into the line category because these departments directly provide street maintenance, sewer plant operation, and water supply and distribution. At the same time, the public works administrative staff handles budget preparation and policy advisory responsibilities that go beyond day-to-day service.

Particularly in local governments having fewer than 200 employees and in departments having fewer than 20 employees, line and staff functions tend to blur in favor of getting the job done. Employees in smaller organizations may not know whether they are carrying out a line or a staff function, and it is not important to them which of the two categories they fall into.

Examples of various organizational structures that have been tried in selected cities are described below.

Centralized planning and budgeting

Three cities that have sought to bring planning, policy analysis, and budgeting into the chief executive's office on a day-to-day basis are Seattle, Atlanta, and Baltimore. Enough experience has been gained in these cities to provide prototypes for other local governments.

Seattle   In 1973 the Seattle 2000 Commission produced a set of goals for the city to achieve by the end of the century.[17] The mayor had proposed the consolidation of all city planning activities into a single organization. An Office of Policy Planning (OPP) was to be established (it was to be accountable to both the mayor and the city council) to prepare and oversee the implementation of plans cutting across all functions of city government. The new office was to be staffed by seventy employees from planning positions in the city's line departments. The OPP, though formally responsible to both the council and the mayor, was located in the mayor's office. A separate Office of Management and Budget within the mayor's office was responsible for the budget. By 1974 OPP had a staff of ninety people.

After two years of experience, two views of the world of OPP emerged. One was that OPP should spend its time developing broad policy statements that could be endorsed by the city's elected officials so that specific decisions would follow. The other was that the office should help the mayor initiate policy and run the line departments. OPP went in the latter direction and became very useful to the mayor in his day-to-day responsibilities. Through its control of federal Community Development Block Grant (CDBG) funds and the capital improvement program, OPP made the largest share of discretionary spending decisions in the city. At the same time OPP monitored line department progress and asserted increased control over their decisions.

In 1979 OPP was replaced by an Office of Policy and Evaluation (OPE) with about forty staff members. Its responsibilities included administering the CDBG program and monitoring line departments in accordance with the mayor's objectives. Most of the staff positions lost in the transition from OPP to OPE were allocated to line departments for planning and analysis at the departmental level. A new deputy mayor was appointed and was made responsible for relations between line departments and the mayor's office. Each council member was given one professional and one clerical staff member, and the whole council was to share a staff of ten audit and analysis personnel.

In addition to the planning and policy advisory staff assigned to the mayor and members of the city council, Seattle has two departments with primary responsibility for planning. Since 1974, the Department of Community Development has managed urban renewal projects, housing programs, historic preservation, and neighborhood planning. In 1979 environmental planning and zoning activities were moved to the new Department of Construction and Land Use, which consolidated the former building department duties with land use regulation and administration. The engineering, parks, human resources, and other departments continued with their own planning staffs.

The housing and community development block grant staff was moved from OPE to the Office of Management and Budget in 1981; and OPE was replaced by a limited-purpose Office of Land Use and Transportation.

Lessons learned from Seattle's experience are relevant to planning practice today because of the current trend toward executive and staff strategic planning: "The Executive Planning Agency is typically a plan making rather than a plan implementation department, with responsibility for long-range, comprehensive or policy planning."[18]

That experience points up many of the elements that local government executive planning agencies should consider:

1.   In order to help demonstrate success, the agency must complete technically competent long-range or policy plans in a timely manner.
2.   The more agencies and citizens groups involved in the plan-making process, the more time it takes to prepare those plans and the more difficult it is to reach a consensus.
3.   Planning staff expertise has to be regularly demonstrated. The staff is not taken for granted and must repeatedly prove itself.

4. Results of planning agency work programs must show how their activities contribute useful information to the planning process, and present understandable information.
5. Clear definitions of the agency's work can help in demonstrating progress and achieving purposes.
6. Unlike mature planning agencies, a new agency needs to develop a strong internal organization and gain public acceptance before it can initiate political innovation. Experts may want to acquire power and expand activities by controlling information, but an information monopoly is unlikely, given the vagaries of planning processes, citizen participation, and planning methods.
7. Public agencies need support not only from the chief administrator but also from the legislative branch and citizens. An executive plan-making agency can never relax in accommodating the public, line department, and legislative interests represented in the community.

Atlanta   In 1974 Atlanta adopted a new city charter that institutionalized a comprehensive development planning process by means of a major policy statement on how the city manages its resources.[19] It was accompanied by a reorganization ordinance consolidating twenty-six departments and agencies into nine departments. The charter and ordinance distinguished the comprehensive planning and policy-making processes from past practices in three ways: (1) by specifically linking planning and budgeting, (2) by strengthening the planning process, and (3) by requiring substantial citizen involvement.

Under the old charter, the council exercised legislative and executive functions through small committees for city departments. Acknowledging differences between long-term research and planning and short-term development permission responsibilities, the council had a planning and development committee and a zoning committee to work on these functions. The departments staffed these committees, and department heads worked directly with council committee chairpersons. Together they defined work programs, drafted budgets, and jointly approved major departmental activities. No one was responsible for interdepartmental program coordination or overall policy direction. Mayors had little formal authority but typically exercised strong personal leadership. There was little evaluation of programs.

The reorganization ordinance established a new Bureau of Budget Policy and Evaluation to join the existing Bureau of Planning in the Department of Budget and Planning. The new bureau was to monitor and evaluate programs to make certain that they were consistent with predetermined priorities, and it was to formulate budget and computer utilization priorities. With the two bureaus in the same department, it became easier to develop budget policies that would be consistent with the comprehensive plan.

Each year the mayor prepares a comprehensive development plan for one-, five-, and fifteen-year periods. The charter requires citizen participation in the preparation of this plan. The council reviews, amends, and adopts the plan. Because of the size of the city's budget and the complexity of the process (especially the relatively elaborate citizen participation requirements), planning and budgeting have become a continuous process. The plan, including the capital budget and program, is adopted in June, the operating budget in January (when they both become effective). The plan includes an annual rezoning plan. Petitions for zoning changes require a formal change by the council in the comprehensive development plan.

The city's neighborhood planning units are the geographic basis for the Bureau of Planning's annual neighborhood planning process. Neighborhood plans are submitted annually for inclusion in the five-year element of the comprehensive development plan and therefore become a part of the annually adopted budget.

The following eight programs have been used:

1. Urban development and neighborhood preservation
2. Transportation
3. Economic development
4. Human development
5. Recreation and cultural opportunities
6. Environmental protection and enhancement
7. Protection of persons and property
8. General government.

These eight programs have been broken down into subprograms, activities, cost centers, and line items. This specific format clearly shows what is to be done by whom. If the city is engaged in an activity that is not in the plan, then the agency justification or the plan itself is reviewed. Since the plan as well as the budget are adopted by ordinance, they have the standing of law.

The requirements for citizen input encourage citizens to become better organized and more articulate. The plan and budget format are closely interrelated because both bureaus are within the same department. Since a planner and a budget policy analyst are assigned to each department in the city government, there is feedback to the Department of Planning and Budget. This helps staff members share know-how about the operating agency's function. Thus, planning and budgeting are conditioned by the realities of operating agency experience.

Baltimore   In 1966 the Baltimore city charter was amended to require the city planning commission to adopt annually a six-year capital improvement program. Capital improvements are defined as all new projects or improvements, except those costing less than $5,000; vehicular equipment; items of repair or maintenance, except those costing less than $100,000; and emergency projects. The capital improvement program is prepared by the city planning department, and adopted annually by the city planning commission, the board of estimates, and the city council.

City agency submissions to the planning department provide a brief description, justification, detailed cost estimate, and sources of funding for each capital improvement. In the event costs exceed available funds, the planning staff assigns priorities to specific projects or groups of projects. As the staff recommendations are formulated, they are presented to the planning commission's capital improvement program committee, which discusses both the overall policy and the merits of individual projects. The committee then presents recommendations to the full planning commission for review. Agencies are requested to make presentations of their programs to the commission, which adopts the program. The commission forwards the program to the director of finance and the board of estimates for review and recommendations. After the board of estimates approves the capital improvement program, it is forwarded to the city council.

Only after the city council has approved the first year of the program as part of the ordinance of estimates (city budget) is the city actually committed to finance the adopted projects. Since the board of estimates is composed of the mayor, president of the city council, and the controller, adoption of the capital improvement program by the board indicates a serious commitment on the part of the city to implement the projects in the six-year program.

Each capital project request is evaluated according to its level of priority, the expressed needs of citizens, and the financial constraints imposed by the board of estimate's policies. The planning staff tries to increase the efficiency of capital expenditures by coordinating function, timing, and location in each project. The capital improvement program is published annually as the city's development plan. Seven separate reports are prepared on the program, one for each of the city's six council districts and for downtown Baltimore.

Baltimore Briefing Center The Baltimore Briefing Center, built adjacent to the Baltimore Economic Development Corporation (BEDCO), provides offices, meeting rooms, and reception areas where BEDCO, other representatives of the city, the Economic Development Council, or the Maryland Department of Economic and Community Development can provide information to business prospects. Displays, large-scale photographs, maps, and models provide information on transportation, labor supply, quality of life, utilities, and other attractions for firms that might relocate to the city. Of special interest is a large, table-top model (about ten feet square) showing the central business district and the Inner Harbor area. Prepared multi-projector audio-visual

shows are available, and tailored presentations can be arranged in rooms with conference, theater, or living room seating. The center facilities are available without charge to local business and professional groups.

The center, constructed at a cost of about $250,000, operates on a budget of approximately $200,000 per year. Support comes from the city of Baltimore, through BEDCO; from the private sector, through the Economic Development Council of the Greater Baltimore Committee; and from the state of Maryland, through the Department of Economic and Community Development.

In order to control cost-and-time overruns, a capital improvement program management team was appointed in 1974 consisting of the physical development coordinator, the director of finance, and the director of public works. The team established a Project Scheduling and Tracking System with a data base that includes general descriptive data, project manager comments concerning schedule and status, design development data, bid/award data, construction data, and basic financial data. The Project Scheduling and Tracking System controls a project from authorization through preliminary design, final design, site acquisition, bid/award process, and construction, to utilization. Because each department's computer is interactive, it can update information in the system, as required. The Project Scheduling and Tracking System provides the data for analytical studies of project activity costs and time for each step. Benefits of this system include:

1. A data base of project information
2. Specific reports for every level of management
3. Consolidated information flow
4. The ability to identify and respond to problems at optimum times
5. Information for modeling the financial impact of budget decisions
6. Management confidence in the accuracy of data
7. A basis for upper-level management to utilize Management by Objectives (MBO) techniques for capital projects.[20]

Separate development permission and policy planning staffs

One of the weaknesses of city planners in the past is said to have been their "ignorance" of the many factors that affect development projects:

Private enterprise is far more familiar with the objectives, political and bureaucratic realities, and attitudes of municipal government with respect to land development and project design than city planners are with the world of business. Ignorance of all factors significantly affecting an intended project is bliss that private enterprise cannot afford. Bankruptcy is the consequence of underestimating the problems and pitfalls of project approval at city hall.

City planners—municipal legislators, and all those in city planning and other municipal departments involved in recommending, establishing, and policing regulations affecting land in project development—are under much less pressure of time and cost than private enterprise. Few bureaucrats are sufficiently familiar with the economics of land development and the requirements of efficient project management to appreciate the private developer's needs or to challenge his professed problems factually.[21]

It was the same view that led the city of Carlsbad, California, to reevaluate the organizational structure of its planning and building departments. The planning function had been carried out in two divisions: current development processing, and research and analysis. The building department was responsible for building inspections and building codes. In 1982 the planning and building departments were reorganized. The planning division of the planning department became the land use planning division of the building and planning department; and the advance planning division of the planning department became the research/analysis group reporting directly to the city manager.

The staff of the current planning division is responsible for development permission processing and implementation of the planning program. Planners work closely with building inspectors, zoning enforcement officials, engineers, redevelopment staff, and other city employees concerned with day-to-day processing of development activities. The goals of the division are to build the city by (1) making planning operational, (2) cultivating better communication with developers, and (3) streamlining the development permission processing function. By increasing the development project review and building permit fee schedules, the division expects to become financially self-sufficient.

The research/analysis staff, working directly for the city manager, studies policy issues and collects information on these issues for decision makers. The staff's role is similar to the strategic planning role found in private corporations. In a sense, the staff functions as a private consultant, undertaking selected studies of the highest priority for the council on economic, social, and environmental issues. These people are responsible for preparing population and revenue forecasts, managing the capital improvement program, analyzing environmental degradation, amending the general plan, and conducting any other studies that are directed by the city council. Each of the research/analysis group projects is costed out and specifically approved before it is undertaken. This group strives to be financially self-sufficient by soliciting grants from various sources. The organizational structure for Carlsbad's two planning functions—current and policy— is shown in Figure 3-4.

Planning and social services

Planning and social services have traditionally been fragmented in the United States; many such services depend on nonprofit delivery institutions that are built on voluntary contributions for major portions of their budgets, combinations of paid and volunteer staff, and occupancy of second-quality building space.

In contrast, in some Canadian cities, social services advisory commissions comparable to planning commissions have been in existence for many years. For example, the Community Services Advisory Commission of West Vancouver, British Columbia, has defined its responsibilities as follows:

1. Identify social needs and recommend priorities to assure the availability of services in close cooperation with the various departments, boards, and agencies of West Vancouver, of the North Shore, and of the provincial government.
2. Assess community social programs to prevent duplication and to encourage coordination and cooperation of such services to increase efficiency, effectiveness, and economy of program costs.
3. Advise council on proper society amenities within neighborhood boundaries of the municipality.

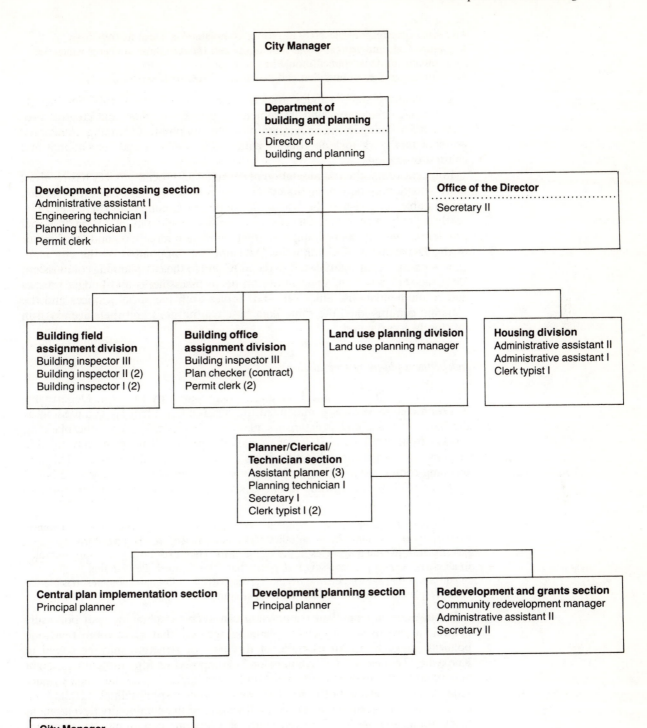

Figure 3–4   Organization for planning, research, and analysis in Carlsbad, California. The Building and Planning Department handles development processing, building inspection, land use planning, and related activities. The Research/Analysis Group is a separate unit in the Office of the City Manager.

4.   Act as the responsible body to receive complaints on social matters from individuals and groups in the community and forward those concerns which the commission feels council should be aware of.
5.   Encourage the continuation and extension of volunteer services.[22]

The planning staff includes a social planner whose responsibilities include researching, developing, and implementing preventive plans and creative programs and assisting in the integration of social and physical planning. Functional areas of this work include educational, health, welfare, and recreational and cultural operations.

In recent years, the fragmentation of planning and social services has received more attention in the United States. The city council of Charlottesville, Virginia, for example, established the Social Development Commission (SDC) in 1974, partly to help assure that the city government would pay attention to social problems. The city council appoints the commission members, and the director of the Department of Community Development—appointed by the city manager—assigns departmental staff to the SDC and to the city planning commission. Both the staff and SDC concentrate on needs assessments and budget reviews and recommendations. Since one staff serves both the social services and the planning commissions, the same data base can be used and their agendas can be closely coordinated.

Independent planning commission

The Standard City Planning Enabling Act, prepared by the U.S. Department of Commerce in 1928, recommended the quasi-independent lay commission as the best organizational structure for planning. It was to separate the planning process from city politics in order to staff the process with technically capable persons and to prepare objective plans for use by decision makers. The first planning commissions established by many cities across the country were based on this model, but, according to one observer, it was by no means appropriate for every situation:

It appears that while the independent commission may be especially useful in some circumstances, it is undesirable in others. The more recent trends toward the placement of planning agencies in the office of the chief executive is no more suitable to all cities than its predecessor. It appears that there is no single planning organization that best meets the needs of every city. . . . Organizations responsible for effective planning vary with differing local circumstances.[23]

Because the independent commission can keep the planning staff politically neutral, it is a useful model for planning agencies that serve more than one political jurisdiction. An example of this type of structure may be found in Knoxville, Tennessee. The commission is composed of fifteen members, eight appointed by the mayor of Knoxville and seven appointed by the Knox County judge (the chief elected official). The commission's responsibilities include both current and long-term planning. Administration of the community development block grant program is the responsibility of a separate community development department reporting to the mayor. The housing authority, responsible for redevelopment and housing programs, is separately appointed and staffed. Commission budgets are provided by the city and county governments and by intergovernmental grants.

Under the independent commission approach, feedback among staff, commission members, and elected officials has a formal structure of reports and memoranda together with budget and project decisions that dictate the staff's work. However, the predecision exchange of information between the elected officials and the staff members is highly informal and is based on interpersonal relations among elected officials and staff.

Because a strong central planning agency has not been established, Knoxville's planning process in the chief executive's office is looked after by a small number of managers and administrative assistants responsible for program development and budgeting. Planning commission members participate in this process on an informal basis. Thus, the planning function is highly decentralized among the mayor's office, city council, planning commission, planning staff, and city and independent operating agencies. It is strongly influenced by citizen groups and informal coalitions.

Recap

In planning there is no single road to organizational salvation. Legal restrictions, competing needs and interests, money, community traditions, and citizen self-expression are among the many variables that influence the formal organization for planning, management, and city council or county board decisions.

A variety of arrangements have been summarized in the preceding pages. In Seattle, planning and policy making are housed in the mayor's office to facilitate executive control. In Atlanta, planning and budget making are housed in the same department to facilitate the common elements of planning and budgeting. In Baltimore, the planning department serves as the capital budgeting and programming agency for city departments. The common element in all three cities is the careful attention given to coordinated planning and budgeting for both one-year and multiyear periods.

Planning vis-à-vis social services is built into the organizational arrangements for physical planning in West Vancouver, British Columbia, and Charlottesville, Virginia.

Short- and long-term planning are formally recognized in Carlsbad, California, where development permission (project) planning takes place in the building and planning department, and research and analysis (comprehensive) planning takes place in the office of the city manager.

Finally, the planning agency serving the city of Knoxville and Knox County, Tennessee, is an example of an independent planning commission that serves two local governments.

Conclusion

Strategic/nonstrategic

Comprehensive/functional

Comprehensive/project

Citywide/neighborhood

Centralized/decentralized

Management centered/independent

These are the appositional pairs that this chapter has dealt with in defining and locating comprehensive planning within city and county government. The first three clearly separate comprehensive and project planning. Citywide and neighborhood is a geographic separation that could involve both comprehensive and project planning. The last two pairs involve organizational structure and management practices.

In organizing for comprehensive planning, the chief administrator, the planning director, and others concerned need to think first about the many possible ideas, places, methods, and groups that can be the "focus," the point of emphasis, for the planning/management program. This chapter has covered a number of such points: budgeting, executive management, research and analysis, political input, citizen participation, economics and public finance, neighborhoods, and social services.

These are the "data" that underlie the goals and objectives to be set by the city or county government. The goals and objectives, in turn, are the foundation of the political decisions, appropriation ordinances, work programs, activities, and tasks that make up local government services.

1 Francine F. Rabinovitz, *City Politics and Planning* (New York: Atherton Press, 1969), 8.
2 See: T. J. Kent, *The Urban General Plan* (San Francisco: Chandler Publishers, 1964).
3 Robert C. Einsweiler, "What the Top People Are Saying about Central City Planning," *Planning* 46 (December 1980): 16. Copyright © 1980 by the American Planning Association.
4 Caner Oner, "The Methodology and Results of the 'Planning Effectiveness' Survey," presented at the annual meeting of the Urban Affairs Association, Flint, Michigan, 24 March 1983.
5 Robert Rider, "Decentralizing Land Use Decisions," *Public Administration Review* 40 (November/December 1980): 596.
6 Ibid., 597.
7 Dorn C. McGrath, Jr., "D.C.'s Blueprint for Chaos: A Comprehensive Plan That Only Zoning Lawyers Could Love," *Washington Post*, 6 December 1983.
8 City of Long Beach, California, *Community Development Strategy: 1980*, 6.
9 Interview with Michael Gleason, City Manager, Eugene, Oregon, 12 August 1982.
10 City of Phoenix, City Planning Commission, *Phoenix Concept Plan 2000: A Program for Planning* (1979), 7.
11 City of Lexington and Fayette County, Kentucky, Lexington-Fayette Urban County Planning Commission, *1980 Comprehensive Plan: Growth Planning System* (1980), 13.
12 Corporation of the District of West Vancouver, British Columbia, *West Vancouver Community Plan* (1980), 3.
13 Prince William County, Virginia, *Major Issues: Prince William County* (1980).
14 Prince William County, Virginia, *Governing the Government: Prince William County's Program Plan* (1981).
15 City of Modesto, California, *Four-Year Revenue and Expenditure Forecast: 1981–82 to 1984–85* (1981), i.
16 Rabinovitz, *City Politics and Planning*, 44–45.
17 See: Richard F. Elmore, "Staffing the Mayor and Council: Analysis and Political Power in Seattle," in *Washington Public Policy Notes* (Seattle: University of Washington, 1980), unpaginated.
18 L. Fitzpatrick, *Office of Planning and Policy* (Seattle: University of Washington, 1982), 2.
19 David E. Rivers, "Atlanta's Planning Process: Comprehensive, Coordinated," *Municipal Government, Politics, and Policy: A Reader*, ed. Gunnar Wikstrom, Jr., and Nelson Wikstrom (Washington, D.C.: University Press of America, 1982), 338–43.
20 City of Baltimore, Department of Planning and Department of Public Works, *A Summary Description of the Project Data Display System and the Project Scheduling and Tracking System* by George D. Becker and John Moscato (February 1979), 10.
21 Melville C. Branch, "Sins of City Planners," *Public Administration Review* 42 (January/February 1982): 1–2.
22 Corporation of the District of West Vancouver, British Columbia, "Terms of Reference for Community Services Advisory Commission," I. T. Lester (14 May 1980), photocopy.
23 Rabinovitz, *City Politics and Planning*, 34.

Organizing for project planning

Whatever the size of a land development or redevelopment project, the project planning is usually built around the development permission process. Unlike comprehensive planning—which, as Chapter 3 pointed out, is concerned with strategy (that is, information, probable effects, possible policies, and decisions)—project planning is concerned with implementation. That means the zoning code, subdivision regulations, and other regulations on land use will come into play here. This is the level of planning at which negotiation takes place between the city or county government and the developers.

This chapter examines first the procedures, staffing, locations, and facilities involved in project planning. Remember, the person requesting permission to develop a project may not be a real estate professional; such a person will need all the help he or she can get in filling out forms, paying fees, and going through the entire permission process step by step. For the neophyte, the process can be irritating, frustrating, and expensive.

The chapter also sets forth specific guidelines for planners and other local government employees responsible for project negotiations. Public-private partnerships and a striving for consensus are emphasized. This chapter also covers organization for economic development at the local government scale, which involves power, risk, need for privacy, finances, and the coordination of the many details that come together in a project. The chapter concludes with discussions of neighborhood input to development decisions, sources of funding, and the feasibility of public-private partnerships.

Development permission organization

Organizing for the project planning process differs from comprehensive planning in several ways. First, the project and approval process typically requires irrevocable decisions, many of which must be made on the spur of the moment. Development permission regulations are an example. Second, detailed reference information must be available to the planner as needed. Third, the planning agency frequently contacts other agencies to make sure that their substantive information is available for development permission decisions and coordination of project review. Fourth, project planning typically involves frequent contact with the public, including developers and interested citizens.

Streamlining procedures

Many local governments across the country adopted development management regulations in the 1970s to meet the pressures of population growth, environmental degradation, and cost-revenue squeezes that accompanied the conversion of unimproved land to improved sites. These regulations and administrative procedures were seen as impediments to growth by many progrowth constituencies. Meanwhile, both the orderly-growth and the antigrowth constituencies grasped the opportunity presented by the regulations and procedures to influence—through the political process—the type, timing, location, and density of

Date	Event	Comment
Pre-1789	European concept of municipal government powers	Cities were municipal corporations of considerable authority, commonly capable of owning and disposing of all vacant land in the city, of holding monopolies on certain aspects of trade, and of approving or disapproving physical changes to the city.
1785	The Ordinance of 1785	An opening of a century of cheap land that resulted in rampant land speculation for private gain.
1789	U.S. Constitution	American cities become creatures of the state. State gives municipal corporations limited powers; little ability to control land development.
1790–1810	Plans for Washington, D.C., Detroit, and New York	Plans for these cities were rejected, changed, ignored, in keeping with the concept of minimal government responsibility, rampant land speculation, and minimal interference with private property.
1856	Site for Central Park in New York City purchased	The first of a series of municipal purchases made in various cities for park purposes.
1867	New York City Tenement House Law	Legitimized the railroad flat with a few improvements, precluding by law the development of anything worse.
	San Francisco ordinance	Prohibited development of slaughterhouses, hog storage facilities, and hide curing plants in certain districts of the city.
1877	*Munn* v. *Illinois,* 94 U.S. 113, 126 (1877)	A landmark decision that paved the way for future governmental intervention in private development.
1879	New York City Tenement House Law	Known as the Old Law, the ordinance required that new tenement buildings be constructed on a dumbbell plan, providing a narrow air shaft. Also, two toilets were required on each floor.
1893	The World's Columbian Exposition	The White City becomes a model for what is possible in urban America.
1898	Ebenezer Howard, *Tomorrow: A Peaceful Path to Real Reform*	The birth of the concept of the New Town movement, wherein the public took a stand on urban expansion. Greenbelt garden cities were to be constructed, surrounded by greenbelts of publicly held land permanently committed to agriculture, thus precluding urban expansion and eliminating speculative land costs.
1907	The Hartford Commission on a City Plan	The first official, local, and permanent town planning board in the United States.
1909	Burnham's plan for Chicago	The generally acknowledged beginning of modern city planning. Proposed public housing as a proper government function, but early city plans proposed no changes to or control over private property.
	Welch v. *Swasey,* 214 U.S. 91 (1909)	The first clear-cut nationwide authority for communities to regulate development of private property through limitation of building heights, and to vary these heights by zone.
	Wisconsin Planning Enabling Act	The first enabling act granting a clear right to cities to engage in city planning.
	Land use zoning ordinance passed in Los Angeles	The beginning of the zoning concept.

Figure 4–1   (caption on facing page).

Date	Event	Comment
1912	*Eubank* v. *City of Richmond,* 226 U.S. 137 (1912)	Setback legislation declared constitutional.
1915	*Hadacheck* v. *Sebastian,* 239 U.S. 394, 408 (1915)	Provided that the restriction of future profitable uses was not a taking of property without just compensation.
1916	New York City Zoning Code adopted	The first comprehensive zoning code in America, prepared under the leadership of Edward Bassett.
1920	*Town of Windsor* v. *Whitney,* 95 Conn. 357, 111 A.3 54 (1920)	Made land subdivision regulations possible by holding that dedication of streets as a prerequisite to platting was possible.
1925	Cincinnati adopts comprehensive plan	The first officially adopted plan; a legal connection between zoning and the plan.
1926	*Village of Euclid* v. *Ambler Realty Company,* 272 U.S. 365 (1926)	Established the constitutionality of comprehensive zoning—the Supreme Court's basic constitutional building block for American city planning and zoning.
1928	Radburn, New Jersey	One of the first and most influential of American new towns.
	Standard City Planning Enabling Act	Provided the basic model ordinance adopted by city councils for the next fifty years.
1934	U.S. Housing Act of 1934	The federal government enters the housing field.
1937	U.S. Housing Act of 1937	The foundation for most federal public housing programs for the next forty years. Local housing authorities use state granted eminent domain to acquire housing sites.
1949	U.S. Housing Act of 1949	The beginning of urban redevelopment whereby cities interfere substantially in the local private land market.
1954	U.S. Housing Act of 1954	Extended the clearance program of the 1949 act to include rehabilitation and conservation, thus increasing the degree of public involvement in land use decisions.
Late 1960s– 1970s	The Quiet Revolution	A movement in states such as Hawaii, Massachusetts, California, Oregon, and Florida, in which state government reasserted its involvement in local land use decisions. Examples: Florida established the concept of developments of regional impact and areas of critical concern wherein the state participated in local land use decisions; Massachusetts passed a law authorizing the state to review and override local zoning ordinances if they discriminated against low income families.
1975	*A Model Land Development Code* adopted by the American Law Institute	A new model code that "replaces" the standard enabling acts of the 1920s. Considerable emphasis on the relationship between state and local governments in the land use control regulatory system.

Figure 4–1 Highlights in the evolution of public intervention in private property in the United States. Land development regulations are not new, but since the late 1960s, population growth, environmental degradation, and revenue limitations have added to the pressures for regulation.

development. Still other communities streamlined their development permission procedures to seek a middle ground between unregulated and overly regulated development.

In its guidebook for streamlining local land use regulations, the U.S. Department of Housing and Urban Development lists eight reasons for considering such action:

1. Contain rising administrative costs
2. Control one of the factors that increases the cost of new housing
3. Save time for public officials responsible for project proposal review
4. Encourage the kind of development the community wants
5. Establish better working relations between applicants and reviewers
6. Structure constructive citizen participation
7. Make the regulatory system more accountable
8. Assure fairness and protect the rights of all participants in the process.[1]

Development takes place in project-by-project decisions made by investors and the local governments regulating their investments. It is at the point of individual project development, however, that the investor's and the public's interests are negotiated. Local governments cannot, however, draft ordinances that will anticipate all possible project circumstances—that is, laws cannot be written to cover all eventualities affecting use, density, setbacks, accessibility, and other project characteristics. With the recent increase in explicit public-private partnerships, financial as well as physical characteristics of projects have become the subject of intense negotiations between developers and land use regulation staffs.

Substantially increased land use regulation means that the quality of development will be better but that it will cost more. Better quality is the direct result of high technical development standards, of sophisticated and competitive markets, and of a hard-nosed attitude about acceptable development among local elected officials. The striving for design, structural, and environmental quality is praiseworthy, but it comes at a price. The additional regulation required to achieve it complicates developers' lives. Not only are there more regulations to comply with, but more effort has to be put into reconciling the regulations and the realities of the marketplace in order to maintain project feasibility, and thus more time (read *money*) has to be devoted to the development permission process. Otherwise reasonable regulations may be the surrogate for delaying or killing projects that would serve the public interest and meet recognized market demands.[2]

Three management guidelines should be adhered to in the regulation of development. First, the regulations, and the procedures used to administer them, should be readily understood by the average citizen. Whenever a law or procedure appears complicated to citizens who do not work with it daily, it will be equally complicated to the occasional developer and to the elected official. Second, the regulations should be relatively simple to administer so that they will be cost-effective. Although the public generally supports the imposition of land use regulations, the public's interest will not be served if the marginal cost of administering a given regulation is greater than the expected public benefit. Third, regulations or administrative procedures should not be changed too often. Frequent tinkering surprises developers, reduces political support, and increases the costs incurred by the development community.

Costly and often contested development permission processes have also resulted in developers using alternative procedures to win approval. Less frequently are proposed projects cloaked in secrecy because you cannot keep a secret where the public is involved. Less frequently are generalized advantages to the community advanced because the public and elected officials have heard a litany of unrealized promises before. In some cases developers are using public forums

Figure 4–2 The developer brings his plans, hopes, and dreams to the permissions process.

to help them define projects before they are submitted to public agencies for review. This cooptation approach can reduce litigious posturing by the developer, neighborhood representatives, and staff members.

Staff review

Although the frequency of contact between developers and the development permission staff might vary, successful development permission processes generally have the following characteristics:

1. A full range of information is available at one or a small number of locations.
2. Ordinances, regulations, and procedures are clearly printed or photocopied, are always in stock at the information desk, and are well organized in bins or on shelves.
3. Knowledgeable personnel who can work well with the public are on duty.
4. Applicants have ready access to key employees in the application evaluation process.
5. Printed or photocopied descriptions of fees and application schedules are on hand.
6. Standardized forms are used for the staff to record highlights of discussions with applicants.

Two principal objectives in designing development permission application forms should be to assist the public in understanding and complying with regulations, and to simplify data storage and retrieval. Too many forms and instructions unnecessarily complicate the process, particularly when approval is sought for relatively simple and uncontroversial projects. A rule of thumb for designing applications is to request only the necessary information that can be stored and easily retrieved when the need arises.

In 1982 the District of Columbia redesigned its building applications process by consolidating twenty-nine applications into four forms (see Figure 4–3). These

How to make an omelette   Many attempts have been made over the past generation to bring planning, public administration, and the policy sciences together and thus bridge these fields for planning and management practitioners.

Planning theory was developed from the work of Rexford Guy Tugwell and others in the thirties and forties; public administration usually is dated from the

At least a dozen universities have tried to make an omelette, starting with the Tugwell planning program at the University of Chicago that ran from the midforties to the midfifties. These programs have attempted to put public administration, planning, and policy analysis together in a variety of recipes to meet the needs of students in public, quasi-public, and private sectors. The academic world (disciplines, professions, schools, departments, and

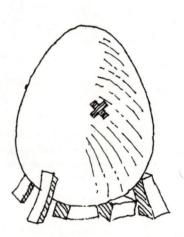

work of Woodrow Wilson in the late nineteenth century with many scholarly permutations since then that encompass planning and other subjects; the policy sciences are the most recently developed, building on operations research, cybernetics, and systems analysis, and drawing on the computer and a variety of quantitative methods.

The ideal way to bridge these worlds is to make an omelette—to "delicately emulsify" the eggs, add the seasoning, heat carefully, and fold over for presentation. When the ingredients are so blended, all will be well: planning, public administration, and the policy sciences will become one omelette, and practitioners will happily work together in an integrated environment.

programs) is concerned, however, about the need for autonomy on the one hand and the merging requirements of students and practitioners on the other.

The omelette will evolve of course; these things usually do; but the recipe and the ingredients have to be worked out. The attempts will accelerate to bridge the worlds of the academic and the practitioner because the real world demands a merger.

Source: Abstracted from a discussion paper prepared in October 1982 by Lawrence D. Mann, Professor, Regional Development and Urban Planning, Faculty of Social and Behavioral Sciences, University of Arizona.

Application for Construction Permits on Private Property	Application for Permits to Install Supplemental Systems in a Building
New building, addition, or alteration	Electrical
Razing a building	Plumbing
Retaining wall	Refrigeration
Fence	Fuel burning
Shed/garage	Miniature boiler
Awning	Pressure vessel
Sign	

Application for Water or Sewer Excavation Permits	Application for Public Space Permits
Water excavation	Trees: new building, driveway, trimming, removal, planting
Sewer excavation	Rental of public space: sidewalk cafe, parking lot, fuel oil tank or line

Figure 4–3 Streamlined construction permit forms, Washington, D.C. In late 1982, 4 forms replaced 29 application and permit forms. The Application for Construction Permits on Private Property replaces 13 forms; the Application for Permits To Install Supplemental Systems in a Building replaces 6 forms; the Application for Public Space Permits replaces 8 forms; and the Application for Water or Sewer Excavation Permits replaces 2 forms. Separate instructions cover deposit requirements, reviewing officials, office locations, phone numbers, and other information.

forms are all available at one location, and staff members are on duty to assist applicants and explain the instructions accompanying each form.

Phoenix, Arizona, has also established a one-stop application processing center. Its Development Coordination Office (DCO) is headed by the deputy planning director, who has the title of development services manager. This person chairs a three-member committee charged with facilitating, coordinating, and expeditiously reviewing development activities. Before 1974 the planning commission and the city council had the job of reviewing site plans and subdivisions in detail during their rezoning hearings. Now the head of DCO, together with representatives from the engineering and traffic engineering departments, is responsible for conferring and negotiating with developers and for making decisions at several check points in the process (see Figure 4–4). DCO has become the single point of entry into the process for project application review, evaluation, and approval.

In cities and counties smaller than Phoenix (1980 population, 789,704), the site plan and subdivision review procedures, to the extent that they are required by ordinance or regulation, remain pertinent. The principal difference is that in smaller places, since fewer people are involved in the review process, less interdepartmental and interpersonal coordination is required. Some steps that local governments can take to streamline their procedures are:

1. Hold a presubmittal conference between the local government's development permission office and the applicant. Review policies, procedures and forms, and the timetable with the applicant.

Figure 4–4   Development Coordination Office (DCO), Phoenix, Arizona. This office is responsible for processing site plans, subdivision plats, and plats or maps of dedication. Before the plat or map can go to the city council for final approval, construction plans must be reviewed and approved, as applicable, by the Engineering, Traffic Engineering, and Water and Sewer Departments. Such plans cover grading and drainage, paving, landscaping, and water and sewage service.

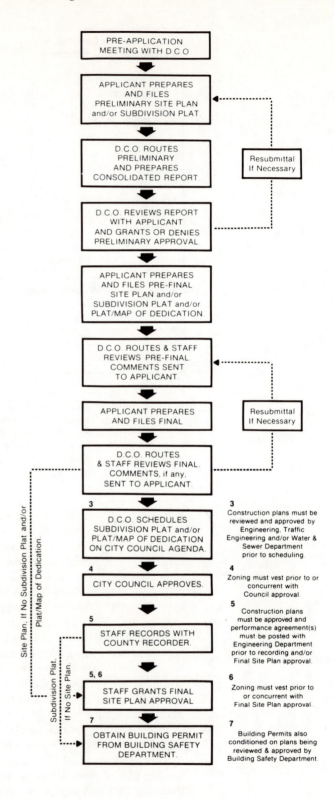

2. After the applicant has filed completed applications and paid the required fees, review the plan or subdivision with the applicant in person and discuss preliminary stipulations. Route the submission to affected departments for comments. At this time, written notice of any rezoning of the property should be posted on the property and sent to adjacent property owners.
3. Consolidate written departmental and public comments, following a standard format and identifying conflicts between departmental reviews.
4. At the time the preliminary plan is filed, review the preliminary report with the applicant and representatives of opposition groups. If agreement is reached, complete the report and mail it to the applicant, the opposition, if any, and affected departments. If the applicant requests, in writing, an extension of time to review stipulations required by the staff, preliminary approval of the application should be withheld until the applicant's review is completed and comments are submitted.
5. Hold a public hearing if an appeal of the recommendations is filed. Typically, stipulations resulting from the application review process require additional information from the applicant and additional review by affected departments. Often, more detailed information is required, including cost estimates to cover all off-site improvements such as street paving, driveway cuts, drainage facilities, water lines, sewerage, landscaping, and site grading.
6. Submit plans and subdivisions to the city council for approval in accordance with local and state laws and administrative practices.[3]

According to the above prescription, there appear to be five keys to success here—that is, to achieving comprehensive, coordinated, and rapid application review.

The first is centralized management, which allows departmental staff members to make immediate commitments to clear projects for staff approval. The planning staff should have authority to approve site plans, knowing that their decisions can be appealed to the planning commission and the city council.

Second, the staff should be able to isolate unresolved issues so that only those issues, rather than the entire application, are submitted for appeal.

Third, a high-level staff member such as the assistant city manager should act as an ombudsman to further expedite project review and implementation, but only if his or her involvement is necessary.

Fourth, the board of zoning appeals should only hear appeals from decisions made by the staff or a zoning hearing examiner (an office that is found only in a few large local governments). These appeals should be limited to zoning matters that involve interpretations of the zoning ordinance. Such a measure would reduce the time for appeals, and thereby save the developers time and money.

Fifth, and very important, a high-level person, such as the planning director, should be available to absorb case-by-case political pressure to free the administrative staff for objective decisions. The absorber of political heat need not be familiar with development permission application details.

Any development permission process will function smoothly and rapidly if it distinguishes responsibilities for policies from responsibilities for procedures. Together they are the basis for administrative interpretation on a project-by-project basis. The first set of responsibilities is embodied in the development permission ordinances (zoning, subdivision, drainage, and others). The second set of responsibilities can be described in a policies and procedures manual that may be supplemented by interpretations during application meetings and by application review memoranda. This legal and administrative framework should be augmented by the written record of appeals, administrative decisions, and court rulings so that "exceptions" (the elements in applications that do not fit

Abuse of the development permission process The many land use development regulations of local governments have worthy objectives, particularly the orderly development of land so that local governments can cope with the high start-up costs for roads, utility services, police and fire protection, and schools. The use of such controls, however, has generated bitter controversies among advocates of no growth, controlled growth (everybody is in favor of that of course), and unlimited growth. Bernard Frieden, a long-time student of housing and urban development, reviewed growth/no growth in his book, *The Environmental Protection Hustle*. The following excerpts from this book show three aspects of the issue: the politics of no growth, the abuse of land use controls, and the stretch-out of development time.

The politics of no-growth required the invention of new tactics to discourage homebuilding. Local government staff and consultants rose to the occasion. Their tactics included putting land into agricultural preserves, declaring moratoria on new water and sewer connections, setting explicit growth quotas, establishing service boundaries beyond which there would be no extensions of utility lines, charging thousands of dollars in "hook-up" fees for each new house as a price for local public services, and creating a climate of hostility that encouraged all opposition groups to bring pressure against proposed new developments. Residents opposed to growth tested and polished their own techniques, which included making strategic use of public hearings, putting development issues on the ballot for popular vote, and bringing lawsuits that could tie up housing proposals for years.

. . . .

How the system [zoning and subdivision regulations] worked in practice became evident from a 1970 study of four suburban counties in northern New Jersey. These counties contain most of the vacant land available for future suburban development around the western edge of the New York–New Jersey metropolitan area. Their land use regulations will affect the housing prospects of millions of families, and by 1970 these regulations added up to a policy of keeping out almost all inexpensive housing. Local ordinances prohibited all mobile homes and allowed apartment buildings on only one-half of 1 percent of all the land zoned for housing. Single-family zones were also drawn to keep out moderately priced houses. Only 5 percent of the land zoned for housing allowed single-family homes on lots of 20,000 square feet or less, while more than three-quarters of the land required minimum lot sizes of an acre or more.

. . . .

The stretch-out of development time noted in California appears to hold true in much of the country. On this point, a nationwide homebuilder survey tells a clear story. In 1976 some 2,500 homebuilders estimated the length of time it took them in 1970 and in 1975 to go from their decision to develop a project to the day when a building permit was issued. More than three-fourths reported development times of six months or less in 1970 while half the builders reported development times of more than a year in 1975. The average periods were 5 months in 1970 and 13.3 months in 1975. Extra development time adds extra carrying charges to the sales price. It also prevents builders from responding quickly to market changes, as in California when construction delays led to major price inflation because the volume of homebuilding lagged too far behind current demand.

Source: Bernard J. Frieden, *The Environmental Protection Hustle* (Cambridge, Mass.: MIT Press, 1979), 5, 158–59, 164–65. Copyright © 1979 by The Massachusetts Institute of Technology.

within laws and procedures) are seldom encountered. By maintaining extensive written records of each application, the local government will be able to develop a body of administrative practices. Taken together with the ordinances, this body of material will provide the staff with a sound basis for recommending decisions on applications to elected officials. Phoenix, Arizona, estimates that streamlining development permission processing has saved developers 15 to 22 percent of land development costs.

Where new development regulations or procedures are controversial, they may be tested on a temporary basis. Salinas, California, did this by attaching a sunset clause to proposed regulatory changes: "The effect of the sunset clause is to enact changes for a limited period—usually twelve to eighteen months. Unless the city council takes positive action to re-enact the regulatory change at the end of that period, it dies. The sunset clause has made it easier for the city council to take a risk where some changes appear desirable, but where it was not clear from the outset what the results would be."[4]

Staff requirements

The point at which the project planning staff and the public interact generally occurs during the development permission process. Alien to many citizens and to less sophisticated developers is the highly structured nature of the law, administrative regulations, and procedures for determining the extent to which these requirements apply to a given project proposal. Applicants with prior development experience and persons representing applicants are less cowed by what is expected.

Regardless of the familiarity that applicants have with laws, regulations, and procedures, the city or county employees assigned to meet with them and to interpret their questions should be qualified to do so. Just any city or county staff member who happens to be available will not do. The staff members assigned to these duties should

1. Get along well with people—even those who are hostile or who threaten to use political pressure while seeking a favorable answer.
2. Understand the substance of state and local development permission laws, regulations, and procedures and be able to discuss them in detail.
3. Read and understand site plans and building plans in relation to development requirements.
4. Program time for on-the-job training. This applies to both the office responsible for inspections and the plan-making section of the planning office. Learning about the inspector's problems in administering construction ordinances will make the development permission staff aware of how sites are actually developed and what types of problems developers encounter. Experience in comprehensive land use planning will round out the staff members' understanding of the relationships among the major elements of the planning-implementation continuum: planning, development permission, and construction.

One technique for building communication bridges between applicants and staff members is to hold meetings on each other's "turf." For example, as part of the development permissions staff's continuing "sensitivity training," the city of Carlsbad, California, encourages occasional meetings between the staff and applicants in the applicant's office. Such meetings allow the people to become better acquainted and to increase their informal dialogue, which helps reduce the adversarial relationship that sometimes develops.

The one-stop permit center has been adopted by many local governments that have had problems with time-consuming and complicated regulations or that have allowed several agencies to issue permits. In these governments, "permit requirements have usually been adopted one at a time, mainly in response to difficulties made apparent by lack of regulation" of real estate development.[5] Communities have adopted the one-stop application center to combat other problems as well, particularly when they have found that

1. Too many employees have been spending too much time providing, explaining, processing, filing, and retrieving applications.
2. Applicants have been irritated (occasionally infuriated) by a slow, cumbersome, complicated, confusing, and ill-defined application process.
3. Applicants have complained about the employees who handled the applications.
4. Too many permits have been required by the local government when fewer could have done the job.
5. The process has been costly and irritating for applicants and has generated poor public relations for the local government.

One of the communities to come up against these issues is Salem, Oregon, which set up a one-stop development permission application center in order to

1. Establish one place for the applicant to apply for and later receive appropriate documents, and thus help to save time
2. Catalog the ninety activities which the city regulates for easy reference and retrieval by employees so that more accurate information can be conveyed to applicants
3. Implement a revenue accounting system to more easily identify the costs and revenues associated with each permit and license
4. Develop a batch filing system so that each of the city's eleven permit issuing agencies can retain internal files while providing an address-based file in the permit application center
5. Standardize, consolidate, and eliminate application forms to reduce the annual volume of 35,000 documents while increasing staff productivity.[6]

Physical location and operation

The application center should be accessible to the public. To augment this service, local governments often locate application centers at high-visibility public service counters on the first floor. If the application center is not visible from the main entrance, well-placed signs should guide prospective applicants there.

In Walnut Creek, California, the community development department distributes a series of applicant's guides for various private investments that require permits. These guides contain details about the purpose of the permit, the application procedure, estimated time of the entire process, and application requirements. Each guide is of a standard size but is printed on paper of a different color, which allows staff and applicant alike to recognize each one readily. Explanations of the guides and procedures are provided on the spot by the staff.

Related materials should also be available at the application center. Development-related documents from all departments should be listed in a bibliography, preferably annotated, with price information. The bibliography should be updated as additions to the community's development-related literature are made available for public distribution, and the documents should be on hand for free distribution or sale.

The application center should be open at least during the hours the city hall or county courthouse is open. Nothing irritates the citizen more than to find that an application center is only open from nine to four while the building is open to the public from eight to five thirty. Every possible effort should be made

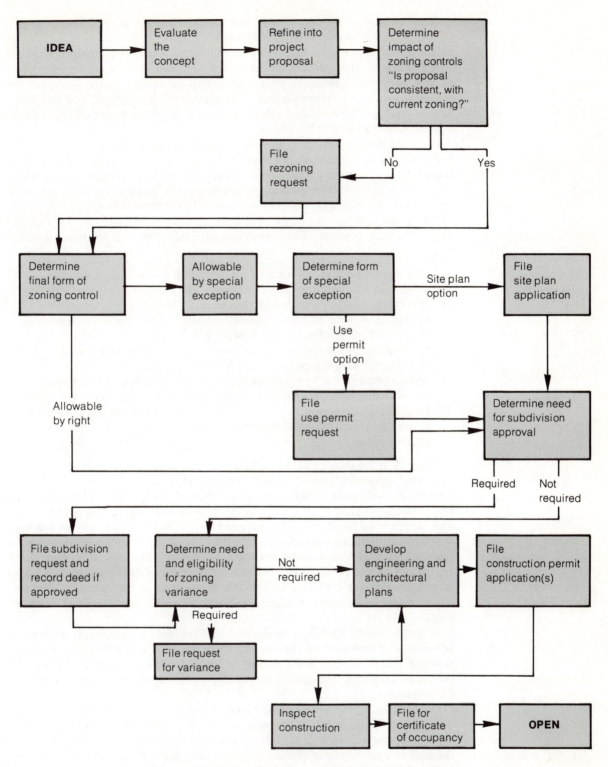

Figure 4–5 A generalized diagram of this kind can show the developer/applicant the major steps that must be considered in planning a project from the original idea to the time when the project is completed and ready for use.

to keep the center open for sixty to ninety minutes after "normal" hours to give people a chance to stop in after *their* working hours.

The application center supervisor should monitor staff performance to guard against burnout. If employees are rotated, several can staff the application center in any given year. Because such centers will have high public visibility, the supervisor should frequently check the substantive, procedural, and public relations aspects of this assignment to make sure they are being carried out according to departmental standards.

In delineating the political, policy, and procedural aspects of the application center's work load, the staff supervisor should be especially sensitive to protecting the procedural responsibilities from political influence. The allocation of these responsibilities should be guided by two principles: (1) procedural work loads should be delegated as far down in the organization as possible; (2) interpretation of the politics of development permission should be retained as high in the organization as possible. These principles are based on the following assumptions:

1. The higher the level of concern for executing procedures within the context of adopted laws and regulations, the less time there is for policy.
2. It is costly to add procedural responsibilities to policy interpretation and management responsibilities because of salary differentials between the staff members involved in these two types of tasks.
3. It is inefficient for staff members throughout an organization to spend time interpreting the political ramifications of their jobs. Persons below a certain point in the hierarchy probably cannot influence those politics anyway. Idle political speculation robs staff members of productive time.
4. Once the legal, administrative, and procedural directions have been set by elected officials and administrators, only they are responsible for altering them.

Changes in the development permission process are to be expected. Pressures to change generally evolve slowly and a monitoring system can identify the sources and substance of these pressures. Records should be kept on questions and complaints of any consequence so that the city or county's chief administrator and the planning director will be prepared for the changes that may be needed.

Wherever applicants are charged for time spent on reviewing and processing applications, that time *must* be recorded. In addition, the substance of applicant discussions should be recorded as a part of the project file so that persons who do not have direct contact with the applicant—such as the planning director, city manager, and elected officials—will have access to the dialogue in summary form.

A simple record form can be devised to show date, time, names of those in attendance, a summary of the discussion, decisions reached (if any), questions pending, and next steps. Such records are available for recording problems with ordinance language, substantive complaints about regulations, and knotty procedural issues.

Periodically, complaints can be summarized in standard format and shared with others who do not staff the application center and are therefore not regularly exposed to these issues. In addition, periodic debriefing sessions would enable the staff to stay on top of problems by resolving those that can be resolved and by clarifying and recording those that cannot be resolved.

Another useful source of information and feedback is a committee of nonstaff persons familiar with the process such as developers, citizens who have been applicants, and persons who are familiar with regulations and procedures elsewhere. Systematic monitoring and feedback will increase the orderliness of subsequent changes in the legal, administrative, and procedural requirements for development.

Ordinance compliance negotiation

Negotiation is likely to be part of the development permission process when large and complex projects are being proposed, when public-private funding is required, and when an adversarial situation develops between planning staff and applicants. The larger the outlay, the more intense the negotiations, and the longer it will take to go through the process. Higher financial stakes also increase the likelihood that the applicant and his or her representative will clearly understand development permission requirements and how things are done in the community.

A common and often well-founded complaint about public employees who negotiate the development permission process is that they are too enthusiastic about constraints placed on the developer. Yet many local government staff members do not really understand the problems of the developer since they are neither schooled nor experienced in the complexities or realities of real estate finance. Therefore, it is important to exercise care in selecting local government representatives for the negotiating team.

Organizational principles

A number of useful practices have evolved with the increasing experience in development permission negotiation. First, one person should be made responsible for representing the local government. The greater the authority this person has to speak on behalf of the local government, the better it is for the applicant. The major issues should be defined at the outset so that subsequent agendas can be prioritized; this arrangement helps to ensure that the greatest amount of time will be allowed for the most controversial issues. Staff members should be selected to participate in the negotiations on the basis of the issues. For example, Rockville, Maryland, brings staff members into negotiations with developers only when their expertise is required. If there are overarching issues, the appropriate staff members are more frequent participants than other staff members. The selection of participants and coordination of their contributions is the responsibility of the city manager or the person he or she designates.[7]

Each negotiating session should have a written agenda agreed to by both parties. While the city or county manager and the planning director need not attend every session, it is important to keep a written record so that the manager and others can keep abreast of developments. The manager need not attend any sessions if he or she determines the issues can be handled by a department head or by someone lower in the hierarchy.

Development incentives

All levels of government have made capital investments which have improved the value of privately owned vacant land. The increased value is capitalized by private enterprise. Although cities have always been caught up in continuous cycles of building and disinvestment, it was not until the federal Workable Program for Community Improvement was introduced in 1949 that land clearance and multi-use redevelopment were legislated and funded. This program required a demolition plan, a construction plan, and public-private financing for reinvestment as a part of urban renewal applications.

As long as market demand was sustained and social objectives were satisfied, urban renewal projects were considered successful. The developers' potential for profit became less certain, however, as markets tightened and citizens began influencing project implementation to better suit their needs. To sustain or increase their competitiveness for new investment, local governments began

Figure 4–6 The planner provides a balanced interface
during project negotiations between the developer
and the city or county manager.

increasing their role in what before 1949 had been largely privately owned real estate investments.

Today individual cities and counties can offer numerous incentives to attract real estate development. A great number of communities from coast to coast offer such incentives. They are also available from the federal and state governments and from special-purpose districts. While the landmark residential and commercial incentive was the urban renewal program, the landmark manufacturing incentive was a program of tax forgiveness, established in 1935 by the Mississippi legislature, which agreed to forgive real property taxes if a factory located in that state. Since the mid-1960s, incentives have become more sophisticated, as can be seen from the following sample:

Real property tax forgiveness for nonmanufacturing land uses

Density bonuses

Utility construction

Public facility construction

Speculative building construction

Grants

Loans

Guaranteed purchase contracts

Interest buydowns

Lease-purchase agreements.

Greater public participation in the real estate market has placed more demands on the skills of planners and managers. Taken together, these incentives and the financial implications they represent place an extremely high priority on local initiative. At one time, communities could wait for developers to propose projects and then react to the proposals. As competition for those projects increased, however, cities began to seek out developers and deals, with the result that the broad comprehensive planning process gave way to the selling of specific projects.

In recent years the collaboration between public and private agencies has influenced real estate markets at the same time that it has addressed local economic and social problems. One result has been greater corporate involvement in community problem solving. Businesses protect their interests by participating in and monitoring solutions to local development issues for a number of reasons:

1. Business needs adequate public services to operate and expand.
2. Business requires adequate protection of its property, equipment, and personnel.
3. Business needs a well-trained labor supply.
4. Business needs to help assure an acceptable quality of life in order to attract and retain workers, especially managers.
5. Business needs to have healthy employees.
6. Business needs to keep down tax burdens to reduce operating expenses.
7. Business wants to be perceived as a "good citizen."
8. Business is expected to keep its end of the implicit bargain with the federal government's philosophy to allocate services, taxes, and voluntary contributions among levels of government and philanthropic institutions.[8]

Shrinking public tax bases and private profit margins have fostered these public-private partnerships. Both sectors appear to have a significant financial stake in successful project implementation. For one thing, the public tax base can be increased and the community's competitiveness can be enhanced. For another, the corporation is better able to finance a project, and its investment is protected through the provision of public services.

Project negotiation

Prior to project commitment, discreet informal meetings will help identify the private and public interests at issue. Usually the community's manager, chief executive officer, or chief elected official is invited by a corporate representative to a face-to-face meeting to explore each other's interest in pursuing the project. Participation in this and subsequent meetings is generally restricted to persons who need to know about any conflicting interests and those who have pertinent information about them. The agendas of subsequent meetings are determined by the issues that need to be resolved and the data required to forge a partnership agreement. Past experience with forming partnerships indicates that participants tend to approach these partnerships with some false assumptions:

1. The private sector assumes that government officials support business development per se because of its importance to the financial viability of the community.
2. Public representatives are convinced that they are familiar with issues facing their jurisdictions and that their projects and programs are effectively communicated to the public.
3. Public and private leaders understand the institutional and procedural constraints faced by the other's internal organization and management missions.[9]

Private development issues Our approach to handling private development issues, the small as well as the large, was fairly straightforward. . . . We took the position that, for the kinds of development proposals that had to come to the planning commission for approval, our positive recommendation (if we were prepared to agree to the use at all) would be dependent upon the developer's meeting what we called "urban design terms of reference." These terms amounted to conditions that we felt to be important from a planning standpoint, generally related to function and design, but at times with social overtones as well. . . .

The success of this approach depended on many things, not the least of which was early consultation with developers and their architects. No one wants to change a design once it's completed.

We encouraged developers to see us early so that they would be aware of our concerns before the designs went very far. . . .

Inevitably, the process led to conflicts. The developers, being people, didn't follow "the rules." They never do. They did talk to and influence the mayor and the commissioners. Even when the developers agreed to our conditions, that didn't guarantee that interested citizens agreed or were pleased. Sometimes there were honest differences of opinion. We won some and lost some, although for the most part I think we won more than we lost.

Source: Allan B. Jacobs, *Making City Planning Work* (Chicago: American Society of Planning Officials, 1978), 139.

Nothing should be taken for granted in negotiations. Negotiating session agendas should be established in advance. One person should be designated as the chairperson of each formal meeting. The chairperson should request background information far enough in advance so that staff members will have time to pull it together. If the public and private representatives have not worked together before, they will be able to start with a clean slate. If they have worked together, prejudices, rumors, animosities, and personal relations may cloud the prospect for agreement. In such circumstances, it may be desirable to ask a third party to bring his or her expertise and neutrality into the negotiations at the outset. The following general model for initiating and fostering partnerships using third party conveners is instructive:

1. Jointly agree on a third party. Because of prospective demands on that person's time, funds should be made available in an agreed upon proportion to pay the third party.
2. Avoid hostility between business and local government leadership.

3. The third party "broker" should meet individually with the public and private leaders prior to meeting with them together. The purposes of these one-on-one confidential meetings are to listen to explanations of city priorities, demonstrate the credentials of a neutral facilitator, determine if there were prior examples of unsuccessful or successful partnerships in the community and the reasons they failed or succeeded, and impress on them the necessity of high-level participation in meetings in order that peers will be talking to each other and decisions can be reached as issues are discussed.

4. Hold the first meeting on neutral turf and precede it with a social event, if the persons do not know each other, to permit participants to become acquainted outside the restrictions of their jobs. All participants should receive approximately equal time. Place local leaders in charge of both the agenda and the discussion.

5. The local government staff should assess its technical capabilities to work with developers or their representatives. If any outside expertise is required, it is typically real estate finance. You should not expect developers who want to build a competitive project to expose their plans and financial *pro forma* (quantification of costs and revenues over time). Therefore, participation by local private business leaders may retard negotiations. If the community feels it needs nonstaff expertise, it is available from peers in other communities which have had comparable experience and from consultants. Peers from other communities who are willing to share their experiences are especially helpful if those experiences are directly relevant and if the person sharing them is well prepared and convincing.

6. Agendas for subsequent meetings should be carefully determined to assure substantive progress is made. There should be attempts to keep participants informed and involved between meetings. It is equally important that any outside experts are fully aware of the issues at hand and are well prepared for meetings. The agenda is also useful in making sure that there is closure on each of its items during the meeting or that someone is assigned to cover that item in between meetings.[10]

Staff members responsible for negotiating can learn a great deal from the experience of others. According to the following keys to successful negotiation with developers, public staff members should negotiate in the context of existing policy, should be substantively prepared, and should anticipate almost any eventuality.

1. *Policy framework*. Negotiations should take place within the existing economic development policy of the city or county. If such a policy does not exist, it should be prepared by the staff and adopted by elected officials. If a proposed project is outside the policy framework, consideration should be given to not pursuing it. The community's chief negotiator should be responsible for making this judgment and conveying it to elected officials. Without their support, later agreement on the project may be difficult to obtain.

2. *Be prepared*. Staff members should take the time to gather and analyze facts. Once the negotiating schedule is determined, it is too late to begin filling substantive voids in staff capability or in data required to represent effectively the community's posture. If, at this late date, weaknesses become apparent, the chief negotiator should acknowledge them and seek outside assistance. This assistance is readily available from consultants and is also available from peers in other cities with negotiation experience.

3. *Avoid delays*. Time is money and should not be frittered away by bureaucratic or regulatory delays. Private-sector representatives expect the chief negotiator to be able to make commitments and expect other members of the community's negotiating team to be able to bring relevant information to the table. If the community wants the project it should deal in good faith. If the community does not want the project, the developer should be told of this at the earliest possible time.

4. *Anticipate issues*. The need for negotiation is based on two factors: unresolved issues and unknown positions on issues by both parties. Commonly, as negotiations evolve, the agenda is redefined. Before terminating negotiations as hopeless, it is important that there be agreement between elected officials and staff members that their community objectives or resources will make further negotiations fruitless.

5. *Give credit*. It is the elected officials who are at public risk in accepting or rejecting the results of negotiation. Regardless of the amount of staff work involved, there should be adequate acknowledgment of this risk. The relative competitive risk brought to the negotiating table by developers leads them to conclude that they are at greater risk than the community. A fair profit is not guaranteed. Therefore, the staff should acknowledge the developer's risk as a negotiating constraint. Although the staff is at least risk, it can only fairly represent the community's interest if it is well prepared by fully understanding the limits of the elected officials' and developers' risks that are imposed on the negotiating process.

6. *Write it down*. Good records are vital in any public activity that has multiple participants, that takes place over a reasonably long period of time, and that is relatively complex. Records encourage a higher degree of discipline in the negotiations. Unless there are legal requirements to the contrary, all parts of the written record need not be revealed. To encourage frank discussion, negotiating sessions should not be recorded. One approach is to have at least one person representing the public interest and one person representing the private interest exchange notes on each formal meeting. The differences in these notes could be the first subject taken up at the next meeting.

7. *Keep informed*. In selecting a chief negotiator, it is important to consider that person's ability to work with people, be sensitive to communicating information from the negotiations, and have a substantive background to discuss details. Guidelines for this role are neither cut and dried nor prescriptive. In most cases, however, the number of chief negotiator candidates will be sharply limited by the criteria discussed here.

Organizing resources

In some communities the politically palatable approach to planning is to define objectives in terms of economic development since that is perceived as a source of job opportunities. The 1974 Economic Development and Public Works Act established economic development as the centerpiece of comprehensive planning espoused by the U.S. Department of Commerce. Citizen participation was required; a written product was required in the form of an Overall Economic Development Program (OEDP); and the analytical methodology was parallel to the comprehensive planning process: gathering information, identifying issues, describing resources, developing the plan, locating the financing, carrying out the strategy, and periodically reviewing and revising the process.

OEDP communities were required to have elected-official and broad-based citizen-group representation. Many localities assumed that the citizen-group requirement meant a quota requirement for representatives of groups even if they were not perceived as having political or financial leverage. It was during this period (the middle 1970s) that many OEDPs were established with the encouragement of the U.S. Economic Development Administration (EDA). At the same time, a recessionary economy stimulated the creation of economic development policy groups throughout the country.

Prevailing local circumstances coupled with the experience of other communities are guidelines for organizing economic development agencies or corporations. No organizational formulas can guarantee that predetermined objectives will be achieved. One reason is that there are many variables—such as money supply, interest rates, energy pricing, and intergovernmental grants—over which local officials have little or no control. Such variables are often more important to the success or failure of economic development programs than organizational structure.

The experience of communities in recent years does not show clear advantages or disadvantages in creating private economic development corporations outside the local governmental structure. The following seven points should be considered, however, when organizing or reorganizing the economic development function in setting up a private development corporation:

1. *Power*. The state government can grant only limited local government powers to private development corporations. If, for economic development purposes, a local government is willing to share its taxing, tax forgiveness, eminent domain, development permission, grant or loan priority setting, and other powers, the private corporation will be in a position to make deals. If, on the other hand, the local government does not give up these powers which are needed to sweeten a private sector deal, the private development corporation has too small an arsenal to negotiate effectively.
2. *Risk*. The private development corporation can shield both sectors from liabilities and risks which may have to be incurred as part of the negotiated agreement. They include land writedowns, reducing development restrictions, a potential for economic failure, and other risks inherent in deals requiring public or quasi-public participation.
3. *Privacy*. Sunshine laws, active citizen participation, and citizens' right-to-know allow for public scrutiny of public business. Developers wishing to avoid this scrutiny may prefer negotiations with private development corporations over negotiations with local governments which may be susceptible to more open exchange of information with the public.
4. *Coordination*. Private development corporations are not necessarily required to coordinate their resources and actions with those of public agencies. This can work to the disadvantage of negotiating parties and of the local government if deals depend on cooperation with public agencies and it is not forthcoming.
5. *Financial independence*. Single-mission private development corporations account for their own budgets and may not be subject to public audit and oversight. This is an advantage when the private corporation needs to react quickly to economic opportunities and needs to spend travel or entertainment funds to meet the competition from other areas. More frugal standards typically apply to public agencies; their more stringent financial practices may increase response times to intolerable levels from the developer's perspective.
6. *Employees*. Public civil service requirements, pay scales, and work rules may discourage the kinds of people who are needed for economic development work. The leeway provided by working outside the civil service system may attract a superior staff. Once this is done, however, the local government tends to lose control of those employees.

7.   *Access to decision makers*. By opening up the policy board to wider
     representation, private development corporations can increase their
     network and gain better access to technical and financial resources in the
     local private sector. The policy board's ability to influence the allocation
     of resources for job-generating development is the principal selection
     criterion. However, once public policy-making responsibility is shared by
     elected officials, it is diffused in the community and is less subject to
     coordination by the chief executive officer.[11]

In summary, private development corporations are generally more responsive
and more willing to share the risk of economic development, can negotiate with
greater privacy, can attract a superior staff, and may have access to greater
resources than economic development programs housed within the existing local
government. On the other hand, economic development agencies in the public
sector must compete for policy and financial attention on an equal footing with
other public agencies, are subject to greater public scrutiny, may be able to
coordinate their affairs better, and have greater control over the substance of
economic development programs than the private corporations. Communities
wishing to establish or reorganize their economic development efforts should
consider these factors in doing so.

Geographic scale

The location, use, and design of community development plans are determined
both by site requirements and by neighborhood needs. As far back as the 1920s,
new community planning, such as that for Radburn, New Jersey, advocated
planning for change at the neighborhood scale. This approach was reinforced
for neighborhood reinvestment planning by the workable program requirements
incorporated in the Housing Act of 1949. The 1974 Economic Development and
Public Works Act, however, established a comprehensive communitywide approach to identifying and solving local economic issues. Nonetheless, communities have invariably depended on neighborhood development organizations as
the bottom-up vehicle for reinvestment planning in their effort to organize an
effective response to these issues.

For a number of reasons the neighborhood remains the most viable geographic
area to organize for planning and development activities:

1.   Elected officials in many cities are either nominated from or nominated
     and elected from councilmanic districts. This procedure establishes a
     political base for the planning process that is keyed to representation of
     neighborhood interests.
2.   People tend to think of themselves as living in neighborhoods rather than
     in cities or counties. In communities of perhaps 2,000 people or more,
     the number of personal acquaintances rapidly diminishes and the
     perception of the geographic area becomes hazy.
3.   The hierarchy of development issues is built up from the perceptions of
     individuals. Most of these issues are located in and affect only one or two
     neighborhoods.
4.   In reacting to development issues, local elected officials can influence and
     change endogenous (local) variables. Therefore, local elected officials are
     in a much better position to repeatedly fill street potholes than to reduce
     traffic on that street by constructing a bypass or by increasing the price of
     gasoline.
5.   It is much easier for citizens and elected officials alike to comprehend
     development issues at the neighborhood scale than at communitywide or
     areawide scales. Cause-and-effect relationships are easier to establish and
     they produce more direct solutions to development issues.

How to use development plans The good planning agency does not keep its plans on dusty shelves but uses plans in day-to-day decision making. This example shows how planning agencies use plans.

Let us say that a private developer wants to build a 150-acre development that is predominantly residential (135 acres) and partly commercial (15 acres). Let us assume that a mixture of housing types—single family homes, rental apartments, and condominium apartments—is proposed. How does the planning agency use plans in reviewing such a development?

The agency would first check the land use plan to determine whether the general area is designated residential, then examine the proposed densities to see how well they fit with the plan's proposals and projections. The planning staff would also check to determine any physiographic characteristics—soil conditions, stream profiles, and important stands of trees—to see the environmental constraints that will influence site planning. The staff will also determine the land use plan policies concerning the amount and location of commercial space in the center of the community.

On the basis of the land uses and anticipated population to be served, the staff will, in turn, check other plans for sanitary sewers, storm runoff, major and minor streets, and public facilities to determine how well the proposed development "fits into" the community's plans. For example, the parks and recreation plan may call for a neighborhood park site within this general area. Or the school plan may have identified the area as being served by an existing school; therefore, no additional school facilities are anticipated. The staff will also examine the capital improvements program to determine how public facilities that are or are not programmed in the future will serve the new development.

There will be times when the development raises major policy issues not covered by general plans. Perhaps the plan is out-of-date, or perhaps it was not detailed enough to make a judgment. In these cases planning staffs will carry out supplemental studies that amplify or update a plan element.

Finally, the planning staff will prepare a staff report that will be presented to various decision makers in government, such as the planning commission, the mayor, the city manager, and the city council.

6. Development issues of concern to private corporations are those that most directly affect their property and employees. Therefore, corporate development issues have to do with plant and office locations and the activities of the employees when they are on site. In that sense, private sector approaches to protecting their own interests also have a geographic focus.

Government and private sector approaches to neighborhood improvement should be based on the following considerations:

1. Preserving and enhancing the existing assets of neighborhoods. Efforts should be made to develop assets already available, recognizing the ways in which housing and commercial rehabilitation and supporting social institutions can be mutually beneficial.
2. Promoting new housing and commercial and industrial development compatible with the existing assets and character of neighborhoods. Plans for new development need to be sensitive to their impact on neighborhood assets.
3. Facilitating and supporting self-help efforts. Citizens' associations, merchants' organizations, neighborhood development corporations, and

volunteer neighborhood crime watches offer vehicles for responding to neighborhood development issues. They tend to be knowledgeable about constituent needs, able to articulate local resident interests, motivated to perform in their own interests, and held accountable for results by those who stand to benefit from them.[12]

Funding sources

Private sector contributions to neighborhood revitalization should be discussed during the negotiations between the corporations involved and the agencies, including the local government that provides the neighborhood services. Companies may donate money directly or through their corporate foundations.

Corporations also may lend staff members or encourage employee involvement in community organizations. Other corporate resources that may be available include management assistance, and loans of physical facilities and equipment. In addition, struggling neighborhood groups may find it encouraging to be associated with well-known corporate philanthropies. In negotiating these types of corporate contributions, the local government staff should point out that there are sound reasons for the corporation to contribute to the development effort, that there are cause-and-effect relationships between physical improvements and corporate benefits.

Private foundations are another source of grants and program-related investments. The funds here may be channeled to various nonprofit groups for economic development, housing, open space preservation, public television, street furniture, and other improvements. The local government staff can provide technical assistance to understaffed nonprofit corporations representing neighborhood interests by seeking corporate or foundation funding; as well, they can provide direct, "hands-on" assistance with ongoing programs.

Resources may also be obtained from expertise brokers, sometimes called "intermediary organizations," which can provide not only financing, but also information, training, and technical assistance to neighborhood-scale community development organizations. The burden of complex work and financial demands placed on volunteer and nonprofit development organizations attests to the need for grants, loans, technical assistance, management advice, and networking (which enables development organizations to benefit from the experience of others).

There are five common types of neighborhood-based enterprises devoted to self-help.

Community development corporations are organized and controlled by persons living in neighborhoods where household incomes are below average. They plan, promote, finance, and operate businesses for the purpose of generating employment and income. These corporations are backed by a combination of public and private funds.

Cooperatives are owned and controlled by their members, who elect a board of directors. The board is responsible for identifying issues, solving problems, and implementing projects. The cooperatives are supported by a combination of public and private funding.

Community development credit unions are financial cooperatives owned by depositors and borrowers and governed by a board of directors elected by the members. Their lending policy is oriented toward helping the neighborhood or community with its own improvements and extending credit to residents who have been unable to obtain credit through conventional lenders.

Community investment trusts are established by individuals for charitable or business purposes. Their pool of money is available for specifically defined and limited purposes.

Community organizations are self-help groups whose goal is to increase the organizational capacity of residents and business representatives. They can be especially helpful in gaining a consensus on issues and in influencing the investment priorities of local governments, private corporations, and foundations wanting to invest in their areas.

Conclusion

Project planning and the development permission process are carried out in accordance with ordinances, administrative regulations, and procedures. Do not underestimate the importance of the forms, procedures, fees, staff qualifications, records, even office hours, that constitute the process. The development permission process will work much better when the planning staff is well prepared, records are accessible and pertinent, the office is conveniently located, and the forms and other documentation are streamlined. Careful work will not eliminate the applicant's pain in coping with the costs, delays, complications, and tedious tasks, but it will make the process as effective and pleasant as possible.

Project negotiations should be carefully planned so that the agendas are arranged in order of priority, background information has been compiled and analyzed, and schedules have been agreed upon. Nothing is guaranteed in negotiations, but the meetings should not be conducted like collective bargaining sessions between labor and management. If the sessions are not going well (from the point of view of either party), a third-party facilitator often can help to improve the situation. Among the seven keys to successful negotiation, perhaps the most important are

Do your homework.

Leave nothing to interpretation or chance.

The local government staff can lay the groundwork for identifying the interests that hold benefits for both the public and private sectors. The private sector will be expected not only to invest but also to modify business policies, share business manpower and facilities, and provide corporate leadership for community improvements. The habits of project-by-project partnerships, one-shot grants, or sporadic plans for investment are hard to change, but steps can be taken to standardize or institutionalize the process by which public-private partnerships are formed, including privatization or the leveraging of private investments. These and other steps would facilitate public-private partnerships, which will no doubt be the means by which many projects are planned, built, and paid for during the 1980s.

1 John Vranicar, Welford Sanders, and David Mosena, *Streamlining Land Use Regulation: A Guidebook for Local Governments*, American Planning Association and Urban Land Institute.

2 For a discussion of selected cases showing the use of federal and state environmental regulations to obfuscate the development process, see: Bernard J. Frieden, *The Environmental Protection Hustle* (Cambridge: MIT Press, 1979).

3 For an example of these types of procedures, see: City of Phoenix, Development Coordination Office, *Policy & Procedures Manual* (n.d.), 9–10.

4 Michael J. Murphy, "Reforming Local Development Regulations: Approaches in Five Cities," Municipal Management Innovation Series, no. 35 (Washington, D.C.: International City Management Association, Spring 1982), 12.

5 Michael D. Rancer, "The Permit Application Center: Time, Money Saved," Municipal Management Innovation Series, no. 25 (Washington, D.C.: International City Management Association, Spring 1978), 1.

6 Ibid.

7 Interview with James M. Davis, 14 October 1982.

8 Abstracted from: Terrence Cullinan, *In Good Company: Corporate Community Action and How to Do It in Your Community* (Menlo Park, Calif.: SRI International, 1982), unpaginated.

9 W. C. Grindley et al., *Forming Urban Partnerships* (Menlo Park, Calif.: SRI International, 1982), II-6.

10 Ibid., III-4.

11 Committee for Economic Development, Research and Policy Committee, *Public-Private Partnership: An Opportunity for Urban Communities* (New York and Washington, D.C.: CED, 1982), 44.

12 Ibid., 48–50.

5 Managing financial planning

The cost-revenue squeeze facing local government today has stimulated increased planning in the finance department and increased budgeting and financial analysis in the planning department. Advocates of capital improvement programming and of linkages between planning, programming, and budgeting have been calling for planning for finance for many years. Data collected and used by planning and finance staffs are useful to both. The chief administrator, who oversees both departments, is responsible for bringing finance and planning linkages to bear on the allocation of resources.

This chapter reviews budgeting as a continuous process that involves allocating resources and making decisions. Thus, budgeting is discussed within the contexts of control, management, and planning. The chapter includes examples for setting financial policies, and covers planning for financial policy as measured by the capital improvements program and the operating budget.[1]

Budgeting functions and roles

Typically, the local government budget is a single unified document prepared by the chief executive or prepared by the staff for the chief executive's review, endorsement, and submission to the city council or county board. Because the budget affects all residents in that it gives to some persons and keeps from others, it is the most political of all documents regularly prepared by local governments. Persons who influence the budget have influence in the community.

At the same time, these people know how little they can actually change the budget from one year to the next. One long-time participant in and analyst of local government budget making estimates that the manager can influence only about 5 percent of the annual budget.[2] There are many reasons for this:

1. Local ordinances and policies require selected services to be provided and do not permit the provision of others.
2. State and federal funds are always accompanied by restrictions on their use.
3. Budgets are decreasing or are not increasing fast enough (in constant dollars) to provide "maneuvering room" to alter priorities.
4. Financially conservative constituencies will not support rapid increases in the budget or changes in priorities.
5. Budgets cannot change exogenous variables such as rising interest rates, energy costs, labor costs fixed by contract, declining tax bases, and the loss of revenue legislated by all levels of government.

To the extent that expenditures and revenues are "locked in," little policy or administrative leverage is available. Nonetheless, the budget remains the one document that triggers the implementation of plans and programs. The chief executive, governing body, budget agency, and line departments are the principal budget makers. Each is influenced by the political will of the citizens at large and by the constituencies they work with. Some elected officials do not want financial forecasts, because they may portend bad news for which citizens will demand answers.

The chief executive, whether elected or appointed, is responsible for preparing and submitting the budget and for enforcing adherence after it is adopted. The legislature is the city council, county board of supervisors, or elected officials having another name. Collectively these people determine revenues to be raised and expenditures to be allowed. These responsibilities are accompanied by an oversight role for which accountability is determined and enforced.

The budget agency, if it exists, actually prepares the budget and monitors the execution of the document during the fiscal year. In many communities having a population under 10,000, these responsibilities are performed by the chief administrator. The operating agencies of local government not only perform the services funded in the budget, but they also perform planning, programming, and budgeting functions themselves. These functions may embrace accounting, monitoring, and auditing the services they perform. Because these functions permeate local government, most employees are involved in them to one degree or another. Figure 5–1 shows the principal persons involved in the budget and their major responsibilities.

If looked at in the context of the annual fiscal planning process, these roles appear to be inextricably interwoven within the three basic functions of budgeting: control, management, and planning.[3]

Budgeting would obviously be useless if expenditures were not controlled. Control provides the assurance that funds are spent for the purposes for which they were appropriated, that spending is limited to the amounts appropriated, and that appropriations cover the budget period.

The management function of budgeting has grown out of the need to provide efficient public services. The performance of public functions has to be managed

Council, commission, assembly, or other legislative body
Authorizes programs
Identifies sources of revenue
Appropriates funds
Adopts budgets
Orders and reviews external audits

Manager, mayor, or other executive officer
Maintains overall management
Prepares and submits annual budgets
Administers adopted budgets

City attorney
Prepares ordinances
Reviews contracts
Ensures legality of financial operations

Finance officer
Directs department of finance
Assists chief executive in preparing budget estimates and in budget administration
Conducts economic and fiscal analyses
Maintains general accounting records
Issues bills, taxes, and assessments
Issues payments and payrolls
Maintains inventory of city property
Conducts the internal audit

Assessor
Assesses property values
Maintains property tax maps and records

Treasurer
Collects revenues
Disburses funds
Maintains city treasury
Issues licenses

Auditor (external)
Conducts audit of financial operations
Prepares and submits report to the legislative body

Planner
Conducts basic economic research and policy analysis
Assists with planning and programming functions
Prepares capital budget

Department head
Formulates programs
Prepares budget estimates

Figure 5–1   Principal officials and employees involved in the local government budget and the activities they are responsible for.

efficiently if local government is to stay within budget constraints while doing its job. Managers are the connecting link between what should be done (strategic planning) and what is done (operational control).

The planning function of budgeting emphasizes the rational resolution of policy choices in raising revenues and proposing expenditures. The planning approach to budgeting has the following characteristics:

1. Government operations are defined by their objectives.
2. The budget is organized by programs.
3. The emphasis is on budget decision making rather than budget administration.
4. Program choices are based on cost effectiveness in comparison with alternative means of achieving the same objective.
5. Multiyear planning is an explicit part of the process.
6. The skills and perspectives of economists, systems analysts, and planners are stressed over those of accountants and politicians.[4]

The broad programs of the planning-oriented budget can be subdivided into the activities and tasks of the management budget. Meanwhile program analysis for the planning-oriented budget looks at operating issues over a longer term than does the management-oriented budget.

The budget process[5]

Competition and conflict in the budgetary process are endemic, even if they are usually muted. This is not so surprising in view of the many different responsibilities, roles, values, preferences, and goals that are wrapped up in budget making. Spenders (departments) struggle with economizers (chief executive), and both are subject to the decisions of the overseers (legislators). Who wins and who loses depends on the influence each brings to bear on the decisions of others. The organization called government can be considered a coalition of semi-independent units held together by the distribution of material resources—the budget. Since power is a major determinant of the outcome of the bargaining for "who gets what," spending preferences of the politically strong will be evident in the municipal budget.

The question is, who holds this power? The answer is complicated and it varies from locality to locality. Where formal authority is concentrated in the chief executive, the elected mayor or the appointed manager is the central power figure. In these cases, the council and department heads generally have little to say about resource allocation on a macrolevel unless the chief executive wants to share his or her power. Influence consists of both formal and informal elements.

In some places, the executive is vulnerable to the pressures of the departments. Here, executive recommendations will emerge as a result of bargaining, negotiation, and compromise. In other places, consultation occurs infrequently and unilateral reductions are imposed. Some departments may not even meet with the executive or know what their budgets are before they go to the city council or county board.

The executive and the legislature assert their formal authority by making independent assessments of the amount of spending. The legislature does not depend on the executive to make the decisions; when disagreements arise over spending preferences, legislative choices prevail.

A strong executive is able to limit the contact between the departments and the legislature so that departments will not be able to "go over the executive's head" and appeal to the legislature. Departmental representatives may not even appear at city council or county board meetings; when they do, they usually act as agents of the executive and support the recommendations made for their department. They are not autonomous and cannot make an "end run" to the council. The legislature, meanwhile, may not see the initial spending requests from each department. The legislature thus is denied an alternative voice, and is compelled to rely on the information supplied by the executive. The council members thus are prevented from forming a coalition with the departments (and vice versa) as both a resource of and strategy for influence. When they are able to do so, both the departments and the legislature have greater influence over the executive and the determination of budget outlays.

Formal budget authority is only one of the "two faces of power." Power is also exercised in a less obvious and less direct fashion. That is to say, the politically powerful may create barriers to spending proposals they do not favor, or they may keep budget items from entering the public arena and record. Thus, the elimination or modification of official proposals may rest on discussions that never take place in public. Overt disagreements are muted. Explicit actions are minimized. The items that are "likely to go" are anticipated with cues and signals. In the end, the choices of others are shaped and limited by the behind-the-scenes communication, which clears an item before it is formally put forward.

Interest groups and external pressure

Municipal budgeting tends to be isolated from specific, organized community pressure. Even though constituency support may be widespread in the political process, when it comes to real participation and influence in the budgetary process, interest groups either are not involved or are not influential.

Formal budgeting is relatively free of the specific pressures of organized interest groups in the community because it is an internal, bureaucratic affair, dominated by those occupying administrative offices. Accountability is indirect and ambiguous but, by implication, it rests with the chief executive. However, two mechanisms are available to enhance the public's influence: public opinion surveys, and decentralized, community-based budgeting. Both have grown out of the movement for greater citizen participation in government. Although both seek to provide greater input into the budgetary process to achieve closer correspondence between governmental spending and the public's values, preferences, and priorities, their effectiveness in this regard is somewhat limited.

Opinion surveys do indicate what people want and what they are willing to pay for. The particular advantage of a scientifically conducted, representative sampling of the entire community is that it reflects the attitudes of all residents, not just the voters, the politically active, or the influential.

Some of these surveys employ the concept of the budget pie to determine public attitudes. Respondents are provided with a drawing of a circle—which is meant to represent the whole governmental budget—and are asked about relative program shares (see Figure 5–2). This pictorial representation of spending examines the intensity of spending preferences relative to limited resources, which correspond to the real world of municipal budgeting. The pie chart is a useful way of depicting the trade-offs among individual programs in the total budget.[6]

Community access and influence could be expanded if the sequence of budget stages were restructured in a way that would increase public participation. For example, public hearings could be conducted more often, and they could take place earlier in the budget cycle (perhaps by the departments themselves), and at various sites throughout the community. Furthermore, an outreach effort could be made to disseminate information and to encourage citizen involvement. On-site workshops could be held to disclose financial information in a clear and

Assume that you are in charge of deciding how the police should spend their budget dollars on the following three activities:

A: Patrolling (crime prevention)
B: Detective work (criminal investigation)
C: Administration

Indicate by dividing this budget dollar into three separate sections the way *you* would like to see the police spend their budget. Identify each section by writing the letter A, B, or C in the corresponding sector.

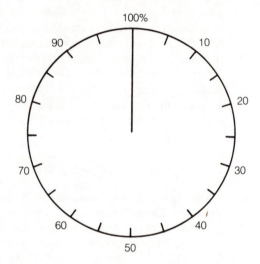

Figure 5–2   Budget pie
questionnaire form.

understandable fashion and facilitate public access and influence, and budget meetings could be televised using two-way audio and pictures.

Decision-making models

There are two general views about how budget decisions are made: comprehensive-analytic and incremental.

In *comprehensive-analytic budgeting*, the first task is to identify and rank goals according to relative importance. This step is followed by a comprehensive analysis of possible methods for reaching these goals. The consequences of each are then compared in a formal, systematic manner, and the single best way to optimize the desired goal is identified. This model's application to budgeting has been summarized as follows:

1. Governmental objectives should be as clearly and explicitly defined as possible.
2. Alternative policies should be explicitly regarded as alternative means toward the achievement of objectives.
3. Expenditure decisions should be made explicitly in the light of all objectives they are intended to achieve.
4. In the interests of a rational comparison of alternatives, final expenditure decisions should not be made until all claims on the budget can be considered.
5. Revenue and expenditure decisions should be deliberately coordinated.
6. For each expenditure, some systematic and deliberate appraisal of benefits and costs should be made.

7.   Policy making, including budgetary policy making, should achieve a unified policy.[7]

Some view comprehensive-analytic decision making as a normative (that is, prescriptive and authoritative) statement of how decisions should be made rather than an empirical description of how they actually are made. They argue that in fact problem-solving capabilities are limited here; information and time are scarce; analysis has a cost; knowledge is insufficient to forecast the impact of public programs; goals cannot be isolated; priorities cannot be clearly set; and social preferences often overlap, change rapidly, and conflict with one another.

Incremental budgeting uses existing spending (defined as the level of funds appropriated in the current year), and the annual increment as its base, and thus works outside the purview of the annual budget cycle. It claims legitimacy as the foundation on which next year's budget is built. Policy commitments of current programs and their spending levels are not reevaluated. Thus, the range of options is limited, and the margins—the narrow range of increases and decreases from one budget year to the next—become the focus of the budgeting process.

The most important factor in the current year's budget is the amount in last year's budget. The future is an extension of the present, just as the present is a continuation of the past. The marginal differences in costs from one year to the next are often highlighted by forms showing the dollar or percentage change in spending from one year to another.

In incremental budgeting the annual review is limited to financial considerations. By and large, new policy objectives, options, and impacts are excluded. Spending choices do not emphasize the worth of programs in attaining goals; values and priorities are minimized; and conflict is contained. The annual change in the cost of "doing business" is the issue at hand. Since essentially only dollars-and-cents data are available, budget making is guided by rules of thumb such as "fair share," across-the-board percentage adjustments, and balancing out.

The significant feature of incremental decision making is that the seemingly inexorable increases occur every year. The cumulative consequences of annual marginal choices are ever-growing expenditures. Therefore, incrementalism is institutionalized. This means that decisions on the major, long-range amount of spending lie outside the formal cycle of budgeting and are beyond the effective power of its participants. Little leeway exists to affect the flow of funds since choices are locked in by the past, the mandatory, and the fixed expenses.

During the past several years these two budget decision-making models have found expression in two systematic approaches. One is the Planning, Programming and Budgeting System (PPBS) (which was adopted by Atlanta, as discussed in Chapter 3). PPBS bases budgets on programs, and programs on plans. Thus, budget items can be directly traced to adopted plans. The second approach, Zero Based Budgeting (ZBB), annually assumes that each budget item starts from scratch, or zero. To the extent that these items are fixed in law or are politically unyielding, their justification, but not the level of effort, is a given.

Achieving budget objectives

The budget process should be carried out to achieve its three primary objectives of control, management, and planning.[8] Any one of these objectives, it has been pointed out, is a complex undertaking because:

The public budget is a political document—a record of the outcome of combat among important groups for a slice of the public pie. Giving out money is a political reward. Withholding resources is a political punishment. The legislature and the executive compete for the use of resources to reward their favorite constituency or program. . . . As a result, budgets have become useless for planning purposes.[9]

Most local governments are guided by a policy of minimizing locally raised taxes and maximizing the services that can be provided within that revenue. This policy establishes the context within which the local public budget is managed.

Budgeting as control

Traditionally, the purpose of the budget has been to assure financial compliance and accountability and the propriety and rectitude of public officials who have authority over the public purse. Limited discretion to spend ensures that funds are disbursed throughout the fiscal year only in the amounts and for the purposes set forth in the adopted budget. Techniques of "counting and watching" have been developed so that at any given time the government will know how much is available to be spent, on what, and by whom.

Control budgeting tends to be negative in its orientation. Its objective is to curb spending. By limiting the budget at its inception and by keeping a tight rein throughout the year, the increases are minimized from one year to the next. In this way, the balance between revenues and expenditures can be maintained, tax increases forestalled or lessened, and borrowing costs reduced.

About fifty years ago, a set of budgeting principles for financial accountability was defined on the basis of the characteristics of budgeting for expenditure control. These characteristics—comprehensiveness, exclusiveness, unity, specification, annual basis, accuracy, clarity, and publicity[10]—are described briefly in somewhat new forms in the following paragraphs.

Budgets are detailed Expenditures are authorized line by line, item by item. These form an "object-expense" budget format. Each expense for hundreds of specific items is enumerated and listed from groupings such as waste collection, economic assistance, personnel, and other categories (Figure 5–3). Personnel position schedules are often included. Each account line is coded numerically to identify every transaction. Line items are supposed to limit precisely the amount and narrowly define what can be spent. The greater the detail and the more specific the appropriations, the easier it is to monitor outlays. This is the hallmark of control budgeting.

Budgeting is annual The authority to spend is restricted to the fiscal year. Each year the regular budgeting cycle is repeated. Frequent review provides a regular opportunity for close supervision over what has happened to the funds appropriated. Discretion is limited and autonomy restricted. Almost all local governments adhere to this doctrine of control.

Budgeting is comprehensive The budget includes a one-year forecast of all financial transactions. Total receipts and outlays are reviewed together, including such special-purpose and earmarked revenues as those received from federal and state governments, all other funds, special districts and authorities, and public benefit corporations that are tied to the general-purpose municipality.

The budget is unified The budget should be organized so that the relationship of one part to another is clear. All budget items should be presented uniformly, and incorporated into a single budget. Although it is acceptable in governmental accounting to segregate revenues and expenditures, according to the rule of expenditure control, the budget should make clear the connections between the financial transactions in one part and those in another.

The demarcation of capital expenditures from operating expenses, however, is an exception to the principle of budgetary unity. This means that in most municipalities the effects of long-term investments in physical facilities on future annual operating expenses tend to be obscured.

SCHEDULE 1-1

APPROPRIATIONS - GENERAL FUND

	EXPENDED 1981	BUDGET AS MODIFIED 1982	BUDGET ADOPTED 1983
CENTRAL GARAGE			
.4000 Contractual Expense	60,044.49	95,000.00	95,000.00
1-50-5000-5132			
SNOW REMOVAL			
.1000 Personal Services	81,333.74	96,973.00	100,523.00
.4000 Contractual Expense	57,167.60	71,500.00	79,528.00
1-50-5000-5142	138,501.34	168,473.00	180,051.00
WASTE COLLECTION			
.1000 Personal Services	106,940.25	118,442.00	125,072.00
.2000 Equipment	440.82	650.00	893.00
.4000 Contractual Expense	12,530.00	11,300.00	12,300.00
1-80-5000-8160	119,911.07	130,392.00	138,265.00
SANITARY LANDFILL			
.1000 Personal Services	536.82	-0-	-0-
1-80-5000-8161			
PARKS & BEAUTIFICATION			
.1000 Personal Services	10,129.69	11,395.00	12,698.00
.2000 Equipment	753.93	2,510.00	1,965.00
.4000 Contractual Expense	4,429.30	5,610.00	5,325.00
1-80-5000-8510	15,312.92	19,515.00	19,988.00
1-0-5000 TOTAL PUBLIC WORKS	621,844.93	838,108.00	937,322.00
ECONOMIC ASSISTANCE			
.6310 Community Action Administration	8,866.45	9,048.00	9,048.00
.6342 LC/LG Planning Commission	1,250.00	1,250.00	1,250.00
.6415 Plattsburgh Dev. Association	5,000.00	5,000.00	5,000.00
1-60	15,116.45	15,298.00	15,298.00
CULTURE & RECREATION			
RECREATION ADMINISTRATION			
.1000 Personal Services	35,629.20	50,478.00	45,927.00
.2000 Equipment	-0-	375.00	4,400.00
.4000 Contractual Expense	9,278.87	10,495.00	15,786.00
1-70-7072	44,908.07	61,348.00	66,113.00
PARKS & PLAYGROUNDS			
.1000 Personal Services	24,834.93	32,897.00	33,916.00
.2000 Equipment	-0-	2,274.00	-0-
.3000 Capital Outlay	-0-	-0-	4,000.00
.4000 Contractual Expense	12,459.68	22,758.00	19,890.00
1-70-7140	37,294.61	57,929.00	57,806.00
CITY HISTORIAN			
.4000 Contractual Expense	-0-	125.00	250.00
1-70-7510			
CELEBRATIONS			
.4000 Contractual Expense	-0-	235.00	1,000.00
1-70-7550			

Figure 5-3 A page from the line-item budget for Plattsburgh, New York.

Figure 5–4 The budget has to be comprehensive to get the job done.

Spending is preaudited The budget does not constitute a mandate to spend, only the authority to do so. Although legislative action establishes boundaries for expenditures, the actual disbursement of funds is neither automatic nor certain. Departments do not write the checks. Many rules and regulations must be followed and many layers of approval must be obtained before any funds are legally obligated and any money is paid out. Bids and quotations must be assembled and reviewed, and requisitions, vouchers, and other documents must be completed by various departments and reviewed by the controller and the purchasing agent before the purchase order can be issued.

The preaudit, or "first instance" review, of the expansionary departments by the economizer is meant to verify that money is available and that it will be used in accordance with accounting standards and legally authorized appropriations. A preaudit is uniform as all agencies are treated alike and are subject to the same rules and regulations. It is comprehensive as it covers all transactions. It is routine as it does not require a special rationale and justification but is built into daily operations.

Budgeting for control focuses on the execution stage of the budget cycle through a process of central regulations, monitoring, and approval.[11] The major components can be summarized as follows:

1. Personnel classification, position allocation, and compensation plans are either in the budget or closely linked to it. Filling a position vacancy, transferring an employee to another job, or any other personnel action involves both the personnel and finance departments. Such control helps ensure that the position is legally authorized, that personnel roles are observed, that the funds are available, and that the established salary is paid.
2. Purchasing supplies, materials, equipment, and other tangible commodities (even when specifically included in the budget) requires special forms and documents and the approval of the accounting office, or chief executive in small communities.
3. An apportionment/allotment system times the outlays according to the life cycle of the program. The purpose here is to ensure that appropriations are available for the entire fiscal year.
4. For the most part, budget amendments throughout the year are regulated by the central budget office. Discretion is limited, and rules and

procedures govern alterations in line-item amounts within a department or shifts of funds between departments.

5. When a charge is made to an appropriation account, an encumbrance accounting system records the amount at the time that a purchase order is first issued or bids are accepted on a contract. The expenditure is first recognized in the accounting system when an obligation that must be paid is incurred.

6. An internal audit for the actual disbursement of budget money throughout the fiscal year is designed to ensure that transactions are recorded accurately and that governmental assets are protected properly. An internal audit is achieved by checks and balances. Authority over funds is shared by a number of individuals; no single person can handle a transaction from beginning to end. When necessary, employees sign for work; other employees may countersign. Forms are numbered in sequence to ensure that all transactions are recorded. Some records are independently confirmed by physical evidence, by inventory, and by external controls. These and other internal audit methods offer a continuous opportunity to prevent misfeasance, malfeasance, and nonfeasance in office.

Generally accepted accounting principles   Although the private sector takes for granted adherence to the Generally Accepted Accounting Principles (GAAP), local government tends to overlook them. These accounting standards were begun by the Municipal Finance Officers Association (MFOA) back in 1934, through what is now the National Council on Governmental Accounting.[12] Consistent and universal accounting principles are especially helpful when the accuracy of the numbers is in question, or when fiscal sleights of hand obscure a municipality's financial position.

Full disclosure   Financial stringency and the inability of a few cities to meet their debt obligations have led many to insist that the financial condition of municipal governments should be fully disclosed. Investors, creditors, and others now are asking for information that presents fairly the financial position of local governments. Unlike corporate instruments of indebtedness, the multibillion-dollar-a-year issuance of municipal bonds and notes is not regulated by the Securities and Exchange Commission. Instead, local governments voluntarily comply with the standards developed by the Municipal Finance Officers Association and the incentives of the marketplace. Whatever form full disclosure takes, it places new requirements on the financial information system for valid and reliable information about the financial viability of local government.[13]

Financial reporting   To track funds throughout the fiscal year, a municipality develops monthly or quarterly projections of spending and then plots actual outlays against the projections. This type of financial report shows the rate of spending, which is particularly useful for maintaining a balanced budget and cash flow and for preventing unexpected shortages.

Such a report typically includes (1) appropriations adopted at the start of the fiscal year; (2) the amount disbursed for the last month (or quarter); (3) the amount disbursed for the year to date; (4) the amount encumbered (which is separate from the amount disbursed); and (5) the available balance (which is the original appropriation minus the disbursements and encumbrances). A report of this kind may also show comparative information on disbursements for the same month in the previous year, ratios of total expenditures to the available balance and the original appropriation, and the total expenditures to date compared with the prior year to date. The most important item is the unencumbered balance. These breakdowns can be shown at any desired level of expenditure (for example, salaries and wages, police pension fund contributions, insurance, and automotive maintenance), depending on the accounting system and account classifications. In addition to this object (or function) breakdown, reports can be prepared by department or agency programs, geographic districts or neighborhoods, and specific activities.[14]

Postaudit   The final component of the budgetary process is the postaudit. Its purpose is to detect and prevent fraud and the misuse of funds. Traditionally, audits for financial compliance examine (1) the proprietary, legal, and mathematical accuracy of accounts to ensure that receipts have been recorded properly and expenditures made in accordance with authorizations; (2) the fairness and accuracy of accounting statements in presenting the financial position of the jurisdiction; and (3) the adherence of financial transactions to generally accepted accounting principles.[15]

Conclusion   If control were the sole criterion for budget preparation, the result would be a narrow and cumbersome financial management system, characterized by paperwork, detail, duplication, complexity, and inflexibility. Technique ultimately triumphs over purpose, and procedures often become counterproductive if control is your single purpose. In the pursuit of "nickel and dime" savings, outlays are delayed and control is circumvented. For every rule there are various interpretations, and for every procedure there are exceptions.

In an era of increasingly scarce resources, however, the importance of budgeting for expenditure control must not be undervalued. Despite excesses of red tape and delay, control is a vital part of budgetary and financial management. It helps to ensure legality, public trust, financial responsibility, and the financial solvency of local governments. Good budgeting recognizes these pluses and minuses and builds effective control into the larger framework of operations and planning and management.

Budgeting as management

Management budgeting, long known as "performance" budgeting, takes the budget process beyond the level of control to translate the things bought by government into the things done by government. Management budgeting establishes performance goals and objectives and focuses on quantitative indicators of output and achievement. Spending choices thus become a vehicle for operational direction and control. Budget review extends beyond the cost of purchases to include the work of the departments and the processes that lead to the completion of programs and tasks.

Expenditures are classified by activity   In management budgeting the control format of line items is augmented by the classification of spending activities. Line items by themselves do not indicate the kind and amount of activities undertaken, goods produced, and services rendered. As the Hoover Commission once noted of performance budgeting, the focus is "upon the general character and relative importance of the work to be done, or upon the service to be rendered."[16]

The end products of government now assume prominence. With the control format, the budget not only documents past payments, current outlays, and expected purchases; it also shows how dollars are used and what kinds of work are projected.

Narrative statements are provided   Narrative statements defining activities are another means by which management budgeting provides information on what things are being done by government. These introductory statements relate

CITY OF DAVIS

PROGRAM BUDGET SUMMARY

Division/Program ___CURRENT PLANNING___ (_262_)
Name (No.)

Dept. ___COMMUNITY DEVELOPMENT___ (_30_)
Name (No.)

Page No. _79_

PROGRAM PURPOSE

Assist with, and/or coordinate, the efforts to achieve the community's development goals and objectives as stated in the approved General Plan and various supportive specific plans, and in the subdivision and zoning ordinances.

PROGRAM DESCRIPTION

Review public and private development proposals, land use changes, and site utilization/building designs, in the context of approved City policies and regulations, and process them, as appropriate, through appropriate staff representatives, the Planning Commission, Housing Development Review Board, and the Design Review Commission, and coordinate the preparation and processing of environmental assessments of public and private development proposals; develop and process through the appropriate advisory groups proposed changes to the City's development policies, procedures and regulations which will make them more effective planning devices and which will reflect changes in state and federal laws; provide information to developers and the public on the City's development policies, procedures and regulations; provide data to the State Department of Finance in order to obtain an update of the City's official Population Estimate for state subvention and planning purposes.

Emphasis this fiscal year will be on continuation of a comprehensive revision to the Zoning and Subdivision Ordinances; completion of the Core Area Design Manual and design guidelines for the Commercial Highway area; continued enforcement of the sign and other ordinances; implementation of a one-stop, permit information counter for the City's development process in accordance with State law; and improved coordination with other City departments involved in the development review process.

Fiscal Year	Work Hours	Total Resources
1980-81 Actual Expend. & Encumb.	6,684	79,500
1981-82 Current Approved	6,616	89,260
1981-82 Estimated Expenditure	6,167	86,665
1982-83 City Manager Recommendation	6,785	107,988

FISCAL YEAR BUDGET

REVENUE SOURCE		FY 1980-81 Actual Revenue	FY 1981-82 Current Approved	FY 1981-82 Estimated Rev.	FY 1982-83 City Manager Recommendation
General Fund Support	(01)	24,831	35,760	17,755	77,088
3303-Design Review	(01)	16,005	17,825	14,260	11,750
3304-Tnt Subdv/Par Maps	(01)	8,670	9,650	9,650	5,500
3305-Rezoning/Prezoning	(01)	-0-	500	500	3,100
3306-Variances	(01)	1,400	1,050	1,200	1,050
3307-Appeals	(01)	1,025	1,000	1,000	800
3308-Zoning Verifications	(01)	180	225	100	100
3310-Maps-Sale of	(01)	318	200	200	200
3311-Annex/Ag Pres Apps	(01)	-0-	1,000	1,000	500
3312-Planned Development	(01)	20,295	7,700	20,000	2,600
3314-Condl Use Permits	(01)	2,855	5,500	4,500	2,000
3320-Vacation of Easemnts	(01)	500	300	300	300
3321-Housing Alloc Appls	(01)	-0-	5,250	12,800	-0-
3333-Zoning Permits	(01)	3,421	3,300	3,400	3,000

Figure 5–5 A page from the program budget, Planning Division, Department of Community Development, Davis, California.

agency responsibilities and goals to the specific jobs and tasks identified by the classifications of expenditure activity. They help show how appropriations serve the purposes of the agency (see Figure 5–6).

Work load is measured   Management budgeting also measures work load—that is, it compiles quantitative indicators of work actually accomplished. This amounts to a simple counting of the units of work completed, which is intended to correspond to the activity classification of expenditures. These measurements provide a record of the goods and services produced.

Efficiency is measured   Once the information about costs and services becomes available, the efficiency of the programs and tasks can be measured. Efficiency, usually defined as the ratio of the measurable work done to the measurable resources used in doing that work, often takes the form of the average cost per unit or employee days per unit of work load. Cost accounting is a way to calculate these measures.

Efficiency is also a criterion for spending choices. Decisions are based both on costs and on the end-products; decisions are not based on services alone. If two alternatives cost the same, the one that yields the greater return will be selected. Given the same outlay, the one that costs less will be chosen.

Efficiency cannot be used to decide what goals and programs to pursue, or to assess the benefits of government. Given the goals of government, efficiency relates services to costs. Once programs are selected, efficiency is crucial to the assessment of alternate paths to those ends. A management approach to budgeting pinpoints activities that are not performing well, and thereby signals the need for corrective action.

Work planning   Budgets can be built around the kind and amount of work to be undertaken in the fiscal year. These work load targets are the "programming" part of budget preparation and involve scheduling work, developing an organizational structure, and establishing procedures to reach the proposed plan. Alternative methods of achieving this volume of work should also be considered at this time. Budgeting the work plan is next; the personnel, equipment, materials, and supplies needed to attain the chosen level of work are priced in terms such as money, personnel, and equipment.

Performance projections offer another way to calculate the budget. The relationship between a designated level of service and the funds required to achieve that service can be established, by linking the input of resources to the output of the activities and work performed.

Performance reporting   Management budgeting is identified by a performance monitoring system. Feedback is obtained by checking and adjusting specific and measurable productivity targets. Monthly and quarterly estimates of work load and other performance indicators can be established at the beginning of the year and routinely reported as illustrated in Figure 5–7. Actual performance can then be compared with the plan.

Periodic reports on budget execution help instill financial sensitivity in day-to-day management. Meetings to compare spending with the plan provide an arena for decision making that will include not only those who are spending budget money but also those who are delivering the services.

Sharp or sudden deviations from expected outlays suggest (1) unrealistic estimates of revenue or expenditure, (2) inadequate accounting controls, (3) capricious management decisions that inflate the rate and amount of spending, and (4) unplanned inflationary cost increases. Performance reports make it clear to department heads and other program managers that they must know the budget, the expenses that can be charged to it, and the controls they must exercise over their subordinates.

Modification of preaudit controls   A management budget also enables the budget office to modify controls. The once automatic and mandatory requirement that departments obtain central approval before incurring financial obligations is not in effect here since authority over the execution of the budget is decentralized to those who spend the money. The budget office's surveillance and intervention in the many routine expenditure decisions is minimized, and departmental discretion is enhanced.

Management budgeting rejects the traditional and still widely held view that without central direction, departments would abuse their spending power and, as a result, overspend. Instead, it contends that internal cost consciousness complements reduced central supervision. A condensed focus on performance replaces the tug-of-war over dollars and cents.

As long as aggregate spending totals are maintained and personnel rules and procedures followed, departments will have greater latitude in spending. Appropriations will be less detailed, line items grouped, and forms and procedures simplified.

Performance auditing   The postaudit increases efficiency and productivity by examining: "Whether the entity is managing or utilizing its resources (personnel, property, space and so forth) in an economical and efficient manner and the causes of any inefficiencies or uneconomical practices, including inadequacies in management information systems, administrative procedures, or organizational structure."[17]

Performance auditing evaluates such points as (1) the need for the purchase; (2) the reasonableness of costs incurred (for example, those in the purchase of products that have a low price initially but a high maintenance cost and a short life span); (3) the adequacy of safeguards over resources acquired (for example, inventory control); (4) the adequacy of revenues received for goods and services sold (for example, franchises); (5) the duplication of effort by employees or by organizational units; (6) overstaffing in relation to work to be done; and (7) simplification of forms, procedures, and the flow of paperwork.

Conclusion   Budgeting as a management tool measures what a local government accomplishes in order to compare it with what it intended to accomplish. Systematic quantification and description of budget items and work performed allow periodic review of progress toward achieving goals. This is a useful way for the planning office to husband resources, take note of activities demanding too much time and money, and justify next year's budget. The lack of procedures to measure efficiency casts doubt on the usefulness of the endeavor. Existence of a measurement system is an indication of the commitment to productivity. Budgeting for management is not employed in many municipalities. Although local governments are concerned with productivity and performance, most are not linked formally and systematically to budgeting.

Budgeting as planning

Budgeting also provides program and financial planning with a public policy agenda; the budget provides a basis for deciding what government should be doing, for whom, why, and with what effects. Budgeting for planning, it has been said, asks its own set of questions: "What are the long-range goals and policies of the government and how are they related to particular expenditure choices? What criteria should be used in appraising the requests of the agencies?

Objective #1. To make environmental and fiscal analyses, as needed, for approximately 870 development proposals and to support the County Attorney's office in approximately 13 cases of litigation related to County action on such proposals using no more than 8,780 staff hours.

Management indicator	FY 1980 Actual	FY 1981 Actual	FY 1982 Estimate 1/	FY 1982 Actual	FY 1983 Plan 2/	FY 1983 Estimate 3/	FY 1984 Projection
Workload							
No. of studies undertaken	494	475	535	464	640	600	870
Rezonings							140
Special exceptions							180
DPA, PCA, FDP							50
Section 456							25
Special permits							95
Variances							60
Local reviews							60
Street vacations							20
Site plans	N/A	N/A	N/A	N/A	N/A	N/A	90
(trials only)							
Agric. districts	N/A	1	N/A	1	N/A	N/A	100
Cluster subdivisions	N/A	N/A	N/A	N/A	N/A	N/A	50
Cases of litigation	20	20	20	10	20	15	13
No. of public inquiries	N/A	N/A	N/A	N/A	N/A	145	175
Productivity							
Staff hours/analysis	9	7	8	10	7.25	9	9
Staff hours/litigation	69	69	60	62	60	60	60
Staff hours/public inquiry	N/A	.24	.25	.75	.24	.75	1.0

1/ FY 1982 estimate reflects estimate shown in FY 1983 Advertised Fiscal plan.
2/ FY 1983 plan reflects projection shown in FY 1983 Advertised Fiscal Plan plus Board approved program additions.
3/ FY 1984 estimate reflects Agency current estimate.

Objective #1 (continued)

Management indicator	FY 1981 Actual	FY 1982 Actual	FY 1983 Estimate 1/	FY 1983 Actual	FY 1984 Plan 2/	FY 1984 Estimate 3/	FY 1985 Projection
Effectiveness							
% of analyses prepared on timely schedule	N/A	100%	100%	98%	100%	100%	100%
% of recommendations adopted	N/A	N/A	N/A	N/A	90%	90%	90%
% of litigation support studies prepared on timely schedule	100%	100%	100%	100%	100%	100%	100%
% of public inquiries responded to on timely schedule	N/A	90%	95%	98%	95%	98%	100%

1/ FY 1982 estimate reflects estimate shown in FY 1983 Advertised Fiscal Plan.
2/ FY 1983 plan reflects projection shown in FY 1983 Advertised Fiscal Plan plus Board approved additions.
3/ FY 1984 estimate reflects Agency current estimate.

Figure 5–6 Management indicators, Planning Cost Center, Environment and Policy Division, Fairfax County, Virginia, fiscal years 1980–1985. The goal of the Planning Cost Center is "to research, analyze, propose, and participate in the implementation of policies, plans, and ordinances that conserve and protect environmental, economic, and social resources." Six objectives are set forth within this goal. Objective no. 1 is shown here.

Indicator	Fiscal year 1979, annual actual	Fiscal year 1980		
		Annual plan	4-month plan	4-month actual
Agency-wide indicators				
Absence rate (% of scheduled hours)				
Uniformed—paid sick leave	2.5%	2.4%	2.3%	2.4%
Uniformed—line of duty	2.9%	2.6%	2.6%	2.0%
Civilian—paid sick leave (city funded)	3.6%	3.5%	3.4%	3.9%
Civilian—paid sick leave (CETA)	4.4%	3.9%	3.6%	5.4%
Complaints—civilian complaint review board	3,772	3,000	1,000	1,118
Percent of complaints resolved within 90 days	81%	82%	82%	66%
Police officers scheduled daily by chart (average)	10,740	10,343	10,373	10,299
Police officers on patrol per day (average)	6,705	6,636	6,595	6,251
12 midnight to 8am tour	1,191	1,148	1,182	1,097
8am to 4pm tour	2,712	2,674	2,674	2,531
4pm to 12 midnight tour	2,802	2,814	2,739	2,623
Crime complaints (000)	1,301	1,256	419	DNA
Felony complaints (000)	508	509	170	DNA
NYCPD apprehensions (000)	493	432	144	DNA
NYCPD felony arrests (000)	92	94	31	DNA
Summonses issued (department-wide):				
Parking violations (000)	4,508	3,400	1,074	1,195
Moving violations (000)	925	791	252	288
Major mission indicators				
Crime prevention and control				
RMP cars on patrol per day (average)	1,558	1,535	1,534	1,447
One-officer RMP cars on patrol per day (average)	125	122	133	95
911 calls (000)	6,327	6,103	2,094	2,224
Radio runs (000)	2,612	2,563	879	957
Required time to dispatch police unit in response to "crime-in-progress" call (minutes):				
Median	2.6	2.0	2.0	2.3
Mean	4.8	4.0	4.0	5.7
Investigation and apprehension				
Cases investigated	10,323	10,381	3,499	3,772
Percent of investigated cases cleared:				
Homicide	63%	70%	70%	53%
Sex crime	55%	57%	57%	57%
Robbery	27%	30%	30%	16%
Burglary	28%	31%	31%	11%
Warrants outstanding (000)	216	248	227	228
Warrants received (000)	114	122	41	34

Figure 5–7   Management report, New York City, showing
agency-wide and mission indicators for the police department.

What programs should be initiated or terminated and which expanded or curtailed?"[18]

A planning budget has been most closely associated with planning-programming-budgeting (PPB), which gained prominence in the 1960s.

A budget process that is planning oriented first plans, then programs, and finally budgets. The initial step is to determine the goals and objectives of spending. These goals and objectives are then translated into operational pro-

Figure 5–8 Planning, programming, and budgeting, by process and result.

	Plans	Programs	Budget
Process	Establish spending objectives	Translate objectives into operational programs	Calculate financial requirements
Result	Policy formulation	Management for service delivery	Financial management system

grams. Finally, the financial requirements of such plans and programs are calculated and shown in the budget. (Figure 5–8 depicts the entire process.)

In incremental budgeting, the budget is put together from the bottom up. The budget sequence begins at a low level of the organization and successively travels upward to the chief executive and the legislature. Departments usually prepare their initial requests, without specific program guidance from those above. As a result, initial spending figures usually are unrealistically high.

Consequently, by the time the budget reaches the chief executive, he or she is compelled to cut it in order to achieve the required balance between revenues and expenditures and to implant his or her program preferences. Nevertheless, any reductions are imposed on the base established previously by the departments. The range of options thus is limited to relatively small modifications in areas of special interest and major political consequence. The same constraints apply to evaluation by the legislature. Once the budget reaches the city council or county board members, the momentum of the process compels the legislature to accept it.

Budgeting for planning seeks to change this pattern to more explicit and formal policy guidance by the executive (and the legislature) during the department's initial preparation of spending requests. The "budget call" includes strategic guidance on what the chief executive thinks is important; program issues that are likely to emerge; fiscal guidance in terms of targets; and general assumptions, constraints, and other factors that need to be taken into account. These instructions go beyond the prevailing vague plea to "hold the line." Thus, setting goals, determining priorities, and planning financial and programmatic implementation are the initial steps in the budget cycle. Issues and controversies are purposefully brought to the surface before the dollars-and-cents element of budgeting begins.

Because the goals to be achieved and their relative priority are identified first, a criterion for spending can be established. Moreover, because the intent of budgeting for planning is to reexamine, all past commitments, goals, objectives, and previously adopted programs are reconsidered. Reallocations are made by giving less to what is now less vital.

Further, funds are distributed on the basis of program results. Once the goals have been accepted, a second set of evaluative questions examines the effectiveness of programs in performing their function, satisfying demand, meeting needs, and solving the problems to which they were addressed. The relative success and failure in producing achievements takes its place as a budgetary criterion. Is the program worth the money? What is the ratio of costs to benefits? Are there alternative means of accomplishing the same goal?

A program structure is devised Another feature that sets a planning budget apart from a control and management budget is the rearrangement of line items into a program structure. This format helps identify and clarify the fundamental

OBJECTIVE	QUALITY CHARACTERISTIC	MEASURE	DATA SOURCES
Prevention of Crime	Reported crime rates	1. Number of reported crimes per 1,000 population, total and by type of crime.	Incident reports
	Victimization rates	2. Number of reported plus nonreported crimes per 1,000 households (or residents or businesses), by type of crime.	General citizen survey
	Different households and businesses victimized	3. Percentage of (a) households, (b) businesses victimized.	General citizen survey, business survey
	Physical casualties	4. Number and rate of persons (a) physically injured, (b) killed in course of crimes or nontraffic, crime-related police work.	Incident reports
	Property loss	5. Dollar property loss from crimes per 1,000 population (or, for businesses, per $1,000 sales).	Incident reports
	Patrol effectiveness	6. Number of crimes observable from the street per 1,000 population.	Incident reports
	Inspection effectiveness	7. Number of crimes per 1,000 businesses in relation to time since last crime prevention inspection.	Incident reports, inspection records
	Peacekeeping in domestic quarrels and other localized disturbances	8. Percentage of domestic quarrels and other disturbance calls with no arrest and no second call within "x" hours.	Dispatch records, incident reports
Apprehension of Offenders	Crimes "solved" at least in part	9. Percentage of reported crimes cleared, by type of crime and whether cleared by arrest or by "exception."	Incident reports
	Completeness of apprehension	10. Percentage of known "person-crimes" cleared, by type of crime①	Incident reports, arrest reports
	Quality/ effectiveness of arrest	11. Percentage of adult arrests that survive preliminary court hearing (or state attorney's investigation) and percentage dropped for police-related reasons, by type of crime.	Arrest and court records
		12. Percentage of adult arrests resulting in conviction or treatment (a) on at least one charge, (b) on highest initial charge, by type of crime.	Arrest and court records
	Speed of apprehension	13. Percentage of cases cleared in less than "x" days (with "x" selected for each crime category).	Incident reports, arrest reports
	Stolen property recovery	14. Percentage of stolen property that is subsequently recovered: (a) vehicles; (b) vehicle value; (c) other property value.	Incident reports, arrest or special property records
Responsiveness of Police	Response time	15. Percentage of emergency or high-priority calls responded to within "x" minutes and percentage of nonemergency calls responded to within "y" minutes.	Dispatch records
	Perceived responsiveness	16. Percentage of (a) citizens, (b) businesses that feel police come fast enough when called.	General citizen survey, business survey, and complainant survey
Feeling of Security	Citizen perception	17. Percentage of (a) citizens, (b) businesspersons who feel safe (or unsafe) walking in their neighborhoods at night.	Citizen survey, business survey
Honesty② Fairness, Courtesy (and general satisfaction)	Fairness	18. Percentage of (a) citizens, (b) businesses that feel police are generally fair in dealing with them.	General citizen survey, business survey, and complainant survey
	Courtesy	19. Percentage of (a) citizens, (b) businesses who feel police are generally courteous in dealing with them.	General citizen survey, business survey, and complainant survey
	Police behavior	20. Number of reported incidents or complaints of police misbehavior, and the number resulting in judgment against the government or employee (by type of complaint (civil charge, criminal charge other service complaints), per 100 police.	Police and mayor's office records
	Citizen satisfaction with police handling of miscellaneous incidents	21. Percentage of persons requesting assistance for other than serious crimes who are satisfied (or dissatisfied) with police handling of their problems, categorized by reason for dissatisfaction, and by type of call.	Complainant survey
	Citizen satisfaction with overall performance	22. Percentage of (a) citizens, (b) businesses rating police performance as excellent or good (or fair or poor), by reason for satisfaction (or dissatisfaction).	General citizen survey, business survey, and complainant survey

Figure 5–9   Effectiveness measures for crime control (see facing page for notes applicable to Specific Measure 10 and the Objective of "Honesty, Fairness, Courtesy").

purposes of public spending and the priorities among alternative ways to achieve established ends. As a result, complementary activities can be grouped by common objectives without regard to existing organizational location. The Davis, California, budget for the services listed was $5.8 million in fiscal year 1983. Because many services are contracted out, the Palos Verdes budget was $3.6 million in 1982, at which time the city had thirty-four full-time employees.

Budgets are planned   While the budget is always a plan in the sense that it is directed toward the next year, the budget is not necessarily a product of a planning process. Planning has two meanings in budgeting.

First, planning may mean assessing the consequences of the present in the future. An explicit and deliberate search for anticipated consequences several years hence is made.

Second, planning may refer to shaping the future. Decisions made in one year are meant to bring desired results in a subsequent year. A series of annual decisions and actions, according to some determinable schedule, may be required to meet a goal. In this sense, each budget is a one-year installment in the implementation of a long-range plan.

Multiyear forecasts of both revenues and expenditures three to five years hence represent the future orientation of a planning budget. Revenue projections establish the framework of available resources and highlight the prospect for tax increases and their probable consequences. When coupled with data about general community conditions, a planning budget can contribute to an economic development strategy. Obviously, available resources set the boundaries for expenditures so that probable imbalances can be identified in advance. The long-range requirements of uncontrollable and fixed costs can be uncovered, as well as the future impact of current commitments.

Multiyear forecasts can show the rapid escalation of spending that sometimes results from program choices. The future financial impact of contracts can be assessed. Federal and state payments can also be forecast, as well as their expiration dates, matching requirements, and possible residual costs. Cash management and the scheduling of short- and long-term borrowing also depend on multiyear revenue and expenditure projections.

Effectiveness is measured   Budgeting for planning attempts to measure program effectiveness. Some types of effectiveness indicators are the improvement and change in conditions that result from programs; client satisfaction; the extent to which needs and demands have been met (that is, the ratio of actual to potential recipients); the quality of service delivery, which takes into account the degree of excellence; accessibility (that is, distance traveled); equity of the distribution of services among economic groups, neighborhoods, and other relevant features; and the cost effectiveness ratio that determines the expenditure per unit of achieved results. (Specific examples of effectiveness measures for criminal justice planning are presented in Figure 5–9.)

Measures of effectiveness indicate the level of program performance in the same way that the financial and management information systems do. Although the reliability and validity of these indicators are difficult to determine, once developed and accepted, the indicators can augment the existing performance reporting system.

1. One person committing four crimes or four persons committing one crime would be four "person-crimes." When the number of offenders involved in a crime is unknown, as may frequently happen with such crimes as burglary, "one" criminal can be assumed for this statistic (or the historical average number of offenders for that type of crime could be used).

2. A satisfactory approach to measuring the degree of corruption, malfeasance, or negligence is lacking. Data on the number of complaints received by the city on these problems should be examined, particularly when their number increases substantially.

Program audits   Another element of budgeting for planning is the redefinition of the postaudit to appraise results. This is called program auditing by the Government Accounting Office because it "determines whether the desired results or benefits are being achieved, whether the objectives established by the legislature or other authorizing bodies are being met, and whether the agency has considered alternatives which might yield desired results at a lower cost."[19]

Conclusion   Although budgeting for financial and program planning has not been undertaken to any extent in most cities, the pressures for more productivity, the constraints of tax and expenditure limitations, and the volatile municipal bond market may force cities and other local governments to adopt more precise and diagnostic forms of budgeting and financial planning.

Establishing financial policies[20]

Too often city or county administrators—especially the chief administrator, the planning director, and the finance director—are so immersed in the day-to-day work on the budget that it is hard to see the forest for the trees. When the details become all-important, the big picture is lost. Every city and county should try for a larger measure of planning for revenue and expenditure forecasts that go beyond one fiscal year. If revenues are limited in what they can produce, as they almost always are, and expenditures continue to rise, as they so often do, then the consequences must be planned for.[21]

Good financial management *is more than balancing the budget.* . . . By knowing what lies ahead in the coming two or three years. . ., a city council can take action to help reduce the painful consequences. For instance, if an impending financial crisis will necessitate layoffs within two years time, it may be beneficial to allow employee reductions to occur gradually, beginning now, as attrition takes its course, rather than experiencing the demoralizing effects of layoffs. By keeping the future in mind, municipal officials can determine the long-term, as well as the immediate, consequences of actions taken today.[22]

Property tax limitations, expenditure limitations, bond disclosure requirements, lowered credit ratings, and revenue shortfalls are among the financial problems and conditions that local governments will be living with for the foreseeable future. A financial policy framework builds on sophisticated revenue forecasting, realistically and conservatively prepared budgets, strong accounting and internal auditing, and reserve, debt, and investment policies that protect the financial position of the local government. In a word, "financial policies provide a systematic approach for financial decision making."[23]

Stated more specifically, financial policies are interwoven with the budget, revenue forecasting, capital improvements, the debt load, and short- and long-term planning. A systematic procedure for establishing, reviewing, and updating financial policies is described in the paragraphs that follow.

Benefits of policies

Establishing financial policies helps local officials view financial management from an overall, long-range vantage point. In most communities, financial policies already exist in budgets, capital improvement programs, functional and comprehensive plans, charter, grant applications, council resolutions, and administrative practices. When financial policies are scattered among these kinds of documents, are unwritten, or are developed on a case-by-case basis, it is likely that decisions will be made without consideration of other current policy decisions, past policy decisions, or future policy alternatives. This kind of policy making can lead to

1. *Conflicting policies*. The governing board may be making decisions that are in conflict with each other.
2. *Inconsistent policies*. The governing board may be making certain decisions and following certain policies on one issue, then reversing itself on a similar issue.
3. *Incomplete policies*. The governing board may not be making any policy or reaching any decision on a particular aspect of financial management.

A formal set of policies helps the chief executive and the governing board see where these conflicts, inconsistencies, and gaps lie. There are other benefits to establishing financial policy:

1. Publicly adopted policy statements contribute greatly to the credibility of and public confidence in the local government. To the credit-rating industry and prospective investors, such statements show a city or county's commitment to sound financial management and fiscal integrity.
2. Established policy can save time and energy for both the manager and council. Once certain decisions are made at the policy level, the issues do not need to be discussed each time a subsequent decision has to be made.
3. The process of developing overall policy directs the attention of management and council members to the city or county's *total* financial condition rather than single issues. Moreover, this process requires management and council to think about linking long-run financial planning with day-to-day operations.
4. As overall policies are developed and an effort is made to tie issues together, new information may come to the surface and reveal further issues that need to be addressed.
5. By discussing financial policy, the council can become more aware of the importance of their policy-making role in maintaining a sound financial condition.
6. By discussing the financial issues and adopting a formal position, the council will be prepared for a financial emergency and can thereby avoid relying on short-run solutions that may be creating worse problems in the long run.
7. Setting policy can improve city or county fiscal stability. It can help officials look down the road, set tax rates and plan expenditures for a two- to three-year period, and create a consistent planning approach.
8. Finally, an explicit policy contributes to continuity in the handling of financial affairs. The manager and membership of the council may change over time, but policies can still guide those holding these positions.

In summary, an explicit financial policy can help both management and elected officials make effective financial decisions.

Approaches to setting policies

There is no best way to set financial policy. In any particular community, successful policy setting will depend on such variables as the relationship between the manager and the council, the financial policies that already exist, the uses to be made of the policies, and the present and projected financial condition of the city or county. A comprehensive, systematic approach may work in communities where a variety of financial management policies have to be considered at one time. A step-by-step approach may work better in communities where selected financial policies have to be considered incrementally over a period of years. Whatever the approach, the steps to be taken will be similar:

1. Determine who will be active in setting policy.
2. Identify areas of financial management to be addressed.
3. Establish content and format of the actual policy statements.

First, a policy study group could be selected to identify the policy issues to be dealt with. This group could include the manager, the finance director, the finance assistants, the department heads, the finance committee of the council, the council as a whole, citizen groups, or other appropriate persons. Strong council involvement and leadership at this initial stage is the key to the acceptability of the financial policies eventually established.

After this group has been selected, its first task should be to choose the areas of financial management that it will study. The field of choice might consist of just the basic areas of financial management: budgeting, accounting, capital programming, debt management, and cash management. Alternatively, policy areas could be selected from a list of current financial problems such as tax policy and debt management.

The next step is to develop the actual policy statements. If policy statements are to be formulated for budgeting, for instance, the following procedure could be used:

1. *Pull together existing explicit and implicit policies*. This can lay the groundwork and indicate what further policy work is needed. Internal documents and manuals are probably the best place to start. Local and state laws that apply to financial management also should be considered.
2. *Use department heads*. Ask department heads to submit recommendations, both for setting new policy and changing existing policy. The finance director in particular should be active in part of the process.
3. *Focus on problems*. If a community undertakes a systematic evaluation of its financial condition, the problem areas will indicate where policy statements need to be made. The planning director especially should be active in part of the process.
4. *Use technical assistance and people*. Many organizations and individuals can be resources in policy setting. Organizations such as public interest groups, state departments of community affairs, bond rating firms, consultants, and municipal leagues may be able to provide handbooks and other written materials. Persons connected with these organizations may be able to contribute their expertise.
5. *Talk with people in other communities*.
6. *Get community input*. A sense of how citizens view the future is valuable in gaining community support. Key business organizations (such as the chamber of commerce and banks) and existing citizen groups (such as a homeowners association) can participate in developing policy statements.

Financial policy framework examples

The following examples of policies are the types for which the planning department can often provide the data base. By taking the initiative in providing data and helping to formulate policies, planners can establish a planning perspective in budgeting processes.

These policy frameworks are based on a wide variety of existing policy statements. Not all of these policy statements will be applicable to every community, and possibly a few should not even be considered since they may conflict with state and local laws and the local political environment. Nonetheless, each statement raises an important *issue* in financial management. A city or county should be able to pick and choose among these issues, modify them as needed, and prepare a statement to express its policies on the issues chosen.

These frameworks can be used as tools for setting policy in three ways. First, they provide a means of identifying financial issues that should be considered by the policy study group or the council. Second, they illustrate one possible format for organizing and articulating policy ideas. Third, they offer a city a starting point for preparing its own policy statement.

Sample operating budget policies   The city will pay for all current expenditures with current revenues. The city will avoid budgetary procedures (such as postponing expenditures, accruing future years' revenues, or rolling over short-term debt) that balance current expenditures at the expense of meeting future years' expenses.

The budget will provide for adequate maintenance of capital plant and equipment, and for orderly replacement.

The budget will provide for adequate funding of all retirement systems.

The city will maintain a budgetary control system to help it adhere to the budget.

The city administration will prepare regular reports comparing actual revenues and expenditures to budgeted amounts.

The city will update expenditure projections annually for the next (three/five/other) years. Projections will include estimated operating costs of future capital improvements that are included in the capital budget.

Where possible, the city will integrate performance measurement and productivity indicators with the budget.

Sample revenue policies   The city will try to maintain a diversified system to shelter itself from short-run fluctuations in any one revenue source.

The city will estimate its annual revenues by an objective, analytical process.

The city will project revenues for the next (three/five/other) years and will update this projection annually. Each existing and potential revenue source will be reexamined annually.

The city will maintain sound appraisal procedures to keep property value current. Property will be assessed at _____ percent of full market value.

The year-to-year increase of actual revenue from the property tax will not exceed _____ percent. Reassessments will be made of all property at least once every _____ years.

The city will follow an aggressive policy of collecting property tax revenues. The annual level of uncollected property taxes will generally not exceed _____ percent.

The city will establish all user charges and fees at a level that supports the cost of providing the services. Each year, the city will recalculate the full costs of activities supported by user fees to assess the impact of inflation and other cost increases.

Sample capital improvement program and budget policies   The city will make all capital improvements in accordance with an adopted capital improvement program.

The city will develop a (five/six year) plan for capital improvements and will update it annually on the basis of the city's comprehensive and functional plans.

The city will enact an annual capital budget on the basis of the multiyear capital improvement plan. Future capital expenditures necessitated by changes in population, real estate development, or the economic base will be calculated and included in capital budget projects. These forecasts will be based on the city's comprehensive planning process.

The city will coordinate development of the capital improvement budget with development of the operating budget. Future operating costs associated with new capital improvement will be projected and included in operating budget forecasts.

The city will use intergovernmental assistance to finance only those capital improvements that are consistent with the capital improvement plan and city priorities, and for which the operating and maintenance costs have been included in operating budget forecasts.

The city will maintain all its assets at a level adequate to protect the city's capital investment and to minimize future maintenance and replacement costs.

The city will project its equipment replacement and maintenance needs for the next several years and will update this project each year. From this projection a maintenance and replacement schedule will be developed and followed.

The city will identify the estimated costs and potential funding sources for each capital project proposal before it is submitted to the council for approval.

Sample debt policies   The city will confine long-term borrowing to capital improvements or projects that cannot be financed from current revenues.

When the city finances capital projects by issuing bonds, it will pay back the bonds within a period that is not to exceed the expected useful life of the project.

The city will try to keep the average maturity of general obligation bonds at or below _____ years.

On all debt-financed projects, the city will make a down payment of at least _____ percent of total project cost from current revenues.

Total debt service for general obligation debt will not exceed _____ percent of total annual locally generated operating revenue.

Total general obligation debt will not exceed _____ percent of the assessed valuation of taxable property.

Where possible, the city will use special assessment, revenue, or other self-supporting bonds instead of general obligation bonds.

The city will not use long-term debt for current operations.

The city will retire tax anticipation debt annually and will retire bond anticipation debt within six months after completion of the project.

The city will keep bond rating agencies informed about its financial condition. The city will follow a policy of full disclosure on every financial report and bond prospectus.

Sample reserve policies   The city will establish an emergency reserve to pay for needs caused by unforeseen emergencies. This fund will be estimated on the basis of the city's contingency plan but in no event will it be maintained at less than _____ percent of the general operating fund.

The city will establish a contingency reserve to provide for unanticipated expenditures of a nonrecurring nature, or to meet unexpected small increases in service delivery costs. This reserve will be maintained at _____ percent of the general operating fund.

The city will establish an equipment reserve fund and will appropriate funds to it annually to provide for timely replacement of equipment. The amount in the reserve will be maintained at $_____ . The amount of $_____ will be added annually.

Financial policies will differ from community to community, depending on the participants, policy-setting process, format, and content. Given the leadership role of the elected or appointed chief executive, citizen, department head, consultant, and staff roles are molded to serve local circumstances. The following examples illustrate the potential importance of planning departments in the policy-setting process.

Planning for financial policy

Figure 5–8 illustrates how the planning process can be placed in a pivotal role in financial policy making. Described below are the results of such action in four communities (one county and three cities) that gave their planning departments roles ranging from complete responsibility to consultation. Two of these communities prepared a capital improvement program (CIP), and two an operating budget. A model CIP is also described.

Capital improvement programming[24]

Typically, the agency responsible for preparing the CIP gives the departments instructions on preparing project proposals. The instructions usually include a calendar of events, project request forms, and criteria for evaluating projects. Departments should indicate priorities on their project requests.

Project requests are reviewed for plan implementation, prospective use, technical feasibility, cost, sources of funding, funding limitations, political acceptability, and other criteria. This review should produce a provisional priority list within functional areas. Then interfunctional project requests must be compared so that interlocking and conflicting projects can be identified and an overall priority list developed. This list becomes the draft CIP (see Figure 5–10).

As the reviewing agency, the planning department must synthesize many factors to prepare a CIP that (1) is acceptable to the public, planning commission, mayor, and council; (2) is agreed to by the operating departments; (3) implements the goals and objectives of the long-range plan; and (4) stays within the fiscal capacity of the municipality. The CIP may also recommend projects for bond referenda.

Planning commission review of the proposed CIP may overlap with staff review and analysis. The commission may conduct departmental and public hearings to ensure that the CIP meets intermediate and long-range plannning goals, that priorities are proper, and that cost estimates are reasonable. The commission provides a sounding board for the program and an opportunity to detect and correct problems.

Roles of the planning commission in the CIP process vary. In some municipalities the recommendation of the commission is passed through to the council virtually as is; in other municipalities the CIP is handled administratively and is never presented to the planning commission. The model opts for a middle ground—the commission should review and if necessary modify the proposed CIP.

The mayor and council should conduct informal meetings with departments prior to public hearings. Such hearings may be part of general budget hearings. The council must ensure that the CIP is in harmony, or at least not in conflict, with community values, as well as provide the funds to support the capital budget. Council adoption of the CIP and capital budget, with or without amendments, permits the municipal administration to proceed.

Mayors or managers may or may not make significant inputs into the CIP, depending on such factors as their management styles, the competence of and their confidence in their staffs, personal interest, and the political situation. The technical complexity of the CIP makes it difficult for a council to make major changes. The influence of the council should not be underestimated, though. Councils can and will push pet projects; favor some departments over others; modify project costs, schedules, and sites; and advocate or block projects thought to be affecting their districts.

Council consideration involves intangible factors such as relations between planning commission and council, mayor and council, and council and department heads. These factors may not be measurable, but they are real and cannot

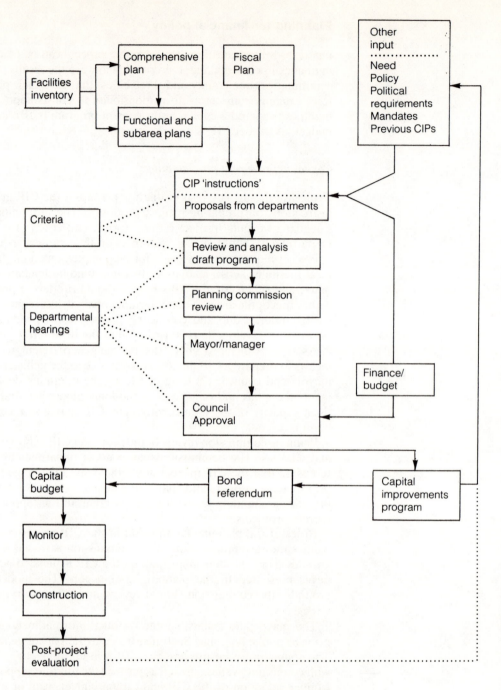

Figure 5–10 Developmental, analytical, evaluative, and decision-making steps in the process for capital improvement programming. Note the circularity of the process with both the capital improvement program and the post-project evaluation feeding back into the inputs.

be ignored. But the CIP also is a creature of many technical considerations. Its successful formulation and implementation will reflect the art and science of the CIP process, including political debate, negotiation, and resolution.

Montgomery County, Maryland[25]   The CIP in Montgomery County, Maryland, links the planning process with capital project demand and funding. The county's fiscal impact model uses total county population, number of single-family and multifamily dwelling units from twelve areas, and number of employees from six areas as demand bases. These demand generators are multiplied by a number of cost and revenue factors in each budget subsystem to generate the total fiscal result from the development mix being tested. Geographic sensitivity is built in by including different numbers of students per household and household sizes for the expenditure calculations and property values and income tax yields for the revenue calculations.

   The assumptions for preparing the data and the fiscal model parameters are:

1.   In general, new development has the same service demand characteristics as existing development of the same type—for example, single family, multifamily or employment, in the same area.
2.   Future multifamily housing construction will be 75 percent condominium and 25 percent rental.
3.   Rental apartments and condominium apartments share the same characteristics other than assessed value and turnover rate.
4.   The costs of delivering public services do not vary significantly by subarea within the urbanized area of the county.
5.   The costs of providing service to a new dwelling, person, or job will remain level in terms of constant dollars—that is, a constant level of service will be maintained as measured in real dollars per person, household, or job.
6.   Programs will expand no faster than the growth of population, households, and jobs.
7.   School yields are constant over time.
8.   Per household costs do vary by geographic subarea because of varying household sizes and school yields, but costs per person or student do not vary.
9.   The present tax rate of _____ is used in deriving fiscal impacts.
10. Single-family units (including townhouses) appreciate at 2.5 percent per year in constant dollars; other units do not appreciate or depreciate.
11. Only 20 percent of new rental apartments and business space is subject to real estate transfer tax.
12. Average sales turnover rates are assumed to be once every ten years for single-family homes and condominiums, once every twenty years for rental apartments and business property.
13. Debt service expenses for programmed capital improvements are divided between existing development and future growth, on the basis of information in the CIP.

   These assumptions are used to translate the distribution, timing, and amount of growth into public service requirements based on standard size and locally sensitive indexes. These requirements are costed and programmed.

Baltimore, Maryland[26]   Baltimore's capital programming process is initiated when the planning department distributes a special form on which city agencies indicate their requests for particular projects in the new six-year CIP. The agency provides a brief description, justification, and detailed cost estimate of the project being proposed. The agency also lists its appropriation requests, by fund sources, for the six-year program period. This form is forwarded to the planning commission.

The planning commission prepares a recommended capital improvement program. During this three-month period the planning department staff meets with each agency to discuss each project. The major criteria used in reviewing requested projects are:

1.   Relationship of the requested projects to the major policy statements and master plan elements of the city's comprehensive plan.
2.   Degree of coordination possible between various projects.
3.   Community sentiment.
4.   Availability of financing from both city and noncity sources. Among the factors considered are the city's capacity to borrow, expected revenue from the property tax, anticipated federal and state aid, and anticipated motor vehicle revenue.

After specific projects have been reviewed and found to be consistent with these criteria, the total cost often exceeds the funds available. In such cases, the staff must assign priorities to specific projects or groups of projects. In determining priorities, the planners assess where the greatest needs exist and where the city will benefit most. As might be expected, consideration is given both to *relative* deficiencies in facilities or services in specific functional areas and in specific geographic areas, age groups, and income groups. Also considered is the *relative* effect of a project—for example, a new road might make vacant industrial land accessible and hence available for development. Finally, the planners consider the impact of each separate project on other projects and programs—for example, by constructing a recreation center adjacent to a school, the city may reduce the capital and operating costs of both facilities.

On the basis of all these conditions, certain projects are included as requested; others are rearranged within the six-year period; and still others are not recommended for inclusion.

As the staff recommendations are formulated, they are presented to the capital improvement program committee of the planning commission. After review and modification by the CIP committee, the six-year program recommendations are presented to the full planning commission for review.

During the planning commission's review, agencies are asked to present their programs to the commission. After weighing all considerations, the commission adopts a six-year recommended program that is forwarded to the city board of estimates.

Next, the board of estimates forwards the program to the director of finance and the board of finance for review. Once the recommendations of the finance director and the board of finance have been received, the board of estimates officially adopts the six-year program. Board of estimates approval does not, however, legally bind the city to appropriate funds. Only city council approval of the first year of the program as part of the ordinance of estimates (city budget) actually commits the city to finance projects. The adopted first year then becomes the city's capital budget. However, since the board of estimates is composed of the mayor, the president of the city council, and the comptroller, adoption of the capital improvement program by the board indicates a serious commitment on the part of the city to implement the projects in the six-year program. The city's development plan and capital program are published in the same document. The capital program is also published as separate compilations for each councilmanic district.

Forecasting operating budgets

Planning departments generally have access to much of the data required to forecast local government operating budgets. The types of data required are shown in Figure 5–11, a Financial Trend Monitoring System. This figure shows

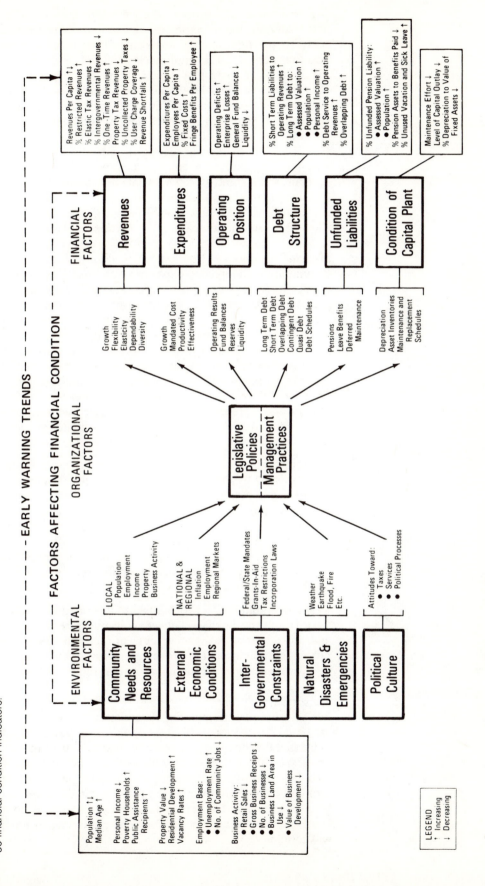

Figure 5–11 Financial Trend Monitoring System showing 12 financial condition factors (5 environmental factors, 1 organizational factor, and 6 financial factors), definitional and descriptive elements, and 36 financial condition indicators.

five environmental factors to the left. With the exception of community needs and resources, these factors are almost entirely controlled by exogenous variables. To the right are six financial factors: revenues, expenditures, operating position, debt structure, unfunded liabilities, and condition of capital plant. In the center is the controlling organizational factor: legislative policies/management practices. To the outside left and right are thirty-six financial condition indicators; almost all are economic and financial measures. These indicators feed into all six financial factors and one of the environmental factors, which in turn feed into the organizational factor of legislative policies/management practices. The flow from left to right is suggestive only, but the framework is illustrative of how planning builds on employment, population, household, business, development, and income data. These data are among the quantitative bases for many planning methods and techniques.[27]

The following examples for Modesto, California, and Kansas City, Missouri, show how revenue forecasting can be done by using generally available data.

Modesto, California[28] In Modesto, California, the finance and planning, and community development departments annually prepare a four-year operating budget forecast with revenue and expenditure estimates for the current fiscal year and each of the following three years. The primary purpose of the multiyear forecast is to offer a preview of the city's financial position and, in doing so, extend the reaction time for addressing financial issues.

The revenue and expenditure forecasts are considered to be guidelines requiring refinement when the operating budget for each year is prepared. The multiyear forecast includes operating projections for the general downtown improvement district, comprehensive employment and training, housing and community development, parking, water, sewer service, airport, bus service, and Tuolumne River Regional Park funds. Estimates are modified as necessary to allow for

1. Growth at an annual rate of 4.5 percent based on statistical information furnished by the planning and community development department, including population, dwelling units, and commercial development projections. Growth adjustments are also made for the added operating costs associated with projects appearing in the city's four-year capital improvement program.
2. Inflation at 10 percent, 9 percent, and 8 percent, through the forecast period based on economic data published by a variety of research and banking institutions.

The operating budget forecasts are illustrated in Figures 5–12, 5–13, and 5–14 to show the linkages between revenue forecasts, expenditure projections, and the resultant balances or deficits for each fund. Figure 5–15 carries this process into the capital improvement program by showing revenue and expenditure projections by capital improvement funds.

Kansas City, Missouri[29]   The Kansas City budget and systems office prepares a five-year forecast of operating revenues and expenditures. Revenue projections are based on an analysis of thirty-one years of history (see Figure 5–16). Twelve individual revenue projections were made. Four of these—earnings and profits taxes, sales and service taxes, utilities and franchise taxes, and interest and rental income—were made using the statistical technique of regression analysis. Deterministic techniques were used to project federal and state grants and miscellaneous revenues. The remaining projections were made using time-series analysis, which assumes that the previous pattern of incremental revenue growth will continue.

FUND 01 GENERAL FUND	1981–82	1982–83	1983–84	1984–85
EXPENDITURE FORECAST	$27,489,089	$31,562,250	$35,147,871	$38,409,517
REVENUE FORECAST	27,001,268	29,525,595	31,813,421	34,375,918
BALANCE (DEFICIT)	$ (487,821*)	$(2,036,655)	$(3,334,450)	$(4,033,599)

REMARKS:

Percent increase over prior year:

Expenditures	14.8%	11.4%	9.3%
Revenue	9.3%	7.7%	8.1%

The revenue forecast does not reflect additional reductions in state subventions that may occur after the current fiscal year.

*Available from prior year to cover deficit - $2,422,274

Figure 5–12   The four-year operating budget forecasts in Modesto, California, are based on linkages between available current revenues, projected expenditures, and the balance or deficit for each fund for each of the four years. This figure shows the expenditure and revenue forecasts for the General Fund. Note how sharply the projected deficit rises in the second and third years. This kind of information is shown for all ten operating funds used by the city of Modesto.

These revenue projections are based on several assumptions, the most significant being that current tax rates will not change.

Property tax revenue was projected by means of time-series analysis, which assumed that the trend in the past will continue in the future. The incremental growth over time explains 99.2 percent of the growth in property tax revenue. The increase in this revenue source is projected at 2 percent annually, compared with the historical average of 3 percent.

It was assumed that earnings and profits tax revenue would continue to follow the growth of per capita national personal income. Historically, per capita national personal income has successfully explained 99.8 percent of the growth in earnings and profits tax revenue. The growth in this revenue source is projected at 10.6 percent annually, just exceeding the historical average of 10.2 percent.

Sales and service tax revenues were assumed to be following the growth of inflation as measured by the national Consumer Price Index (CPI). Historically, the CPI has successfully explained 98.2 percent of the growth in sales and service tax revenue. The growth in this revenue source is projected at 7.2 percent annually, which is close to the historical average of 7.0 percent.

Utility and franchise tax revenues were assumed to be following the growth in the inflation rate as measured by the CPI. Historically, the CPI has successfully explained 99.6 percent of the growth in utility and franchise tax revenue. The growth in this revenue source is projected at 9.0 percent, well below the historical five-year average of 13.5 percent. This lower growth rate reflects adjustments downward for the recently enacted increase of residential exemptions and the

CITY OF MODESTO FOUR YEAR FORECAST - GENERAL FUND REVENUE (BY SOURCE)				
REVENUE SOURCE	1981-82	1982-83	1983-84	1984-85
Property Tax & State Replacements	$ 3,780,900	$ 4,117,600	$ 4,557,100	$ 4,998,200
Sales Tax	6,107,700	6,886,500	7,731,500	8,684,000
Other Taxes	3,782,100	4,312,500	4,828,200	5,403,700
Apportionment and Grants	2,423,915	2,235,300	2,312,000	2,419,000
License Fees and Permits	3,225,860	3,477,790	3,851,830	4,270,280
Fines and Penalties	210,060	191,780	193,290	195,400
Franchises	552,600	623,000	697,400	780,900
Interest and Rent	3,054,480	3,347,940	3,050,125	2,775,290
Special Services	152,300	176,000	193,500	212,900
Parks and Recreation Fees	506,500	606,000	651,900	697,700
Miscellaneous Revenue	135,800	139,100	147,950	156,900
Transferred Revenues From:				
Local Transportation Fund	600,000	650,000	650,000	650,000
Traffic Safety Fund	500,000	650,000	708,500	765,180
Gas Tax Fund	600,000	600,000	600,000	600,000
CETA Fund	2,046	-	-	-
Housing & Community Development	44,000	74,000	81,000	89,000
Water Fund	332,905	366,195	399,152	431,084
Sewer Service Fund	450,971	495,518	540,114	583,323
Airport Fund	29,900	32,890	35,850	38,718
Bus Service Fund	27,800	30,588	33,333	36,000
Self Insurance Fund	657,274	723,001	788,071	851,117
Transfers to Other Funds	(175,843)	(210,107)	(237,394)	(262,774)
TOTAL REVENUE - GENERAL FUND	$27,001,268	$29,525,595	$31,813,421	$34,375,918

Figure 5–13 Four-year revenue forecast, General Fund, by source, Modesto, California. The information shown in the first row is broken down by sales taxes, grants, and other sources, including revenues transferred from other city funds. The totals in the last row tie back to the revenue forecasts in Figure 5-12.

FUND	01	GENERAL FUND	CITY OF MODESTO
DEPT.	18	FIRE	EXPENDITURE FORECAST BY MAJOR BUDGET CATEGORY

FUNCTION / PURPOSE

The purpose of the Fire Department is to provide around-the-clock emergency services, consisting of fire suppression, rescue and first aid, investigation, and fire prevention for all citizens and property located inside of the City limits.

CATEGORY	1981-82	1982-83	1983-84	1984-85
EMPLOYEE SERVICES	$ 4,617,720	$ 5,433,303	$ 6,296,063	$ 6,828,683
PROFESSIONAL and CONTRACTUAL SERVICES	346,836	383,005	419,274	452,816
MATERIALS and SUPPLIES	97,538	109,712	130,675	141,259
OTHER	5,907	16,398	17,874	19,304
DEBT SERVICE				
CAPITAL OUTLAY	23,072	770	11,195	907
SUBTOTAL	$ 5,091,073	$ 5,943,188	$ 6,875,081	$ 7,442,969
LESS SERVICE CREDITS	-	-	-	-
NET BUDGET	$ 5,091,073	$ 5,943,188	$ 6,875,081	$ 7,442,969

ANTICIPATED CHANGES IN SERVICE LEVEL OR OTHER

Increases in administrative work load and the need for increased staff effectiveness make desirable the addition of an Administrative Assistant. The opening of Fire Station #9 will require nine additional positions in 1982-83. The addition of a new pumper, ladder, and water apparatus at Fire Station #4 and the need for relief personnel will each require six additional positions in 1983-84. Increases in technical inspection work load will require a Fire Prevention Technician in 1984-85.

1982-83	Administrative Assistant Fire Fighter (3), Engr. (3), Lt. (3)
1983-84	Lieutenant (6) Engineer (6)
1984-85	Fire Prevention Technician

Figure 5-14   Sample page showing four-year operating expenditure forecast, General Fund, Fire Department, Modesto, California. The same format was used for the expenditure forecasts for all departments and agencies within the General Fund and for nine other operating funds. Note the brevity and clarity of the information. Any council or board member, neighborhood association representative, union representative, or individual citizen can get the essentials at a glance and then ask for the details if he or she wants to know more.

	1982-83		1983-84		1984-85		1985-86	
1	Locally Derived (2)	Inter-Governmental (3)	Locally Derived (4)	Inter-Governmental (5)	Locally Derived (6)	Inter-Governmental (7)	Locally Derived (8)	Inter-Governmental (9)
13 Special Fund for Capital Outlays								
Sales Tax	$ –	$ –	$2,577,133	$ –	$2,894,635	$ –	$3,126,206	$ –
City-Other	69,000	–	83,000	–	69,000	–	69,000	–
County Contribution	–	8,000	–	20,000	–	8,000	–	–
Storm Drain Assess. & Developer Fees	42,000	–	84,000	–	453,000	–	1,163,000	–
Available Balance	1,105,200	–	(37,000)	–	(37,000)	–	(37,000)	–
TOTAL FUND 13 $	1,216,200	8,000	2,707,133	20,000	3,379,635	8,000	4,321,206	–
%	99	1	99	1	99	1	100	–
05 Local Transportation Fund								
Sales Tax (Local Trans. Fund)	$ 850,895	$ –	$ 8,500	$ –	$ 70,500	$ –	$ 94,500	$ –
City-Other	100,000	–	5,000	–	105,000	–	16,000	–
Federal	–	258,000	–	–	–	–	–	267,000
State and County	–	57,000	–	–	–	58,000	–	69,000
Available Balance	487,191	–	–	–	–	–	–	–
TOTAL FUND 05 $	1,438,086	315,000	13,500	–	175,500	58,000	110,500	336,000
%	82	18	100	–	75	25	25	75
07 Gas Tax Fund								
Gas Tax	$1,242,000	$ –	$1,568,495	$ –	$1,568,495	$ –	$1,568,495	$ –
City-Other	58,000	–	55,000	–	58,000	–	55,000	–
Federal	–	4,000	–	119,000	–	8,000	–	452,000
State	–	–	–	–	–	5,000	–	49,000
Available Balance	(550,000)	–	(600,000)	–	(600,000)	–	(600,000)	–
TOTAL FUND 07 $	750,000	4,000	1,023,495	119,000	1,026,495	13,000	1,023,495	501,000
%	99	1	90	10	99	1	67	33

Figure 5–15   Four-year revenue projections of funds available for capital improvement, Modesto, California. Three of the thirteen revenue funds are shown here. The first column shows the principal sources of revenue flowing into each fund. "Available Balance" shows any amount carried forward from a previous period into the first year of the current four-year program, interfund transfers, and amounts excluded to finance operating components of the fund. A separate section of the capital improvement program shows each capital project with information on revenue fund sources and expenditure projections for four fiscal years.

Revenue projections are based on an analysis of thirty-one years of history. Twelve individual revenue projections were made. Four of these, Earnings and Profits Taxes, Sales and Service Taxes, Utilities and Franchise Taxes and Interest and Rental Income, were made using the statistical technique of regression analysis. Deterministic techniques were used to project Federal and State Grants and Miscellaneous Revenues. The remaining revenue projections were made using time-series analysis, which assumes that the previous pattern of incremental revenue growth will continue.

These revenue projections are based on several assumptions. The most significant of these assumptions is that tax rates currently in effect will not change.

Property tax revenue is projected using time series analysis which assumes the trend that has been evidenced in the past will continue in the future. The incremental growth over time explains 99.2 percent of the growth in property tax revenue.

Sales and service tax revenue will continue to follow the growth of inflation as measured by the national Consumer Price Index (CPI). Historically, the national CPI has successfully

explained 98.2 percent of the growth in sales and service tax revenue.

Utility and franchise tax revenue will continue to follow the growth in the inflation rate as measured by the national Consumer Price Index (CPI). Historically, the CPI has successfully explained 99.6 percent of the growth in utility and franchise tax revenue. The growth in this revenue source is projected at 9.0 percent, well below the historical five-year average of 13.5 percent. This lower growth rate reflects adjustments downward for the recently enacted increase of residential exemptions and the residential tax reduction.

Federal and state grant revenue is assumed to remain constant over the forecast period. Revenue Sharing and Community Development Block Grant revenues are assumed to remain constant at their historical averages.

All other revenue sources are projected to grow at an average annual rate of 6.4 percent. This rate is lower than the five-year average of 12.6 percent due to a decrease in revenue from interest and rental income. All other revenue sources are forecast using regression analysis, continuing historical trends, or averaging historical information.

Operating and debt fund revenue projections, 1982–83 to 1986–87 ($ millions)

Revenue source	82–83	83–84	84–85	85–86	86–87	Average annual growth
Property tax	$ 28.1	$ 28.7	$ 29.3	$ 29.8	$ 30.4	2.0%
Earnings and profits taxes	69.4	76.8	85.1	94.1	103.7	10.6
Sales and service taxes	38.9	42.0	45.0	48.1	51.2	7.2
Utility and franchise taxes	55.3	60.3	65.3	70.3	75.3	9.0
Federal and state grants	34.0	34.0	34.0	34.0	34.0	—
All other revenue sources	43.0	46.0	49.0	52.0	55.1	6.4
Total revenues	$268.7	$287.7	$307.7	$328.4	$349.8	6.8%

Figure 5–16   Revenue projections, 1982–83 to 1986–87, Kansas City, Missouri.

residential tax reduction. In addition, the lower growth rate anticipated lower utility rate increases tied to a moderating inflation rate.

Federal and state grant revenues were assumed to remain constant over the forecast period. Revenue sharing and community development block grant revenues were assumed to remain constant at their historical averages. Other grant revenues were forecast to remain at a level consistent with the 1982 federal budget.

All other revenue sources were projected to grow at an average annual rate of 6.4 percent. This rate was lower than the five-year average of 12.6 percent owing to a decrease in revenue from interest and rental income. All other revenue sources were forecast using regression analysis, continuing historical trends, or averaging historical information.

Budget preparation

The two ingredients for preparing the planning department budget are money and time. The budget also should include estimates for grants that may or *may not* be received. Only through frequent communication can the planning director decide how to treat grant prospects. Evaluation of grant criteria, preparation of preliminary applications, and discussions with representatives of grantors are a sound basis for deciding to include or exclude a prospective grant.

Matching work, time, and people

The way to allocate hours and dollars realistically is to list tasks, and subtasks if necessary, along one side of a matrix and personnel across the other. Task assignments cumulatively represent the work to be performed during the year to achieve the department's objectives. This exercise requires sensitivity to the complexity of the task in comparison with the abilities of the persons assigned. It is assumed that the more a person is paid, the greater is the number and complexity of tasks he or she can perform, and the faster they will be performed. Staff assessments described in Chapter 7 will yield valuable information on staff abilities and their willingness to take on new assignments.

A number of variables over which the planning director has little control are inherent in the budgeting process. Staff members may resign or be absent for long periods as a result of illness. Anticipated grants may not be awarded. The council may request additional studies that could not be anticipated. Natural or manmade disasters may occur and require new priorities. The number of meetings called and their length may increase. The number of public inquiries requiring response may increase as issues "heat up." But these variables, except for disasters, tend to average out over the long term.

Extemporaneous council requests for special studies can wreak havoc with the planning department's schedule and budget. Persons requesting these studies sometimes think that data bases and methodologies are readily available. Even if they are not, a critical part of local planning is to fulfill requests for quantification of consequences of alternative development decisions. Not only can these studies help establish a record of the usefulness of planning in the eyes of local elected officials, but they can also help influence imminent development decisions. Therefore, the planning director should anticipate these types of requests and include staff time for them in the budget.

Budget formats are too terse and "pigeonholed" to adequately explain the research to be performed and the interrelatedness of individual tasks. Therefore, an off-budget memorandum should be prepared to describe nonroutine work to be performed and its level of effort, purposes, and timing. The planning director should send copies to elected and appointed officials and citizens who are especially interested in planning activities. This memorandum should be carefully labeled "draft" to avoid any implication that final decisions have been made on all aspects of the department's program.

Cutback budgeting

The planner's view of the world calls for more planning. Yet the competition for scarce dollars and the demand for greater employee productivity will lead the chief executive to ask the planning department to cut back program, staff, equipment, travel, or all of them. Where does the planner begin if a cutback is inevitable? What tests need to be applied to a planning program to determine where to cut back and when? What questions will the planner face in justifying the remaining program? The effective cutback manager needs to look at the program carefully before making painful decisions to reduce the level of effort he or she sincerely believes is required for a viable planning program. The following kinds of rethinking illustrate the questions that should be answered by the planning director before any budget decreases are recommended.

1. Are the program goals clear and precise?
2. Have all feasible alternatives been presented?
3. Have realistic costs and benefits been assigned to each alternative?
4. Have the unseen trade-offs for the entire community been brought out?
5. Are the criteria for making the choices clear?
6. Are there alternative or nongovernmental means to solve the problem?
7. Are there technological breakthroughs that can help improve local government productivity?[30]

The planning director who can successfully answer questions such as these will have reevaluated the program and responded in ways that are useful to the chief executive who has overall responsibility for making program cutback recommendations and decisions.

One approach to answering these questions is to establish a formal agency evaluation process. This process, however, requires substantial staff time and reopens fundamental questions about an agency's goals, objectives, programs, activities, and tasks.

Another possibility is to establish an evaluation committee composed of planning commission members and citizens knowledgeable about the planning process. Outside opinion may also be sought from consultants or representatives of planning and management associations familiar with experience elsewhere. These and other outside experts help reduce the likelihood of charges of political expediency if no outsiders are included in the process. It is likely that the committee will need the type of information that can be obtained through a survey. Questions asked of political leaders, business leaders, and citizens should provide feedback on the most important elements of the planning program and on any problems that the respondent may have had with it or may have heard about.

The staff should convey feedback from the questionnaires and discussions to evaluation committee members. The staff should also prepare answers to questions and should comment on points of misunderstanding in the feedback. Critical and lucid respondents should be invited to present their views to an evaluation committee meeting.

The staff should then be able to draft a list of planning department program changes in response to guidance from the evaluation committee. Upon agreement between the committee and staff, a report of the committee's findings should be drafted by the staff. Agreed-upon changes should be incorporated into the next annual budget.

The evaluation committee approach has the advantage of bringing in outside perspectives and of rethinking priorities. It may also have the secondary benefit of broadening and deepening political support. Evaluation committee members may become "salespersons" for sustaining rather than cutting back the planning program.

Conclusion

Financial planning is both broader and deeper than the typical budget routine of most local governments. It goes beyond the earliest budgeting objective of financial control, and the later budgeting objective of management information, to the current objective of a policy agenda with revenues and expenditures attached. Each builds on the other.

For almost every city and county, most of the annual operating budget is locked in by immutable commitments: bond payments, pension fund contributions, wages and salaries with a probable across-the-board increase every year, replacement of worn-out police cars and other motor equipment, materials and supplies, building maintenance, and other predictable obligations. What is left is that small discretionary amount "at the margin." One city manager has estimated this amount to be only 5 percent of the annual budget. Some managers and planners would put it at 10 percent, but very few would put it any higher.

It is this relatively small amount that is studied, appraised, fought over, and finally allocated through the governmental process. It is here that financial planning makes its most important contribution to community development. Although a city or county decision at the margin may be small in dollars, the leveraging of other public and private investment may be substantial. The location of new water and sewer lines is a well-known example.

Planners are most commonly involved in the CIP because capital facilities strongly influence the location, timing, and type of development. Fewer planners use three- to five-year forecasts of operating revenues and expenditures. By building in financial plans and forecasts—and the quantitative analyses upon which they are based—finance departments can produce strategic planning budgets. Such budgets add a forward looking perspective to the control and management purposes of the budget.

1 Much of this chapter has been excerpted, with appropriate citations, from: Lewis Friedman, "Budgeting," in *Management Policies in Local Government Finance*, 2d ed., ed. J. Richard Aronson and Eli Schwartz (Washington, D.C.: International City Management Association, 1981).

2 Interview with Thomas W. Fletcher, 18 August 1982.

3 James C. Snyder, *Fiscal Management and Planning for Local Government* (Lexington, Mass.: Lexington Books, 1977), 79.

4 Abstracted from: Frederick O'R. Hayes et al., *Linkages: Improving Financial Management in Local Government* (Washington, D.C.: Urban Institute, 1982), 24–27.

5 This section, "The budget process," has been excerpted, with editorial changes, from: Friedman, "Budgeting," 95–99.

6 See: Terry N. Clark, "Can You Cut a Budget Pie?" *Policy and Politics* 3 (1974): 3–31; and John P. McIver and Elinor Ostrom, "Using Budget Pies to Reveal Preferences: Validity of a Survey Instrument," in *Citizens Preferences and Urban Public Policy: Models, Measures, Uses*, ed. Terry N. Clark, Sage Contemporary Social Science Issues (Beverly Hills, Calif.: Sage Publications, 1976).

7 Charles Lindblom, "Decision Making in Taxation and Expenditures," in *Public Finances: Needs, Sources, and Utilization*, National Bureau of Economic Research (Princeton, N.J.: Princeton University Press, 1961), 297–98.

8 This section, "Achieving budget objectives," has been excerpted, with editorial changes, from: Friedman, "Budgeting," 99–111.

9 Jacob B. Ukeles, *Doing More With Less: Turning Public Management Around* (New York: AMACOM, 1982), 81.

10 J. Wilner Sundelson, "Budgeting Principles," *Political Science Quarterly* 50 (June 1935): 236–63.

11 George E. Hale and Scott R. Douglas, "The Politics of Budget Execution: Financial Manipulation of State and Local Government," *Administration and Society* 3 (1977): 367–78; George E. Hale, "State Budget Execution: The Legislature's Role," *National Civic Review* 66 (June 1977): 284–90; Allen Schick, "Control Patterns in State Budget Execution," *Public Administration Review* 24 (June 1964): 97–106.

12 See: Robert Anthony, *Financial Accounting in Non-Business Organizations* (Stamford, Conn.: Financial Accounting Standards Board, 1978); National Council on Governmental Accounting, *Governmental Accounting and Financial Reporting Principles—Statement 1* (Chicago: Municipal Finance Officers Association, 1979); William W. Holder, *A Study of Selected Concepts for Government Financial Accounting and Reporting* (Chicago: National Council on Governmental Accounting, 1980).

13 See: Municipal Finance Officers Association, *Disclosure Guidelines for Offerings of Securities by State and Local Governments* (Chicago: Municipal Finance Officers Association, 1976).

14 See: Jan M. Lodal, "Improving Local Government Financial Information Systems," *Duke Law Journal* (1976): 1133–55; The Urban Academy, *An Introduction to "IFMS"* (New York: Urban Academy, 1976); Roger Mansfield, "The Financial Reporting Practices of Government: A Time for Reflection," *Public Administration Review* 39 (January/February 1979): 157–62; "Financial Reporting by Governmental Units," *Governmental Finance* 7 (May 1978): 2–39.

15 Comptroller General of the U.S., *Standard for Audits of Governmental Organizations, Programs, Activities and Functions* (Washington, D.C.: Government Printing Office, 1972), 2.

16 U.S. Commission on the Organization of the Ex-

ecutive Branch of the Government, *Budgeting and Accounting* (Washington, D.C.: Government Printing Office, 1949), 8.

17 Comptroller General of the U.S., *Standards for Audits*, 2.

18 Allen Schick, "The Road to PPB: The Stages of Budget Reform," *Public Administration Review* 26 (December 1966): 243–58.

19 Comptroller General of the U.S., *Standards for Audits*, 2.

20 With the exception of the first four paragraphs, this section, "Establishing financial policies," has been excerpted, with editorial changes, from: W. Maureen Godsey, *Financial Performance Goals: A Guide for Setting Long-Range Policies*, handbook 4 in *Evaluating Local Government Financial Condition* (Washington, D.C.: International City Management Association, 1980), 1–9, 11.

21 Abstracted from: Karl Nollenberger, "It's More than Balancing the Budget," *Public Management* 62 (April 1980): 2–3.

22 Ibid. Italics in original.

23 Abstracted with the closing quote from: John Matzer, Jr., "Financial Policies Payoff," *Public Management* 62 (April 1980): 6.

24 Excerpted, with minor editorial revisions, from: S. Wayne Kohlwes, "The Capital Improvements Program: An Implementation Technique for the Comprehensive Plan?" (Master's thesis, The Graduate School, Pennsylvania State University, 1982), 210–16.

25 Excerpted, with minor editorial changes, from: Maryland-National Capital Park and Planning Commission, *Planning, Staging and Regulating* (Silver Spring, Md.: The Commission, 1979), 4–3 to 4–5.

26 Excerpted, with minor editorial changes, from: City of Baltimore, Department of Planning, *Baltimore's Development Program* (1982), 6.

27 For a more detailed discussion of these techniques and methods, see: Anthony James Catanese, "Information for Planning," in *The Practice of Local Government Planning*, ed. Frank S. So et al. (Washington, D.C.: International City Management Association, 1979), 90–114.

28 Excerpted, with minor editorial changes, from: City of Modesto, California, *City of Modesto Four-Year Operating Revenue and Expenditure Forecast, 1981–82 to 1984–85*, prepared by Garth Lipsky (19 November 1981).

29 Excerpted, with minor editorial changes, from: City of Kansas City, Missouri, *Five-Year Financial Forecast, 1982–1983 to 1986–87*, prepared by Shirley Weglarz et al. (1 October 1981).

30 Wayne F. Anderson et al., "Promoting the Community's Future," in *The Effective Local Government Manager* (Washington, D.C.: International City Management Association, 1983), 161.

6 Working with councils, boards, and commissions

Planners work with and report to boards, councils, and commissions. An integral part of their work is to make recommendations to policy makers. In a democracy their work is subject to a variety of checks and balances. Planners, who define technical processes, report to elected and appointed officials and citizens who define the public interest that planners serve. That public interest is pluralistic: it differs between communities, and it is continually refined by changing coalitions. These circumstances call for great skill on the part of local government department heads in general, and planners in particular, if they are to identify and respond to the public interest in the context of contemporary issues.

Changes in the planning process

Before the 1950s, it was taken for granted that the planner was a professional whose expert advice reflected community interests. Administering development regulations and preparing the master plan for land use were the principal responsibilities of most planners. That role changed with the development problems brought about by rapid economic growth after World War II and the increased funding of planning provided by the Federal Housing Act of 1954. Consequently, more planners were hired, and increasingly sophisticated planning methods were applied.

Three changes that occurred in the 1950s and the 1960s are thought to have fundamentally altered the way local government planning is carried out: (1) the emergence of functional planning, (2) citizen participation, and (3) the dispersion of the decision-making process.[1]

Functional or single-purpose planning has actually been around for decades, but it did not become very noticeable until the passage in 1956 of the Interstate Defense Highway Act. Although adopted by Congress without a planning requirement (that was added six years later), the "interstates" soon made an impact on communities, both in the form of bypasses that went around the smaller places and the urban links that began to bifurcate the larger, central cities. Although a continuing, cooperative, and coordinated planning process was mandated and funded by Congress beginning in 1962, the program still involved functional planning, albeit on very large scales. The geographic scale was the metropolitan area. The data-base scale consisted of large quantities of land use and transportation behavior information.

Similarly, wastewater collection and treatment facility grants were provided by the federal government several years before watershed planning requirements were mandated and funded. The same was true of planning for health facilities, recreation facilities, and other public services. The consequence was the establishment of functional planning staffs (health services planning, transportation facilities planning, park planning, and so on) that complemented the comprehensive planning staffs that had existed. These functional planning staffs have been oriented toward the delivery of a service or the construction of projects rather than overall community goal setting and implementation.

In 1962 Governor Terry Sanford of North Carolina appointed an economic opportunity commission to look at social and economic problems in that state. Its staff set up programs that would remove obstacles to individual development, education, and job opportunities and lead to higher personal income and less dependence on public assistance. In order to aid the staff and its policy board in navigating these relatively uncharted waters, prospective program participants were questioned about the problems they faced and possible solutions. Thus was born the systematic citizen participation process for social growth and development.

At about the same time, citizens in many states were complaining about controversial highway projects, especially people in central cities in the states that were aggressively implementing the Interstate Defense Highway Act. Their organized political pressure produced a Federal Highway Administration regulation requiring that public meetings be held before project construction began.

Both functional and comprehensive planning brought forth new information on the development issues faced by local governments. In addition, increased citizen participation brought multiple lay perspectives to bear on the evaluation of these issues. With more information to process and multiple constituencies to respond to, local governments found decision making more complicated. Citizen groups, meanwhile, took advantage of the information available and became skilled in building and presenting their cases to local officials. Furthermore, citizen group coalitions were created in response to single issues and then were dissolved as issues were resolved. The legacy of more planning and citizen participation is a pluralistic decision-making process in local government.

Demand for community relations

Demand for community relations and citizen participation increased rapidly with the creation of federal social programs in the late 1960s and environmental programs in the early 1970s. Both technical and political uncertainties affected the social and environmental laws passed at that time. Urban renewal had been roundly condemned by some critics as a social and ecological failure, and the interstate highway program was deemed a divisive (some said destructive) force.

As a consequence, congressional constituents demanded, and got, a voice in the definition and execution of these and other federal programs. Legislatively mandated citizen participation was the result. The federal Model Cities Program of 1966 required participation of residents from center city neighborhoods in which the program was administered; and the federal Community Development Block Grant program of 1974 required opportunities for participation of representatives from all community groups in setting local expenditure priorities. Meanwhile, the Federal National Environmental Policy Act of 1969 required analysis of the consequences of proposed federal investments, and areawide agencies receiving Section 701 comprehensive planning funds from the federal government were urged to include a cross section of elected officials and citizen members on their policy boards.

Citizen participation has affected both the decisions of elected officials in local government and the programs, methods, and actions of planners who gather and analyze information. Elected officials depend on organized citizen participation so that they will not become overly dependent on technicians in their effort to recognize major courses of action and make project decisions. Citizen groups are seen as sources of information and major links to constituencies. This tendency to rely on citizen groups can, of course, produce decisions that reflect narrow preferences rather than broader and more diverse interests. At the same time, the interaction of technical complexity and citizen participation has strengthened the sophistication of planners and the planning process.

Now that the citizen participation process has been institutionalized, it has

The interstates and the people

When Congress enacted the Federal-aid Highway Act of 1956, which provided for the National System of Interstate and Defense Highways, it was heralded as "the beginning of a new era in . . . highway transportation." And indeed it was. The program was projected in 1956, at a cost of $33 billion, to provide an interstate network of 41,000 miles linking 42 state capitals and 90 percent of the cities over 50,000 population.

The benefits were to include creation of 500,000 full-time jobs; huge requirements for cement, steel, and other construction materials and equipment; lower car operating costs; increased property values; and substantial improvements in ease of travel and highway safety.

The euphoria of the moment did not include the reaction of citizens when work got under way, but two persons, an economist and an engineer, did foresee in 1956 some of the difficulties in highway location that might occur.

"The location of a major freeway or parkway—as all of the interstate high-

ways must be—is a difficult undertaking in our larger urban areas, involving the uprooting of many people and businesses. Bitter emotions are stirred up. . . . The federal act specifically requires public hearings whenever a federal-aid highway project involves bypasses or going through a city. Experience indicates that on many occasions the objectors to a particular location are vocal at a public hearing while the supporters appear to be non-existent. Even in a state such as California, where . . . the advantages of limited access, bypasses, and through-passes are rather widely understood, the location problem continues to be a source of considerable irritation and delay. One can well imagine that the problems will be magnified many times in communities where the concepts of modern highway design are just beginning to take shape."

Source: Partly abstracted and partly excerpted from: Richard M. Zettel and Norman Kennedy, "Effect of New Highway Act on Urban Areas," *Public Management* 38 (December 1956): 270–73.

altered the allocation of powers. Formerly, elected officials dominated, but as their need for information prior to making decisions increased, the role of the technical staff increased commensurately. As citizens protested that their interests were not being served, either by the elected officials or by the professional staffs, responsibility for plan making was redefined to give politically acceptable shares of responsibility to citizens, elected officials, and staff.

Community relations pitfalls[2]

Planners focus their work on two particularly issue-laden subjects: (1) the use of land and buildings (which have a high potential for windfalls and wipeouts), and (2) the future of the community (in which there is sufficient uncertainty to make almost all opinions equal in importance).

Controversy continuously surrounds the planning process. Although their exposure and intensity might vary, the most prominent issues in the local planning process are those that involve the most people, the most important people, or large amounts of money. As city managers, county managers, and planning directors know, it is not easy to work with councils, boards, and commissions on the firing line. They deal with contentious issues that strike at peoples' values. The working relations are highly personal. These are reasons why the planner who participates in resolving issues has one of the most interesting jobs in local government.

A feature of planning—a feature that creates the challenge, excitement, and indeed the central problem—is that the professional local planner must work constantly in the swim of community life with its shifting standards, values, ideas, and ideals. The push and pull of community groups ensures that yesterday's goals may not be appropriate for today or tomorrow. Developing an effective relationship with the community is therefore one of the most demanding and complex tasks facing any local planner. The planner must nurture this relationship with great care for, above all else, the planner's success or failure—his or her professional survival—in this line of work depends on it. At least four pitfalls can stand in the way of success here.

Why worry about community relations?

The planner who does not worry about community relations is living dangerously. Once upon a time, the planner thought mainly about zoning and long-range plans and was not expected to participate in policy formulation or budgeting. Such noninvolvement no longer applies. Modern local planning demands continuous work on "people issues." The policy formation role played by planners can be one of their most valuable and significant contributions to their communities. Disregard of this essential fact is the shortest route to early, involuntary retirement. Planners are more likely to lose their jobs for failing to work well with people issues than for failing to work out the technical aspects of their jobs.

"Glad handing" is not enough

It takes considerably more than the glad hand, a sales pitch, or the easy smile to build effective community relations. It takes skill and understanding. Some planners, despite being somewhat introverted or at least not highly communicative, succeed in developing positive, strong ties with the communities they serve.

Figure 6–1

"Would a study shut them up?"

Overemphasizing community relations

The notion that community relations are the sole key to successful local planning is just as false as the idea that community relations are unimportant. A planner is hired because he or she can perform specific tasks required by the community. Skill, expertise, a sense of responsibility, good judgment, and common sense are important for on-the-job effectiveness. And these are the capabilities that the planners' immediate bosses and elected officials most admire. Simply put, the planner is hired for technical effectiveness but is most likely to get in trouble because of his or her inability to deal with people.

Delegating community relations

Everyone, including the planning director, must be responsible for building effective community relations. For a number of reasons, the planner cannot delegate this job to someone else, such as a public information officer or a personal staff assistant.

First, most local governments do not have the money to hire a public information officer or to organize a public relations (PR) department. And citizens often resent spending tax dollars for PR purposes.

In any case, PR should be the planning director's job. The director sets the tone for the planning department, the organization, or the agency where he or she works. Thus, if the director is conscious of the importance of community relations, subordinates will take the cue.

Furthermore, the planning director's efforts in this regard can provide local government with considerable information about the community, its problems, its needs, and its concerns.

Determining community relations needs[3]

The world of the local planner is not composed of a neat set of individual mathematical problems for which there are correct answers. Nor do the problems occur in a logical pattern, as they might in a chess game. Rather, the life of the planner is fragmented and full of surprises. Unexpected requests and complications undermine the best-laid plans, and no one has any idea what the final result will be. Local planning is frenetic work.

Obviously, developing effective community relations is not a simple matter of choosing a set of right and wrong things to do. Rather, this undertaking is more like a quest toward an ideal model. A model provides a target to shoot for. It offers a way of thinking, not a specific list of tasks; a quest, not an end; a process, not a solution.

What then is a useful model for thinking about effective planner-community relations? Figure 6–2 illustrates one possible model—though by no means the only one. Each level consists of problems or issues the planner must address. The order in which these issues are raised is important. The one at the base may be considered the most critical and complex and therefore should be examined first. The others build progressively on the first, in order of priority. In reality, of course, a busy planner has to be involved in all the levels at once. Still, ranking the issues is helpful to any planner who wants to think systematically about achieving overall effectiveness in community relations. The thought process represented by this model consists of several steps:

1. Sizing up personal community relations style. First, the planner must size up his or her style in relating with others by wrestling with such questions as: Who am I? What are my values? Ideals? Strengths? Weaknesses?
2. Understanding what community relations capabilities the community

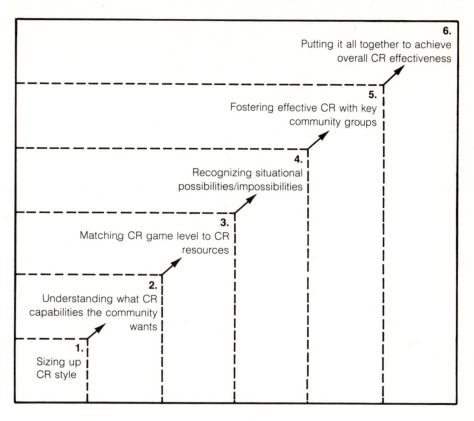

Figure 6–2 A model for developing
effective community relations (CR).

wants. Next, and of almost equal importance, what does the community
want from the planner in terms of relating to the public?

3.   Matching community relations "game level" to community relations
     resources. What are the institutional capabilities—formal and informal
     resources—of the planning office? What is the best fit for the application
     of these resources in the different types of public activities or "game
     levels" of community involvement?
4.   Recognizing the situational possibilities or impossibilities of community
     relations. How does the political landscape in the community limit or
     enhance the planner's community relations capabilities? Given the unique
     political configurations of the community, how do they shape local
     strategy for building support, coalitions, and allies for programs?
5.   Fostering effective community relations with key community groups.
     What community groups, organizations, and interests are especially
     important to the planner's on-the-job success or failure? Why are they
     critical? How can the planner best gain their support?
6.   Putting it all together to achieve overall community relations
     effectiveness. How can the planner put it all together to achieve overall
     effectiveness in community relations?

Relationships with others

To be effective in dealing with others, a local public planner must first come to
grips with his or her own values, views, and ideals. A personal inventory of
strengths and weaknesses helps give the planner a clear idea of what he or she
can reasonably accomplish. Conversely, self-assessment may indicate what tasks,

Who are the influentials?   I learned quite a bit about San Francisco and its people during the public hearings and negotiations. For one thing, I learned that the chamber of commerce was extremely well funded and had a large staff. It had extensive associations with elected officials, commissioners, architects, and the media, and it was understandably opposed to constraints on development. Bigger is better was the prevailing philosophy at the chamber. Government should keep its hands off. Although that position was predictable, the chamber's strength was a modest surprise. More surprising was the philosophy of the committee of the local chapter of the American Institute of Architects that was monitoring the proposed ordinance. Its chairman and some of its members seemed philosophically in tune with Ayn Rand's Howard Roark and were at heart opposed to any zoning. Later, I was to find that this committee was not wholly representative.

Others voiced opinions too. Chinatown business interests were looking ahead to opportunities for future development (and profits) by replacing modest structures (that house poor Chinese) with new high rises. They were not above claiming, through the Human Rights Commission, that the proposed height restrictions would cause hardship to low-income people. Organized labor demanded that the new zoning eliminate the low paying, nonunion garment shops of Chinatown. Over and over I was surprised to learn that this property owner and that lawyer knew individual planning commissioners, not necessarily in any improper or conspiratorial sense, but as schoolmates, club members, neighbors, or old acquaintances. It seemed a very small city.

Source: Allan B. Jacobs, *Making City Planning Work* (Chicago: American Society of Planning Officials, 1978), 10–11.

---

programs, or activities the planner should not undertake—or at least those that might well be frustrating in view of particular strengths and weaknesses. Furthermore, self-awareness can help anyone gain self-confidence. By having a firm grasp of the skills that you have and those that you lack, you will convey to others a lasting impression of personal conviction, integrity, and knowledge—priceless treasures for establishing solid and effective human relationships.

One way to size up community relations abilities may be to compare yourself with other local planners in terms of operational goals, values, outlooks, activities, interests, procedures, and practices. Despite the great variety among city and county planners, studies of managers show four styles of local management that can serve as reference points for self-assessment: (1) the community leader, (2) the chief executive, (3) the administrative planner, and (4) the caretaker planner.[4]

The community leader   Community leaders take the broadest view of their job. They visualize themselves as community change agents, innovators, "idea men," and "doers" in a broad range of community issues and concerns.

This community relations style is characteristic of planners who are energetic and idealistic, and have a few battle scars from previous policy fights. Examples that come to mind are strong mayors elected on a reform ticket—mayors whose popularity gained them broad mandates to initiate sweeping changes in their cities. In general, today's community leaders are well educated, keep up with current professional literature, and are active participants at conferences of their peers.

This type of professional tends to ask the following kinds of questions:

1.   What are the big problems and needs facing my community?

2. How can I best keep citizens informed of these problems/needs?
3. How can I tap the human and physical resources of the community to work out solutions?
4. How can I apply current knowledge, technology, and techniques to these issues?

The chief executive   Chief executives are generally seasoned veterans who know from experience the practical limitations their political environments impose on them and who are more circumspect than community leaders about plunging into a community controversy. They are more pragmatic and less idealistic about the possibility of promoting social change and therefore less willing to stick their necks out for a good cause unless all their ducks are lined up ahead of time. This kind of planner is the realist who firmly believes the old saw that "often the ideal kills the possible."

In terms of education, on-the-job-training, and active involvement with professional associations, chief executive types are fairly similar to community leader types. Only age and length of tenure differentiate them—and they may at one time have been "young Turks" themselves. They may also be more prudent in joining local organizations—belonging only to groups that help further their management aims.

The chief executive tends to ask cautious questions:

1. What can I do for my community that is realistic and possible?
2. How can I encourage others in the community to speak out for this idea and push its development?
3. How can I lead the community from behind the scenes and even give credit to others for what may in fact be my initiatives?
4. Is now a good time to push this idea onto the community's agenda, or would it be better to wait a while?

The administrative planner   Administrative planners, like the first two types, are interested in change, but they prefer to initiate change primarily within the organization or agency. In their view, the planner's community involvement should be kept in line with the strict legal terms of the charter or the planner's job description. In other words, their job is to administer policy, not make it. They consider setting the political agenda to be the sole responsibility of the chief administrator and the city council or the county board. Indeed, the administrative planner may even view community relations activities with some distaste—"time-wasting nonsense"—and may therefore dwell on the pitfalls and drawbacks of such activities beyond obligatory speaking engagements and meeting appearances. Still, he or she recognizes, perhaps reluctantly, that community relations are part of the job, something that "comes with the territory."

Nevertheless, within the confines of "administration" (which may have fairly wide boundaries), the administrative planner finds ample room to apply creativity and innovation. This planner's professional pride and satisfaction frequently come from technical achievements in the community (a new zoning ordinance, a community center, or adopted land use policies) or from administrative innovations (for example, a new development permission processing system) he or she has introduced to make the organization function more efficiently. Administrative planners often achieve substantial recognition as specialists in such problem-solving areas as urban renewal, historic preservation, and transportation.

The typical administrative planner asks questions that are quite different from those asked by the community leader or the chief executive:

1. What policies and programs do the council and manager want me to carry out?

The mayor and planner team   William H. Lucy, Chairman of the Urban and Environmental Planning Program at the University of Virginia, Charlottesville, served in the late sixties and early seventies as Director of Policy Planning in the Office of the Mayor, Syracuse, New York. At that time he wrote three memoranda to Mayor Lee Alexander on policy questions in relation to the work of the chief administrator. The memoranda covered revenue sources, financial policies, education, police service, and public relations, but the memoranda also gave extensive attention to strategic planning, although it was not called that. The following excerpts, with a few editorial interpolations, illustrate how planning, management, and policy choices can work together.

When I assumed a policy advisor role to the mayor in mid-November, 1970, Mayor Alexander had been in office more than 10 months. I learned by listening and observing that decision making often occurred in an ad hoc manner . . . and without satisfactory consideration for how other policy concerns would be affected by each decision. I decided to confront these two decision-making characteristics [and argue] the case for more attention to long-range achievement of policy objectives.

The first and overriding principle is that public persuasion follows only from a combination of strong policy and effective communication.

Second, the public impression of accomplishments by the chief executive will flow from one, two, or at most three projects or programs with which he has repeatedly been identified.

Third, it is essential that strategies of crisis management be devised so that crises can be defused and made ambiguous.

Fourth, since crises and controversies are more noticeable to the public . . . it is important to try [to take] the initiative and . . . define the issues.

Fifth, . . . scenarios should be developed for the key programs and projects.

The key elements of policy are that it be consistent with the course of recent history, that the bureaucracy have the ability and the will to carry it out, that the decision be within the scope of what a chief executive can hope to affect, that it be within financial reach, that it be timely, and that the entire purpose and process of policy be explainable to the general public.

2. How can I implement these policies wisely, creatively, and efficiently?
3. How can I get the council to clarify any ambiguity about what they want me to do?
4. What administrative activities within the organization are most in need of repair, reform, or improvement?
5. Should I buck this issue up the administrative ladder or avoid it altogether since it smacks of politics?

The caretaker planner   The caretaker planners, unlike the other three types, are interested not in change or innovation but in order and routine. They view themselves strictly as administrators, and thus concentrate on housekeeping or maintenance functions in the local governments they serve. Often they glory in their knowledge of specific administrative routines, budgetary procedures, and zoning regulations. Frequently they have little formal education in planning, lack interest in improving their professional skills, and harbor few aspirations for higher, more responsible jobs in government or elsewhere. The caretaker prefers to make few waves in the community. In fact, the caretaker may enjoy

[Turning to four specific applications of policy and implementation, Professor Lucy made the following observations.]

If some tax funds are going to be available, the question then is how to use them to achieve a significant result. This will vary from community to community, but I would focus on tangible, visible, and deeply felt needs. These would include garbage collection, street and maintenance, crime control, and school facilities.

It is important that the service be regular and universal, like garbage collection, or that it involve physical observations, like certain kinds of police programs.

Chief executives, feeling the pressure at times of violent crisis, may exaggerate the extent to which their constituents seem to have a blood lust. Chief executives may even stimulate a backlash inadvertently. They may be unaware of, or lack a program for, longstanding anxieties felt by some people, especially lower middle income whites, that blacks are getting preferential attention, and that kids are taking advantage of their elders who never had the same opportunities. These are neither irrational nor unreasonable feelings. However, they are unbalanced and de-

scribe only a small part of the circumstance of both blacks and young people, and the attitudes and policies of public officials toward them.

Some policies can be adopted that will reduce this prevalent feeling of one sided public policy . . . garbage is a problem for everyone, the poor more than the rich, but still for everyone. Crime is a problem, and education is a problem, in the same way, worse for the poor but problems for everyone with the middle class perhaps more vocal than others. Policies that focus on problems that everyone can identify as being "for them" do not have the same potential for backlash.

This is the broad policy goal: communicate the city's financial problem, fight for a viable alternative, minimize the liabilities from the inevitable tax increases, increase the possibility that a windfall will create a surplus, and establish a policy framework within which people can recognize the problems of running the city. Part of that need to communicate must be met by describing genuine efforts to conserve resources and save money. The most important of these would be the elimination of jobs, which has already been carried out.

the office and its title purely for the status and the paycheck it affords, and his or her major interest in the job may be personal survival.

The questions that concern a caretaker planner include:

1. How can I avoid this potential hot potato?
2. Since the council and manager have not made up their minds on this issue, how can I best play it safe and do nothing?
3. Have I handled the budget and personnel procedures according to law?
4. Is my in-basket getting too full?

Summary

The community leader generally exhibits a high level of skill in dealing with people and a low to mid-range level of technical competency (see Figure 6–3). The chief executive has a slightly lower orientation to people owing to lower expectations about what managers can reasonably achieve coupled with higher

High people orientation

Community leader
Interested in broad community-wide changes; willing to be active in pursuit of goals

Chief executive
Interested in community change but realistic and prudent; willing to work within and through formal organizational routes

Low technical orientation ◄——————————► **High technical orientation**

Administrative caretaker
Focuses mainly on keeping things going as they are

Administrative innovator
Focuses mainly on change within the organization; takes careful cues on policy directions from council

Low people orientation

Figure 6–3 Planning and management in terms of people orientation versus technical orientation.

technical concerns about doing the job. The administrative planner, as the title implies, has high technical capabilities and generally less orientation toward people. The caretaker planner is a bureaucrat in the pejorative sense who is deeply involved in routines, forms, procedures and the perquisites of the job.

Conducting a community relations program

One model for conducting a community relations program is the "scoping" process used for preparing environmental impact statements. The staff member responsible for preparing the statement identifies the issues—which may come from city or county council members, planning commission members, textbooks, other staff, or personal observations—and writes a set of definitions representing the tentative scope of the technical work to be done. Selected agencies or individuals are then asked to review the tentative scope and comment on it. They are typically persons who shared the ideas in the first place.

Once their comments are incorporated into the draft, the staff member is ready to add ideas from predetermined citizen groups. These groups are expected to add substantive contributions to the technical material in the "scope." This information is gathered from as many citizen groups as is determined desirable or necessary and is incorporated into the technical work program.

The advantages of this approach are that it provides the planning staff with a systematic method of analyzing local issues and expanding the substance of the work beyond expressly technical considerations. A disadvantage is the time (and cost) it takes to touch base with many interest groups. The more reviews there are, the longer and more expensive the process. Nevertheless, as the preceding sections of this chapter have pointed out, community relations is a built-in part of the planning process. Community relations and citizen involvement can be approached from several points of view. The following pages will review community relations as: power structure, political setting, feedback (citizen surveys and complaint logs), public involvement and accommodation, and informal networking.

Power structure

The first step for the planner is to look at the power structure in the community. A good understanding of the power structure helps the planner to work effectively with official and unofficial groups; communicate with many kinds of people; visualize both the large and small elements in countywide, citywide, and neighborhood proposals; and persuade others of the worth of his or her recommendations. The planner's recommendations will be evaluated by those responsible for acting on them.

Students of the community often classify community power holders within three groups:

Various approaches have been developed to determine who are the holders of community power. Among them are the *reputational*, *positional*, and *decisional* approaches. In the reputational approach, people are asked to identify those persons in the community who exert the most influence. . . . The same technique may be used to determine the power holders and leaders within subcommunities or groups. In the positional approach it is assumed that certain positions (mayor, superintendent) within the formal structures are more powerful and influential than others and, therefore, those people who hold key positions are persons of power. The decisional approach assumes that individuals take on power as they are involved in the decision-making process—that as one learns the techniques of decision making one begins to use them and, in fact, to exert power.[5]

The planner considers organizational charts and titles, reviews decisions attributed to persons of authority, interprets votes, and obtains the latest facts from his or her communication network prior to deciding the relative power structure roles of individuals and agencies.

Political setting

In politically volatile situations an adversarial relationship may develop between representatives of citizen groups and local governments. It is too much to expect that the divergent purposes of dramatizing an issue and resolving it with available resources can be achieved either quickly or with a small number of people. Experienced planners know that the posturing, implied guilt, delaying tactics, misdirected criticism, and hyperbole characteristic of confrontational community relations are difficult if not impossible to avoid in the most controversial development issues. As a public employee, you must minimize their occurrence by being well prepared and accepting confrontation as part of the job.

Citizen input requires special attention so that the input will be channeled into the community's decision-making process. In the best of all possible worlds, information required from the public would be received at appropriate times to guide and support the decision-making process, and extemporaneous, out-of-context citizen input would be held to a minimum. Citizen involvement cannot be turned on and off like a spigot, but it will have a much greater effect if citizen groups participate with accurate information.

Experience with community relations can lead to innovative organizational structures for accommodating the many contributions citizen groups can make to the planning process.

Planning in Charlottesville, Virginia, for example, is done with a task force: A task force is appointed on a particular issue to advise the appropriate commission, which in turn advises the city council. A task force usually includes three types of people: provider of the service, consumer or receiver of the service, and policymakers of the service—thus affording all parties involved an opportunity to plan cooperatively from

Means and ends for municipal policy   Municipal policy questions are not usually concerned with issues that are all "black" or all "white," all right or all wrong, to be answered by well-established dogmas or even by so-called principles. City government is a means to an end, a means by which the people in a municipality, according to their cultural values, secure satisfactory conditions under which to live, to work, and to play.

The city council possesses the ultimate authority and at the same time cannot escape the ultimate responsibility for the total exercise of municipal power. Hierarchy in city government is the formalized structure of relationships between the legislative body and the administrative organization. This hierarchy ordinarily is outlined by state statutes, by the city charter, or by city ordinances.

Source: Clarence E. Ridley, *The Role of the City Manager in Policy Formulation* (Chicago: International City Managers' Association, 1958), 10.

the start. It is the aim of the City of Charlottesville to have the overall planning done by the people, with the people and for the people, in that order of importance and priority.[6]

This approach channels the substance and energy brought by citizens into the issues of greatest concern. At the same time, their inputs go directly into official channels of communication with the staff, planning commission, and city council. These contributions are relevant because they are about current issues, substantive because they use data supplied by the staff and other sources, and timely because they flow through the policy boards responsible for budgeting and priority setting.

A recently proposed system for determining the interrelation of the planning process and citizen participation indicates that an adequate public involvement program will focus on:

1. The decision-making process
2. The public involvement objectives for each stage in the decision-making process
3. The information exchange needed to complete each step in the decision-making process
4. The publics with which information must be exchanged
5. Any special circumstances surrounding the issue and the public you will be working with that could affect selection of public involvement techniques
6. The appropriate techniques—and their sequence—to accomplish the required information exchange.[7]

Bringing planning and citizen participation together involves multiple publics, complex development projects, and a long period of time for information gathering, analysis, hearings of many kinds, and other steps. Thus planning and citizen participation tend to be one continuous process that is of continuous concern to the planner. The planning organization in Charlottesville, Virginia, can accommodate and staff almost any citizen group that wishes to be heard and consulted (see Figure 6–4). The Department of Community Development works with both the Social Development Commission and the Planning Commission, depending on the nature of the problem, and is responsible for physical, social, and economic planning. The primary responsibility of the Social Development Commission is to review and evaluate the budget requests of social service agencies in the community and to make recommendations to the city council. Both the Social Development Commission and the Charlottesville Planning Commission use task forces for special studies and short-term projects. Both commissions and the Department of Community Development work with

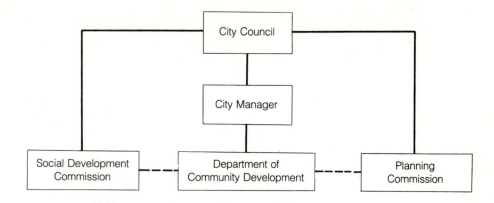

Figure 6–4   Planning relationships in Charlottesville, Virginia.
In addition to traditional planning activities, the Department of
Community Development provides technical assistance
to boards, commissions, and city departments; works with
neighborhood groups on special studies; provides a range of
social services under the aegis of the Social Development Commission;
coordinates grant activities; prepares the capital improvement
program; provides mapping and graphic services; and works with
the University of Virginia on project reviews and special studies.

various other boards and commissions for zoning appeals, architectural review, historic landmarks, and housing and redevelopment.

Feedback

Two major sources of feedback on community relations are citizen opinion data and the complaint log. The city of Walnut Creek, California, conducts a biennial survey to obtain feedback on community development and other issues. Since 1977, this survey has sought opinions from a 2 percent sample of city residents. The survey is structured by asking the same questions in subsequent years and by adding a few new ones pertaining to current issues. After the first year, the respondents were structured into two groups: those who had participated in the past survey and those who had not. This composition was maintained so that opinions about service quality could be obtained from the same people while the input was broadened to ensure that all residents were represented.

While Walnut Creek department heads are encouraged to suggest questions to ask, the city manager and the city council have the final say in selecting questions for the survey. The phrasing of questions is controlled by a professional polling firm. All questions are relevant to the city's comprehensive planning program. They cover the following topics:

1. Frequency of usage of twelve city services
2. Reasons for not using those services
3. Level of satisfaction with those services and with city planning, design of downtown buildings, and police services
4. Level of satisfaction with services and facilities
5. Citizens' budget cutting preferences
6. Importance of selected services to the quality of life and the city
7. Housing problems
8. Perceived need for a major hotel in the city.[8]

This approach not only provides elected and appointed officials and the staff with continuity of hard data on citizen opinions, but it also gives citizens an opportunity to "sound off" formally.

Some cities and counties have established referral offices to receive and handle inquiries and complaints. They work especially well when the staff is well-trained, the information most often needed is on hand, and people are referred promptly and courteously to the right agencies and offices. But such centers cannot do it all.

Some localities have established referral offices to receive and respond to complaints. These can offer significant advantages to the organization by having competent and well-trained staffs and systems of dealing with the complaints of citizens. They can serve as early warning points for problems that need to be resolved, and they can also deal effectively with crank or unjustified complaints without undue stress to the organization. They are most effective when they have the support and the ear of the manager and when they serve as supplements or circuit-breakers for the organization. They should not create the impression that they alone handle complaints. Every office in the organization should be sensitive to negative feedback and be prepared to handle it within certain limits. The need for a centralized referral office to which all complaints are referred does not reflect favorably on the responsiveness of operating offices of the organization.[9]

The usefulness of such complaint centers to the planner lies in the monitoring and periodic reporting. Therefore, it is particularly important for the persons receiving complaints in the general complaint office, as well as in the departmental office, to accurately describe and systematically report them so that responses may be prepared. Because complaints come in all types, shapes, and sizes, it is important to distinguish among them in terms of the relative importance of the complainer and the seriousness of the complaint.

If the complainer is someone with substantial influence over the planning department budget or staff tenure, human nature calls for more responsiveness than would otherwise be the case. Serious complaints must be distinguished by the planning director or a designated employee. Examples of serious complaints include inaccurate data, patently inferior analytical methodology, or incorrect spelling of the mayor's name. Less serious complaints have included the color of paper used for a report and the effect of the world's population increase on the neighborhood rehabilitation program.

Public involvement

Public involvement in the planning process will help the planning staff to think through their objectives, some examples of which follow.

1. Satisfy legal requirements
2. Define next year's planning program in a way that will maximize political support
3. Honor planning department promises made last year to include certain citizen groups in planning for certain development issues
4. Obtain feedback from neighborhood groups to be shared with department heads
5. Co-opt a group that has played a nettlesome, obstructionist role in a technically sound neighborhood or sound planning process
6. Obtain critiques of technical work to make it more relevant to citizen concerns.

The first step is to identify the publics with which information must be exchanged:

During relatively technical or early stages you may be dealing primarily with a leadership group—government staff, leaders of interest groups, etc.—because they alone have sufficient background to understand the technical content. But if you are dealing with the issue of how things "should" be, then you must communicate with a much larger public.[10]

Figure 6-5   A ladder
for advocacy planning
and public involvement.

High impact	**Policies**
	7. Legal enactments
	6. Executive decisions, judicial determinations
Moderate impact	**Programs**
	5. Interstate-wide programs, intercity-wide programs
	4. Citywide programs
	3. Poverty areawide programs
Low impact	**Projects**
	2. Organization-sponsored projects
	1. Individually sponsored projects

Many of the agencies and individuals designated for involvement will have been preselected. Legislation mandates certain public hearing and citizen participation activities. Circular A-95, issued by the U.S. Office of Management and Budget in the late 1960s, mandated intergovernmental comments on many federal grant proposals, and for more than a decade was a part of local planning and development processes. A-95 has been eliminated as a federal requirement, but its effect still is felt when local and state governments confer on projects, large and small, with intergovernmental implications. In addition, planning commission bylaws and a host of state laws and local ordinances may require the planner to consult with others before making recommendations. Alternatively, some citizen involvement may simply be "the way it's always been done."

Citizen participation programs are not expected to be identical. A major difference is the level of management support which in many local governments does not even exist. Some of the reasons for these differences are suggested by the experience of the regional municipality of Ottawa-Carleton (Ontario, Canada) during a thirteen-year period when almost one-third of the planning agency budget for staff studies was devoted to citizen participation:

1. At an early stage, the citizen participation program may lack support. This may be due to the lack of a constituency which translates into a low priority issue; or lack of support may be based on the perceived thoroughness of the staff's work which makes the layman feel inadequate.
2. Strident opposition to planning work may develop. It generally results in each side posturing, by overstating its case, refusing to compromise or reason, and labeling every position or gesture by the planning staff as favoring one side or the other.
3. The study process may not attract early public interest, perhaps because the planners are unable to provide adequate information early enough as to how people will be affected.

4. Advisory committees may not represent vital constituencies, in which case these constituencies will become passive and find technical information difficult to relate to. Or, they may view the committee as the tool to control both the planning process and its outcomes. Planners should be careful not to rush the process; committee members need time to learn about the problem and to consult with their constituencies. Sometimes planners are too eager to publicize committee support, and committee members withdraw and become cautious.

5. Because most public participation is carried out to satisfy a legal or political obligation, it may be too time consuming, and resource exhausting, and not closely tied to the planning process.[11]

This litany of problems has been repeated in other communities. Too much strife has accompanied the search for accommodation strategies to resolve development issues. Some participants feel that planners have already made up their minds and that public participation is a perfunctory exercise—imposed with good faith and carried out in bad faith.

The time between issue identification and project implementation is often too long. This delay becomes a financial burden for the developer (who has construction financing commitments), and a harassment for volunteer citizens, part-time elected officials, and staff members (who have many other demands on their time). With turnover, participants may feel obliged to support positions they inherited or to establish new positions to distinguish themselves from past actions. So much time can be consumed that earlier solutions will become obsolete. In addition, staff burnout may become a problem if it takes five, or more, hours to prepare for meetings and still more time to follow up on decisions made in them.

Further problems can arise in connection with the structured nature of meetings, workshops, and public hearings. The more formal they become, the more rigid the communication flow. As the rigidity increases, the amount of useful information decreases. Persons unfamiliar with highly structured meetings may find their format reminiscent of parliamentary procedures and rigid formality.

Networking

If participants could be better prepared for formal meetings and could use such meetings for the record and for decision making, more and better information could be brought to bear on development decisions. One method participants can use to become better informed is called "networking." This is the process of informally contacting other people to obtain information and to influence courses of action. Most planners and public administrators depend heavily on networking to get their jobs done. Honesty and confidentiality are hallmarks of successful network participants. Planners will lose "participation rights" if their integrity is successfully challenged.[12]

Informal networking is fundamental to both the political and technical aspects of planning. Since a great deal of time in networking is spent on one-on-one communication, the planner must determine whom he or she needs to talk to and who needs to talk to him or her. The planner needs to talk to both the formal leadership, elected and appointed officials, and the informal leadership (that is, the people the elected and appointed officials depend on for advice). Exchanging information with these people is the political foundation for the planning process. Next to quantitative methods, the networking approach, although inexact, offers the planner the best method available for obtaining current information on citizen values.

The planner will find networking information to be of great interest to managers and others. Although there are too many persons in the typical network for any one staff member to have time to talk to, information can be pooled. The planning director and the local government manager therefore will depend on each other and on their staffs for feedback from contacts with citizens and with elected and appointed officials at all levels of government. The "givens" that establish the political framework for planning are determined by this process.

Equally important is the group of persons who want to talk to the planner. They too can provide valuable information. These two-way contacts are a good opportunity for the planner to test ideas before they are committed to paper. These ideas need not be fully thought-out proposals. Indeed, such ideas may be too complicated for the planner to express clearly or for the listener to comprehend!

Continuing use of the informal, one-on-one networking approach depends on the integrity of its participants. Planners and managers must be able to talk to persons at all levels of understanding of the planning process—from the highest to the lowest levels of technical sophistication. They must be able to absorb a good deal of irrelevant information over a considerable period of time before the really applicable information becomes available. They must not share information told them in confidence or information that would embarrass another person. Violators of these principles soon become former participants in the planning information network.

Conducting citizen surveys

Systematic citizen opinion surveys can be designed to measure a cross section of opinion and obtain comparable information from individuals. Unlike informal networking, surveys are quantifiable, and the data obtained can be compared among neighborhoods, socioeconomic characteristics, and over time.

"Citizens surveys," as has been noted elsewhere, "are distinguished on the basis of how they are conducted and types of information they seek."[13] Surveys may be conducted by personal interviews, telephone interviews, or mail-back questionnaires. The types of information typically sought include data, opinions, demand for goods or services, and evaluation.

Methods and techniques

Determining what information is to be obtained is the first step in designing the survey. Topics to be considered for the survey should be sought from elected officials, planning commission members, and program managers. A number of questions will be apparent from the interest that generated the survey in the first place.

If the community is not yet committed to the survey, the staff should review topic suggestions and reduce them to a manageable number. If there is a question as to priority, advice can be sought from the council or local government manager. The type of survey conducted will depend on the information needed and the money available. The least expensive surveys use mail-back questionnaires. Because many recipients fail to return these questionnaires, however, this type of survey cannot be relied on to produce enough usable replies to meet the criteria for a statistically valid sample.

There is less uncertainty with telephone surveys because additional respondents can be dialed until the target number has been reached. The most expensive approach is the personal interview because it takes more time and depends on highly trained persons to conduct structured interviews, and a standard format to produce statistically valid replies. But the personal interview permits, and often encourages, more open-ended responses. This approach is particularly useful if you are uncertain about what topics should be covered or how the questions should be phrased.

The major cost variables to consider are

1. Time of staff and consultants
2. Number and complexity of topics
3. Size of the sample
4. Number and complexity of cross-tabulation of responses
5   Cost of writing computer programs
6. Postage.

If cost is *the* constraint on whether the survey will be conducted, and if the staff has not had experience in conducting citizen surveys, it would be wise to seek outside counsel to estimate the total cost of proposed surveys. The primary variable is staff time, which tends to be greater than anticipated.

The questionnaire should be designed so that it is easy to administer, easy to answer, and easy to tabulate. The greater the number of questions, the more likely it is that respondents will be turned off, and the response rate reduced. The sampling plan can be based on a variety of variables, including neighborhood residents, age, income, and consumers of selected services. Respondents can be selected from those with telephones, those registered to vote, those owning property, and other bases.

If the personal interview or telephone interview is used, interviewers must be recruited and trained. Interviewers must not build resistance into respondent attitudes because it will take more time, will cost more money to conduct the survey, and will compromise its statistical viability. Part of the training should include a pretest of the interview questionnaire to pinpoint questions that are superfluous, ambiguously worded, and unnecessarily provocative.

The final survey instrument should not be printed until it has been reviewed and approved by the local government manager or the next highest ranking person in the hierarchy who will receive the heat if something goes wrong. A small number of the persons surveyed can be expected to resist participation and to complain about the survey and the way it is conducted.

The next step is to conduct the survey. Surveys should not be conducted when people are not likely to be at home or are watching popular television programs (such as Sunday afternoon football). Survey supervisors should check that each surveyor is actually doing his or her work and should be available to answer any questions that may arise during the survey.

The next step is to edit, code, and tabulate the results of the survey. A good source of people to accomplish this task is a local college or university, which will probably have both the people and the computer (usually available at inexpensive rates) to perform these tasks.

The analysis and interpretation of survey findings should be left to experienced professionals. Often results are not clear-cut, and interpretation may require broad and deep knowledge of the community that the inexperienced observer does not have. The interpretation should be written in report or memorandum form to ensure that it is available to interested persons and that each of them receives the same information.

Planners should be aware of the pitfalls in citizen surveys. If caution is not used, the unique and sensitive data from surveys can cause embarrassment. The following pitfalls have been identified:

1. Beware of opinion polls on complex issues about which citizens lack information.
2. Beware of citizens' responses reflecting short-run considerations to the neglect of long-term problems.

3. Beware of surveys that appear to interfere with elections or referenda.
4. Beware of using surveys to hide from controversy and responsibility.
5. Beware of question wording—what is said or not said can be misleading.
6. Beware of sensitive issues and questions that tend to elicit silence or misleading answers.
7. Beware of nonrepresentative results if inadequate procedures are used.
8. Beware of antagonizing citizens who consider interviews or interviewers to be an invasion of privacy.
9. Beware that dissemination of survey findings may be a two-edged sword—raising false hopes among citizens and providing political fodder to candidates.[14]

The survey can be designed both for broad citizen participation and comparisons of attitudes and opinions over time. Broad participation can be achieved by selecting a sample of persons who have not participated in the past. Changes in attitudes and opinions over time can be obtained by including the same respondents each time the survey is taken.

Staff responsibilities

In assigning responsibility for citizen surveys, a balance should be struck between the management responsibilities of the planning director and planning program managers and the professional responsibilities of the technically oriented planning staff.

The planning director and, in larger agencies, program managers should assume the greatest responsibility for public involvement, dealing with the contentious issues that may come to the fore in survey work, and protecting the planning staff from harassment. These skills in dealing with the public are so important that they have been added to the criteria for selecting planning directors and program managers in many cities and counties.

Because of the prospective demands on time, management tends to let this responsibility devolve to lower paid and more technically oriented staff members, but it is dangerous for the planning director and the program managers to be too remote from the details of the program. The higher the level of the staff member, the more personal is the network and the more politically oriented is the involvement. The lower the level of the staff member, the more responsive is the network and the more technically oriented is the involvement. Each planning director, or his or her chief executive, must determine the level in the hierarchy and the personnel most suited for the politically oriented and technically oriented public involvement responsibilities.

In selecting staff for these assignments, remember that in some cases these people will have to work directly with angry citizens. The language and demeanor of angry citizens can put the staff member on the defensive, especially when the citizen is more knowledgeable about the issue at hand than the staff member. The following principles should help planners deal with this situation:

1. Try to understand the citizen's anger.
2. Try to find out the real problem, concern, or issue that caused the citizen to talk to you in the first place; remember, some of these calls may be made by cranks.
3. Be positive in your tone and attitude; don't let the citizen annoy or upset you.
4. Either resolve the problem or personally take responsibility for shepherding the question to another staff member who can resolve it.
5. Make notes of the conversation so that the facts are available at a later time if needed.

Formal alternatives for citizen input

Many different approaches are available to the planning department that wants to increase or change citizen involvement. Whereas only one informal process—networking—is used to establish community relations, many formal structures are available for this purpose including commissions, temporary committees, and formal plan review and adoption.

Commission

In 1978 King County, Washington, which includes the city of Seattle and many of its suburbs, established a policy development commission by ordinance to provide citizens with the opportunity to advise elected officials on "planning for land use, transportation systems, utilities, public facilities, recreation, housing, community development, conservation, human services and capital improvements. The basic purpose of the policy development commission is to provide effective opportunities for the citizens of King County to participate in the policy-making processes of county government."[15]

The commission is composed of 100 citizens appointed by the elected county executive and confirmed by the county council. The commission is staffed by the policy development commission administrator and by appropriate staff members of each department of the county government. Because the commission has no executive or legislative authority, its power comes from its ability to persuade elected and appointed officials about their point of view. The county planning commission, a separate organization with powers and duties typical of those organizations, is staffed by the community development department.

The policy development commission is supposed to bring a countywide perspective to development issues, but the tendency has been to focus on neighborhood- and project-level issues. In all probability, interest in nomination and appointment to such a commission is based on concern for neighborhoods as opposed to countywide development.

This multitiered approach is also used in Sacramento County, California. In 1975 the county created two planning commissions. One is responsible for project review and comments; the other is responsible for formulating policy recommendations for consideration by elected officials.

In the same year, eight community planning advisory councils were established by the county board of supervisors. Like the two planning commissions, these community councils have bylaws and regular meeting schedules. Unlike the planning commissions, the community planning advisory councils do not have decision-making authority, but they can review and comment on any short- and long-term development problems. The county planning department staffs the two planning commissions as well as the eight community planning advisory councils.

According to a review of these community councils in Sacramento County, the following types of problems are relatively common to citizen advisory groups:

1. There is a lack of consensus as to the role, duties, and requirements of members of the community councils. The planning staff sees the councils' role as determining the compatibility of proposed projects with plans, goals, and objectives. The board of supervisors and the community councils see their role as providing advisory inputs into the planning process.
2. The nature and quality of council inputs varies markedly. Some provide advice on narrow technical aspects of planning; others take a broader view.
3. Some council members agree to participate without realizing the personal

time commitment required and the amount of information they are expected to review. Insufficient planning staff time was devoted to training prospective members.

4. There was a lack of feedback to the councils on their recommendations and on their performance. No monitoring system was established to report back to the councils on the disposition of items on which they took positions.

5. Insufficient operating funds were provided for councils interested in pursuing issues in more depth. The budget constraint also hindered the councils' ability to carry out administrative tasks, distribute materials to members, and operate efficiently.

6. The broad-based citizen inputs to elected officials did not occur because of poor council meeting attendance and difficulties in recruiting members for the councils.

7. The countywide perspective of the planners and of the elected officials was at odds with the smaller geographic perspective of the councils.[16]

Temporary committee

Another method of obtaining citizen input is to appoint a temporary committee that can capitalize on intense citizen interest in development issues. Many issues at the national, state, substate, and local levels have been approached in this way. One of the most systematic and far-reaching national committees ever established went so far as to produce a book—*Goals for Americans*, published in 1960—in which it identified a broad spectrum of issues and suggested a wide range of goals. The states of Texas, Washington, Utah, and Idaho, among others, have established similar goals commissions to air issues and recommend solutions.

A number of cities also have established goals commissions to encourage dialogue on urban issues. At a minimum, these goal-setting activities intensified the awareness of elected and appointed officials and citizens of the community's greatest problems, the difficult and cumbersome process of trying to solve them, and the general composition of the various power bases. Temporary goals committees have been criticized for their lack of achievements on the implementation side of the ledger. Yet, these committees have typically not had the mandate, tenure, or funding to ameliorate the problems they identified.

An example of both state and local approaches to goal setting can be found in Idaho. The Idaho Tomorrow Program was established in 1976 with a ten-member advisory commission. A statewide meeting of citizens consolidated their views on the Idaho they wished to see in 1995. Follow-up meetings were held in six regions and in several cities and counties. A public opinion poll was conducted to obtain reactions to the issues and conclusions at the state and regional meetings, and reports were published on the findings.

Two years later the Coeur d'Alene Tomorrow Program was established and staffed by North Idaho College. Unlike the one-time state program, the city's goal setting was to take place every two years. Information therefrom was to be systematically used, and citizen attitudes and priorities were to be measured. The major elements of the program included: a citywide telephone survey in which a sample of the public was asked to react to twenty issues, and a conference of city leaders to discuss proposed city policies. The results of the telephone survey and conference were summarized for the news media and placed on file at the city hall for the general public.

The Coeur d'Alene Tomorrow Program is repeated biennially, and information is systematically collected, analyzed, and distributed to provide input to the planning process and the provision of services. The program notifies the staff that when the process is reconvened it will look at performance during the past two years. Therefore, it has a direct effect on policy, measurements of progress toward meeting goals, and accountability. Critical elements of the program are the willingness of the news media to recruit citizens and the willingness of those citizens to take their assignments seriously.[17]

Why doesn't anybody understand me? Do you have trouble getting a message across at a meeting of the city council or the county board? Many planners and managers do. The city manager of Southfield, Michigan, looked at this problem and concluded that there are nine major reasons why the city council has trouble understanding proposals at meetings.

Language. PUD, CPU, 48K, and down-zoning are examples of the jargon that needs to be used carefully.

Time. Almost all city council and county board members serve part-time and have to consider local government policies alongside their personal and business concerns.

Attention span. It is hard to concentrate on a long and complex agenda.

Audience. All council and board deliberations are conducted in public, and the public forum always must be considered.

Elections. The first six months for a new council or board member is the learning season; the last six months is the time for campaigning. The time in between is when most of the work gets done.

Background. Council and board members are not monolithic in personality, education, income, and interests. The council or board members must be considered individually as well as collectively.

Diversity of the group. A presentation for the council, whether formal or informal, must address the different interests, personalities, and objectives of each member of the council or board.

Conflicting objectives. Even if the group is homogeneous, individual objectives can be strikingly different.

Staff relationships. The city or county staff must not be overly professional in gaining the understanding of the council. Staff must not be aloof to the overall objectives of the government or too engrossed in the purity of the product, forgetting the process.

Source: Abstracted from "How To Translate Complex Development Issues into Policy Options That a Council Can Support," paper presented by Del D. Borgsdorf at the annual conference of the International City Management Association, Kansas City, Missouri, 12 October 1983.

Formal plan review and adoption

Federal regulations, state laws, local ordinances, and planning commission by-laws require the formal adoption and amendment of comprehensive plans. The authority to adopt such plans may rest with the local elected officials or the planning commission. Adoption by elected officials carries more weight in generating revenue to implement plan recommendations. Because planning commissions are almost always appointed rather than elected, their plan adoptions carry less weight. Plans that are not adopted by either planning commissions or elected officials are widely considered to be technical documents that are not officially sanctioned and that are more important to the planning agency than to people responsible for implementation.

An approach that has been used for several years in Fairfax County, Virginia, a jurisdiction of approximately six hundred thousand people outside Washington, brings together the efforts of both the appointed county planning commission and the elected county board of supervisors. Since adoption of the comprehensive plan in 1975 by the board of supervisors, the plan has been reviewed annually. The key to the process is that citizens, landowners, civic associations, professional groups, staff members, and elected and appointed officials are encouraged to nominate matters for consideration as possible plan amendments.

The board determines whether the annual plan review is to be open or limited. In an open review, it accepts all kinds of suggested amendments. In a limited review, proposed changes must be supported by substantial reasons for changing the plan. Such reasons may include significant points about content or geographic coverage; the need to delete unreasonable limitations on the county's ability to achieve its objectives; and corrections of oversights, inconsistencies, and inequities.

Persons wishing to nominate matters for consideration are required to submit one-page summaries to the planning commission. This summary includes information on the item's location, reasons for the nomination, and the changes proposed by the nominator. The planning staff is given about one hundred days to review nominations and make their own recommendations to the planning commission. The planning commission holds public hearings on them as does the county board of supervisors.

The advantages of this approach are several. One is that frivolous plan amendments are avoided. Second, ample time is provided for the consideration of plan amendments. Third, proposed changes are available to persons in favor of and against plan amendments, and they are given enough time to build their cases.

Among the disadvantages of this approach is that it takes a great deal of staff time to receive, assemble, analyze, and make recommendations on each nomination. Second, the long lead time for nomination and consideration of changes increases the time between proposed plan amendments and their implementation. Third, some would argue there is no need for two public hearings on the same question—one by the planning commission and one by the county board of supervisors. In communities where the staff is limited, plans are less complex, and the demand for development is low, fewer restrictions on plan amendments are necessary, and the plan review process can be shortened.

Person power identification

During the governmental reform movement of the early 1900s, the independent commission was thought to be the best organizational structure for planning. Its advocates argued that community leaders would lend their prestige to planning by becoming commission members; the views of citizens would be brought to bear on the technical planning process; and corrupting political influences would be minimized. The citizen participation movement of the 1960s and 1970s altered the process. Citizen advisory groups, often neighborhood based, were formed to offer new perspectives and advice on development issues. As with any volunteer approach, the results have been mixed. Here are some of the reasons that volunteer service may fall short of expectations:

1. Lack of understanding about what the volunteer is expected to do
2. Lack of volunteer preparation for making a substantive contribution
3. Acceptance of the appointment merely as a stepping stone to bigger and better things
4. Lack of time to fulfill the commitment
5. Absence of anticipated staff support to prepare background information and help in other ways
6. Resentment of criticism while trying to do a good job
7. Emotional burnout resulting from the pressures of volunteer activity

8.   Disappearance of the issue(s) that stimulated original interest in the volunteer effort.

In addition, some persons appointed to citizen advisory committees and other boards and commissions lack the interest and capacity to do the work.

To help remedy the problems associated with ineffective volunteer contributions, techniques have been developed for evaluating performance and encouraging turnover. The cities of Eugene, Oregon, and East Lansing, Michigan, for example, require applications for neighborhood advisory boards and other volunteer positions.

In Eugene, citizen-awareness open houses are held annually to encourage people to come to city hall and learn about the activities of their local government. Staff members are present to answer questions, describe activities, and identify persons who have not served on voluntary boards and commissions in the past but who show interest in doing so. Interested persons are encouraged to apply for citizen participation activities, and their applications are accepted and evaluated once a year.

In East Lansing, a similar process has brought "new blood" into the government. Among the criteria for appointing volunteers are (1) sound reasons for interest in appointment, (2) experience in dealing with community development and other issues, (3) neighborhood of residence, (4) references, including city officials and others, and (5) testimony that the applicant will stick with the job.

Annual appointments allow the city council or county board to appoint new persons frequently. Within a year's time, the volunteer's willingness to do the work, to attend meetings regularly, and to stick with assignments will be evident. The planning staff can rely on the informal networking process and personal observation to judge the quality of the contributions. This information can be provided to the council or board, at their request, before the volunteer is considered for reappointment.

Putting community relations together[18]

Effective community relations at the local level are complex and demanding. Yet the challenge of local public planning—indeed, its fascination—is "putting it all together" to make things happen. Although this chapter has offered many ideas, much depends on the planner—how *and whether* he or she puts these ideas together to achieve overall success at fostering community relations.

To translate these ideas into action, the local planner should not try to do everything at once. He or she may also have to learn to juggle apparent opposites. In other words, the planner must accept an agenda that is at times paradoxical— riding herd on opposing ideas and activities simultaneously. An action list of paradoxes shows elements paired as opposites: whole community/self, possibilities/impossibilities, effective speaking/listening, networking/renetworking, special interests/public interest, and learning/relearning.

Perception of the whole community/yourself

The most difficult paradox may be to know yourself as a planner (your abilities as well as your limitations) and your community (what it wants and expects). In other words, to be effective at community relations you must keep in mind both the big picture and your own style and abilities.

Situational possibilities/impossibilities

Many savvy planners speak of a "window" for action, meaning that there is an opening (or a lack of one) for taking a specific step. Effective planners (and managers too) must have a keen sense of the possibilities or impossibilities of a given situation. "Now is the time" or "it can't fly" are judgment calls that good planners have the wisdom (and luck) to make correctly.

Effective speaking/listening

Much of the advice in this chapter stresses open lines of communication. Getting your message across, however, is only half the answer. Listening is equally important if you are to gain a knowledge and understanding of community relations. Cultivating the ability to listen may be more difficult, but it is fully as fruitful as learning to express ideas effectively.

Networking/renetworking

A major way to foster effective relations with community groups is to create networks, or links, among groups and individuals, but "renetworking" also may be needed. When one tangled web of connections doesn't work out, the planner will start again, reweaving and reconnecting to bring about the desired result. Such activity may demand as much inventiveness on the planner's part as any technical achievement.

Special interests/public interest

A frank assessment of the nature, purposes, and activities of the many interest groups that confront a planner is part of the job. To deal with interest groups realistically and know how to cope with their designs is a major task. It is equally important, though, to have a clear vision of the public interest, of what is in the best interest of the community *as a whole*. Without such a clear ideal, planning can deteriorate into dealing with the petty pushes and pulls of groups.

Learning/relearning

It is important to learn the art of relating well with the public, but it is equally important to give up the worn out lessons of the past, rethink old ways, and rediscover other, perhaps better, ways. Since change is an enduring aspect of the modern community, any planner unwilling to adapt to new terms of the planning process may quickly become its victim.

Conclusion

Community relations always have been an ongoing part of local government planning. Citizen study groups date back at least to the McMillan Committee, which in 1902 reported on restoring the Mall and making other public improvements in Washington, D.C. A big change, however, occurred in the 1960s and 1970s when citizen participation was (to use the ponderous language of political science and sociology) legitimized by law and institutionalized by public expectations.

Before the 1960s, citizen boards, commissions, and committees were mostly "establishmentarian." Lawyers, bankers, and businessmen dominated; and their advice was often accepted. How this has changed! Neighborhood groups, even in places where the population is under 25,000, are a strong political force in planning, budgeting, and project implementation. Their membership is more broadly based, and their concerns are more personal and immediate. Even in communities where citizen groups are relatively placid, planners and managers prudently build community relations into their value systems, administrative processes, and work habits.

Although community relations are tied up with intangibles like power structure, political considerations, feedback, and networking, they can be learned. Part of learning is paying close attention to what is going on around you, listening to people, and steering clear of snap judgments. Practice empathy. Put yourself in the other person's shoes; you may not agree with his or her assertions, but you will discover that the person is not stupid or irrational.

There are overt methods to nurture community relations, too. Two of the methods—networking and citizen surveys—are covered in some detail here because they are important and relatively easy to learn and apply.

The preceding section of this chapter emphasizes achieving a balance in your approach to planning and management by learning to handle a paradoxical agenda. Perhaps the most important items on it are:

1. Know yourself *and* your community.
2. Balance special interests *and* the community interest.

1 Edmund M. Burke, *A Participatory Approach to Urban Planning* (New York: Human Sciences Press, 1979), 12.

2 This section has been abstracted and excerpted from: Wayne F. Anderson et al., *The Effective Local Government Manager* (Washington, D.C.: International City Management Association, 1983), 13–15.

3 This section has been abstracted and excerpted from: Anderson et al., *Effective Local Government Manager*, 15–22.

4 These composite "ideal local management types" are drawn from three books: Richard J. Stillman II, *The Rise of the City Manager* (Albuquerque: University of New Mexico Press, 1974); Ronald O. Loveridge, *City Managers in Legislative Politics* (Indianapolis: Bobbs-Merrill, 1971); and John P. Kotter and Paul R. Lawrence, *Mayors in Action: Five Approaches to Urban Governance* (New York: John Wiley & Sons, 1974).

5 H. Douglas Sessoms, "Community Development Social Planning," in *Managing Municipal Leisure Services* (Washington, D.C.: International City Management Association, 1980), 128–29.

6 City of Charlottesville, Virginia, "Department of Community Development," Satyendra Singh Huja (1981?), four-page public information statement.

7 James L. Creighton, *The Public Involvement Manual* (Cambridge, Mass.: Abt Books, 1981), 57.

8 City of Walnut Creek, California, "Walnut Creek Citizens Survey: Wave III," prepared by Corey, Canapary and Galanis (7 December 1981), photocopy.

9 Kenneth M. Wheeler, "Serving the Citizen," in *Effective Communication: Getting the Message Across*, ed. David S. Arnold, Christine S. Becker, and Elizabeth K. Kellar (Washington, D.C.: International City Management Association, 1983), 26.

10 Creighton, *Public Involvement Manual*, 63.

11 Chris Bradshaw, "Beyond Public Participation: Networking Approach to Planning" (Background paper for workshop at annual conference of the Canadian Institute of Planners, Hull, Quebec, 22 June 1982, photocopy), 2–3.

12 Ibid., 5.

13 See: Camille Cates, "Using Citizens Surveys: Three Approaches," Municipal Management Innovation Series, no. 15 (Washington, D.C.: International City Management Association, February 1977).

14 Kenneth Webb and Harry Hatry, *Obtaining Citizen Feedback: The Application of Citizen Surveys to Local Government* (Washington, D.C.: Urban Institute, 1973), 33–42.

15 King County, Washington, *Laws of King County*, Title 20, Chapter 20, 726.

16 R. Lance Bailey and Cortus T. Koehler, "Citizens in the Planning Process: How Sacramento County Does It," *National Civic Review* 71 (September 1982): 421–23.

17 Information on this program is based on: Tony Stewart and Sydney Duncombe, "Coeur d'Alene Tomorrow: A Look at Citizen Input," *National Civic Review* 70 (September 1981): 410–14.

18 This section has been abstracted and excerpted from: Anderson et al., *Effective Local Government Manager*, 42–44.

7 Personnel management

Some of the organizational structure and much of the effectiveness of local government depends on the technical and personal qualifications of employees, especially professional and management staff. Because people are individuals and because circumstances vary from community to community, a planner who might be successful in one community might not do so well in another. Thus, the selection of staff members to serve local needs deserves special attention.

Once they have been selected, the performance and potential of planners should be evaluated in terms of agency goals, and continuing education should be encouraged.

This chapter reviews these and other aspects of personnel management in the context of planning. The principal topic is the work of professional planners from this aspect of personnel management, which means employee selection, motivation, performance evaluation, training, and the use of consultants.

Roles of the planner

The planning director's job varies with the legislative mandate, size of the planning department, professional and personal background, and community expectations. The larger the program, the more time required for management. Small planning programs require both technical and management skills of the same person since no one else is available to do the job.

Skills of the planning director

Like the planning process itself, the skills applied by the planning director tend to be highly situational. In many communities, there is a continuing need to legitimize the position, although influential citizens in nearly every community are strongly in favor of planning. In general, the director's rank in the bureaucracy has an effect on his or her role. The higher the level in the bureaucracy, the greater the need to communicate with nontechnical persons—elected officials, appointed officials, and citizens—both inside and outside the organization.

Seven major roles of the planner have been identified. Orchestrating these roles is the job of the planner as manager.

1. *Analyst*. An expert in the analysis of data, applying parameters of the scientific method.
2. *Organizer*. Develops a constituency in support of the planning process. Assesses decision-making processes and determines how to participate in them to influence decisions.
3. *Broker*. Mediates issues and negotiates decisions.
4. *Advocate*. Assists client groups with information and advice.
5. *Enabler*. Indirect leadership to guide others to achieve their objectives. Encourages and supports client groups to develop their own leadership skills.
6. *Educator*. Outreach activities to educate the public on the purposes and

Figure 7–1 Public
management roles
and competencies.

Managerial roles
1. Policy/program implementation and evaluation of results
2. Organizational maintenance and development
3. Policy, program, and organizational innovation
4. Conceptual leadership

Managerial competencies
1. Brokerage and interorganizational competencies
    a. Internal/external leadership
    b. Facilitative/linkage skills
2. Policy/program analysis and knowledge of functional services
    a. Social, economic, political, and governmental forces and democratic institutions
    b. Public policies and programs
3. Organization management
    a. Services management
        1. Setting policy/program objectives; planning; assembling resources; determining priorities
        2. Services programming and implementation
        3. Evaluation of performance and results
    b. Administrative management
        1. Personnel and labor–management relations
        2. Finance and budgeting
        3. Property and general services
        4. Information systems
4. Personal and organizational development
    a. Organizational
        1. Leadership styles and skills
        2. Counseling and coaching skills
        3. Organizational change and development skills
    b. Personal
        1. Self-assessment, professional development, and self-renewal
        2. Communication skills

functions of planning and to share training and experience with aspiring planners.

7. *Publicist*. Creates an awareness of planning. Publicizes information useful to the planning constituency.[1]

The roles and competencies of the public manager are identified in Figure 7–1. They emphasize the importance of the manager as someone who facilitates the process of getting from where you are to where you want to be.

With the technical sophistication of local government services, both the planner and the manager are now required to have greater professional skills. Moreover, the increasingly sophisticated citizen participation and negotiation have meant that greater interpersonal skills are also required.

Leadership is one of the management skills that always gets attention in the research and writing on the subject. Some would say that it is *the* management skill, and all would agree that it is important in both the public and private sectors. Furthermore, all would undoubtedly agree that leadership has several meanings. Those that best fit planning directors are community leadership, policy leadership, situational leadership, and agency and staff leadership.

Planners should take a conceptual leadership position in the community. Even where there are arguments cast against doing so—"the city's not growing," "we can't pay for it anyway," and "we have enough problems without thinking about the future"—there is a need for this type of thinking. It is centered on priorities, interrelatedness of issues, and long-term consequences of current actions. If the planning director is not going to do this on behalf of the community, who will?

This leadership role can be isolated and lonely at times because it is at the "cutting edge" of community development. Much of its stimulus comes from similarly inclined people on the planning staff, in other local government departments, and among other groups.

Employees in other departments may have a special interest in conceptualizing the community's future, depending on their interests and program responsibilities. In some communities, formal or informal groups representing several professions meet regularly to discuss city issues and the future. Participants' networking has helped bring political relevancy to these issues.

From the internal management point of view, research has indicated that successful leaders will:

1. Define the managerial roles as an individual leader rather than a member of a group or team.
2. Explain objectives with high expectations of fulfillment; allow employees autonomy to get the work done.
3. Manage subordinates as a team, not one-on-one; provide opportunities for interaction with individual employees.
4. Impress upon workers the value of productivity.[2]

Planning directors who achieve managerial excellence place a high premium on the timely delivery of the products of the planning process that are thought, by their clients, to lead to results. The results might be the construction of a project, a public investment decision, an improved development regulation, or saving an elected or appointed official from taking an embarrassing public position. Because time costs money, the planner's work may be the critical path to important public decisions; punctual delivery of promised products is a leadership characteristic to be emulated by staff.

Skills of the technician

The planning manager strives to obtain the best results possible from the personnel and equipment available. It has even been said that "In a strict sense, management is more the development of people than the direction of things. In this context, management and personnel administration are one and the same."[3] The manager's burden is that many of the ingredients needed to achieve these best results are totally or partly outside his or her control. The efficient approach therefore is to isolate the most controllable factors and minimize the obstacles to that control.

Personnel management, like most other local government services, has achieved higher professional standards in the last two decades. Because the central personnel agency has been strengthened in many local governments, personnel professionals can now deal with the entire range of new personnel issues, including job-relevant testing, affirmative action, civil rights, comparable worth, executive compensation, fringe benefits, and productivity. The planning department and other local government agencies, however, are still responsible for the recruitment, transfer, promotion, training, and discipline of their employees.

Legal and technical changes have been accompanied by two notable changes outside the planning director's control. First, the personal values of people entering the planning profession have changed. The pre-1960 enthusiasm of pathfinders in a new field has been replaced in the minds of some by a pragmatic attitude that planning is a job to be done with nonwork-related aspirations considered equally important. Second, the job market has shrunk. With fewer jobs available, there is less job mobility and fewer opportunities to advance. The resulting apprehension tends to heighten job-related initiatives and productivity, but to depress morale.

Another recent development is that planning process skills have multiplied. In the early years of the profession, the term *planner* generally referred to the person who came up with future land use recommendations. The term was then broadened to include staff members responsible for administering zoning and subdivision regulations. In recent years, the definition has been further broadened to include persons engaged in programming, budgeting, citizen participation, project packaging, issue negotiation and other tasks.

Under these circumstances, professional specialization has been inevitable. The question for the planning manager is whether to encourage or discourage specialization. It can be encouraged by narrow job descriptions, highly selective job assignments, selective communication, and limitations on midcareer training opportunities. Many would argue, however, that the price of specialization is too high. The results are all too likely to be circumscribed thinking, indifference to the political realities of the development process, and insensitivity to the constraints, on developers, of an arduous development process.

One remedy for narrowness is to expose employees to job assignments cutting across lines of specialization. For example, the zoning administrator could be asked to prepare an employment forecast; or the transportation planner could be asked to prepare a park plan. In communities with small staffs, this is a standard operating procedure because there are so few people with training and experience to draw upon.

The Phoenix, Arizona, planning department has transferred divisional managers within the department for limited periods of time. In addition, planning staff members are loaned to other departments for specified periods. For example, the wastewater quality planner may be transferred for a few months to the sewer department to assist with its plans and programs.[4]

The planning staff

In addition to the director of the planning agency, who is almost always a person with experience and training in planning, the planning staff includes professional, preprofessional, and support personnel. Although the lines between these three groups, when judged by specific assignments, are often indistinct, some distinguishing characteristics can be identified. These are summarized in the following paragraphs.

Professionals

A planning professional may be most easily identified by educational background. If a person holds a master's degree in planning from a school that is recognized by the American Institute of Certified Planners, then that person is considered a professional planner. Perhaps a planning professional may be most accurately identified by the work he or she is doing. Of the many types of jobs that have been described, professional planning work primarily entails influencing public decision making; introducing a comprehensive point of view to research, analysis, findings, and recommendations; and dealing with complex linkages of land, money, laws, and other variables. This work involves many kinds of people in the public and private sectors. The recognized credential for a planning professional is membership in the American Institute of Certified Planners. New Jersey licenses and Michigan registers planners.

Preprofessionals

Persons without training or experience in planning may be considered preprofessionals until they obtain either or both qualifications. Perhaps the clearest distinction between typical responsibilities is that the preprofessional collects but does not analyze information. The preprofessional may conduct and tabulate land use surveys, organize census data, and tabulate results from questionnaires. It is the responsibility of the professional to analyze and interpret results. This procedure can be a good training ground for the preprofessional who becomes familiar with such information and the analyst's interpretation of this material.

Support personnel

The planning office environment is one in which many reports have to be written by a certain time. Skilled persons are needed to prepare and deliver such reports, particularly accurate and fast typists, design-sensitive graphic artists, and dependable photocopyists and delivery persons.

Exposure of the planning office's written products to the public makes their graphic quality especially important. Timeliness is equally important. Planning products that are late, regardless of quality, may lose their usefulness in the decision-making process and may create a poor impression of the planning department's quality of management and technical ability to address contemporary issues.

Employment criteria

The criteria for planning positions should be balanced between (1) training and experience in the preparation and presentation of technical work, and (2) experience in networking. Obviously, the desirable proportions will vary from one planning job to another, but the proportions will also vary between large and small planning agencies. In a large agency, it may be desirable to authorize one or more planning jobs that heavily emphasize urban design, long-range planning studies, and other technical work. In a small agency (where perhaps only two professional planners are budgeted), it is likely that both positions will call for a balance of the two sets of skills. In both large and small agencies, however, the higher the level of the job, the greater the proportion of networking skills the job will require.

This generalized look at planning jobs can serve as the starting point for developing an inventory of jobs in the planning agency. Because recruitment is so important for a vital planning program, the following paragraphs will concentrate on three parts of employment: (1) the job description, which is the tool for classifying positions and establishing salary scales, and the framework for recruitment; (2) pay and other incentives; and (3) the general process by which employees are recruited and selected.

Job descriptions

No single criterion applies across the board to the description of planning positions. Whoever describes the position will do so on the basis of his or her perceptions. The person holding the job, the personnel office, a recruiting firm, the planning commission chairperson, the local government chief administrator, and the mayor may each describe the same position but emphasize different qualities in the prospective employee and different blends of experience and education. In general, the incumbent is best able to describe the responsibilities and tasks that make up the job, and the skills needed by the community in that position.

There is a tendency for personnel offices to pigeonhole job descriptions by drawing on secondhand information. Such information may come from planning commissioners—who may describe staff jobs so as to minimize controversy—

Figure 7–2   Classified
ad for a city planner.

PLANNER
CITY OF NEWPORT NEWS

Qualified individual desired to be responsible for
managing in a lead role a variety of major planning projects as an Assistant to the Director. Requires broad expertise & thorough knowledge of
principles & objectives of planning & statistical
analyses, research & the ability to carry these into
implementation in areas of comprehensive,
neighborhood, physical, urban & capital improvement planning. Requires ability to prepare & present oral & written reports. Requires any combination of education & exper. equivalent to a
master's degree in urban planning or related field
& extensive exper. in professional planning, to
include urban & physical planning, w/consider-
able supervisory exper. Desirable to have familiarity w/cost-benefits analyses & computer application; AICP. Chief Planner salary range:
$24,150 to $32,550. Reply w/resume, references, salary history & non-returnable examples
of work to: Personnel Director, 2400 Washington
Avenue, Newport News, Va. 23607. EOE.

and from elected officials—who may say the work requires skills leading to
politically acceptable recommendations.

Figure 7–2 shows a classified ad for a chief planner in Newport News, Virginia.
Note the clear description of the work to be performed, the requirements for
experience and education, and the desirable background in cost-benefit analysis
and computers.

Job descriptions for planners should tell the applicant and others what is
expected but they should also be open-ended so that the work can be redefined
as the employee's skills mature and as the department's program objectives are
modified. Phrases such as "and other duties as he or she may be called upon
from time to time to perform" are sufficient to encourage the employee to meet
new challenges. Figure 7–3 is the job description of the Southfield, Michigan,
director of city planning and economic development. It shows a wide range of
prospective assignments: from I-696 (a controversial interstate highway) to communication tasks.

Pay and other incentives

Establishing salaries for each class of positions requires a reasonably accurate
assessment of what the market will bear and the level required to attract and
keep employees. Whenever the need arises to compare salaries with work responsibilities, detailed job descriptions and salary histories of those jobs should
be available. Pay levels by title of planning personnel are published annually by
the American Planning Association (APA) (its information is based on a survey
of members). In addition, personnel offices of other local governments can
provide job descriptions and salary histories while maintaining personal ano-
nymity.

DIRECTOR OF CITY PLANNING AND ECONOMIC DEVELOPMENT

General Statement of Duties: To administer the Department of City
Planning and Economic Development which consists of city planning and
engineering. To coordinate activities which are essential to the
economic well being of the City. To develop long range plans consisting
of city planning and engineering activities. To promote the economic
development of the community.

Appointment: The Director of City Planning and Economic Development is
appointed by the Mayor and is responsible to the City Council, receiving
direction from the Director of Public Services.

Typical Examples of Work: This employee will be responsible for the
following:

Manage the city planning and engineering functions of the department.
Coordinate and prepare a Capital Improvement Program.
Administer the Community Development Block Grant Program.
Be staff liaison to the Economic Development Corporation and the Tax
    Increment Finance Authority.
Administer and coordinate state and county improvement programs (including
    I-696).
Submit and administer State and Federal grants.
Prepare and implement Economic Development Programs.
Review recommendations made regarding planning and engineering proposals
    to the City Council.
Prepare and keep current a long range plan for the development of the
    community.
Confer and meet with business groups, organizations and companies in pro-
    moting Southfield.

Desirable Qualifications for Employment:

An extensive knowledge of city planning and engineering principles.
An understanding of Public Administration and Community Development.
A Masters Degree in City Planning, Public Administration or related field.
Five years of increasingly responsible experience in local government
    community development field.
Ability to effectively communicate orally and written.

Figure 7–3 Job description for city
planning director (Southfield, Michigan).

Nonsalary benefits have become particularly important to employee morale
as a source of in-kind income. Cumulatively, it is not unusual for the nonsalary
income to be as high as 15 to 25 percent of the salary for work performed.
Monetary components of the nonsalary income include retirement contributions,
social security payments, health insurance, life insurance, dental insurance, income maintenance insurance, and disability insurance. Vacation time may amount
to ten to twenty working days per year, and holidays may account for seven to
ten additional days. Time off for midcareer training is also a competitive fringe
benefit along with paid membership in professional associations and paid attendance at their national, state, and local meetings.[5]

Salary ranges and fringe benefits should be highlighted in advertisements for
planning positions. This information together with the brief job description and
the identification of the community in which the job is located will help prospective applicants determine if they should apply. Competitive job descriptions
should entice the most qualified persons to ask for more information.

What to look for in a résumé   The following paragraphs show the views of the vice mayor of Falls Church, Virginia (population 9,515), on résumés, based on his experience when the city council recruited a city manager in 1982. His comments apply equally well to the recruitment of many planning directors and other planning staff. Note the importance of writing for the information packet (many applicants did not do this), reading it carefully, and using the information to tailor the résumé for the concerns of the specific local government:

Our small city recently received 152 applications for the position of city manager.

We agreed on criteria for selection that . . . dealt with (1) education, (2) years of experience managing a city-type organization, (3) success in recruiting professional staff, (4) effective supervision, (5) use of modern management techniques, and effective relationships with the (6) council, (7) public (including media), and (8) neighboring jurisdictions. The applicants had not been told what the criteria were, although the notices we published implied most of them. Despite the silence of many résumés about several criteria, we somehow winnowed the total of 152 candidates down to 22 [semifinalists] whose references we checked.

After comparing notes, we agreed on eight people to interview. Each interview lasted three hours, with a fairly standard structure.

The council made its choice. The mayor and I negotiated an employment agreement. We think we have an excellent new manager and are looking forward to a long and productive working relationship. We are pleased with ourselves for the process we followed and for the results.

Nevertheless, we wonder about some of the 130 candidates who did not survive the first cut. Some we know are really able, but they did not seem to fit our particular needs. Perhaps others could have brought more to our community than some of the 22 on whom we sought more information. But then we shrug and say, "If they can't write good résumés, they wouldn't be good managers."

Each of our announcements in the newsletters of the ICMA, ASPA, and Virginia Municipal League urged people to write for an information packet before submitting a résumé. The packet also included a standard résumé cover sheet.

A surprising number sent in applications without writing for our information packet. The city clerk then sent the packet to them and asked them to return the cover sheet. Some didn't take the trouble.

Many people accompanied their applications with a letter commenting on the information. Some simply said that the community sounded like a pleasant place and reinforced their eagerness for the job. Others told about aspects of their experience or communities that paralleled our needs. We often found the letters more useful than the bureaucratic job descriptions in the résumés.

But only one person obviously wrote his application to fit our position. For each of the city's goals and objectives, he told how his experience or education was pertinent. For some, he confessed a gap in experience. This candidate was relatively junior level and was not one of our semifinalists. Never-

---

Recruitment and selection

The selection and development of staff is perhaps the most important single task of the planning director. For effective results, the director and the key agency staff should work closely with the central personnel agency in the local government, carefully observing all legal requirements (a formidable task because of

theless, I plan to give his application to our personnel officer and suggest that he might be considered as an assistant department head.

Do some advertisements or articles like this specify that résumés should not exceed three pages? It seems so, because some people crowded their pages, with narrow margins and little paragraphing. These résumés were hard to read. A few short résumés conveyed a flavor of informed competence, but I preferred longer ones with well-organized sections that facilitated reference during council discussions.

The best résumés gave a little background about the cities or counties where the applicant had served. Were they central cities, suburbs, or isolated farm-market towns? Does the economy depend on industry or services? Are they established communities with solid institutions or new corporations with growing pains? What is the size of the population, government budget, and government staff?

With applications from 35 states, our personal knowledge did not include answers to such questions. An atlas would give locations and population but little else. But why should the employer have to do the research? We felt better able to judge the difficulty of the applicants' situations and the worth of their accomplishments if we could sense the context in which they worked.

We were disappointed that the usual résumé told us little about several of the selection criteria mentioned earlier. Sometimes omissions concerned such topics as recruitment, supervision, or management techniques, but the most frequent blanks concerned relationships with the governing body, public, and neighboring jurisdictions.

Dealing with these topics in a résumé is not easy. A declarative statement that relationships are good is not enough. Citing specific examples may appear too detailed or too boastful. But it seemed to me that those who succeeded in transmitting a sense of successful relationships in their written applications were also the ones who easily established rapport in their interviews.

In the first executive session of the council after we had read all 152 applications, we commented that for many applicants we knew all about management and nothing about community results. We knew that productivity had increased, staff had been reduced, positions classified, capital budgeting introduced, accounting reformed and computers installed, purchasing consolidated, and so forth. We wondered whether the quality of life was any different: How were social services? What cultural activities were in progress? Was there any urban design? What was the mix of housing by type and cost?

One could almost think that some candidates derived their job satisfactions entirely from the mechanics or process and cared nothing about the well-being of the citizens!

After 152 applications, my conclusion was that the applicant whose résumé conveyed an impression of competence, philosophy about community values, and low-keyed poise had the best chance to be among the semifinalists.

Source: Robert L. Hubbell, "Problems with Résumés," *Public Management* 65 (December 1983): 20–23.

the strict requirement of the civil rights laws and numerous court decisions on equal opportunity and nondiscrimination), and conducting open recruitment.

Occasionally private recruiting companies, commonly known as executive search firms, are a part of the process. Because of the cost, such companies are usually used only for the recruitment of planning directors and a few other key employees. As with any other consulting service, reports are mixed on the value and appropriateness of this approach. Among the advantages are that an executive search:

1. Saves time in screening candidates' résumés and conducting preliminary interviews
2. Provides applicants with more objective information about the community and its planning staff needs
3. Keeps applicants better informed about the selection process
4. Advises rejected candidates of the disposition of their applications, somewhat more diplomatically than if it were handled by a staff member
5. More readily identifies special groups of candidates such as minorities.

The experiences of various communities point to the following disadvantages of employing private recruiters:

1. Firms may play favorites.
2. Firms may sell other consulting services to former clients who have been placed.
3. Candidates are sometimes required to agree to accept jobs if they are offered.
4. A candidate for two jobs being brokered by the same firm at the same time may be "steered" to one of the jobs.
5. Firms may prevent candidates from gaining direct access to local government representatives; such access might allow the candidate to sell himself without the need for the recruiting firm.
6. Communications between the recruiting firm and local government may not fully convey the competitive attributes of selected applicants.[6]

Before an executive search firm is employed, a decision must be made about recruiting within the agency, within the local area, within the state, or nationally. It is a sham to go to the time and expense of large-scale recruiting when the intention is to fill the job by appointing someone on the staff. Widespread recruitment often is the preferred way to hire, but it does have its drawbacks.

Irrespective of the range of recruiting, the applicant's résumé is the most important and widely used screening device to reduce the number of candidates to a small, reasonably qualified group.

Résumés are designed to summarize rather than completely describe a person's training and experience. Because résumés are most often an introduction to strangers, they should be carefully prepared and well presented. The most recent job should be described in the greatest detail. The three key elements of a résumé explain responsibilities, duties, and accomplishments.

Résumés also provide factual information about education, jobs held, honors and awards, and personal interests. When the recruitment process has narrowed the candidates down to a small number, the factual information on the résumés should be verified. This is a separate step from checking references by mail and phone. The verification process means checking the facts: that a claimed degree has actually been awarded, that a claimed job actually was held during the dates set forth on the résumé, and that there are no false statements. Recruiters' experience is that "Lying on résumés booms in troubled times, . . . of the thousands of résumés we investigate, there are outright lies on 22 percent."[7]

Interpersonal "chemistry" is a major consideration for someone who is expected to participate in the local development network. Therefore, it is especially important to conduct personal interviews, but there is no need to interview more than three or four persons for any given position. This number of persons is likely to include all of the requisite qualifications in one mix or another.

It is more costly to interview more persons if they come from out of town. Therefore, sufficient information needs to be made available in the résumés,

How not to recruit Another sidebar in this chapter describes the excellent process used for selecting a city manager in Falls Church, Virginia, and the shortcomings of almost all of the résumés submitted. An instructive contrast is provided in this description, based on an actual event, of a self-destructive recruiting process.

An experienced communications consultant heard that the local office of a federal government department was looking for help in his area of expertise. The consultant called the office to inquire. He was told a package of information sheets and job applications would be mailed immediately. Two weeks later the package arrived.

Inside was a standard federal job application that applied to anyone from a laborer to a top-line civil servant. Two other enclosures, a description of the qualifications of the person being sought and a description of the tasks to be performed, were confusing and contradictory examples of the cut-and-patch school of writing. The qualifications demanded a high-level executive with a strong marketing background, while the tasks described could be performed by almost anyone with a college degree and no experience. The mismatched descriptions indicated that the writer had consulted the appropriate civil service manuals, but did not know the job or its problems. The consultant later learned that the prospective employer was attempting to circumvent the constraints of the civil service hiring procedure in order to hire a more "creative" person.

The consultant did his homework by reviewing various materials on the agency's program, particularly the work in his area of interest, so that he would be well prepared for an interview.

After a long period of time the person in charge of recruitment called the consultant and set a time for an interview. The interview began 30 minutes late. It took that long to get the three-person interview panel together. The person in charge opened the interview by saying to his group, "Where do you think we should start?" The discussion began in a random way with a loose description of the work of the organization. Goals, needs, and objectives were not mentioned. Finally the consultant took the bull by the horns and began tactfully to define problems and solutions as he saw them.

The panel members were impressed, and the interview ended on a high note. As the interview broke up, the person in charge indicated that the consultant would get the job, saying "When you begin this project . . . the first thing I want you to do. . . ." He went on to say, "Regulations require that we interview the rest of the applicants, all five of them, but the interview confirmed what the application form told us—that you are the most qualified person for the job, and you really understand our problems."

Three weeks went by. The consultant called the person who had been in charge of the interview, but the calls were not returned. When he finally reached the interviewer, a long and equivocal conversation ensued. The interviewer at last implied that the consultant would not get the job. That was the end of the process. No further word, by mail or phone, was ever received.

Planners, managers, and personnel officers can draw two important lessons from this description of the wrong way to recruit. First, learn about your organization and what is required for the job you are filling so that you can write an accurate job description and conduct an organized interview. Second, treat the job applicant with the dignity and respect he or she deserves as a person who is striving to find the best opportunity to use his or her unique talents.

applications, and telephone discussions to permit the selection person or committee to winnow the candidates to those who are most highly qualified. Organizations recruiting for several positions at one time and placing recruitment responsibilities in the hands of only one or two persons would save money if the recruiters visited the candidates rather than bringing them from dispersed places to a central place for interviews.

The interview committee should be chosen for its knowledge of the characteristics required of the successful applicants. A broad-based committee might include an elected official, a member of the planning commission, a member of the planning staff, a citizen, a developer, and the city or county manager.

Prospective applicants should be given every opportunity to present their best case. Some rules of thumb might be to schedule interviews during regular business hours, hold interviews at places that are easy to get to, be as informal as practical to set the applicant at ease, and avoid irrelevant questions. When many applicants are interviewed during the course of more than one day, they should be systematically evaluated by rating criteria.

Figure 7–4 illustrates the use of the rating form. The selection criteria should be drafted by the planning director and submitted to the local government manager and personnel department for review before it is used. These criteria represent the most important concerns of the council and manager at the time the applicants were interviewed. Each criterion is ranked from 1 (lowest) to 10 (highest) by each selection committee member. The criteria weights are multiplied by the committee's ranking to determine the score of each applicant. These scores are taken into consideration, but are not the sole basis for determining who should be offered the job first. These scores are kept as a part of the applicant's file. They are supplemented by written notes from each selection committee member reflecting that member's personal impressions.

Applicants welcome a quick response after being evaluated for a job opportunity. It is a matter of courtesy to notify the highest rated candidate of the community's intention to negotiate responsibilities and compensation with him or her. Losing candidates also welcome immediate notification of the decision.

Letters of notification are more appropriate than phone calls because letters can be kept for future reference and because they eliminate emotional discussions between selection committee representatives and losing candidates. Until the winning candidate has agreed to the terms and conditions of his or her new employment, losing candidates who are considered competitive for the job should be told that they will remain under consideration until agreement has been reached with the winning candidate. Once that agreement is reached, another

Criterion	Person		
	1	2	3
Appearance	10	9	7
Responsiveness to questions	4	8	8
Technical knowledge	6	7	9
Oral communications skills	7	8	6
Written communications skills	7	6	9
References' evaluation	9	8	9
Leadership capabilities	5	7	9
Total	48	53	57

Ranking system: 1 lowest to 10 highest.

Figure 7–4 Prospective employee rating form.

Figure 7–5 The recruiting firm and the local government may not be looking for the same skills in a prospective employee.

written communication should be sent to the losing candidates telling them that they are no longer under consideration.

Motivation

Motivating employees has become one of the most difficult and sensitive of management tasks. Human relations prescriptions will be ineffective unless coupled with an in-depth understanding of prevailing circumstances. Planning managers therefore should tailor their motivational efforts to the employee's education, experience, responsibilities, and personal objectives.

Most motivational research in recent years emphasizes stressing goals and accountability, which links responsibility for getting the job done with receiving rewards or disincentives. This approach assumes that

1. Workers are capable of understanding the organization's goals and the relation of a given assignment to those goals.
2. Workers are substantively capable of carrying out the assignment.
3. The time of delivery is a very important part of determining the effectiveness of the product or process.
4. Workers are capable of receiving criticism of their work and thereby of improving performance.
5. Workers understand that they will not receive rewards or that they will be "punished" if they do not help achieve the organization's objectives in a timely manner.

Because of the current local government cost-revenue squeezes, planning managers and citizens have begun to demand increased employee productivity. Where productivity levels were high anyway, this demand has been translated into new priorities regarding how employee time is spent. Where productivity gains are achievable, the demand is that more be produced either in the same amount of time or by working longer hours. If more is to be produced in the same number of hours, production will have to be more intensive; that means eliminating frivolous activities and using machinery to complete tasks in less time.

The broad subject of motivation was reviewed briefly in Chapter 2. The five major concepts of motivation have led researchers to propose three sets of ideas that have become widely accepted today:

1. Motivation depends on the situation, and individual and group differences must be taken into account.
2. Goals, objectives, and targets provide essential frameworks for improved performance.
3. People change and can be changed in motivation and performance.[8]

Among the motivational factors of special value for the management of local government planning are employee needs, income, and recognition, which are discussed in the immediately following paragraphs. Subsequent sections examine two other important factors—performance evaluation and continuing education.

What is motivation?   When we talk about motivation we are really talking about the amount of physical and mental energy that a worker is willing to invest in his or her job. Note that this definition covers three points:

Motivation is already within people. The task of the supervisor is not to provide motivation. What is important for the supervisor is to know how to *release* higher levels of motivation to do the work.

Different people are willing to invest different amounts of energy and enthusiasm in their work. Not everyone is a rate buster, an overachiever. On the other hand, not everyone by any means is lazy or "poorly motivated."

The return in personal satisfaction that an employee receives from an investment of energy in the job affects the level of that employee's motivation. In other words, a low return in need satisfaction results in a low level of motivation; a high return in need satisfaction results in a high level of motivation.

Source: Kenneth K. Henning and Sam Mitchell, "Motivating Employees," in *Effective Supervisory Practices,* ed. Harold F. Holtz and Kenneth K. Henning (Washington, D.C.: International City Management Association, 1978), 91.

Needs levels of motivation

Basic human needs must be satisfied if the individual is to be motivated to increase productivity. Motivational research has shown that a hierarchy of needs governs human behavior:

1. Psychological needs: food, shelter, and clothing; environment that sustains life
2. Security needs: absence of threats to life, health, and safety; orderly environment
3. Social needs: sense of belonging; group membership; love; acceptance
4. Esteem needs: self-respect and the respect of others
5. Self-actualization: full development of abilities; creativity; fulfilled personal life.[9]

Employment standards in local government have evolved to the point where basic needs (levels one and two above) are generally assumed, but planning directors and managers can help provide the framework for planners who want to strive for levels three, four, and five.

The level and intensity of these needs vary from person to person, as do the opportunities to achieve them. Persons selecting a public planning career should recognize at the outset that rewards are more likely to be found in personal satisfaction from a job well done, recognition of that performance by peers, and personal intellectual growth, than in money or decision-making power achievable in other careers. Persons seeking more than a middle-class income and more than responsibility for making recommendations rather than decisions would do well to consider other careers. Planners, like most other public employees, are motivated by the need for a reasonable income and by the prospect of positive recognition for accomplishment. For the planning director and planning program managers, these are the two primary motives for increasing productivity.

Income

The local government planning manager's leverage over employee income usually is limited to a salary schedule recommended by the personnel office and approved by elected officials. Only under special circumstances can major (more than 6 to 8 percent) income increases occur. When, for example, an employee is strongly identified with what is widely considered to be a successful project or pattern of successes over a number of years, that employee's salary may be adjusted radically upward, or a special one-time bonus may be provided. Or, when an employee possesses a skill that is thought to be unique or in great demand, the job description may be amended and pay substantially increased to retain him or her.

In most cases, however, employee income tends to be locked into a relatively narrow range when measured in constant dollars. (Constant dollars represent the effective buying potential of a person's income by calculating the effects of inflation. Current dollars exclude changes in the value of the dollar over time.)

Although planning directors have little to say about fringe benefits from one employee to another, they do have the same influence as other department heads when advising the city or county manager on benefit levels, both across the board and for groups of employees. The planning director can, for example, present the case for professional education and training in terms of tuition reimbursement and educational leave with full or partial pay. Full or partial reimbursement of expenses to attend professional conferences and workshops is a strong nonmonetary incentive, especially for the younger professionals. Retirement plans—with both employer and employee contributions, portability, and immediate "vesting" (immediate employee ownership of employer contributions)—are a strong monetary incentive, especially for older employees.

The annual salary review for each employee is the time for the planning director to give careful thought to income as a motivator. Consider, for example, three employees with identical annual salaries: $24,000. Assume that the planning director has authority to grant individual raises from 0 percent to 6 percent and that the consumer price index went up by 3 percent in the past year. Assume further that one employee has done outstanding work; the second has done competent work; and the third has done work that is marginal, barely acceptable. With raises of 6, 3, and 0 percent, the outstanding employee receives a raise of $1,440 (a good raise proportionately in constant dollars); the competent employee receives a raise of $720 (enough to keep pace with inflation); and the marginal employee receives no raise (a pay cut in constant dollars and a warning that his or her job is in jeopardy). This example is an oversimplification, of course, because the planning director should also conduct an evaluation interview

---

Compensation for work well done

"One of the most prevalent myths of public management is that supervisors can do little to reward productive employees because of inflexible pay and benefit systems. This is patently false, however, because like their private sector counterparts, public managers occupy positions of considerable power and influence over subordinates. They have the authority to design jobs, set objectives, and monitor task accomplishment. They have many rewards available to induce employee participation and recognize employee productivity."

Statutes and ordinances fix many of the pay scales and benefits such as health insurance, retirement, annual leave,

and sick leave. Other benefits are flexible in many local governments and provide the planning manager with rewards to offer for outstanding performance. Some examples include: promotions, extra salary increases, tuition loans and reimbursement, increased job autonomy, opportunities to attend professional meetings and conferences, letters of commendation to be placed in the employee's personnel file, and prompt and open recognition of superior performance.

Source: Partly excerpted and partly abstracted from Donald E. Klingner, *Public Personnel Management: Contexts and Strategies* (Englewood Cliffs, N.J.: Prentice-Hall, 1980), 296–99.

---

to review each employee's performance, set objectives for the next year, and, for the marginal employee, put him or her on notice that the work must improve.

Recognition

Recognition of superior performance is an especially effective means of encouraging employees to raise the quality of their work, especially those who are already intellectually motivated and to whom marginal income increases pale in comparison with the stimulus of doing a good job. The planning director and planning program managers should always watch for opportunities to recognize staff accomplishments. Here are some examples of such recognition:

1. Drop by to seek the extemporaneous advice of a staff member on an important current issue. This type of action tells the staff member that his or her views are important to the success of the agency.
2. Praise an individual for a job well done and give reasons why it was well done.
3. Praise an individual's good work in the presence of others.
4. Send a letter or memorandum to the mayor, city manager, or county manager to cite outstanding work on a specific assignment.
5. Change a person's title to a more impressive sounding title.
6. Publish a report or paper produced by a staff member that was especially well done but that would not otherwise have been published. For example, the Phoenix, Arizona, planning department published "The Best of 81's Issue Papers," a series that began in 1980. These papers describe staff members' investigations of problems of special interest that might have potential value for plan implementation. Among the subjects covered during the first two years of this program were population estimates, housing costs, high-rise development, office space, and school enrollments.
7. Encourage staff members to prepare and submit papers for national, regional, and local professional conferences. If the paper is selected for delivery, pay the staff member's way to the conference.

8. Provide midcareer training opportunities. Encourage employees to take correspondence courses, attend seminars, and take courses for college credit, whether or not the work leads to a degree.
9. Establish an awards program. This may include a certificate for the employee and an announcement in the employee newsletter. Jackson County, Mississippi, has had a planner-of-the-month award that acknowledges good performance.
10. Acknowledge superior contributions over a long period of time by allocating the best located or largest offices that are available to the staff members responsible.

Performance evaluation

Performance evaluation systems help managers to determine how well an employee is doing in his or her job or how well the employee might do in another job in which he or she has interests and skills. The local planning manager needs to look beyond performance in existing jobs to potential for other work. Evaluating potential requires finding out which employees have skills they are not using, identifying special employee interests, and determining employee training needs. Employee assessment centers have been used in private companies and some local governments to assist in the hiring of staff. Such assessment centers can also help in determining which employees to promote and which employees to shift to new responsibilities within the planning agency.

Most local governments evaluate employees regularly as a basis for merit pay increases. These systems must be organized to help the manager or supervisor to

1. Clarify the skills, knowledge, and ability it takes to do an existing job;
2. Identify the tasks, responsibilities, and activities that the employee is expected to carry out in that job;
3. Establish acceptable performance levels for specific tasks, usually for a set time period;
4. Assess how well an employee measures up against those agreed-upon performance standards during a fixed time period;
5. Reward effective performance, reprimand employees for or alert them to unsatisfactory performance, or take other appropriate action based on a careful assessment of the past performance level;
6. Confirm, clarify, or refine an employee's perception of how well he or she is meeting expectations and performing in an existing job;
7. Set program and performance goals for the next time period.[10]

The planning manager also will want to estimate the future staff complement, the skills of existing staff, and the employee potential for professional growth. Assessing potential focuses on what an employee can do, is capable of learning how to do, and is interested in doing. When assessing employee potential, the planning manager should

1. Focus on existing positions that have been or could be expanded and which might provide new opportunities for carefully selected employees;
2. Identify new skills employees might need to take on new responsibilities and new positions;
3. Match employee skills and interests with future job possibilities in the organization;
4. Look for untapped skills, ability, knowledge—and potential.[11]

The importance of evaluating employee potential increases sharply in times of staff and budget cutbacks. Opportunities for advancement decrease as fewer jobs are available and available jobs are redefined. New demands are placed on the planning staff; new equipment such as microcomputers are made available to increase productivity; and personal advancement becomes important. A shrinking

Figure 7–6   The effective planner
never loses sight of the outside world.

staff means there will be greater pressure on existing employees to produce more, and a greater need to fill available positions with the best qualified people. With new programs, new skills will have to be developed along with the knowledge to service the programs. As for new technology, the staff will have to be able to use it before productivity can be increased.

Assessment centers

Employee assessment centers provide a systematic approach to matching individual skills with jobs that need to be performed. Most assessment centers emphasize the following steps:

1. Identifying the management ability, technical skills, and substantive knowledge required to do an existing job or a proposed position;
2. Designing individual assignments and group activities that can be used to assess how skilled or knowledgeable some employees are already and to assess their potential to develop the necessary skills and knowledge;
3. Selecting and training people who will serve as assessors to gauge employee skills and potential;
4. Conducting an assessment session in which a group of employees actually do the assignments and group activities while being observed by trained assessors;
5. Providing information about observed behavior and performance that can be used to make hiring decisions, to plan training programs, and to help employees understand their strengths, weaknesses, and potential.[12]

This approach may be used by the planning department, or the planning department may participate in the local government's assessment center process.

In either event, the planning director should be involved in the following stages of the assessment:

1. Describing the functions of the job. These functions may include preparing plans, making oral presentations, writing memoranda, networking, and chairing meetings.
2. Performing these job functions. High on this list is effectiveness of oral expression, ability to make persuasive oral and written presentations of ideas and facts, and ability to speak extemporaneously.
3. Selecting and training persons who will assess the skills and knowledge of others. These persons should be able to observe behavior accurately, record these observations, prepare a written report summarizing findings, and discuss these findings with the employee and the supervisor.
4. Evaluating the assessment center process. Feedback should be sought from employees who were assessed and from the assessors.

The assessment center can be of particular assistance to planning agencies that want a systematic approach to selecting the best candidate for the job from among many candidates, or that want to increase the likelihood that the selected candidate will perform up to or beyond expectations. It has the added advantage of being able to obtain information beyond that supplied in résumés, job applications, and perfunctory oral interviews. At the same time, this process can improve employee work planning.

Anticipating work load

Planning agencies for many years did not plan their work loads more than one year in advance; this planning was usually part of the annual budget process. One of the earliest multiyear planning agency work programs was prepared by the Tampa Bay Regional Planning Commission in 1965. Its purposes were to interrelate work over the next three-year period, to provide an agenda for discussing future planning grant requirements with federal agency regional representatives, and to keep the agency's policy board informed of issues to be analyzed. Soon thereafter the U.S. Department of Housing and Urban Development began encouraging other Section 701 comprehensive planning grant recipients to prepare similar programs.

In 1975, Salem, Oregon, implemented an employee work planning process based on management by objectives. After being trained to implement the program, each supervisor meets with his or her employees and plans the work each employee is expected to accomplish in the coming months. Each employee work plan identifies

1. Key performance areas of the job
2. Specific objectives to be accomplished in each key performance area
3. Performance standards that measure how well the specific objectives were accomplished
4. Career development needs of the employee
5. Any performance deficiencies that need improvement.

The employee generally prepares a rough draft of his or her work plan as a basis for discussion with the supervisor. The plan period may be anywhere from three to twelve months, depending upon the employee's ability to conceptualize the work load. The work plan is periodically reviewed with the employee to assess performance relative to objectives.

Defining job functions, evaluating the knowledge and skills required, evaluating employee ability and potential, and preparing and monitoring work plans—these tasks require a commitment by the planning director. Since the process represents change in the organization, it will probably meet with some resistance.

Another factor is that it takes time to systematically carry out all phases of the process. It is only worthwhile if the commitment is there and a follow-up takes place.

Continuing education

"Learning has no limit." This is the motto of the Center for Continuing Education at the University of Georgia, Athens. It epitomizes the demand in almost all occupations, trades, and professions to keep up or be left behind. In scholarly disciplines, it means that one must—at the least—keep up with the literature. In planning, finance, personnel, and other local government professions, keeping up means both reading about developments in the field and participating in continuing education, whether it be on-the-job training, midcareer training, or conferences.

The 1970s and 1980s provide three examples of the changing context of local government planning that has affected the skills needed by planners: (1) originally citizen participation skills were not important, but later became the foundation for most planning programs; (2) environmental constraints on development were not quantified at first, but then became important bases for plan preparation; and (3) real estate finance skills were thought to be in the bastion of the "other side" until public-private partnerships became common.

Skills that will be required of the planning staff in the future are being determined now. As staffs continue to dwindle, it will be imperative for future planning programs to deal with questions of productivity. Already equipment is rapidly becoming available to help improve efficiency. Word processors, microcomputers, and telecommunications equipment will soon become common in planning offices. More planning will take place in the office of the city or county manager or other chief administrator as efficiency and political reality become key criteria. More planning will also be done by departments responsible for service delivery such as utilities, recreation, and public works. Greater demands will be placed on planning agency management to motivate employees toward products and processes that are directly useful for elected and appointed officials.

In a 1980 survey of ICMA members, who were asked to identify the issues over which they expected to have greater influence in the future, respondents ranked planning and evaluation above any of the other eight management categories surveyed (Table 7–1). The third highest category was policy recommendations and formulation. Respondents concluded that it was necessary for

Table 7–1   Anticipated degree of influence of various management issues in 2000 in comparison with 1980.

Category	Greater influence (%)	The same influence (%)	Less influence (%)
Planning/evaluation	56	41	3
Labor relations	55	33	12
Policy recommendations/formulation	47	43	10
Public opinion leadership	44	45	11
Budgeting	35	59	6
Administration	31	63	6
Personnel policies	30	56	14
Local politics	24	58	18
Purchasing/procurement	14	60	26

Source: Richard J. Stillman II, "Local Public Management in Transition: A Report on the Current State of the Profession," in *The Municipal Year Book 1982* (Washington, D.C.: International City Management Association, 1982), 171.

them to play a more activist role in the planning process, if they hoped to exercise greater influence over the formulation and recommendation of policies.

The same survey evaluated the public management skills thought to be necessary in 1980 and 2000. Planning and evaluation was ranked the fourth most important skill out of sixteen skills (Table 7–2). Furthermore, 14 percent more respondents thought it would be the fourth most important skill in 2000 compared with 1980. Local government managers foresee the need to increase the amount of planning and evaluation they do or are responsible for. Therefore, planning will no doubt become an increasingly important management tool in the years to come.

On-the-job training

In a formal sense, the term "continuing education" refers to the correspondence courses, workshops, institutes, and seminars offered by university extension agencies, professional and trade associations, and private sector companies. Continuing education also includes on-the-job training (OJT)—which refers to the ongoing, informal efforts of planning agencies and other organizations to draw on their own talent and skills to keep the staff abreast of current issues, methods, and technology. Planning agencies can practice on-the-job training by means of information sharing, quality circles, and in-house training, among other methods.

The information and ideas the planner is exposed to during his or her work include those gleaned from meetings, memoranda, one-on-one discussions, networking with persons outside the office, and reports and books that come across his or her desk.

Common complaints of the planning director and other planning agency man-

Table 7–2 Importance of local public management skills for 1980 and 2000.

Skill	1980		2000	
	No. reporting	Ranking	No. reporting	Ranking
Budgeting/finance	1,435	1	1,039	1
Management and control of programs	737	2	624	2
Personnel/labor relations	686	3	536	3
Planning/evaluation	460	4	525	4
Public relations	459	5	359	7
Human relations	415	6	512	5
Assisting elected officials	384	7	349	8
Brokering/negotiating	304	8	475	6
Building community support	289	9	337	9
Economic development	241	10	247	10
Grantsmanship	125	11	65	14
Maintenance/development of physical infrastructure	104	12	120	13
Development of new programs	92	13	204	12
Data processing	43	14	225	11
Other	28	15	36	16
Emergency (disaster) management	12	16	33	15

Source: Richard J. Stillman II, "Local Public Management in Transition: A Report on the Current State of the Profession," in *The Municipal Year Book 1982* (Washington, D.C.: International City Management Association, 1982), 172.

agers are that they are exposed to too much information and are required to spend too much time in unimportant meetings. Common complaints of lower level planning personnel are that they are not exposed to enough information to know "what is going on" and are not invited to enough important meetings.

The planning director's management style dictates how "tightly the ship is run" in terms of exposure to information. In agencies where productivity improvements are a high priority, it is difficult to add the cost of OJT to an already inadequate budget. There is simply not enough time for all staff members to read all of the material that is available and to attend all of the meetings. It is the director's responsibility to strike a balance between minimizing the exposure of staff members to OJT on a "need to know" basis and maximizing it by including everyone in all phases of the work program. One approach is to provide additional information to those employees who are getting their work done in a timely manner and at an appropriate level of quality.

Another approach is to offer OJT in quality circles, that is, in small working groups that voluntarily get together to identify and try to solve problems in their work unit. By and large, these groups meet to discuss ways of improving productivity, employee growth and development, or organization development. Many planning departments will find it convenient to start their quality circles in the processing of development permission applications because the functions here are more standardized than in long-term research or networking.

In the typical quality circle, the group's first task is to identify the problems to be addressed. The next step is to list problems in order of priority. The first problem "should be important enough that its solution will be considered more than only a minor improvement, but 'achievable' to insure fairly quick success. Ideally, problem selection should be left up to the circle members, because they will know if a problem is something they can solve and because they often will opt to solve the problem that causes them the greatest annoyance or wasted time."[13]

Circle members analyze the problem to determine its causes and what can be done to solve it. Outside opinions may be sought at this time, but it is the group's responsibility to deal with the problem. The next step is to present the problem, findings, and proposed solution to management (that is, the department head) in written form with appropriate graphics and to summarize it orally. Management then is obligated to try to do something about the problem or problems.

Still another approach is to organize in-house training sessions to teach staff members a skill they do not have or that they need to improve. If sessions are held in the office, they will be inexpensive and convenient to get to, and they will be held in a friendly environment. An example is the training provided in the Lansing, Michigan, planning department to help staff overcome a common shortcoming, poor writing. Since the planning department staff included a person who was skilled at writing reports, the department was able to establish an eight-week course in writing improvement taught by the skilled staff member to other staff members. The approach obviously has other applications.

Midcareer training

Many short-term educational programs provide information on the latest methods of discharging planning agency responsibilities. Such programs typically last one to three days and cost about $100 to $500 per person per day. They generally take the form of a seminar featuring several speakers who share printed handouts.[14] Invitations are often extended through advertisements, which bring in attendees representing a broad range of interests. As a result, participants are given the opportunity to hear the same types of problems discussed from a variety of perspectives. Attendees learn from each other as well as from the speakers. Some programs only accept attendees from a single jurisdiction. The

On-the-job training resources
Continuing education, formal or informal, is part of the job for every professional in local government. Planners have long had opportunities for training in zoning, urban design, growth policies, economic development, and many other aspects of city and county development, and management training for planners has been added in recent years. The major sources for such training are summarized.

Planners Training Service. The Planners Training Service provides handbooks and other publications and conducts workshops and seminars in management, supervision, and related fields. The Service is provided by the American Institute of Certified Planners, which, in turn, is affiliated with the American Planning Association.

ICMA Training Institute. The Training Institute, conducted by the International City Management Association since 1934, provides correspondence training for city and county managers, planning directors and staffs, and other local government employees. The Institute provides ten correspondence courses in planning, management, police, finance, communication, housing, and other subjects; offers training packages, group courses, and handbooks; and conducts workshops and seminars.

Institutes of training. Many colleges and universities provide training and educational opportunities designed especially for local government officials. Generally, these programs are offered through a local government research or education division attached to the school's department of political science or public administration. Seminars, workshops, and courses on high-interest topics are scheduled at convenient times so that officials with full-time jobs may attend.

Departments of community affairs. Most states provide direct assistance to local governments through their divisions or departments of community affairs. As part of their assistance efforts, these agencies design and conduct training programs, usually on topics of current concern within the state. Staff from these agencies may also work directly with local officials on topics of shared concern to both the state and the local government.

Cooperative extension services. Land grant colleges and universities offer education programs through their cooperative extension services. These programs serve a wide audience, including citizens, elected officials, and appointed professionals in local government. Cooperative extension agents work closely with local officials in designing and conducting seminars, workshops, and campus-based courses.

Regional agencies. In some areas, regional councils of governments and training agencies are another source of continuing education. Generally, these agencies work very closely with local officials to provide training programs that meet local needs and interests. For example, the Government Training Service in St. Paul, Minnesota, serves as a major source for local government training programs in the Twin Cities metropolitan area.

advantage here is that the analyses and case studies are able to concentrate on that community.

Seminars have several other advantages. One is that they take the participant away from the office and allow him or her to think about everyday problems in a more abstract and theoretical way. Second, they give the employee a chance to talk about common problems with outsiders whose experience and background are different. Third, attendees can generally carry away materials for future reference that are directly applicable to the work back home. Fourth, bibliographies of additional resource material are often provided for future reference.

A possible disadvantage of the seminar approach is that it may attempt to cover too much substance in too short a time. Participants may be inundated by information and provided with little time to cover the written material and in the end questions may not occur to attendees until after the seminar is over, when resource persons are not available.

Correspondence courses extend the study period over several weeks or months and thus cover more material; in addition, participants have more time between study sessions to reflect on questions. Planning, management, economic development, assessment centers, quality circles, and other correspondence courses are available from ICMA, and planning courses have been developed and offered by university extension services.

The lack of personal contact between the instructor and the student in a correspondence course means that the participant will have to work independently. The correspondence course should be selected by those who do not have ready access to comparable college-level courses in the community and to those who want to set their own pace of study.

Many communities have established continuing education opportunities for persons who wish to take college courses leading to a degree in a field related to their work. Often these courses are taken at night so they won't conflict with regular working hours. Courses may also be taken during the day, and employees allowed to attend night meetings (typically an important part of planning staff work) to compensate for any time lost in taking such courses.

If the local government commitment to the employee's continuing college education exceeds one or two courses, a trade-off is often expected—that is, the employee is expected to remain with the local government for a specified time to ensure a partial return on the community's expenditure. For example, the community may require a year of full-time service for each year of course work paid for. Other requirements typically include courses directly relevant to the employee's job and satisfactory completion of the courses. Although some have taken time off with a leave of absence to obtain a college degree, this practice is becoming less common now that sources of funding have been tightened. In some cases, such training is not practicable because trained persons are already available in the marketplace, and full-time employees cannot be spared from their job assignments.

Conferences

One of the most popular forms of continuing education is participation in national and state conferences of professional associations. These meetings provide an opportunity to discuss problems experienced by peers in other communities and to obtain information from experts in a wide variety of subjects. Annual conferences of the ICMA, APA, American Society for Public Administration, Urban and Regional Information Systems Association, and many other associations enable planners and managers to participate in forums in their respective professional networks and obtain information on the "cutting edges" of their respective professions.

These conferences can be even more rewarding when the participant delivers a paper or serves on a panel. Conference participation provides the opportunity for staff members to go to another community to see the physical evidence of the planning process and to discuss it with the responsible planners.

Consultant selection and use

Federal grants for local government planning were sharply increased by the Housing Act of 1954, which required comprehensive city plans to back up urban renewal projects. Section 701 of that act provided for federal sharing of the costs of preparing comprehensive plans. This led to the rapid growth of planning consulting firms serving cities, counties, and regional planning agencies of all sizes. The work was concentrated, however, in nonmetropolitan jurisdictions where most of the federal money was available. The experience that has been gained in widespread consulting work since the mid-1950s indicates that consultants can aid local planning agencies in significant ways by

1. Providing technical skills not available on the staff
2. Assuming responsibility for ideas and recommendations that the staff prefers not to be identified with at that time
3. Providing new sources of information from the consultant's networking that are not available to the staff
4. Preparing products more quickly than the staff can
5. Acting as a sounding board to staff ideas and recommendations that the staff is not ready to air locally.

Reasons for selection

Often consultants are used for several of these reasons. As the complexity of planning and development issues increases, the importance of defensible methods increases; as budget constraints increasingly limit the number of staff members, the need for consulting services increases. A 1979 ICMA survey (Table 7–3)

Table 7–3   Primary reasons for engaging a consultant.

Classification	No. of cities reporting (A)	Limited number of own staff No.	% of (A)	No staff with required expertise No.	% of (A)	Short time frame for project completion No.	% of (A)	Need for independent opinion No.	% of (A)	Other No.	% of (A)
Total, all cities.......	2,311	1,211	52.4	1,874	81.1	547	23.7	603	26.1	84	3.6
Population group											
Over 1,000,000...	1	1	100.0	1	100.0	1	100.0	1	100.0	0	0.0
500,000– 1,000,000.........	7	5	71.4	4	57.1	4	57.1	6	85.7	0	0.0
250,000– 499,999.........	14	11	78.6	14	100.0	8	57.1	11	78.6	3	21.4
100,000– 249,999.........	42	30	71.4	35	83.3	21	50.0	24	57.1	2	4.8
50,000– 99,999.........	110	84	76.4	94	85.5	51	46.4	51	46.4	3	2.7
25,000– 49,999.........	259	191	73.7	201	77.6	94	36.3	104	40.2	8	3.1
10,000– 24,999.........	613	369	60.2	495	80.8	164	26.8	182	29.7	18	2.9
5,000– 9,999.........	545	252	46.2	449	82.4	101	18.5	108	19.8	21	3.9
2,500– 4,999.........	592	218	36.8	480	81.1	85	14.4	92	15.5	23	3.9
Under 2,500	128	50	39.1	101	78.9	18	14.1	24	18.8	6	4.7
Metro status											
Central.............	169	135	79.9	137	81.1	80	47.3	86	50.9	9	5.3
Suburban	1,179	635	53.9	948	80.4	248	21.0	317	26.9	42	3.6
Independent......	963	441	45.8	789	81.9	219	22.7	200	20.8	33	3.4

Source: Tim Maupin, *Municipal Consultants: Patterns and Practices*, Urban Data Service Reports, vol. 11, no. 12 (Washington, D.C.: International City Management Association, December 1979), 2.

provides insight into the primary reasons (beyond the five points listed above) for engaging a consultant.

Other things being equal, the smaller the planning staff, the fewer the skills available. Consultants provide a means of broadening the skills available to do the planning department's work.

For example, real estate finance skills are readily available among consultants, but less so among local planning staff. Local planning programs that require an analysis of proposed public-private partnerships to determine the costs and revenues of projects may temporarily need someone with real estate finance skills. Or, consider what can happen when relatively high construction-loan and permanent-loan interest rates reduce the financial feasibility of community development projects and increase the number of financial techniques used in structuring deals. Deal making thus becomes more complex technically and is beyond the experience of staff members who have not participated in real estate finance. Consultants can shore up the staff and reduce the likelihood of financial errors that might have long-term consequences for the community's budget.

It is hard for the planning agency to get too far out in front on controversial development issues. Planning staff may have well-founded fears that "running a proposal up the flagpole" will lead to public resentment and political heat. The planning consultant, especially if selected from outside the community, can step in to study the situation as a disinterested (not *un*interested) third party. The objectivity of the findings and recommendations lend great strength to the work of the local planning staff. Even if only the consultant's findings are accepted by community and political leaders, that is a big step forward because it is an agreed-upon base for further "dialogue."

Consultants whose practice extends beyond the local community often come up with solutions that can be applied at least in part to problems in other communities. At the same time, their networking exposes them to ideas and sources of information that are not readily available to the planning staff.

Consultants can provide analytical support and written products quickly. Even if the planning staff has the skill, it may not have the time to complete the work when the elected officials need it to make their decisions. Consultant contracts can establish tight deadlines, and consultants typically can program their work and devote sufficient person power to meet such deadlines. Whereas the planning staff has to cope with meetings, ongoing work, management processes, and responses to citizens and elected officials' demands, consultants can isolate themselves from these demands on their time and devote their full energies to the assignment at hand.

Planning managers and chief administrative officers, in particular, have few persons at hand who can be used as a "sounding board" to exchange ideas with. As the person at the top of the planning and management hierarchy, this individual must carefully select the persons he or she talks to frankly about community development and other issues. Similarly, there may be few persons for the planning director to carry on a dialogue with. Peers in other cities are one possible contact here, but they usually have their own busy schedules to follow. Experienced consultants in whom the manager and the planning director have technical and networking confidence can provide this sounding board. This can be done on an issue-by-issue basis or on a retainer whereby the consultant would be on call for extemporaneous advice.

Selection process

The fees paid to consultants are almost always very small as a ratio of the total city or county budget, but the high visibility of consulting work, especially in smaller communities, should be a warning to planners and managers to follow meticulous procedures in selecting consultants. The warning should be heeded by planners in particular because planning agencies generally use consultants more often than most other departments of local government.

It should be recognized at the outset that a consultant's zeal to gain a competitive advantage may lead to questionable representations of qualifications and proposed work. Local favoritism by persons responsible for selecting the consultant may add credence to rumors of unethical practices. Most consultant selection procedures, however, seem reasonable and equitable and show no signs of foul play. In a 1979 study conducted among local officials in Alabama, Kentucky, and Wisconsin, 97 percent voted consultants "usually valuable" (60 percent) or "sometimes valuable" (37 percent).[15] The ICMA 1979 survey came up with similar results (see Table 7–4).

The first step in hiring a consultant, and the most important responsibility of the planning department throughout the course of the contract, is to stipulate the reason for hiring the consultant, the work expected, and the consultant relation to ongoing programs and research activities. The most common reason

Table 7–4   Summary of consultant users by consulting classification.

Consulting classification[1]	No. of cities using consultants	No. of consultants per city (mean avg.)	Average (mean) consultant fee ($)[2]	% of consultant contracts subsidized[3]	Client satisfaction level[4]
Finance and budget					
Audit	575	1.21	11,095	15	3.39
Budget	108	1.13	8,732	11	3.30
Finance	432	1.45	34,421	13	3.35
Utility rate studies	468	1.20	17,077	19	3.28
Planning and development					
Architecture	929	1.79	91,696	51	3.16
Engineering	1,730	2.07	34,206	60	3.21
Housing and community development	595	1.41	23,302	68	3.23
Land use planning	883	1.19	19,788	49	3.17
Management, administration, personnel					
Computer systems	311	1.23	22,879	17	3.08
Grantsmanship	392	1.20	10,586	47	3.14
Management and administration	259	1.39	21,630	33	3.16
Personnel and manpower	568	1.42	28,652	31	3.20
Risk management	280	1.15	5,964	7	3.18
Environment and energy					
Air and water pollution	198	1.23	157,105	69	3.16
Demographic studies	79	1.19	27,396	63	3.18
Energy	82	1.25	16,941	46	2.92
Environment and natural resources	211	1.73	60,463	52	3.16
Solid waste and sewerage	549	1.30	136,203	66	3.16
Miscellaneous					
Communications	118	1.25	84,273	24	3.16
Economic development	330	1.86	37,120	51	3.18
Legal and judicial	447	1.69	17,135	15	3.32
Public information	86	1.47	17,645	25	3.08
Public safety	192	1.52	36,491	50	3.25
Recreation and leisure	440	1.47	20,355	57	3.16
Transportation	439	1.63	81,052	64	3.22

Souce: Tim Maupin, *Municipal Consultants: Patterns and Practices*, Urban Data Service Reports, vol. 11, no. 12 (Washington, D.C.: International City Management Association, December 1979), 4.

1 Items have been omitted where fewer than 75 cities reported.

2 Mean of all fees paid to consultants over a two-year period.

3 Ratio of cities reporting that one or more consultant contracts was subsidized over a two-year period by federal, state, or foundation funds.

4 Satisfaction level on a scale of: 1, "unsatisfactory"; 2, "mediocre"; 3, "satisfactory"; and 4, "very satisfactory."

for undesirable consultant experience is the inability of the client to clearly articulate what is expected of the consultant and to monitor progress.

Some communities have established guidelines on the selection of consultants. Such guidelines usually require competitive bidding rather than sole-source selection and cover ownership of material produced, availability and use of client office space, parties at interest in the consulting firm not having a connection with the community, reasons and procedures for terminating the contract prior to completion, and identification of the client's responsible agent for renegotiating the contract.

The principal steps in selecting a consultant are (1) prepare the request for proposal (RFP); (2) appoint a consultant selection committee; (3) distribute the request for proposal; (4) evaluate proposals; and (5) select the consultant.

Typically, the working relations between planning staff members and employees in other departments highlight issues that are too complex or politically exposed to be handled locally. The planning staff simply does not have the time to tackle these issues. During the course of conversations about these issues and about possible solutions, the seeds of the idea for a request for proposal (RFP) are sown. At other times, networking with elected officals will yield the central topic. This procedure is particularly useful because elected officials usually have to authorize the consulting work and make the ultimate decisions on the consultant's recommendations.

The planning staff member assigned to draft the RFP should review locally produced material on related subjects, reports and other material produced by other planning agencies, and professional coverage in journals and books. The next step is to draft the RFP.

Membership on the consultant selection committee should reflect both technical and political expectations. Members are typically department heads, staff members, planning commissioners, elected officials, and others who have a special interest in and knowledge of the topic. Some of these people will have already contributed ideas for the draft RFP.

The committee will be a short-term, hard-working group. Therefore, persons with only a peripheral interest in the subject should not be invited, nor should those who are unwilling to spend time in committee meetings.

Since the committee will be expected to vote on consultants, it should be composed of an odd number of members. Anywhere from three to seven members is usually large enough to represent community interests yet small enough to encourage interchange between committee members and the consultants to be evaluated.

The best way to determine which firms are to be invited is to send out requests for qualifications (RFQs). The RFQ asks firms to identify themselves by the work they have done and by the qualifications of their employees. This prequalification process can be extended to all interested firms by advertisements in newspapers and periodicals listing the intent of the public agency to purchase goods and services, or to a list of firms recommended by the staff on the basis of personal knowledge. Criteria for evaluating RFQs include (1) substantive studies that are comparable to the work that needs to be done; (2) personnel who have a good reputation for the work that needs to be done; (3) comments on the consultant's work by clients; and (4) the clarity of the RFQ as an indicator of the quality of written products produced by the firm. If this prequalification process is used, then those firms that survive the screening are the ones to receive RFPs.

If prequalification is not used, then the next step is to select the consultants who are to receive RFPs, either by open or limited approaches. There are two schools of thought on which approach is more appropriate. One says that the distribution list should be long to alert the consulting community to the opportunity. This approach emphasizes the openness of the selection process. Its disadvantages include the staff time required to identify RFP recipients, produce and distribute copies of each RFP, and work through the proposals, each of which must be systematically evaluated. The number of respondents can be substantially reduced if the RFP defines precisely the purposes of the analysis, its technical requirements, the level of effort in time or money, and the skills the prospective client thinks will be required. Less than totally qualified consultants will either not respond or will attempt to subcontract for a portion of the work with a firm that decides to respond.

The other school of thought believes that the distribution of RFPs should be limited to firms known to be qualified, or to local firms. Among the disadvantages of this approach are that the staff and selection committee do not necessarily know the best firms to distribute the RFP to or that a short distribution list may imply that one of the firms is already favored by the selection committee.

The RFP should specify what material is to be submitted. More and more committees are asking for two proposals—a technical and a cost proposal. The technical proposal describes the firm's approach to the problem, the work it will perform, the proposed schedule, products that will be delivered, and qualifications of the firm, and it provides résumés of only those persons who will work on the assignment. The selection committee evaluates the technical proposals and ranks them before looking at the cost proposals. Criteria for evaluating technical proposals usually include

1. Responsiveness to the RFP
2. Familiarity with the issue in the client community
3. Experience of the firm with the same or similar issues in other communities
4. Experience of the personnel to be assigned to the job in the client community
5. Reasons given by firm representatives that they are qualified to do the work
6. The firm's record of completing work in a timely fashion and the probability that it will do so in this case.

Each of these criteria may be numerically ranked by selection committee members. Once the scores assigned by member are tabulated, the winning firm can be identified.

Cost proposals are then made available to selection committee members. Often the bottom line is easy to compare, but all professional associations recommend that firms not be selected merely on the basis of the lowest price. One important variable is the cost of travel. If the most distant firm has the best technical proposal but its cost proposal is higher because of its travel costs, it may still be the best firm to hire.

Sometimes selection committees like to introduce subjective criteria into the selection process such as the personal appearance of the firm representative, enthusiasm he or she brings to the presentation, local friendships he or she may have, or alleged access to out-of-town money or decision makers. These attributes may be important for a given project in a given community at a particular time, but such traits and claims are usually not germane to getting the job done well and on time.

Cities should be aware of their ongoing responsibility for compliance with antitrust laws. Therefore,

selection procedures should provide due process, including prior publication of the criteria, an opportunity to be heard, and where appropriate, a right of appeal. In addition, the selection process should avoid closed meetings or other conduct that could give the appearance that the local government is undertaking concerted action with private parties to exclude their competitors. *Even the most innocent meeting behind closed doors is likely to arouse suspicions on the part of unsuccessful bidders*.

Moreover, should that unsuccessful bidder decide to bring an antitrust lawsuit, the discussion in and documents from such a closed meeting may have to be revealed during pre-trial discovery.[16]

Contract negotiation

Once the technical and cost proposals have been evaluated and ranked, the winning firm will be identified. All firms should be contacted immediately by telephone and in writing to notify them of the result. The winning firm should be invited to negotiate a contract. The other firms should be told that if the client is unable to negotiate a satisfactory contract with the winning firm, the runner-up will be contacted for negotiations.

The planning staff then should prepare a draft contract. In addition to the standard or boilerplate language, it should include contractual language representing the winning firm's proposed scope of work and specific delivery dates for interim reports, meetings, and final products. The consultant's proposed coverage should not be wholly appended to the contract as the definition of the work to be done. Contract language is different from proposal language covering the same topics. Contract language should contain precise terms, including mandatory forms such as "shall" and "will," while excluding inappropriate proposal language dealing with items to be determined by the client and references to the firm's past work.

Once the contract has been negotiated, only authorized representatives of the firm and the client local government should sign the contract. Clients should not expect firms to proceed without written authorization. It is unreasonable to expect firms to spend money on a project without assurance that they will be paid.

A key contract item is negotiating the fee and the schedule of payments. The amount of money available to do the research or the number of person days the client wishes the consultant to devote to the assignment should be included in the RFP. The fee is the more precise and relevant figure because most consultant contracts purchase the time of the consultant and therefore the time and cost per day are the most important variables of negotiation. RFPs that do not indicate the level of effort the client expects of the consultant leave the consultants guessing at the amount of money available and level of effort expected. There is nothing to be gained by this guessing game.

Costs of providing professional services are composed of direct costs and overhead costs. Direct costs are those directly chargeable to project work: primarily salaries, travel, photocopying, and telephone calls. Overhead costs are generally items such as office rent, employee fringe benefits, costs of time spent promoting work, secretarial and accounting services, and costs of time for professional development. The overhead costs may be thought of as those necessary to have the consultant available—on call, so to speak—to do the work.

Promotion costs are particularly important because of the unbillable time consumed. These costs of staying in business so as to be available for assignments may range from 1.3 to 1.6 times the direct costs for doing the work. The consultant can reduce this ratio by having an office in an inexpensive location, such as his or her home; only taking work that comes through the door rather than promoting work with prospective clients; and by hiring support services on a piecework basis.

Contract administration

All of the review, definition, and redefinition of the problem, and other steps in the selection process only bring the planning agency to the point where the contract is signed and the consultant is ready to go to work. At this point, even with the best possible consulting firm, the project can fail if the client does not become part of the project team. In other words, the consultant cannot do the job alone. There may have been a time when the efficiency expert could dash into town, dazzle the locals, whip up a report (replete with multicolored charts), pocket the fee, and leave town. This caricature was seldom seen, of course, but even the vestiges were eliminated as consultants and local governments have gained experience with each other.

The local government client must make commitments for a successful effort. The most important of these is management support. In a smaller city or county, both the city or county manager and the planning director should be involved. In addition, the planning agency consultant liaison should invest a minimum of 10 percent of time as a ratio of the total consultant time in the contract. This does not include the time that the planning staff spends on identifying sources of information, gathering and analyzing information, or attending consultant meetings and presentations. To emphasize this point, it is worth quoting a former city manager in two states, a former planning director, and now developer: "The client government should make firm commitments of staff and resources on which the consultant can rely. Failure in this commitment is the most significant risk factor—in terms of both quality of project outcome for the client and economic loss for the consultant—in the entire engagement."[17]

Time is another factor that influences successful consulting work. Usually it is cheaper for the consultant to complete the work in a shorter period of time as long as the time period is reasonable when compared to the amount of work to be done and the number of persons assigned to the project. Better quality consulting projects can emerge when staff members are able to concentrate a great proportion of their time on the assignment. As with any research, inefficiencies are built into assignments that are frequently started and laid aside.

Other elements in the effective administration of consulting contracts include a carefully defined project plan showing tasks and performance milestones, a local government project director who has authority to make decisions expeditiously, progress reports from the consultant, prompt payment of consultant invoices as the project moves along, and consultant access to the planning director and other top management people.

Conclusion

This chapter has touched on many diverse subjects under the heading, "personnel." Some of the subjects—performance evaluation, for example—can become quite technical. Others are managerial, judgmental, and subjective. Among the latter are the responsibilities of the planning director and planning program managers for leadership, motivation, training, and effective use of outside consulting services.

The planning director is the leader of the planning department, and the one who brings a broad range of political, managerial, and technical skills to brokerage, policy analysis, communication, networking, advocacy, counseling, community development issues, staff training, and work with the city or county's chief administrator and elected officials.

Employee motivation is stimulated in many ways, which vary with the individual and prevailing job circumstances. Typical priorities for increasing planner and other employee motivation are income, responsibility with authority, fringe benefits, job security, and opportunities for advancement. Often underestimated is the value of goal setting, opportunities for professional training and advancement, and recognition from peers.

Continuing education becomes more important to planners as they become involved in the dollars and cents of community development issues—a topic that is not usually emphasized in university curricula. Many opportunities are available for participating in seminars and conferences as part of on-the-job training. In-house training using quality circles and staff members to teach other staff members is another important way to upgrade technical and administrative skills.

City, county, and regional planning agencies deal with a wide range of problems. It is likely that some of these problems will be beyond the capacity of the permanent planning staff, or that they will be difficult to handle locally for other reasons. Here is where the planning consultant can provide the skills and third-party objectivity to help resolve specific problems. The consulting work, however, depends on a mutual understanding of the nature and extent of the work to be done. This means careful attention must be given to analysis of the work, to screening bidders and reviewing proposals, drafting a contract, and following through until the consultant has delivered his or her final report.

1   Edmund M. Burke, *A Participatory Approach to Urban Planning* (New York: Human Sciences Press, 1979), 269–74.
2   See: Rensis Likert, *The Human Organization* (New York: McGraw-Hill, 1967).
3   Edward H. Thacker, "Personnel Administration," in *Managing Municipal Leisure Services*, ed. Sidney G. Lutzin (Washington, D.C.: International City Management Association, 1980), 230.
4   Interview with Richard F. Counts, Planning Director, Phoenix, Arizona, Planning Department, 16 October 1982.
5   For several articles and commentaries on employee fringe benefits in city and county governments, most of which cover health care benefits and ways of containing health insurance costs, see: *Public Management* 65 (December 1983).
6   For views on executive search see: *Public Management* 65 (March 1983).
7   "Embellishment Yes, Lying No," *Time*, 9 May 1983, 82.
8   Wayne F. Anderson et al., *The Effective Local Government Manager* (Washington, D.C.: International City Management Association, 1983), 125.
9   Abraham H. Maslow, *Motivation and Personality*, 2d ed. (New York: Harper & Row, 1970).
10 Charles J. Schwabe, *Assessing Employee Potential: Using Assessment Centers in Local Government*,

handbook (Washington, D.C.: International City Management Association, 1982), 2.
11 Ibid.
12 Ibid., 5.
13 W. Maureen Godsey, *Employee Involvement: A Local Government Approach to Quality Circles,* handbook (Washington, D.C.: International City Management Association, 1982), 11.
14 The term "seminar" is used for several kinds of training programs that may include workshops (usually involving a high degree of participation through training exercises and the like), institutes (more formal offerings with lectures and panels), team building (with a high degree of personal and small-group interaction), seminars (small group discussions that are largely self-directed), and others.
15 George P. Barbour, Jr., "How to Get the Most Out of Your Consultant," *Public Management* 63 (April 1981): 2.
16 Martin Michaelson and George Mernick, *Antitrust Exposure of Local Governments—A Guide for the Chief Executive*, Management Information Service Reports, vol. 14, no. 12 (Washington, D.C.: International City Management Association, 1982), 9.
17 Raymond T. Olsen, "Managing Consultants on the Job," *Public Management* 63 (April 1981): 13.

8 Information management

Gathering, analyzing, storing, and distributing information—these activities are at the core of the planning process. That means the collection and manipulation of data are given a high order of priority in planning agencies. "Shooting from the hip" is a luxury the planning agency cannot afford even though circumstances may dictate extemporaneous analysis, especially in public meetings where all questions cannot be anticipated in advance.

In response to the pervasive need for information, some local agencies have organized comprehensive information systems containing useful information that is readily retrievable. Lane County, Oregon; Cincinnati, Ohio; Fairfax County, Virginia; and Orange County, North Carolina, are examples. The information they provide to decision makers is formatted for the greatest utility with a sustained flow of information to monitor trends, refine forecasts, and help justify program priorities. These four information systems, plus other examples of information management in local government, are described and illustrated in subsequent sections of this chapter.

Planning agencies can draw on the extensive technology now available for efficient and low-cost storage and retrieval.

The first such aid is word processing, which permits large-scale storage and retrieval and easy editing, heretofore unavailable with standard typewriters.

Second is the computer, which facilitates the storage and retrieval of large quantities of information with software programs to reduce the drudgery of data manipulation. Hardware developments of the early 1980s allow the planner for the first time to easily access and control complex planning information.

Finally, cable television has opened up opportunities for communication to virtually all citizens heretofore unable or unwilling to attend meetings or acquire copies of reports.

The information framework

The purpose of gathering, organizing, and analyzing information for the management of planning is to provide data that will help achieve objectives. The planning department budget is one of the primary ways of defining such objectives and determining the department's—and therefore the staff's—daily activities.

For many years, the approach to departmental budgeting was to list line items and estimate the expenditures required for each item. The total budget was an accumulation of all these items. However, the line-item budget does not describe what the department plans to achieve and does not say why the listed mix of expenditures will achieve departmental goals.

To remedy this situation, the program budget starts with departmental goals and allocates expenditures to each of several programs directed toward those goals. The result is a budget that forces the planning director, the chief administrator, and elected officials to look at objectives and programs as they approve, modify, or disapprove budget items. But the program budget requires sustained management commitment and the willingness of city council and county board members to work with ideas and programs as well as the details of pay rates and projects. Without this commitment, the program budget will work no better than the line-item budget. The reasons are that

1. Whole programs must be accepted or rejected unless elected officials are sufficiently familiar with the program to restructure it.
2. It is difficult to sort out in sufficient detail programs that are consistent with goals. Interdepartmental and intradepartmental goal overlap is common.
3. Because budget items must be quantified, it is difficult to introduce qualitative, judgmental factors into the budget evaluation process.[1]

Nevertheless, the departmental program budget provides far more information with which to evaluate funding requests, identify objectives, and monitor achievements than the line-item budget. When program budgets are extended by four or five years and are interrelated to other departmental budgets, they become a major part of the strategic plan.

As part of the budgeting process, planning departments need to describe their missions, services to be performed to achieve those missions, and the costs of doing so. Linked to these costs are the sources of anticipated revenues. Although these management tools are identified and prepared separately, they are closely interrelated—that is, the funding constraint is not divorced from, or considered separately from, the planning department missions. Likewise, the depth and breadth of programs reflect not only the department's missions but also the funding that is likely to be available.

Mission statements

The mission statement describes the purposes of the planning department. It is comparable to a justification for creating and sustaining the department as a part of the local government. Therefore, the mission statement is unlikely to

Figure 8–1   Qualification versus quantification for the planning agency.

change from one year to the next. It could change, however, if new programs were added or removed from its responsibilities. For example, if the building inspection division were shifted out of the planning department, the mission statement of the planning department would eliminate reference to the missions of the building inspection division. In like manner, if a mission were added, such as administration of the Community Development Block Grant fund, its purposes would be described among those of the department's.

Accumulation of the mission statements of all governmental agencies represents a description of all the services the local government provides. They might be published in an annual report that describes for citizens and other interested persons the purposes and functions of the local government.

The city of Alexandria, Virginia, prepares an annual report—its subtitle in 1983 was *Analysis of City Conditions and Government Trends.* Unlike communities that do not widely distribute their annual reports or others that publish mundane summaries, Alexandria uses its report to broaden and deepen the dialogue on community development issues. Discussions and quantifications of each major service provided by the city are organized under topics such as "Events During the Past Year," and "Trends and Issues." This highly readable description of what each department does and how it has been doing is prepared by the planning department.

The goals of the Charlottesville, Virginia, planning department listed in Figure 8–2 illustrate the content of a mission statement. Note that it is divided into two parts: an overall goal and twelve "ongoing" goals. The overall goal might be considered for adoption as the goal for the city government as a whole. The ongoing goals range from planning to implementation, include funding from all levels of government, and embrace physical, social, and economic planning.[2]

Figure 8–2 Planning department goals, Charlottesville, Virginia.

Overall goal

To assist in the improvement of the quality of life and the environment, and to facilitate equitable access to opportunities within the City of Charlottesville through comprehensive, physical, social and economic planning and action.

On-going goals

1. To develop and maintain a comprehensive plan for the City of Charlottesville which will contribute towards reaching the overall goal and provide policy directions for community revitalization, maintenance, and growth.
2. To encourage community participation in the planning and decision-making process.
3. To provide planning and decision-making assistance to the City Council, City Manager, Planning Commission, Social Development Commission, Task Forces, City Departments, public, quasi-public, and private agencies, and groups and individuals.
4. To assist and regulate private and public physical development through zoning, subdivision and site plan review, and other relevant legal mechanisms.
5. To assist in economic development opportunities in the community.
6. To assist in the provision of housing opportunities and maintenance of integrity of residential neighborhoods.
7. To conduct social service needs assessments, to assist in needed program development, and effective delivery of social service programs.
8. To plan and assist in the development of a balanced transportation system.
9. To assist in the receiving and coordination of federal, state, local, and private grants and programs to meet community needs.
10. To plan for needed community facilities and services in harmony with the natural, man-made, and social/cultural environment of the community; to include capital programming and budgeting service programs.
11. To assist in the evaluation and monitoring of the impact of programs and proposals for economical, effective, and coordinated delivery of needed services.
12. To implement assigned community development activities.

Objectives

The next step, after the mission statement has been prepared, is to compile a list of one-year and five-year objectives that can be used to establish a framework for the annual budget and the departmental strategic plan. The list of objectives is more specific than the mission statement and is more likely to vary from year to year. Five guidelines for formulating objectives are recommended:

1. An objective should be consistent with authoritative goals, such as charter provisions, legislation, legislative policy, and administrative regulations.
2. An objective should be stated in behavioral terms as a guide for action. That is, it should clearly describe the desired and observable results.
3. An objective should have intermediate targets and a specific completion date—in terms of budget year or other time schedule.
4. An objective should include specific performance criteria, such as number, percent, location, number of persons, or cost.
5. An objective should be both challenging and attainable. No purpose is served by including objectives which are likely to be unattainable.[3]

Because objectives are oriented toward local government needs, they are usually formulated on the basis of signals from elected officials, instructions from the planning director or chief administrative officer, and ideas from staff. At this time, it is important to resolve any conflicts with the objectives of other departments. For example, it would be inappropriate and difficult to justify having both the planning department and recreation department prepare comprehensive county recreation plans. Such a conflict should be ironed out before the budget is submitted.

Time and money

Work planning, control, and measurement in local government are largely based on time and money. There are, of course, other variables; among the best known are purchases of automobiles and other capital items and payments for rented space, utilities, and other outside services. With personnel costs (wages, salaries, and fringe benefits) making up two-thirds or more of the operating budget, however, the most important indicators are time and the money to pay for it.

Personnel time and costs therefore are the major input to departmental budgeting. Time sheets should be designed so that an individual working on each of several projects (separate accounting codes) during the course of the day can record the time devoted to each account. Hours and dollars are the units of measurement for each task. A minimum amount of time, such as 0.5 hour, should be the base for time breakdowns. If an eight-hour day is the norm, each day's eight hours should be accounted for. Even if the finance or personnel department does not require time sheets at this level of detail, the planning director should require them. The resulting data can be organized to indicate what the staff did during the preceding year, to justify increasing or decreasing the level of effort recommended for future tasks, and to provide a base for evaluating employee performance.

Multiyear planning links today's work with tomorrow's targets. Today's information collection process can be amended to accommodate tomorrow's research information needs. For example, if a land use survey were to be conducted in 1985, it could be revised to include building condition data for the housing study that will not be done until 1986. Similarly, if tomorrow's staff funding levels are two persons fewer than today's, positions vacated in the interim could remain unfilled and thereby allow the department to stay within personnel and budget constraints. At a minimum, the planning department programs should be described for three years even if such programming is not required by the

The communication revolution The astonishing developments in television, lasers, video cassette recorders, stereophonic sound, and digital transmission of information have led many to talk about the "information revolution." And indeed it is a revolution. Many predict that the long-term impact of the computer will be as great—from a historical perspective—as the invention of the printing press.

Equally significant, although not nearly so well known, are the developments in communication as a critical variable in political science, sociology, psychology, linguistics, economics, mathematics, engineering, and even the fine arts. Communication has become one of the tools to explain phenomena, including human behavior, cultural patterns, myths, symbols, political decisions, crime patterns, power, and patterns in seemingly unrelated events.

The communications revolution therefore is several revolutions: televised election campaigns; computer analyses of jury panels; computer models for weather forecasting; high-capacity, high-speed indexing and abstracting systems; language translation; analysis of interpersonal perceptions; and targeted advertising. These are phenomena of the last half of the twentieth century.

Communication is a subject searching for boundaries, but the most significant part of the quest is likely to be the simple idea that the computer, with its hardware and software, can change the sequence of its operations through a circular process, evaluate the data, and change, adjust, or modify the process on the basis of the feedback. To that extent, the computer can "think." Much is made of the enormous capacity and high speed of computers, but the revolution for both information and communication lies in the programmed ability to evaluate, modify, check, and reevaluate both the information and the process of analyzing the information.

Sources: Based in part on *The New Encyclopaedia Britannica*, 15th ed., Macropaedia, vol. 3: 1005; and Colin Cherry, *On Human Communication: A Review, a Survey, and a Criticism*, 2d ed. (Cambridge, Mass.: MIT Press, 1966), 52–62.

---

community's budget process. On the other hand, a five-year program is probably the limit for estimating.

Multiyear planning department programming has been used in Eugene, Oregon, to integrate the research program and to provide for a more orderly decrease in the number of personnel. Meanwhile, the Louisville and Jefferson County (Kentucky) Planning Commission assigns priorities to a "menu" of projects requiring departmental participation. First-priority projects are intended to be implemented during the next budget year.

Planning department revenues are more difficult to predict than expenditures, particularly because of fluctuations in grants, local support, and development permission fees. Alternative budgets offer one way of dealing with uncertainty. For example, it might be assumed that no grants will be received, or that selected grants, for which there has been implied state or federal approval, will be received and expended.

In order to increase the likelihood that development permission fee revenue will keep pace with need, Fairfield, California, has indexed its fee structure to the consumer price index. This ensures that the typically negative effects of inflation will be controlled for this portion of the budget.

Time wasters The need to husband time is the central issue wherever project completion dates and other work schedules have not been met. Unrealistic time estimates for accomplishing work, failing to establish deadlines, fighting extemporaneous fires, leaving tasks unfinished, shifting priorities, and not establishing a daily plan of priorities can all cost the planner valuable time. Because of these and many other time wasters, it costs more money to accomplish the same amount of work.

Time is a resource that cannot be stockpiled. Staff members who find they are guilty of wasting time should make a record of how they actually use their time. A format for doing so is shown in Figure 8–3. It organizes time usage by activities and shows who imposed the assignment, the results obtained, and whether the activity could be delegated. By systematically recording the use of time, the individual can pinpoint potential time savings. Following this exercise, the staff should share their experiences and discuss ways of reducing wasted time.

Time management   The most worrisome problem for the planning manager is how to control the use of his or her time and that of the staff. The departmental budget should include both the person-day projections and the starting and completion dates for each major assignment. The implied commitment is not varied unless such a change is authorized by the planning director. The estimated starting and completion dates may be based on staff and consultant time records from earlier years and the planning director's experience.

Experienced schedulers always assume that "if something can go wrong, it will." The larger the project and the further away the deadline, the more gen-

Time analysis form

Day of the week: _____   Date: _____

Record each task during the working day by type (Management or Vocational/technical), who assigned the task, results, and whether the task could have been delegated.

Type of task		Who assigned the task?					Results	Could task have been delegated?
MGT	VOC	BOSS	SYS	SUB	SELF	OUT		YES NO If no, why not?

MGT – Management   SUB – Subordinate
VOC – Vocational (Technical)   SELF – Yourself
BOSS – Boss (Planning Director)   OUT – Person(s) outside
SYS – Supervisor   the office

Figure 8–3 Time analysis form.

erous the ratio for "downtime" should be. Inexperienced work planners and schedulers tend to overlook the inevitable "downtime" that accompanies all local government activities. In a well-run agency, such time is essential for work planning, review, and evaluation. Examples of essential downtime activities that are often overlooked include reports—outline, first draft, subsequent drafts, and final draft—more meetings than anticipated, vacations and sick leave, and changes in short-term priorities that have been mandated by the chief administrator, the city council, or the county board.

Additional time is needed even after a project has been completed and the report draft has been written by the technical staff and approved by the planning director. If the report consists of, say, 80 typewritten pages and a dozen photos and pieces of line art, a minimum of 8 to 10 working days will be needed to produce 100 to 200 neat-looking, spiral-bound copies.

Time is available at a constant rate. It is neither scarce nor plentiful. It's just there, and when it is gone, it is gone. Time can only be controlled when its use is planned. This will not be done until you make a psychological commitment to manage time. This sounds intimidating, but it can be your strongest resource. on your time and plan your work around the time demands that cannot—really cannot—be changed. The following steps may be helpful.

First, tell your co-workers that you are taking steps to make better use of your time, that it will take three or four months, and that you will need their cooperation. This has two immediate benefits: (1) it commits you to action, and (2) it enlists co-workers in the effort.

Second, keep a record of what you do with your time. Start out with records for four weeks in thirty-minute units. Keep such records in real time, continuously; do not try to put the record together at the end of the working day.

Third, review the record at the end of four weeks but not before. Four weeks is needed to get a broad enough picture to cover most activities. Look first for the nonessentials; then look at other tasks to see if they can be grouped or assigned to others. Look for other changes that can be made.

Fourth, plan your time. This means looking at the small as well as the large activities and being realistic about the time that major activities may take. (This point was mentioned above in the discussion of "downtime.") Detailed planning of time does not work for professional and managerial employees. Plan instead by blocks of time—one hour, two hours, or even half days. Be sure to protect the personal time of yourself and your family. Do not include time outside office hours except for activities that cannot be changed; planning commission meetings are an example of unavoidable outside time for many planners. Also, be sure to protect your "do-not-disturb" time for problem solving and (what else!) work planning.

At the end of four weeks, review the work accomplished and not accomplished, revise time estimates as necessary, and continue for another four weeks. At the end of three or four months, you should have a detailed record of what goes on that will enable you to build time management permanently into your work habits.

Quantifying program activities   An example of useful data for preparing the planning department's program budget is the number of person days required to complete detailed tasks. The Thurston Regional Planning Council (TRPC) of Thurston County (Olympia), Washington, maintains such records for budgeting purposes. For example, the current planning services component of the planning staff includes twelve separate services to which time is assigned (see Table 8–1). In addition, records are kept of each of five types of meetings that are regularly attended by current planning services staff members. By main-

Table 8–1 Current planning program monitoring, Thurston County, Washington, 1979–1981, showing number of planning services provided and number of meetings attended.

Activity	1979	1980	1981
Current planning services			
Rezones	9	3	4
Site plan reviews	8	9	31
Subdivisions			
Preliminary	39	17	15
Final	25	29	19
Extensions	3	5	9
Short plats	337	208	134
Administrative appeals	2	7	16
Limited use permits	4	5	15
Nonplatted streets	9	40	78
Shoreline permits	31	27	25
Variances	9	9	8
Conditional use permits	18	15	26
Environmental impact statements			
Negative declarations	142	140	156
Full statements	21	8	4
Project plans	N/A	1,311[1]	1,578
Presubmission conferences	120	89	150
Open space/timber land designation	. . .[2]	16	22
License applications (junk, second hand)	. . .[2]	16	16
Home occupation	N/A	2	18
Mobile home parks	N/A	5	32
Planned residential development (9/80)	N/A	1	1
Total	666	1,962	2,357
Meetings			
Planning commission regular meetings, hearings and study sessions	4/mo.	2/mo.	2/mo.
Field trips	2/mo.	1	1
County commission	weekly	weekly	weekly
Special hearings	3	10	10
Hearings examiner	2/mo.[3]	2/mo.	2/mo.

Source: Thurston Regional Planning Council, *Annual Report '81* (Olympia, Wash.: Thurston Regional Planning Council, 1982), 9.

1 Initiated May 1980, extrapolated to obtain annualized numbers.
2 Not tabulated.
3 Hearings examiner began hearings November 1979.

descriptions of work that was accomplished. These same categories and quantities are then used for the budget process in subsequent years. Alterations in the planning program can be accounted for by changes in any of the line items.

The format for the TRPC shows line items of comparable detail for describing work in the next budget year. The descriptors are both person days and costs. The person days are further broken down by seven staff-member categories. Costs are broken down by two categories: personnel and nonpersonnel, as indicated in Figure 8–4. These allocations illustrate the precision required of the departmental budget-making process.

Management indicators

The term *management indicators* is used here to cover management efforts to control time, set work targets, estimate staffing levels, and measure employee performance in specific ways, and to produce periodic program and performance reports for management evaluation and the recasting of work.

THURSTON COUNTY — PROPOSED 1982 PLANNING WORK PROGRAM

Program	DIRECTOR	SENIOR	ASSOCIATE	ASSISTANT	PLANNING AIDE	GRAPHICS	SECRETARIAL	PERSONNEL	NON-PERSONNEL	TOTAL
I. ADVANCE PLANNING										
A. Comprehensive Planning Services		10	16				5	4,054	542	4,596
B. Floodplain Regulations			12				3	1,767	236	2,003
C. Industrial Siting Policies and Service Options			45				9	7,290	973	8,263
D. Agriculture Committee			6				1	955	128	1,083
E. Yelm/Rainier Sub-Area (partial funding)			56			15	12	12,624	1,685	14,309
								26,690	3,564	30,254
II. CURRENT PLANNING – MANDATED PROGRAMS										
A. Continuing Programs										
1. Hearings Examiner Services										
a. Zoning – Subdivision Review		35			8	6	15	9,115	1,230	10,345
b. Variances – Conditional Use Permits		24			12	4	15	7,346	991	8,337
c. Planned Residential Developments		4			1	1	2	1,111	149	1,260
d. Limited Use Permits – Site Plan Reviews		64	22		32	16	25	18,826	2,541	21,367
e. Shoreline Permits		8			16	8	20	8,652	1,168	9,820
f. Administrative Support	5	12			10		6	4,778	645	5,423
g. Environmental Impact Statements – SEPA			84		4		30	14,040	1,895	15,935
h. Administrative Appeals		4			3		4	1,391	187	1,578
i. Mobile Home Parks/Administrative		4			14		6	3,166	427	3,593
2. County Commissioners Services										
a. Appeals of Zoning, Preliminary Subdivisions, Short Plats; Large Lot Plats (Nonplatted Streets)	3	4		6	2		3	1,808	244	2,052
b. Final Plats		10			8	4	3	2,900	391	3,291
c. Administrative, Response to Emerging Programs and Requests		6		4	8		3	3,216	434	3,650
d. Administrative Appeals		2		4	2		1	1,066	143	1,209
3. Planning Department Services										
a. Short Plats		4		16	75		20	12,023	1,623	13,646
b. Large Lot Plats (Nonplatted Streets)		4		6	48		15	7,718	1,041	8,759
c. Project Permits		2		8	52		20	8,434	1,138	9,572
d. Zoning and Subdivision Inquiries/Public Inquiries		8		40	34		40	12,682	1,712	14,394
e. Case and Regulation Monitoring				20			6	2,580	348	2,928
f. Plan Checking for Zoning Conformance				15				1,530	206	1,736
g. Zoning and Subdivision Enforcement		2		48			4	5,256	709	5,965
h. Shoreline Enforcement		12		12			2	1,762	237	1,999
i. Presubmission Conferences				10			4	3,528	488	4,016
III. FIXED NONPERSONNEL COSTS (PRORATED)									29,245	29,245
										210,374

Figure 8–4   Planning work program by person days and costs for the Thurston Regional Planning Council of Thurston County (Olympia), Washington.

Kansas City, Missouri, for example, has adopted a Comprehensive Program Information System (CPIS) to improve productivity: "By comparing information on actual performance with expected levels of achievement, CPIS should strengthen managers' capabilities to identify emerging problems and to initiate timely corrective actions."[4] CPIS measures program performance, targets specific levels of achievement, and reports program results. This process consists of five steps:

1. Program goals, objectives, and performance measures are developed.
2. Numerical targets are set for each performance. Performance target values are set monthly, and the monthly performance reports show this information.
3. Program performance is reported. This is done monthly and annually so that each report is reviewed by all appropriate levels of departmental management.
4. Program performance is reviewed. Quarterly and annually the planning department prepares a narrative analysis of performance that assesses the performance of the department and indicates areas requiring increased interdepartmental coordination.
5. Productivity improvement projects are initiated to cope with problems identified in the monthly performance reports.

The monthly targets for each performance measure are forecasted on an annual basis. The actual experience is recorded every month so that budget analysts can compare the targeted and actual performances.

Additional examples of management indicators are the work load, productivity, and effectiveness measures used by Fairfax County, Virginia, to define departmental programs, estimate staffing requirements, and conduct year-end program performance reviews. Two separate annual estimates are made. The first estimate is published in the county's annual fiscal plan. The second estimate, which is derived from new information, includes comments on the fiscal plan. The measures of effectiveness allow the planning manager to determine if the staff is meeting its target dates and if its technical reviews are consistent with those of the planning commission.

The two most important ingredients of the department budget are the record of past performance and the opinions of policy makers and staff. In all likelihood, past performance will be measured by means of reporting systems superimposed on all departments by the chief administrator. If such systems are not required, or if the planning director feels those that are required are inadequate, additional measures or new formats should be identified and used.

Most managers would agree that there is no "one best way" to manage public service programs—especially those that seem as mysterious as planning. Nor is there any reason to devise and implement complex reporting systems at the expense of providing planning services. Therefore, designers of budget-making and reporting systems should keep in mind that their objective is to manage the provision of service rather than to actually provide the service.

Another way to maintain a proper perspective on the planning program and possible changes is to ask the following questions during the budget-making process:

1. How much staff time is necessary to properly manage this function?
2. How much city council agenda time is necessary for this function?
3. Is it likely to be controversial? How much time and energy will the controversy drain from the city's resources?
4. How risky is it financially? What is the probability of net revenues to the city being produced, and how much?
5. What kinds of decisions are necessary before it could produce net revenues?

6. Can the program or function be an asset to some other group, if not to the city government?
7. Will city government financial risk be lessened by divesting itself of this activity?
8. Is it politically and legally possible to divest the city of this activity?
9. What can the city do to limit the potential future liability of this program?
10. What can the city do to maximize the asset potential of this program?[5]

Some of these questions have an even greater bearing on a planning department's program if the department is responsible for capital expenditure recommendations. To the extent that these issues are important to elected officials, they are good tests to apply during the planning department's budget-making process. They need not be applied in a quantitative way, but can add a broad perspective of what is important to an efficiently managed agency.

Public performance measurement

Goals, objectives, programs, work load, performance measures, effectiveness—with all these factors to consider, the planning director and program manager may well ask, Where do I begin? Most communities that have gone through the goals-planning process have done so systematically: start with goals, follow them with objectives, and proceed with program definitions. The result is general or "flexible" long-range development plans.

Communities more concerned with middle-range planning (say, five or six years compared with fifteen to twenty years) may wish to reverse this approach and start with performance measures and work back to objectives and goals. This bottom-up approach is comparable to the scientific method—the systematic approach of research that helps solve complex problems.[6] Here, the researcher knows enough about the topic or problem to restrict the data gathering to information that is needed to analyze the problem and write the report. Likewise, if the starting point is knowledge of the overall mission of the agency, the next task is to draft bottom-up performance measures rather than top-down goals statements. What is the appropriate time for a local government to set objectives? It has been suggested that

in the governmental environment the specification of objectives—that is, defining precisely where one would like to come out by a specified date in some measurable term—is certainly not appropriate for a first- or second-year cycle of a performance management system. Perhaps the third or fourth year of a working system is the appropriate time to think about setting some specific objectives.[7]

Some would also argue that it is easier to get people to agree on performance measures than on general goals and that the budget process is simplified and shortened so that staff members can get on with the job of delivering services.

Yet, evaluating many of the activities for which a local planning department is responsible is a soft science. Some activities like networking do not translate into quantifiable performance measures. Although the number of telephone calls placed and received and the number of meetings attended can be measured, the qualitative importance of spending time in these ways is the value of the information obtained and shared rather than the number of calls or meetings. The number of products produced by the planning department is another measure of its productivity that does not necessarily reflect quality of staff performance.

Another problem with trying to measure performance is time lag. Often there is a gestation period of several years for even the partial implementation of plans. If planning implementation is a productivity measure, it may be several years before any measurable results are available. Thus, performance measures may indicate whether research has been done but probably cannot point to many concrete results.

It is easier to apply performance measures to planning department activities with short time fuses and to those that are project oriented. Map preparation, rezoning application review, final subdivision plat review, and zoning board of appeals attendance are examples of activities that readily lend themselves to measurement. Four principles of public performance measurements have been identified:

1. Think incrementally by starting with a rudimentary system and improve it based on discussions with other people and on experience.
2. Select performance measures which a decision maker should and can react to. The measure may not be worth using if a decision maker is indifferent to increases or decreases in the measure.
3. Written explanations of qualitative measures are required. Output, timing, frequency, and progress toward milestones should be provided in enough detail to permit the line manager, department head, chief executive, and elected officials to determine the extent to which they are pleased with progress.
4. Provide sufficient data to compare the relationship of targeted services and actual services. Even if target levels of services have not been selected, actual performance data should be collected as a basis for future comparisons.[8]

Among the performance measures used by the Fairfax County, Virginia, planning office are the number of: environmental and physical analyses undertaken, rezoning applications reviewed and evaluated, special exceptions to the zoning ordinance reviewed and evaluated, proposed street vacations, site plans, cases of litigation, public inquiries, meetings, and training sessions and conferences. This information, to the extent it is available, is provided for the preceding year, the current year, and the next fiscal year as part of the annual budget process.

Data criteria and applications

Information needs of the planning office are centered on data. Beginning in the 1950s, planners and social researchers began to experiment with mathematical models that interrelated social, economic, and physical data to measure and forecast demand for transportation modes and facilities. Because of the large number of variables, vast quantities of data were required to solve the equations and to quantify answers that could be translated into transportation projects. The only practical way to organize, process, and retrieve these data was to use computers. Thus was born the linkage between the planning process and automatic data processing.

In nearly all instances, federal funding was required to support complex transportation planning efforts. By 1962 metropolitan areawide transportation planning was mandated by the Federal Highway Administration, which made funding available for that work. As a result, mathematical interrelationships among variables and indexes for recreation, housing, and other functional planning activities soon were developed.

Without direct experience with the collection and manipulation of large quantities of data, it is impossible for the human mind to understand the data inputs, and the ways that manipulations of the inputs can affect the outputs. Transportation and other planning agencies embarked on computer-dependent processes that used huge quantities of data. Both the data and the analytical processes were inexplicable to the layman. Federal grants were available for this work so the fundamental question (Is this analysis worth doing?) was seldom raised. In

Major technological steps in the information age In 1947 the transistor was developed to replace the vacuum tube, providing a miniaturized electronic switch.

In 1959 the integrated circuit was discovered—essentially a superminiaturization of the transistor that could put many "gates" (chip switches) on a silicon chip.

In 1971, it became possible to interrelate the switches on an integrated circuit "in accordance with a series of predetermined patterns; it became an "integrated entity" that could handle a wide variety of programmed instructions.

In 1973 the Intel 8080 became the first true "computer on a chip," setting the stage for small, powerful computers.

In 1975 the first microcomputer came on the market—the TRS-80 Radio Shack home computer.

"While it is possible to understand the reasons behind the growth of the microcomputer, it is much more difficult to assimilate, intellectually or emotionally, the rate of change. . . . If one recognizes that each of these technological innovations represents a quantum jump, then it is possible . . . to appreciate the impact of this exponential growth.

"In light of the speed and degree of change . . . it is not surprising that many local government officials and professionals simply feel overwhelmed. Yet the change exists, it is real, and it must be dealt with. Microcomputers and the information age are here. . . . The man or woman who does not keep up will be left behind."

Source: Partly abstracted and partly excerpted from James R. Griesemer, *Microcomputers in Local Government* (Washington, D.C.: International City Management Association, 1983), 7–17.

---

the absence of federal money, local elected officials, planning commissioners, and citizen clients of the planning process would undoubtedly have demanded that agencies fully justify the need for massive quantities of inputs and their value as outputs for the planning process.

The large mathematical models used to forecast transportation demand and other community development behavior introduced a number of problems. The principal ones have been identified as the "seven sins of large-scale models":

1. Hypercomprehensiveness: an overly comprehensive structure
2. Grossness: too coarse results for decision makers
3. Hunger: enormous appetite for data
4. Wrongheadedness: deviation between claimed model behavior and actual equations
5. Complicatedness: the problem of error propagation
6. Mechanicalness: the illusion that machines make for rigor and order
7. Expense: very high costs relative to apparent value.[9]

These results were valuable in defining subsequent models and demonstration projects sponsored by the U.S. Department of Housing and Urban Development and others. The lessons learned from gathering, analyzing, and drawing conclusions from vast amounts of data have shaped planners' responses to elected officials' information needs. Good politicians know the importance of good information. A politician depends on accurate, timely, and understandable information to get elected and to carry out his or her responsibilities. Not without reason, it has been pointed out that "the planner who can skillfully analyze data to generate good information and vital intelligence has a great deal of influence on complex political decisions."[10]

Vital statistics, the record of life events   In a time when the efficient collection, analysis, and dissemination of data are taken for granted, it is hard to realize how recent this development is in the span of history. The significance of health statistics was first recognized in the seventeenth century. Until relatively recently, however, vital statistics had to be culled from church registers and other incomplete and often inaccurate sources. The following paragraphs show that vital statistics were not nationwide in the United States until 1933.

Vital statistics are records of life events such as births, marriages, divorces, migration, sickness, and death, and the numerical analysis of these recorded events in the form of rates and trends. The records may pertain to the smallest village or to a whole state or nation.

In medieval Europe ceremonies such as baptisms, burials, and weddings were ordinarily paid for, and the recording of these payments in the parish church produced a rudimentary register. However, what was recorded was the ceremony rather than the event itself, and the entries were confined to parishioners. . . . The forms were not standard from parish to parish, and the collection and compilation of data for whole regions were not attempted.

In the 16th century, efforts were made to improve the church records. These efforts were generally more successful in Protestant countries. By 1608 the first systematic parish register system was established in Sweden, by 1610 in Quebec, by 1628 in Finland, and by 1646 in Denmark. The purpose and control were still religious, and the recording was confined to ceremonies. Consolidation for whole countries was not attempted until the 18th century in France and the early 19th century in England.

Massachusetts Bay and New Plymouth colonies became the first governments in Christendom to require (1) that the actual events rather than the ceremonies be recorded and (2) that this registration be performed by civil authorities rather than the clergy. This important step of secularizing the recording of vital statistics was continued once the United States became independent. The process of settling the continent hindered the establishment of a complete registration. The federal government did not begin collecting death statistics until the "Death Registration Area," comprising ten states, the District of Columbia, and a few cities, was constituted in 1900. The area was gradually expanded until in 1933 it embraced the whole nation. A "Birth Registration Area" with ten states was set up in 1915 and included the whole nation by 1932.

Source: Excerpted, except for the first paragraph, from *The Encyclopedia Americana,* international edition (1979), vol. 28:181–82.

With reliable data, planners are able to forecast the likely consequences of alternative courses of action before elected officials vote on those alternatives. It is important therefore that planners minimize the mystery, complexity, and verbosity of their analytical methods and techniques.

Data criteria

Most successful local elected officials have high standards for the information they need and use. It should be focused, accurate, and timely.

Focused data are those that address only the issues upon which a decision turns and only the realistic alternatives to be considered.

Accurate data are those that are 95 percent, or more, accurate for the circumstances at hand. The planner must make the decision not to incur the additional time and expense to make marginal improvements.

Timely data provide the information in time to be useful for decision making. Late reports, regardless of their thoroughness and quality, are virtually useless in the decision-making process.

Local elected officials, the business community, and citizens are increasingly aware of the need to evaluate their community in terms of the following types of questions:

1. What is the supply of improved land?
2. How long will it take for the supply of improved land to be absorbed by each major land use?
3. What capital improvements are required to improve land so it will be competitive for development?
4. What capital improvement projects are required to improve or replace existing services and infrastructure?
5. What is the five-year forecast of the land-based locally raised revenue?
6. What are the distribution and timing of development within the community?

Much of the data required to answer these and other community development questions can be obtained from other departments or agencies. It is a matter of extracting and compiling the data in a systematic manner so that information can be regularly reported to elected and appointed officials.

Most communities cannot afford the luxury of making a capital investment mistake, and therefore cannot depend solely on intuition for community development decisions. When these decisions are too complex or involve considerable

Figure 8–5   A decision is no better than its information base.

Figure 8–6   Hunch, intuition, and
trial and error are not the best ways
to get information for decisions.

costs, then focused, accurate, and timely information becomes a prerequisite to
sound decisions.

If this information is lacking, planning department research too often is forced
to "reinvent the wheel" each time an important analysis is undertaken. Often
data available do not seem to fit the parameters of the specific issue, for instance,
in units measured, geographic coverage, time period, or validity (level of confidence). A number of problems can arise:

1.   The proportion of research funds required for data collection and analysis
     may become too high—over 25 percent.
2.   Elected and appointed officials, business persons, citizens, and others
     reading each successive report may become more confused by apparent
     discrepancies in the data.
3.   Data analysts may arrive at different conclusions, depending on the data
     available to them.
4.   The credibility of the reports and the planning department may be
     eroded.

As the level of detail in such studies increases, the accuracy and quantity of
data involved also increases. Development permission data are most frequently
needed at the land parcel level. It is at this level—a lowest common denominator—that data bases are built.

Four examples

Highlights of four data bases developed for planning and other local government uses are described below. The Lane County (Eugene), Oregon, geoprocessing and geographic data system was established to help staff researchers obtain data needed for advising city and county elected officials and planning commissioners. The city of Cincinnati, Ohio, conceived the Planning and Management Support System (PAMSS) in 1972 to report on the status of all current planning projects and to help define the planning commission's work program. Fairfax County, Virginia, established the Urban Development Information System (UDIS) to support its development management system conceived in the early 1970s. Orange County (Hillsborough), North Carolina, established a central land records system in 1979 to maintain current information on land ownership and values. Each of these systems was started for a different purpose, but each was intended to provide useful data in a timely manner to decision makers and citizens.

Lane County, Oregon   The Lane County Geographic Data System was built from tax maps of the Eugene-Springfield metropolitan area. The computerized representation of the 750 maps took five person years of work and resulted in a parcel file containing records for each of approximately 60,000 tax lots. Incremental additions to this data base have been made ever since the system was introduced in 1972. Data that are maintained and updated include

Streets	Street number
Sewerage	Street name and type
Soil types	Mailing city
Real property assessments	Tax map and lot number
Parcel size	Census tract
Land use	Zip code
Ownership	Storm draining system
Structures	Fire department routes

This system can group parcels or buildings into subdistricts, generate reports, produce maps at any scale, aggregate selected information by any geographic subarea, access on line more than 425 computer terminals in the Lane County Regional Information System (RIS) network, and perform basic computations.

Administratively, Lane County is responsible for the geoprocessing and geographic data system. The system has been conceived, developed, and incrementally increased as its usefulness has gained political support. It has been found that "the use of shared data base encourages the development of strong horizontal communications between staff members who interact with the data. This horizontal communications network facilitates cooperation between departments, agencies, and the public and private sector."[11]

Lane and Benton counties, the cities of Eugene and Springfield, the University of Oregon, and the U.S. Bureau of Land Management contribute data to the system. These organizations, along with five title insurance companies, use data in the system. Public access is provided.

The Lane Council of Governments runs the system under a cooperative project agreement. A high level of computer programming knowledge is not necessary to use the system (that is, it is "user friendly"); many on-line terminals are available; and the system can store ample information. As for its other features,

the primary computing capability is based on an IBM system 370/3033 operating under the MVS operating system, with ten billion bytes of online storage.

Three general-purpose minicomputers, several special-purpose microcomputers, optical character readers, and approximately 425 terminals are connected to the RIS system. These terminals allow diverse users in many locations to utilize the computer system and access the geographic data base. Additional equipment facilitating the display and use of geographic data includes a drum plotter for creation of three-color maps and several interactive graphics terminals and tablets.[12]

Summaries of data are published quarterly to keep elected and appointed officials and staff members informed of development changes. Ready access to the data increases its visibility and widespread availability. This increases the likelihood that policy makers will depend on the data.

Cincinnati, Ohio In 1972 the city planning staff proposed a Planning Guidance System to report on planning and implementation activities. Later it became known as the Planning and Management Support System (PAMSS), one of the four sections constituting the Cincinnati Planning Commission. The PAMSS office consists of library services, data services, and applied research. The various types of information in the system are kept current.

The library services component includes a document library, vertical files, a project monitoring system, and a slide library. The library's documents are classified by geographic scope and subject. Loose-leaf information consisting of newspaper clippings, newsletters, annual reports, city ordinances, and other materials are stored in vertical files.

The project monitoring system provides current information on the status of active projects, their description, funding, and phase. This information is displayed on a series of 42 × 48-inch functional matrices. Project locations are shown on maps. More than 12,000 slides have been catalogued. The office's monthly newsletter, *Information Update*, highlights information acquired and provides articles of current interest.

The data services component collects, maintains, and disseminates federal, state, and local statistical data. They are stored in the department's main computer and retrieved through the PAMSS computer terminal. The data can be retrieved by various geographic areas, starting at the address level for some data. Data can also be retrieved for special geographic areas by means of the Statistical Package for the Social Sciences. Information on city-owned land is available through the City-Owned Real Estate System.

By integrating the data available on a specific topic or project with the library services and data services components of PAMSS, the applied research staff can compile new data configurations, identify prospective sources, and conduct research on its own. Research agreements are negotiated with government agencies and other groups that are comparable to those reached by planning consultants and their clients.

PAMSS services are available to elected officials, developers, city departments, citizen groups, private organizations, and individuals. Most of the services are free, but a cost recovery fee may be imposed for complex or specialized computer analysis.

The planning director manages the system since the planning department uses most of the information. The department also is responsible for preparing plans and assisting other city departments in plan preparation. The more that staff members become familiar with the system, the greater its utility because they can readily identify and quickly retrieve the pertinent information. Departmental contributions to PAMSS also increase its utility and broaden the base of information available.

Fairfax County, Virginia The Fairfax County Office of Research and Statistics (ORS) operates the county's central processing unit. Many computer systems have been developed and are maintained by ORS. The life of each system varies, depending on its scope and complexity, but on the average it is seven to eight years. The county has a five-stage development process for each system:

1. A feasibility study to identify the need and cost of a proposed system or to evaluate an existing system that is more than seven years old.
2. Definition of what function the system should perform and its scope.
3. Preparation of the logical and physical design, program specifications, input and output formats, and writing or coding programs to make the system operational.
4. Monitoring of the system to ensure that it meets specifications, satisfies user requirements, and accommodates changes.
5. Evaluation of design criteria, documented operation, or user problems during the second year of operation.

Six examples of computer system inputs by the county's planning department or outputs frequently used by the planning department are highlighted below:

1. Urban Development Information System (UDIS). Includes housing, population, building permit, nonresidential structure size, existing land use, and proposed land use data. These data are used to prepare one-year forecasts of the type, location, and amount of development. This information is used as a basis for forecasting solid waste collection, police protection, fire protection, and other services.
2. Rezoning Application System (RAPS). Provides information to monitor rezoning applications.
3. Plan and Agreement Monitoring System (PAMS). Identifies plan development by address, public improvement inspections and violations, and county development bond and other agreements.
4. Inspection Services Information System (ISIS). Maintains information about the building, electrical, mechanical, plumbing, and small appliance permits issued by the county. Monitors the permit application review process and payment of permit fees.
5. The Real Estate Computer-Assisted Appraisal System (CAA). Provides three independent estimates of value for all residential property.
6. The Public Works Sewer Application Tracking System (PUBSAT). Monitors sewer authorizations to track potential sewer flow. Tracking the authorized use of sewer capacity from the issuance of a building permit to the actual generation of sewer flow helps in forecasting when sewerage treatment capacity may be exceeded. This system also records payments made for sewer connections and related charges.

The evolution of information requirements has made the need for computer systems plans just as obvious as the need for land use plans. The ORS computer systems plan has the following objectives:

1. To provide staff resources to maintain existing computer systems at optimum levels.
2. To provide staff resources to continue the development of new systems approved and initiated in prior years.
3. To improve outdated computer systems to a better level of efficiency so as to minimize maintenance requirements and improve system reliability.
4. To perform only those systems enhancements which are cost justified through analysis of qualitative and quantitative benefits.[13]

An example of a computer system improvement request for the Office of Comprehensive Planning is shown in Figure 8–7.

Orange County, North Carolina Begun as a demonstration project funded by the U.S. Department of Housing and Urban Development (HUD), the Orange County Land Records System maintains current parcel location, size, ownership,

Figure 8–7 Computer system improvement request, Office of Comprehensive Planning, Fairfax County, Virginia. This process has been organized for long-range, systematic planning. The stub shows the steps to be undertaken by the county government from system evaluation to contract management, and other essential steps are shown for outside suppliers and contractors. The "Description" shows the planning information requirements that will be handled.

Computer system step	Project Estimate	FY1982 and prior years	FY1983	FY1984	FY1985	FY1986	FY1987
County							
System evaluation							
Feasibility study							
Requirements definition							
System/program design	$ 5,022		$ 5,022				
Programming/program construction	17,333		17,333				
Contract management							
Outside							
System evaluation							
Feasibility study							
Requirements definition							
System/program design							
Programming/program construction							
Hardware/software costs							
Total project	$22,355		$22,355				

Description: The Office of Comprehensive Planning (OCP) is requesting that the Rezoning Application System (RAPS)--the first of the three development process-related systems-- be enhanced to be a totally on-line computer system. (On-line meaning the ability to inquire and/or update computer records by means of a computer cathode-ray tube terminal located at the users work location.) At present, RAPS uses a batch (computer card) update procedure with an on-line inquiry procedure. Also, OCP is asking that information relating to Special Exceptions, Special Use Permits, and Variances be contained on, monitored, and reported through RAPS. It is estimated that this enhancement will save 2,017 staff hours. This effort will allow OCP to update data on RAPS more easily and will help OCP with their present procedures relating to Special Exceptions, Special Use Permits, and Variances.

sales, value, and building permit data. The 1977 North Carolina General Assembly authorized the use of unique numbers as parcel identifiers for an official county indexing system, established a land records management program, and authorized state grants-in-aid to counties to improve their land records systems. HUD funding of model systems was based on the 1974 Federal Real Estate Settlement Procedures Act. Orange County's objective was to "facilitate, simplify, and reduce the cost of processing, storing and retrieving land records."[14] The project also was intended to provide current land-based information supplied by planning and inspection offices.

The computerized master file indexing system permits rapid inquiries into the files of the clerk of superior court, register of deeds, tax supervisor, and tax collector. Representatives of each of those offices assisted in the design and testing of the system before its was put into use.

The land record system is stored on a minicomputer with a capacity of 254 million numbers or letters. Up to thirty-two terminals or printers can be connected with the computer. In particular, the county is pleased with the following features:

1. It provides much information to both officials and citizens in a fraction of the time previously required.
2. It eliminates the need for costly special staff commitments of time in the tax office to update their files and maps on a yearly basis.
3. It makes the tax office better able to reappraise property for assessment purposes without hiring an outside contractor.
4. Data from the transfer of property that used to be entered in five different offices by five different staff members are now entered by one staff member at one location.
5. The system's on-line terminal information-retrieval capability eliminates the need for repeated printouts of updated indexing data, thus saving 400 pounds of paper each month.[15]

Computer criteria

Planners have been among the most ardent advocates of collecting, organizing, analyzing, storing, and retrieving data. The planning process has been the conduit for funding these activities. Had the computer revolution begun with the personal microcomputer, with its "user-friendly" language, most planners would have been computer literate years ago. The same can be said of other local government staff members responsible for quantitative analysis. The computer industry started, however, with very large mainframe machines capable of storing, manipulating, and retrieving vast quantities of data. This hardware had to be operated and managed by specialists, and local government department heads specializing in their own professional fields had little time for and interest in pursuing computer careers.

Before the 1980s, planning relied on computer technology almost exclusively for processing very large quantities of data that lent themselves to quantification by mathematical models. Most early uses were limited to metropolitan transportation analyses.

In more recent years inexpensive hardware and simple programming languages have vastly broadened the prospective applications of computer technology to the planning process. At the same time, more and more local governments are insisting that the use of computer systems be justified in terms of their costs and benefits. The overall result has been a drifting away from central control. Local government computer agency managers no longer control access because of their expert knowledge and hardware proprietorship. Instead, many communities with large central processing units have dispersed access by installing on-line remote terminals that can be operated with limited training.

Decentralization of computers   The movement towards mini- and micro-computers will stem mainly from dissatisfaction with existing centralized computing arrangements. Users complain that computing is dominated by a few big departments, and that the computer staff is unable to satisfy requests for new development because it is overloaded with maintenance of existing systems. There are many other complaints by users. Some claim that department operations are too dependent upon an unresponsive central installation for tasks critical to day-to-day operations. The cost of coordinating one department's development needs and operations with the computing needs of other departments may be viewed as too great. Users may feel that the central computing installation seeks to maintain its monopoly on computer expertise, and that the central installation generally is undemocratic in its relations with users because participation of users is purely instrumental.

Source: John Leslie King and Kenneth L. Kraemer, "Changing Data Processing Organization," *The Bureaucrat* 12 (Summer 1983): 22.

Computer literacy means that the planner must define the output necessary to reduce the drudgery of data storage and manipulation. The planner's second responsibility is to provide some or all of the inputs required to generate the desired output. Planners and other computer users must participate in the formulation of data needs, machine outputs, and the inputs needed to achieve those outputs. Thus, it is important for planners and other staff members in local governments to work with computer system managers and to participate as partners in computer system feasibility, requirements, design, implementation, and maintenance.

Planners who want to explore the use of computers should first learn about the available software and then the hardware required to use it. The software is more important than the hardware and is only now being developed for typical planning applications. Hardware capacity and interactive equipment are already available to meet the needs of most planning agencies. Planners are advised to become familiar with the following areas of computer application if they want to learn more about the evolving computer systems field: professional networking, information dissemination, and the use of appropriate technologies.[16]

Informal discussions should be held by planners familiar with data needs and computer systems specialists familiar with their operations. Together they can address mutual needs and problems, check on available resources, and document the experience of others.

Planning agencies may wish to start with relatively small and inexpensive microcomputers. The rapidly changing technology underscores the importance of starting on a modest scale and, through networking and information dissemination, expanding capacity to fit local needs.

The central processing unit (CPU) interprets instructions and performs arithmetic operations. It not only stores information in the memory but also obtains data and instructions from it. The random-access memory (RAM) sorts instructions and data; its information is stored only while the computer is turned on. The read-only memory (ROM) contains the basic instructions to make a computer operate. Most software is sold on floppy discs, from which the information is transferred to the random-access memory when operations are to be carried out. Hard discs can store data at much greater densities than floppy discs and can transfer information to the random-access memory at higher speeds than floppy discs.

The computer keyboard, which is similar to a typewriter keyboard, is used to put information into the computer. The monitor, a cathode ray tube similar to a television screen, permits the operator to read instructions provided to the computer and to share information with the operator. The modem (modulator/demodulator) allows computers to be linked by telephone to other computers. Two kinds of printers transfer information in the computer to hard copy. The dot matrix printer is faster but the quality of its output may not be suitable for material that is to be shared with people outside the office. The letter quality printer is slower but produces high-quality material that can be readily photo-copied or printed.

Software refers to "the instructions that make the computer open and close its millions of switches in patterns that make sense to perform useful tasks."[17] The operating system, typically a part of the hardware, consists of a set of instructions that tells the hardware how to perform its mechanical tasks such as reading and writing, and receiving and sending information. Task-oriented software is written for specific operating systems. These software "packages" are not interchangeable among different types of hardware.

Once a planning agency's software needs have been identified, they can be compared to standard software available on the market. In many cases, the standard software will have to be modified to meet a given agency's needs. Programming languages enable the user to instruct the computer in a language closer to English than machine language codes understood by the CPU.

Thus, programming language includes a compiler, or interpreter, which translates the programming language into machine code when the program is run. Languages like PASCAL are easy for a person to understand; therefore the language and subsequent modifications are likely to be understood by various users over a long period of time. This feature is particularly helpful in a planning department where several staff members will be using the computer.

In selecting microcomputer software, keep in mind the following factors:

1. It is time-consuming to shop the market. As additional software becomes available, comparison shopping becomes even more complex. Whether seeking word processing, data base and file management, accounting, or electronic spread sheet capacity, each successively more sophisticated product line increases choice and commensurately increases prepurchase analysis time. Time also is required to evaluate software instruction manuals and sort out the sales presentations that emphasize product advantages and ignore limitations.

2. Include staff members who will actually be using the software and hardware in the purchasing decisions. They are the persons most likely to know of procedural and production problems that may arise with new equipment. They are also probably the most apprehensive about job security and their ability to compete with other employees following the introduction of unfamiliar equipment.

3. Do enough background review and first-hand exploration with dealers and computer users to avoid being misled during the extensive evaluation process. The data processing director or computer manager may not cooperate fully in the exploration of microcomputers because of the apparent threat of dispersed, user-friendly systems; may inadvertently mislead planning staff and others by using jargon they are not familiar with; or may fail to explain cost and user trade-offs. A prudent rule: when in doubt, ask.

4. Off-the-shelf software may fail to meet the needs defined for the planning department. Because of copyright protection, software program instructions are typically not available. The department's needs should therefore be as precisely defined as possible to encourage prospective

vendors to try to meet their software needs. Because software instructions and operations are rigorously precise, and because software programs are not prepared with a specific planning department's needs in mind, modification of those programs as the staff gains experience with them is almost always necessary. This will increase the time and cost required to switch from manual to microcomputer manipulation of data.

5. The contract to acquire computer software and hardware should be written in terms of results rather than process. Key features of the contract are to:
   a. Precisely define computer uses before trying out equipment.
   b. Try out equipment before buying it.
   c. Wait until the planning agency needs the equipment before buying it.
   d. Make sure that the hardware is modular, expandable in incremental steps, and compatible with other equipment so the machines can share data, logic, and printing facilities.
   e. When a purchasing decision is imminent, go back and reread computer software periodicals to verify that state-of-the-art equipment is acquired.[18]

Computer system management

Chief administrators, planning directors and other department heads, and other local government managers have a direct stake in information management, particularly with respect to centralization versus decentralization, staff needs, policies and procedures for buying and updating hardware and software, and exploiting the efficiency and economy of microcomputers. The advantages of microcomputers are that they are inexpensive, user-friendly, and small in size and thus can be distributed among offices for decentralized daily use in a wide variety of assignments. Therefore, except in small local governments, their management is likely to be decentralized. Since planning depends so heavily on data, the planning office is likely to find itself in the middle of the computer system management issues.

Computer evaluation

One of the first issues here is what to do with existing computer capacity. Because the technological life span of a computer is less than seven years and demands on the system are continually changing, the first step is to evaluate the existing system. The committee approach to this evaluation is highly desirable because it brings together both data users and computer specialists. The evaluation itself will probably have a shelf life no longer than the time for two curves to cross: availability of technically superior software or hardware and availability of money to replace existing equipment.

Microcomputer requirements should be evaluated when any of the following circumstances arise:

1. Budget constraints require fewer people and more productivity to provide the same work outputs.
2. Elected officials need more information about the consequences of prospective decisions.
3. Data that would not otherwise be readily available need to be accessed quickly.
4. There is a need for greater command over the computer than is available by using a mainframe computer managed by other staff.

Milwaukee, Wisconsin, microcomputer purchases are evaluated by a policy board composed of elected officials, department heads, and citizens who are knowledgeable about data processing. Their criteria are:

1. Can the computer do the job the department wants?
2. Is it the right type of equipment?
3. Will the files be sharable or nonsharable?
4. How will the machine interface with others?

Once the equipment is in place, the department using it describes how it is being used and reports to the policy board every three months. Spot audits of installed systems are conducted to determine their cost effectiveness and ensure that compatible equipment is being used.

Computer usage

Once equipment is up and running, questions will come up regarding greater use, accessibility, use of on-line terminals, and the need for peripheral equipment. The answers to these questions and others about in-house development and transfer of computer applications depend on the following kinds of information:

1. The organizational environment of data processing—where data processing is located, how it is organized, mechanisms for user involvement and executive control, and key contact persons, among other things. Such information will enable one agency to judge whether the governmental environment of another agency is sufficiently comparable to engage in exchanges.
2. The computing environment—hardware and software used or available, the capacities of this technology, and so forth. This information will enable an agency to determine whether its computing environment is compatible with that of another agency. It also will assist agencies which provide software (e.g., firms, nonprofit organizations, universities) in making decisions about the various computing environments in which their software must be capable of operating.
3. The applications currently operational, in development, and planned (over the next 2 to 3 years)—description of the application in some detail: unusual features, computer core requirements, on line versus batch operation, and database operation. This information will need to be collected from suppliers of software as well as from government agencies themselves. It will assist functional groups and agencies in understanding the current availability of software, in making decisions to study and evaluate certain applications more carefully, and in developing recommendations for further software development.
4. The operational performance of the application in technical terms, behavioral terms (e.g., how easy to use, how well liked, etc.), and service delivery terms (e.g., assessment of users and, if possible, quantitative assessments of what difference the application actually has made where it has been applied). This is the most difficult area about which information must be collected, and it should not be addressed initially. The information described above can be used to narrow the choice of applications to be given such careful study. The functional interest groups might perform the actual assessments, or special studies might be conducted in operational settings, or both.[19]

Mapping is one of the most common activities of the planning office, and the computer is one of the most useful tools to reduce sharply the time and cost of routine mapping. Many planning departments with in-house drafting and cartographic expertise can exploit computers to translate mapped information through a digitizer into stored geographic information. Because of memory limitations, microcomputers cannot store enough information to prepare complex maps or a great number of them, but the mainframe usually has the capacity to store adequate data for most mapping purposes. Computerized mapping can produce base maps and overlays, maintain an updated set of maps for use by all departments, provide maps at virtually any scale quickly, ensure that all map users have a consistent information base, and reduce updating and correction time. Computer technology also is available to produce both two- and three-dimensional maps.

Computer management and applications

Computers work best when planned and operated as systems of software, hardware, staff, and applications. As with most systems, however, it takes continuing effort to make the components work together in development, operations, evaluation, and revisions. A number of useful observations and recommendations are available from persons who have gone through software selection, hardware selection, staffing, and designing operational programs:

1. The staff, not the technology, will determine the success of the computer program.
2. Get top management commitment to the program and involvement in determining the computer system goals.
3. Aim toward working applications, regardless of their size, early.
4. Implement high visibility applications first.
5. Carefully choose the combination of in-house data base building and contracting out. The first increases control over the product, while the second allows more time for understanding and satisfying programming needs.
6. Pay particular attention to developing good standards early in the project so products are usable soon after implementation.
7. Measure and closely monitor equipment and staff accuracy and productivity.
8. Adjust program objectives, system planning, and measurements of progress to synchronize equipment and staff performance with realistic achievements.
9. Use equipment as fully as possible to increase cost effectiveness. This generally requires extra shifts of personnel.
10. Consider leasing equipment if possible to avoid obsolescence and build in more frequent review and evaluation processes.[20]

Conclusion

The information needs for planning, especially strategic planning, are greater than ever before. The information needed ranges from data on a single parcel of land to the financial resources, economic base, and exogenous variables that impinge on major decisions.

The information framework includes mission statements, operating objectives and work programs, management indicators, and performance measures. Among these elements, the most important for the planning director and planning program managers may be time, money, and staff. The staff are paid to use their time productively to get the job done. Note that the time wasters briefly described in this chapter do not include the items many people would mention such as going to meetings, visiting on the telephone, chatting with visitors about items that are off the agenda, and daydreaming. Important as it is to control these time wasters, it is even more important to manage time—and this means planning and follow-through. The follow-through can be measured easily enough by checking agreed-upon starting and completion dates for tasks and projects.

As for data—the major information element in planning—keep in mind that data should be focused, accurate, and timely. This sounds platitudinous, but careful perusal of newspaper accounts will show how often findings and recommendations at all levels of government fail to meet these three standards.

The last two sections of this chapter deal with the computer: criteria, evaluation, usage, and management. Planners under the age of forty are (or should be!) quite comfortable in this environment. Planners in the second half of their careers probably have some homework to do. The essential elements of hardware, software, and systems can be learned quickly for those who are not at home in the computer environment. In any case, all planners and managers will need to concentrate on the management implications, including user needs and interests, management commitment, and continuous evaluation and revision of processes and systems. It is an assignment that must be taken up if planners and managers are to become or remain competitive and to make use of the available technology.

1   Robert I. McLaren, *Organizational Dilemmas* (New York: John Wiley & Sons, 1982), 84–87.
2   City of Charlottesville, Virginia, "Department of Community Development," Satyendra Singh Huja (1981?), four-page public information statement.
3   Wayne F. Anderson et al., "Managing for Effectiveness, Efficiency, and Economy," in *The Effective Local Government Manager* (Washington, D.C.: International City Management Association, 1983), 84.
4   City of Kansas City, Missouri, *The Comprehensive Program Information System Operations Manual* (1980), 1.
5   Stephen L. Garman, *The Terminal City* (Pensacola, Fla.: City of Pensacola, 1983), 43–44.
6   *Webster's* defines the scientific method as "the systematic pursuit of knowledge involving the recognition and formulation of a problem, the collection of data through observation and experiment, and the formulation and testing of hypotheses."
7   Jacob B. Ukeles, *Doing More with Less: Turning Public Management Around* (New York: AMACOM, 1982), 230–31.
8   Ibid., 234–41.
9   Douglass B. Lee, Jr., "Requiem for Large-scale Models," *Journal of the American Institute of Planners* 39 (May 1973): 163–78.
10 Anthony James Catanese, "Information for Planning," in *The Practice of Local Government Planning*, ed. Frank S. So et al. (Washington, D.C.: International City Management Association, 1979), 111.
11 A. Lee Gilbert, "Data Sharing as Politics: Policy, Tools, and Access," in *Practical Applications of Computers in Government*, ed. Rolf R. Schmitt and Harlan J. Smolin (Washington, D.C.: International

Science and Technology Institute for the Urban and Regional Information Systems Association, 1982), 353.
12 Ibid., 355–56.
13 Fairfax County, Virginia, Office of Research and Statistics, *Computer System Plan: FY 1983–FY 1987* (April 1982), 1.
14 Orange County, North Carolina, *Central Land Records System User's Manual*, prepared by Roscoe E. Reeve and Janet Van Handel (January 1983), computer print-out, 39.
15 Roscoe E. Reeve, "Computering Land Records in Orange County," *Popular Government* (Summer 1981), 49.
16 Robert J. Lima, "Interfaces between Man, Machine, and the 'System,'" in *Practical Applications*, ed. Schmitt and Smolin, 20.
17 Paul Hoover, *Microcomputers: Tools for Local Government*, Management Information Service Reports, vol. 14, no. 10, (Washington, D.C.: International City Management Association, 1982): 4.
18 Robert I. Berkman and Iris Varlack, *Microcomputers: Applications and Tradeoffs of Decentralized Computers*, Product Information Network Advisory Report, 15 November 1982 (New York: McGraw-Hill), 4.
19 John Leslie King and Kenneth L. Kraemer, "Changing Data Processing Organization," *The Bureaucrat* 12 (Summer 1983): 26–27.
20 Randolf A. Gschwind, Richard K. Allen, and William E. Huxhold, "Creating Magic—An Evaluation in Retrospect of the *M*ilwaukee *A*utomated *G*eographic *I*nformation and *C*ardiographic System," in *Practical Applications*, ed. Schmitt and Smolin, 302.

9 Communication management

ICMA's first book on local planning administration was published in 1941.[1] No book before that time had systematically organized information on what local planning was and how to do planning. Most of the information on methods and techniques was exchanged through the small network of practicing planners who communicated with each other and attended national planning conferences. That book and the four successive editions published by ICMA have been landmarks describing what local planning is and how it can be done.

The first comprehensive book on land use planning appeared in 1957,[2] and since then books and reports on methods and techniques have proliferated. Borrowing from sociology, quantitative methods, design, law, and political science, the art and science of planning rapidly grew more sophisticated in the following years.

Over the four decades in which this progress was achieved, a distressing gap opened between the recommendations of planners and policy makers' expectations of planners. Across the board there was inadequate money to rapidly acquire sites and construct proposed projects. Beyond that, implementation—getting policies adopted, land acquired, and projects built—was sidetracked in the laborious process of translating technical plans into policy makers' decisions. Planners, planning, and plans were criticized for being complicated, unintelligible, verbose, technically mysterious and poorly interpreted, theoretical, and lacking political reality.

Many local government managers believe that communication in the local planning process, above all, needs to be improved.[3] Planners, like others in the local political economy, participate in the competition of ideas. Many decisions rest on winning ideas and reasoning—fewer and fewer on who has the most money or knows the "right" people. Local political processes that are open to competing interests and have reasonably accurate data available are a vast market for ideas on how to solve local problems. The degree to which the planning agency's ideas are embraced by local government managers and elected officials may indeed turn on how well they are understood. In most instances, the better articulated and factual ideas are, the better understood and more widely accepted they will be.

Importance of communication to planning

All types of communication are fundamental to planning. The people involved in the development permission phase of the planning process must interpret ordinances, evaluate development proposals, and present recommendations. These activities depend on communication—among staff members, between them and developers, with citizens, and with planning commissioners and elected officials. There are subdivision regulations to be interpreted, memos to be written, maps to be drawn, and media representatives to be responded to.

The comprehensive planning process also requires a full range of communication skills. Unlike the day-to-day responsibilities of the line agencies, communication for comprehensive planning is likely to include conceptual and goal-oriented dialogue that is intended to establish its context among community services and among programs provided by other governments. Long-range planning is, by definition, conjectural. Although many of its quantitative forecasts may be firmly rooted in trends and experiences, its futuristic orientation makes long-range planning harder to predict, explain, and understand. It is much easier to explain the here and now (the subdivision where construction is under way) than the long range (the airport that may or may not be built within the decade). It is hard to *explain* exogenous variables when even the planning staff is not sure which variables are crucial. It is hard to understand why support for a subsidized housing project for low-income people is uncertain when the need is so obvious.

What is communication? Colin Cherry, in his book, *On Human Communication,* uses five and one-half pages to define communication, but the essence for planning and management is captured in the following quotes:

Communication is essentially a social affair.

The very word "communicate" means "share."

Life in the modern world is coming to depend more and more upon "technical" means of communication, telephone and telegraph, radio and printing. Without such technical aids, the modern city-state could not exist one week, for it is only by means of them that trade and business can proceed; that goods and services can be distributed where needed; that railways can run on a schedule; that law and order are maintained; that education is possible. Communication renders true social life practicable, for communication means organization.

Source: Colin Cherry, *On Human Communication: A Review, a Survey, and a Criticism* (Cambridge, Mass.: MIT Press, 1966), 3, 4–5.

The complexity of the planning process makes it imperative for planners to clearly communicate issues and recommendations. Simultaneously representing their perception of the public interest, protecting elected and appointed officials from making unwise decisions, and maintaining political support for the planning program is no easy task. The planner has to walk a tightrope between a simplistic presentation of ideas that misleads and misinforms and a technical presentation that loses the listener or reader. All people communicate in many ways; the problem is to get the message across.

Clients of good communication

Local government planners are key members of the local government communication team. In the continual process of development permission and policy recommendations, planners are frequently called on to communicate with others on the staff and with the public at large. Communication with other departments, planning commissioners, and elected officials constitutes the major part of the planning staff's communication activities. Although less frequent, external communication with citizens, developers, representatives of other governments, and others also is important in terms of cultivating support for the planning program.

Planners must communicate on complex issues more often than representatives of most other local government departments. The reasons are that community development issues are controversial, and planning is a continuing technical-political process in which the dynamics change over time. Unlike other important departments of local governments—such as solid waste collection and disposal, water supply and distribution, and recreation program development and administration—planning for changing communities means continually redefining and negotiating the public interest. Representatives of other departments tend to negotiate the public interest only for specific issues, but the planning process is concerned with issues that involve simultaneous private and public gains and losses. Land use windfalls or wipeouts make for highly charged decision-making processes.

Citizen interchange

Because winners and losers are inherent in the planning process, planners were among the earliest recipients of the wrath of single-interest or special-purpose groups. When it comes to the full range of local government activities, most citizens are generally apathetic, do not vote in local elections, and do not monitor issues affecting them. Most of the time only a small percentage of citizens are actively involved in a given issue, even if it has communitywide implications, because of the complexity of local government activities and the competition for the limited time available to citizens.

On the other hand, citizens do pay attention to the issues of highest priority to them—those most clearly affecting property values and their family. Since it is incumbent upon staff members, including planners, and elected officials to represent the entire community, conflicts between persons representing community interests and those representing single interests are bound to arise. Communication by planners should balance these interests in an evenhanded manner.

Perhaps this is why city and county managers have placed such high importance on improving their communicating and negotiating skills. A 1980 ICMA survey of local government managers indicated that they expected both "human relations" and "brokering and negotiating" skills to become much more significant over the next twenty years.[4]

Broadening and deepening citizen involvement in development issues can help the planning staff better understand the political ramifications of their recommendations and take those ramifications into account in their daily work. Most metropolitan cities have disaggregated their planning staff assignments to cover the neighborhoods. This practice has produced greater two-way communication between planners and citizens with advantages for both. The staff obtains more detailed information on the likely consequences of recommendations and is much more aware of citizen interests, while citizens learn earlier of development proposals affecting them and of the communitywide implications of those proposals.

Other techniques for encouraging greater staff-citizen communication include personal invitations to public meetings, local government open houses at city hall or the planning office, informal questionnaires, clip-out coupons in routine local government mailings and in newspapers, periodic surveys of citizen opinions, and regular mailings of information on planning to a select group of interested citizens.

Goal-setting programs often are used to communicate with citizens about development issues. Some would state that the primary value of such programs lies in the interchange between planning staff and interested citizens, which enables them to gain a better understanding of their respective priorities. Goal setting also enables planners and elected officials to "test the water" for long-range ideas, differentiate between short- and long-term issues, and help people understand and appreciate that goal setting will not bring overnight results.

Communication failures where citizens are involved often rest with what remains unsaid. Issues, resources, and solutions to problems are not obvious to the average citizen. Community development and the planning process are far too complex to be left to implication. Left to their own impressions, the public may create an image of development issues and plan responses on the basis of gossip or rumor. In spite of the burden it places on limited staffs, frequent communication by planners with citizens is a prerequisite to a politically sound planning program.

Elected and appointed officials

One of the difficult tasks for the planner is to contribute adequately to the flow of information to elected and appointed officials. The competition for the attention of these officials should make planners especially aware of officials' individual needs. Consider the number of times the planning staff is sought out for nonroutine information and opinions. This suggests that elected and appointed officials who maintain a dialogue with the staff are genuinely interested in staff contributions that help resolve community development issues. Another test of the planning program may be the extent to which policy makers include planning staff in their communication network.

Communication for planning and management   For the city or county manager to be a translator between the technical and professional on one side and the political on the other, he or she needs usable information from the planner. The guidelines that most managers would recommend to planning directors are the following:

Planning is perceived as complex to persons not trained in it because it deals with interrelatedness and with the unknown future.

Regardless of the technical aspects of community development, it is a political process, frequently with high financial stakes.

Informal networking is at the root of the decision-making process and is complemented by technical analysis—not the other way around.

Do not spend too much time in the office; most factors influencing development decisions are outside the office.

Do not isolate yourself from other planning staff members; cumulatively they have more information at their disposal than you have.

Extend your network to peers in other communities through conferences, seminars, and the telephone.

Avoid mysterious, verbose, and overly complex agenda communications.

Write as if you (rather than the elected officials you serve) had to make the decision.

Do not be afraid to make recommendations; they are expected of professional staff members.

Communicate on time, not after the decision has been made.

Publish agenda items, information on current issues, and availability of products in a general or departmental newsletter.

Maintain an informal network of social contacts for information exchange before issues become controversial.

Provide orientation materials to new planning commissioners and elected officials to "bring them up to speed."

Source: Abstracted from "The Manager As Translator: Getting Better Information from Your Planner," paper presented by David C. Slater at the annual conference of the International City Management Association, Kansas City, Missouri, 12 October 1983.

Planners contribute to the policy makers' flow of information through personal meetings, meeting agenda communications, formal oral and written presentations at public meetings, and oral and written replies to requests for information.

The informal and spontaneous flow of information is often the basis for formal requests for information and the acceptance or rejection of formal communications. Thus, the importance of informal networking by the planning director and selected staff members cannot be overemphasized. This oral communication network will vary from community to community, but one model goes something like this:

1. At every opportunity, establish and maintain dialogue with elected officials.
2. Identify the five best friends of each elected official and establish and maintain dialogue with them. The purpose is to gain access to other information provided to and influencing policy makers.
3. If political parties are important to the nomination and election of local officials, establish and maintain communication with high-ranking local party officials. The planning director can impartially and simultaneously provide information to both parties.
4. Maintain contacts with a broad spectrum of citizens. Sometimes their perspectives on community development issues reflect the public interest more accurately than do those of elected officials.
5. Read the local newspaper and listen to the local media to supplement your personal network.

Sometimes planners reduce their exposure to the flow of information by spending too much time in the office. Those who do most of their planning at the office may be open to the charge that they are out of touch with reality, in other words, that they are insensitive to citizen needs. Although office work is obviously necessary—to maintain management control, ensure the technical quality of written products, and make it easier for the supervisor to account for the planner's time—there are more important reasons not to be chained to the desk. One of these is the face-to-face contact in networking that is a more personal form of communication than the written document or the telephone conversation and is the best way to obtain confidential information and personal opinions.

It is important for the planner to remember that "many citizens see their elected officials as the court of last resort. They may already have approached the staff with their problem and not been satisfied. By the time they take it to the elected official, their feelings have grown more intense. What may have seemed like a routine problem . . . may become magnified when presented to an elected official."[5] To the extent that networking can obviate such problems, its demands on staff time are justified.

Succinctness   The agenda communication is the easiest and often the most effective way for the staff to communicate with elected officials. The elected official will judge the staff by the quality of agenda communications. Because the subjects of many of these communications will be controversial, complex, spontaneous, or all three, it is more difficult to prepare them than might be anticipated. Some planners, it is said, tend to let the complexity show through with verbosity and to let the technical methods show through with redundancy.[6]

Because agenda communications are a reflection of research, the definition of that research is the first step toward the preparation of a quality agenda communication. If there are options for local elected officials to evaluate, each option needs to be researched, relations among development variables need to be determined, probable consequences need to be laid out, and conclusions need to be drawn.

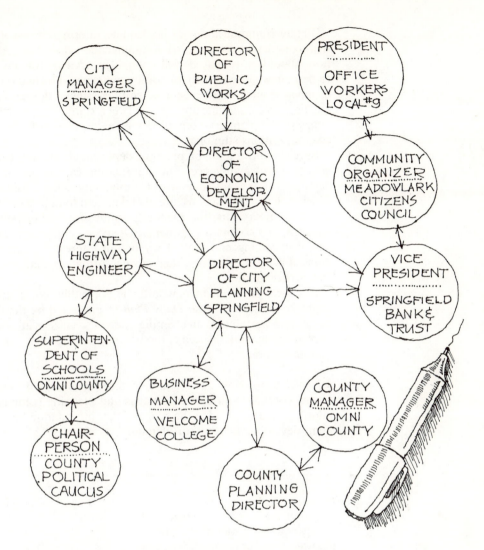

Figure 9–1   Networking includes many people besides elected
officials and the planning commission. Try drawing your
own network. It will clarify a lot of relationships.

The second step is to organize agenda communications properly—as if you
(rather than the elected officials you serve) had to consider all technical and
political ramifications and then make a decision. If it is necessary to include
technical detail, key points should be included in a one-page cover memorandum
on the problem, policy options, and recommendations. In writing the cover
memorandum, the staff should assume that decision makers will not have time
to read the technical details. The technical staff should not forget to take backup
materials to the meeting for reference in answering questions.

Never try to control opinion; the professional planner who tries to do so may
become boxed in. The planning staff, however, has the responsibility to state
clearly its professional recommendation; no one else may have that responsibility
or the capability to do it. All elected officials must receive the same information
so they will not think that one is being treated differently from the other. Special
information requests should be addressed in the agenda communication, and
the manager should be alerted to them before the meeting. Information surprises
from the planning staff are never welcomed.

Timely communication of inadequate information usually is better received than completely documented communication that is late. Agenda communications should be prepared well enough in advance for any last-minute changes to be reviewed by the city or county manager. Information that is not reviewed in advance may cause needless embarrassment during the course of council meetings as communication gaps between staff members become apparent. The image of the planner's competence is undermined if he or she is perceived as a communications stumbler.

Succinct information on planning department activities can also be made available to a wider audience. This information can be part of a local government newsletter. For example, Fairfax County, Virginia, publishes the *Weekly Agenda*, which is devoted to actions already taken and to new agenda items of the county board of supervisors, the planning commission, other policy boards and commissions, and county departments. Of special importance are the detailed agendas of upcoming meetings. They permit interested citizens to identify agenda items of interest to them, obtain more information, and plan for their attendance and participation.

If a local government newsletter is not published, a department newsletter might be considered. The *Daily Plan-It*, published by the Carlsbad, California, planning department is an example. Since few citizens are aware of the full range of planning activities, succinct reports on these activities can help build a broader base of support.

Informal networking   The planning director should develop and maintain informal contacts with elected officials and planning commissioners to exchange information and broaden the scope of that information beyond a specific agenda item, development issue, or planning report.

Plan-It   The planning department in Carlsbad, California, publishes a community newsletter with brief reports on the work of the department for developers, members of the city council, community and neighborhood organizations, and others in the city. The following excerpts from the *Daily Plan-It* for August 10, 1982, show the variety of topics covered in a typical issue.

Mid-block parking area   Final design and bid specifications for a mid-block parking lot in downtown Carlsbad will be presented to City Council at their August 3 meeting. This joint public/private venture will create an attractive public parking area behind the shops and offices on State Street and Roosevelt. The property owners have signed an agreement offering their land for public parking and the city will allocate Federal Community Development Block Grant funds for construction.

PD Ordinance   The new Planned Development Ordinance will be before the City Council for the first reading of the ordinance on August 3. The ordinance will officially go into effect 30 days later. Copies of the ordinance are available at the development services counter.

Office uses in industrial area
Working with input from industrial developers and brokers, the Land Use Office has developed a list of office uses which are permitted in the planned industrial (P-M) zone.

Privately-funded senior housing
The city is now processing its first request for a privately funded senior housing project being developed under the city's Senior Citizens Housing Ordinance. The ordinance allows the city to consider a substantial increase in density if the project is rented exclusively to senior citizens.

Although time-consuming, frequent personal contact will probably yield the greatest results in terms of encouraging the free exchange of off-the-record information. Occasional telephone calls are also effective. Discreet social contacts are another way for planning directors and elected and appointed officials to stretch their communication capital. The extent to which this is carried on will depend on the interests of the parties involved. The risks in doing so are, first, that the relationship between the policy board members and the staff will be altered, and, second, that the staff may be charged with sharing more information with one policy board member than with another.

Regardless of how widespread the communication network, it is not unusual for persons outside that network to be appointed to the planning commission or elected to public office. Often they will need orientation on their legal responsibilities and on current issues. It is the planning department's responsibility to provide new planning commissioners with formal orientation material, to answer questions about the planning program, and to include newly elected officials and new planning commissioners in the informal network of information exchange. One-on-one meetings should be held between the planning director and each new member of the network to go over the issues they will be expected to address as they assume their new responsibilities. However, the staff should not intimidate new commissioners by inundating them with reports and memos.

Planning staff

At the top of the planning department pyramid, the planning director may hesitate to be candid with planning staff, but this may block the flow of communication downward to the staff as well as upward to the director. Personal styles may differ, but the rule of thumb is to share information that is useful to the staff or that will, in return, yield information useful to the director in making decisions. This is yet another reason for the director to cultivate interpersonal trust with staff members.

Since planning staff are an important communication link to citizens, the planning director needs to keep the staff up to date on policy direction and decisions by the council and the chief executive. The planning director cannot assume that the supervisory staff will have access to information from other staff members or will correctly interpret it. Periodic discussions with staff will increase their awareness of top-down policy direction and provide a forum for the free flow of ideas among staff members.

Ideas on what decisions to make under prevailing circumstances should be continually sought. Particularly important are the advice and counsel of disinterested parties, including peers in other communities and friends outside the planning profession. In addition, information on how it was done elsewhere can be obtained from professional conferences, seminars, and intergovernmental committee meetings.

Written communication

Most people find it hard to write, yet the written word is the most common form of communication between planners and their clients. It is the single method of communication that ensures that everyone will receive the same information, and in addition permits widespread distribution, if needed. The challenge for the planner here is to take complicated proposals and background information and explain what they are and what they mean as clearly, concisely, and cogently as possible. Think of these qualities as the three C's of technical writing.

Readers of verbatim transcripts know that the spoken word makes sense when it is heard but may not in written form. Written communication does not provide the opportunity for on-the-spot feedback and correction. Face-to-face communication provides the opportunity to communicate through sight, sound, smell, and touch without saying anything at all.

Writing by dictating words onto a tape is an exercise in which one form of communication is used as an input in order to obtain another form—the written word—as the output. It therefore requires special discipline to organize and produce acceptable written material by means of dictation. An advantage of dictation over handwriting is that, other things being equal, dictation is five times faster. As a rule, dictation should be typed in draft form and edited before being released.

The written work in a planning office may include letters, memoranda, grant-in-aid documentations, budget justifications, news releases . . . and reports. The following paragraphs will deal with planning reports because they usually are the most decisive and long-lasting kinds of writing that planners do.

Report planning

Whether a planning report is dictated, written by hand, or composed on the word processor or typewriter, it should be planned with three points in mind: objectives, audience, and components. The process need not be long and complex, but it should be done every time, even if the publication is relatively routine, like an employee newsletter.[7]

Objectives The author should list the report's objectives because they sum up what he or she is expected to accomplish with the document. These objectives may include trying to persuade elected officials to take a position, providing information, expressing a new set of ideas, or responding to an information request.

Audience The audience for the planning report will determine its substance and style. It is helpful to establish a mental image of the person or persons to whom the report is directed. This might be a composite of the planning commissioners or council. In establishing this image, keep in mind their image of the planning department.

Messages that are conveyed but not understood produce a negative image of the planner and the planning department. Writers should not hesitate to address a broad spectrum of persons such as the citizenry at large. In this instance the writer should identify the most important individuals in this spectrum and address their information needs and level of understanding.

Components The components of a piece of direct mail advertising may include a four-page letter, a brochure, an order card, an insert with testimonials, and a business reply envelope—all enclosed in the "carrier," the outside mailing envelope. A planning report too has components. At the minimum, it probably includes two or more pages of typescript, a cover memo, and a staple in the upper left-hand corner. For more formal reports, the components may include the report body, a separate transmittal letter, a spiral binding, and a mailing or delivery envelope.

Organizing reports

The first step in report writing, obvious as it may seem, is to draft the outline. It should include at least primary and secondary headings that serve as labels for each topic and subtopic. Then themes, in the form of short, descriptive paragraphs, should be written for each topic and subtopic. If time permits, this thematic outline should be reviewed by others, as appropriate, such as the planning director, the finance director, and one or two members of the prospective audience.

It is beyond the scope of this book to include a section on how to write, but one or two suggestions can be offered that apply particularly to planning reports. First, never forget the audience. It is one thing to write a paper for a scholarly journal; it is quite another to write an introductory set of procedural guidelines for a neighborhood association. Second, clear discussions of interrelatedness— a cornerstone of the planning process—are mandatory. Transitional sentences and paragraphs are very helpful in explaining interrelatedness and leading the reader from one idea to the next.

The remaining components of most planning reports are the summary, tables, graphics, and introductory and appendix pages. Tabular data can provide the framework for the report if the central message is the result of quantitative analysis. The writer may wish to prepare the tables first and organize them in sequence, and then organize the text around these tables to explain what they convey to the knowledgeable reader. This approach should not be used in reports where the data are not the most important information.

The purpose of graphics (charts, graphs, statistical maps, diagrams, and the like) is to explain complex information. A general rule is to use graphics only when they help the reader to understand the text more readily.

Written material that is longer than two pages and that is directed principally at elected or appointed officials should always include a summary. Because of the complexity of the methods used to obtain information and because of the political sensitivity of information normally conveyed in planning reports, it is especially important to include concise summaries. The summary should be distinguished from the body of the report by a border or different colored paper, or it can be placed on the first page.

Writing to time and budget

Writing is disciplined work that is constantly done to meet deadlines and to stay within the budget. Those who fret about deadlines, claiming that the creative juices don't flow every day, will not last long as report writers. Each report writing assignment should be translated into the number of person days required. It then becomes a simple matter, depending of course upon the person assigned to write the report, to convert the time to dollars in the budget and adjust accordingly.

The number of person days—the base for planning the work—should be allocated among the major parts of the report outline and among any research components required for the report. A general rule of thumb is to allocate one-half of the time and budget to research and the remainder to writing. If the writing has not started by the time one-half of the budgeted effort has elapsed, it is unlikely that the self-imposed deadline will be met. This allocation of time and money excludes time required for the preparation of report graphics and presentation meetings.

It is especially important to remember that planning reports have to be completed on time. Council, planning commission, staff, and other scheduled meetings often depend on having relevant information at hand. When those meetings include go or no-go decisions, late information can be virtually useless.

One way to ensure that material for policy boards and other groups will be prepared on time is to establish interim deadlines. This technique is especially effective for work that takes more than two weeks. It entails listing detailed tasks to be performed, the persons responsible for them, and the deadlines by

Task	Responsible person	Starting date	Due Date
Prepare topical outline	Jones	1/31	2/17
Review topical outline	Staff Project Committee	2/18	2/25
Respond to comments on draft outline	Jones	2/26	2/28
Prepare thematic outline	Jones	2/28	3/7
Review draft thematic outline	Staff Project Committee	3/8	3/13
Prepare final thematic outline	Jones	3/14	3/16
Prepare tabular data	Smith	3/16	3/23
Review tabular data	Staff Project Committee	3/24	3/25
Prepare first one-third of draft text	Brown	3/26	3/31
Prepare second one-third of draft text	Brown	4/1	4/8
Describe required graphics	Black	4/1	4/2
Prepare third one-third of draft text	Brown	4/10	4/20
Review draft text and proposed graphics	Staff Project Committee	4/21	4/22
Revise draft text	Jones and Brown	4/23	4/26
Prepare final draft	Black	4/27	4/30
Review draft final report	Staff Project Committee	5/1	5/5
Publish final report	Green		5/28
Present report to council	Jones		6/1

Figure 9–2   Tasks, persons responsible, and deadlines for
preparation of hypothetical planning report.

which they are to be completed. Figure 9–2 illustrates the use of interim deadlines to discipline staff performance.

By making assignments explicit, assigning them to individuals, and tying them to specific dates, progress toward achieving the tasks can be readily determined. If a problem comes up in meeting any deadlines, remedial action can be taken. Added pressure to perform may be created by graphing and posting these assignments.

Some persons who frequently write reports are burdened with "writer's block," which reduces their mental capacity to produce written material. Writer's block is attributable to the writer's fear that the information may be inadequate, that the product may be criticized, or that he or she will be unable to organize complex or large volumes of information; or the author may merely feel insecure when under pressure to deliver high-quality materials.

Every writer develops mechanisms to ward off this common affliction. One technique is to observe the conditions under which one writes most easily (early in the morning, late in the day, in absolute quiet, under stress, in short stretches) and then to deliberately create these conditions for the assignment at hand.

Another warm-up activity is to talk about the project with other people. Perhaps the best technique is to begin by writing down anything and everything that comes to mind about the subject—once the writer has some ideas down on paper, other ideas will follow and a structure will begin to emerge. Rewriting can come later. The frustrated writer may find additional motivation in imagining the more desirable uses of time to be enjoyed once the project is finished, or in remembering that other deadlines loom on the horizon.

Writing clearly

An individual's pride of authorship stems from his or her writing style, which is acquired by training, experience, intellect, and personality. "Your writing *is* you, and no amount of mere reading about the subject, or even of hearing a competent lecture on the subject, can of itself bring about improvement."[8] Writing is an acquired skill that is learned and honed over time.

Justifiable ridicule has been heaped on the anonymous authors of government reports and other documents. Such writing frequently has been described as prolix, jargon-ridden, obfuscatory, cumbersome, circuitous, and redundant. But it does not have to be that way: in other words, people will begin to say 'borrow' instead of 'procure on a loan basis' and 'distribute material now' instead of 'initiate such steps toward promulgation of the data as may be appropriate to current situations and the pressure of the time element.'[9]

The job of the writer who wishes to influence opinion is to write effectively. Two of the most useful rules of effective writing are to be sure to understand the written material and to use short sentences.

Planning staff memoranda too often are too long, do not show clear reasons for conclusions that are drawn, and tend to increase, rather than reduce, the complexity of the decision. The remedy is to standardize memoranda format and length to assist decision makers in locating the information they are seeking and to present it more clearly. The length should generally not exceed two pages. The first paragraph should explain the issue; the second paragraph should state the facts; and the third paragraph should set forth the recommendation or preferred alternative. Back-up materials should be readily available.

Additional rules for writing clearly have been prepared by the Gunning-Mueller Clear Writing Institute in Santa Barbara, California. Among the rules of thumb that they advocate are the following:

Be simple, not complex.

Write to express, not impress.

Present ideas simply and directly.

Develop vocabulary by using it.

Avoid extra and unneeded words.

Use active, not passive verbs.

Use terms the reader can picture in his or her mind.

Use a conversational tone.

Word processing

Marriage of the typewriter with computer technology has produced the word processor. Its principal advantages over the electric typewriter are

1. Time and labor savings in the editing/correcting process

Figure 9-3   Clearly expressed ideas
are more readily accepted.

2.   High-quality hard copy
3.   Storage of large quantities of information in a small space
4.   Rapid retrieval of information
5.   The opportunity for linkages between a word processing terminal and
     other terminals in remote locations and high-capacity mainframe
     computers.

Any office producing a large quantity of written material can exploit the
editing/correcting advantages of a word processor. Its hardware comprises a
cathode ray tube (CRT) to display information, a keyboard comparable to that
of the standard typewriter, a memory unit, and a printer. Text, table, and graphic
corrections can be made in the memory unit and immediately displayed on the
CRT to assure the operator they are accurate. The memory unit automatically
and instantaneously makes the changes it is instructed to make, including, for
example, insertions of new material, rearrangements of paragraphs, or relocation
of pages. The document is reprinted faster and more accurately than the human
typist can produce the materials.

The quality of the "hard" (printed) copy is superior for two reasons. First,
the output is exactly the same as the information in the memory unit and,
therefore, as accurate as the input. Second, the hard copy is of uniformly high
quality. Because the information in the memory unit is stored on discs comparable in size to the phonograph record, it requires much less space than the
storage of hard copy. When the disc is inserted into the word processor, all or
a portion of it may be retrieved as hard copy from the printer.

Word processors allow communication with compatible hardware located elsewhere. For example, keyboarding done in another building may be transmitted

by telephone to the planning office and printed on its printer. Likewise, the planning office word processors can be linked to word processors in other departments in the local government office buildings for more rapid communication with each other. Word processors can also be linked by wire to the community's high capacity mainframe computer to input or retrieve data.

In Rockville, Maryland, the planning department's word processor is linked to the mainframe computer located in another department. The planning department stores and retrieves information from the mainframe and it may also retrieve information inputted to the mainframe by another department using appropriate computer instructions.[10]

Oral communication

Planners, like other government employees, communicate regularly with superiors, subordinates, citizens, and persons in their network. Most of this communication is oral and extemporaneous. In general, the higher the employee is in the organization, the greater the amount of time spent on oral communication. Some planning directors spend 75 percent of their time interacting with other people.

Communication channels

The regular channels of organizational communication are formal, informal, and lateral.

Formal communication channels follow predetermined procedural manuals, acknowledged management policies, staff meetings, memoranda, and reports. Typically, formal communication flows downward through the organization.

Informal communication depends much more heavily on oral communication, both structured or unstructured. Informal oral communication is the bulwark of the networking approach to receiving and providing information and is often spontaneous. Therefore, informal communication may, by implication, be considered more timely and accurate. Because it is less subject to control or influence by a planning director or planning supervisor, and because accountability is not easy to pin down, informal oral communication is not part of the planning department's official record.

Lateral communication takes place between or among employees at the same level of an organization or between representatives of other organizations. Depending on organizational level and relations to individuals and groups, lateral communication may emphasize either the written word or oral communication.

Oral communication skills

One of the most important skills for a planning director is to be able to communicate orally. Getting the message across, whether in a carefully planned presentation or spontaneous exchange, requires simultaneous thinking about what is said and what is going to be said. Persons who wish to become planning directors and managers should practice and become skilled at oral communication—the art of thinking on your feet.

The planner uses oral communication principally in extemporaneous responses to persons challenging his or her ideas. The unsympathetic portion of a planner's network requires the planner to develop a keen sense of what he or she believes in—and why. In this sense, "unsympathetic" refers to persons who challenge ideas that planners think are in the public interest. The unsympathetic person in the planner's network today may be a friendly person tomorrow. Therefore, oral communication with temporarily unfriendly constituents requires high levels of understanding of their position and tact in disagreeing with it. Perhaps the most important rule in situations like these is to stick to the facts and avoid simplism and dogma.

Effective oral communication distinguishes hearing (listeners only hear what is said) and understanding (listeners understand what is said). Here are six variables to think about in honing oral communication skills:

1. The sender is the person with something to say who should think about that something before saying it.
2. The message is the information the sender is passing along to others, and it should be understandable.
3. The channel is the speech, presentation, informal discussion, or idle chitchat using the spoken language as the common denominator.
4. The receiver is the person who is supposed to be hearing and understanding the sender's message.
5. Feedback is the response to the message which lets the sender know how well the message is getting across to the receiver.
6. Noise is interference between the sender and the receiver that inhibits the message from getting across. Noise may be confusion in the receiver's mind or the actual sound when cars crash.[11]

Effective senders tend to control these variables, thereby increasing the quality of their oral communication and, by implication, increasing the receiver's receptivity to the sender's ideas.

Because oral communication takes so many forms, the following discussion of oral communication skills will be limited to those most likely to be used by the planning director and planning staff: public speaking, telephone usage, encoding and decoding, and listening.

Public speaking   The planning director, mayor, city manager, county manager, and economic development director usually are experienced public speakers, but planners, assistant city and county managers, assistants to city and county managers, and deputy mayors also are often called on for speeches. They observe certain tested guidelines and practices that begin with a good appearance. Neat, well-groomed speakers are the most acceptable to audiences.

The content should be clear and concise but not heavy. Speakers who take themselves or their message too seriously, compared with the value the receivers place on the sender and his or her message, are not well received. Be aware that receivers vary widely in their receptivity, feedback, and internal noise. Therefore, any adjustments by the sender during the course of the presentation should be keyed to the portion of the audience the sender feels is the most important. The sender should stratify the anticipated audience and the actual audience into key, important, and less important receivers and acknowledge that he or she may not be able to satisfy the interests of all receivers. Recognizing the limitations of a speech helps reduce worry and guilt about not making the perfect presentation.

Telephone usage   Much has been written about effective telephone communication, and local phone companies for many years have provided training in telephone usage and courtesy for employees in all kinds of organizations. Three recommendations are offered for planning agency employees:

1. Make sure the phone system is working the way it is supposed to—the hold button should not be used as a weapon, the phone should be answered promptly (four rings are the maximum), and all employees should speak clearly and cordially.
2. Answer every question or complaint promptly, politely, and accurately. If the information is not at hand, *say so and then call back*.

Figure 9–4 The long-winded speaker
will soon lose the audience.

3. Take notes on important calls to clarify the messages and provide
    information for discussions and queries with others on the planning staff.

Encoding and decoding   The process of translating thoughts—words that can
be shared with others—is called encoding. Highly articulate persons are, by
definition, skillful encoders. They are adept at selecting, managing, and using
words to send messages that are understood by receivers. In the encoding process
words are selected that will translate the message so precisely that the receiver
will understand the intended meaning. Matching words with perceptions is difficult because words may not only have several meanings but may also have
emotional overtones. Networking with representatives of the intended audience
will aid in understanding their language and in selecting words for presentations.

Shared knowledge and language provide a sound foundation for increasing
the effectiveness of oral communication. Admittedly, the content of oral communication is important, but it is equally important to remember that the receiver
is an individual (or group of individuals) with unique characteristics. Personal
values, moods, and internal noise will vary from one communication to another.

The process of receiving messages is called decoding. It means listening to
words and interpreting the meaning. Usually, decoding occurs rapidly and at a
subconscious level in the mind. During the decoding process the receiver tries
to determine what is really being said, how it relates to things already known,
what should be done with the information, and what should be said in response.
The answers determine the feedback the receiver will provide to the sender.

Listening and feedback   Feedback lets the sender know that the receiver has
heard the message and grasps its meaning, and what the receiver thinks about

it. The feedback will assist the sender in modifying the message until it is well understood. If the message is not "accepted," the choices are to respond with a modified message or reinforce the original message to try to convince the receiver that it is a reasonable position, solution, or recommendation.

Communication barriers (inattention, resistance to the message, position already taken, and many other reasons) will block feedback just like highway barricades, and the conversation will break down into two senders talking at each other with no receiver for either message. Conversations that end without either person changing his or her position are in a stalemate. In such cases, it may be necessary for the planner to turn to his or her network to get help from a third party.

If high-quality feedback is expected, the planner should be an attentive listener and interpreter. The following list presents some techniques in the art of listening:

1. The purpose of listening is to give the other person a chance to express his or her point of view.
2. Among the most common mistakes in listening are to assume what the person is going to say is unimportant, uninteresting, too complex, or too elementary; and to listen only for the facts, bottom line, or other point of the conversation.
3. Effective executives avoid the impression of haste and pressure and elicit ideas by paying attention. They do this by practicing and by avoiding interruptions from outside and from themselves.
4. Deep feelings and emotions can be a major barrier to effective communication on topics subject to these feelings and emotions.
5. Emotionally laden "trigger" words can keep you from hearing an idea.
6. Paraphrasing or restating a speaker's message and feelings to his or her satisfaction is one of the most important listening skills.
7. Silence during the course of the conversation can provide you and your listener with a chance to think about what has been said and to collect your thoughts.
8. By listening to the other speaker, organizing your key points, managing your limited time, and actively and periodically seeking feedback, you will become a better listener.[12]

Telecommunications

Television is effective for sharing information with many people at one time. Community Antenna Television (CATV) and video conferencing technologies are available to planners and other local government personnel to communicate with their constituents and with each other. CATV is the wired transmission of pictures and sound to television sets connected to the wire. Television transmission available to these same sets and the public at large is transmitted via the air waves. Direct Broadcasting Satellite (DBS) is a method of communicating television programs to receiving "dishes" that are much more expensive than the typical antenna used to receive network television signals. Low Power Television (LPTV) transmits television signals typically up to twelve miles. Various teletext services that are available by subscription transmit data to television sets equipped with decoders.

Use of television

Planning, among all of the services and responsibilities of local government, seems tailor-made for television transmission of information. Planners evaluate public development issues, receive feedback, and provide recommendations. These issues include a spatial component that is typically easier to describe visually than verbally. Planners communicate a great deal of complex information that television can present in ways that are understandable to the public.

Planners can use CATV to present information on development permission applications, maps to show spatial relationships, discussions of development issues by planning commissioners and city council members, videotapes of existing land use to show spatial relationships and economic development possibilities, teleconferencing between remote sites, and question-and-answer sessions with citizen groups at neighborhood community centers or with individuals at their homes.

Now that information can be transmitted to residents in their homes or to easily accessible central locations, it has become possible to disseminate information on public issues and the planning process over a wide area. Increasing the convenience of receiving this information will increase the likelihood that people will take greater interest in community development issues.

Although it is a powerful tool to convey messages, CATV is not a panacea for broadening and deepening citizen participation in the planning process. CATV cannot duplicate the encoding and decoding that takes place among persons in a room. It is difficult to find persons who have both the technical skills for planning and a television "presence" to get their points across. For these and other reasons, CATV and other electronic technologies will not replace public meetings or networking dynamics.

How do we meet?   Teleconferencing. That is another trend that will not happen. Talking with people via television cannot begin to substitute for the high touch of a meeting, no matter how rational it is in saving fuel and overhead. If it is of little importance, use teleconference. Be appropriate. But we have to face it: There is no end to meetings.

Source: John Naisbitt, *Megatrends: Ten New Directions Transforming Our Lives* (New York: Warner Books, 1982), 46.

An institutional network is a cable network separate from cable subscriber services that transmits nonentertainment information. Institutional networks are still so new that there has been little user experience. The experience with conventional CATV, however, suggests that planning applications could easily be transferred to institutional networks, perhaps in some of the following ways:

1. In-service training. By using an interactive system that allows people to talk to each other, one teacher can reach many students without having the students travel long distances.
2. Monitoring. This service places cameras at strategic locations to transmit what they see. This technology can be used by transportation planners to identify traffic capacity bottlenecks, by water supply planners to monitor reservoirs, and by others.
3. Promotion. Competitive features of the community, such as its tourist, educational, and cultural facilities, and industrial sites can be videotaped for showing locally or elsewhere.
4. Delivery of services. Electronic transmission can be used for development permission application information, housing availability, mass transit schedules, and notices of public meetings.

As CATV technology expands and programming techniques are developed, ideas for local applications will blossom. They will affect the management of the planning office in a number of ways.

Employee productivity will increase as more information can be conveyed to more people in less time.

The need for employees who do *not* manage, analyze, communicate to the public, or operate electronic equipment will decrease.

As information becomes more widely used for decision making, planners will need to learn how to communicate effectively with the technologies available.

Paper will become less important as documents are entered into the computer and reproduced only as the need arises.

Field work will be reduced as surveillance and monitoring are done by camera.

Less time will be spent on attending meetings because they will be brought to the planner rather than having the planner go to them.

More interjurisdictional networking will be done as experience in other communities is brought to the planning staff.

Qualifications of planning directors, in particular, and other staff members will be expanded to include television stage presence.

Local government examples

The opportunities for planning and television to interact are opening up. As might be expected, the approaches vary. In some communities, like Prince William County, Virginia, the free market delivery system has prevailed.[13] In other communities, like Montgomery County, Maryland, county government use of television has been planned and organized through the office of the county executive.[14]

The Montgomery County executive issued a regulation on the planning process for county use of CATV company resources. These resources may be used for communicating with citizens and also for the county's internal business. Montgomery County may contract for special TV programming with the CATV company (franchisee) or with the county's nonprofit corporation for public television. It is expected that specialists in TV equipment, script writing, and oral and visual communication will be assigned to county government offices with the greatest need for this service—the planning office, library system, recreation department, and office of management and budget. The purposes of this system are to deliver information, cover public meetings, and encourage participation in public issues of the day.

CATV use by local governments is growing. Other examples include:

1. Lexington, Kentucky, conducts staff training programs in city department offices.
2. Seattle, Washington, televises public meetings on development issues.
3. Prairie Village, Kansas, uses its local government channel for continuous listing of city news and announcements.
4. Reading, Pennsylvania, uses two-way cable for citizen participation in public meetings.[15]

Graphic presentations

Graphics help planners present visual images that clarify spatial relations, physical development, and other complex information. The subjects, media, and information portrayed, however, should be selected solely to help the planner express ideas and convey recommendations. Graphics are not intended to draw attention to themselves.

Most graphics require advance preparation, and some are time-consuming and costly to produce. For this reason, an effective supplementary graphic technique is spontaneous preparation using a blackboard, blow-up slide, or large piece of paper. Additional rules of thumb for the preparation and showing of visual aids are

1. Be sure letters and numbers are large enough to be read.
2. Do not clutter graphics with extraneous information that is hard to understand. It is better to use two uncluttered graphic pieces than one that is overloaded.
3. Do not use an inexperienced person to operate equipment; inefficient operators disrupt the flow of presentations.
4. Check equipment in advance to be sure it is in working condition; carry spare parts that are easy to install, such as lamps and extension cords, to guard against their failure during the presentation.
5. Reproduce visual aids in an 8½ × 11-inch format to encourage meeting participants who are interested to take copies for further study.
6. Do not use humorous visual aids unless they are likely to have universal appeal; stale humor detracts from the presentation.

The overhead slide is one of the simplest ways to supplement an oral presentation and to clarify complex points. Slides can be quickly printed on photocopying machines and tested before actual use, and overhead slide projectors are easy to transport and operate. Slides of written material should not be read by the person presenting them; they should be clear enough to be read and understood by the audience. It is equally redundant to read graphics to the audience. Photographic slides are an excellent and relatively low-cost medium for supplementing presentations. Their only drawback is the time required to take and develop the photos.

Slides that are on hand should not govern the content of the message. First write the script and then assemble the slides. Show each slide for five to fifteen seconds, depending on its importance. Slide shows on technical topics that run for more than twenty minutes tend to be boring or an information overload. Except for humorous purposes, do not show slides that are out of focus or that exclude a portion of the picture's subject. If photographic slides are used, be sure to take several of each scene to increase the chances that a good slide will be available.

Rules that apply to the use of maps and reports are comparable to those that apply to slides. High-quality maps can be produced for widespread local government use with the digital information in a computer. Information about each parcel in the community is entered into the computer, and, with the aid of a digitizer, the computerized information is converted into lines on a map. As information is recalled, it is automatically drawn from the CRT and can be printed out.

Information can be retrieved for all parcels, or selected characteristics can be retrieved showing which parcels have those features. Available technology permits the use of a "mouse," or cursor, to point at a parcel on a map and immediately obtain information stored in the computer about that parcel. It may include information such as its coordinates, size, zoning classification, assessed valuation, land use, and status of an ongoing activity such as building inspection, construction, or demolition. The only requirement for retrieval is that the information be available, as well as the time and money required to code it for the computer.

Graphic and written information can be digitized and transmitted to conventional television sets in response to requests for the information. This is videotex technology, which requires a television set and a decoder permitting receipt and sending of signals. Because it is a two-way communication network, anyone with a television set and a decoder can participate in the communication linkage over telephone lines, coaxial cables, or fiberoptics. Maps, words, and data can be shared in this way. As the transmission capability becomes available locally, planners can use videotex to communicate graphics, text, and data through all television sets with access to the service. Those television sets connected to a printer can yield hard copy for the interested reader.

Media relations

The work of planners is news, and planning departments should be prepared to communicate with the news media and to think through what needs to be communicated. One day the planner may have a story of interest to him or her but not to the media; the next day the reverse may be the case. Judgment needs to be exercised with regard to what information is confidential and should not be shared with the news media at a given time.

Media relations program

Newspaper, radio, and television reporters are interested in the planning process, not the planner. Planners who are out front in gaining and sustaining community recognition are often not well thought of by others who think they need and deserve the recognition more. Planners who compete with elected officials for news worthiness may compromise their tenure. Planners who try to compete with the local government's public information office are likewise typically frowned upon. Media relations programs have turf implications. The planner therefore should work closely with the person designated by the local government as having central responsibility for coordinating media relations.

The public information officer or other designated person in the city or county government has the primary responsibility for working with the media—newspapers, radio, and television. The "other designated person" may be a deputy to the mayor, an assistant to the city or county manager, or an assistant to a department head. The planning director and the planning staff should expect to work closely with this person. Cooperative working relations can be highly productive. An effective media campaign, for example, can generate valuable results for the planning agency:

Informing the public about all sides of important issues

Persuading a particular neighborhood to support a specific project such as construction of a storm water system

Persuading local voters to approve a bond issue

Garnering local support for a specific position on an issue involving another local government

Helping citizens understand the need for amendments to the zoning ordinance

Throwing out a capital project idea to "test the water" as to its political support.[16]

After determining whether the message is to inform, persuade, or promote, it will be easier to determine the information to be included in a news release or other material. A calendar of planning commission activities alerts editors to the time, location, and purpose of meetings to be held and the dates reports are to be issued. This information helps editors determine news priorities and schedule reporters to cover meetings.

Background meetings with reporters can help them understand the subject matter of the meeting or report. Because they lack familiarity with technical information, and have competing assignments and tight deadlines, reporters are encouraged to seek interpretive advice. It is likely to be time well spent by the planner. Backgrounders lead to more accurate and more in-depth stories. Planners also should refer reporters to key people in local government who are quotable and whose reactions to current issues are important to readers, and they should supply explanatory graphic material to reporters.

Maintaining credibility

Planners can maintain credibility with the media if they do not

Develop phony friendships to influence reporters

Betray the confidence of the reporter who has prepared an exclusive story

Use his or her position as news source for self-promotion

Ignore telephone calls from media representatives

Become identified too closely with one political faction.

The most important purpose of public information activities is to develop a two-way relationship with the media. Honesty is an absolute requisite in establishing this relationship. Newspapers, radio, and television differ in formats, news policies, and deadlines. Therefore information that is news should be organized and presented accordingly. The planning department's media representative should think and write like a reporter to help the department convey its message.

Small group communication

This book has repeatedly stressed the interrelatedness of planning, formally organized citizen associations, and loosely structured groups of influential citizens. Linking these elements to set priorities is a practical way to augment elections, city council and county board meetings, and other parts of the formal processes of local government. One of the most reliable ways to set priorities is to work with small groups drawn from both formal and loosely structured citizen groups through, technically speaking, small group communication. Four approaches to systematically gathering information and setting priorities within small groups are polling, the nominal group technique, Delphi, and interpretive structural modeling.

Polling

Polling brings together three groups who discuss issues and priorities with each other: experts, planning staff, and policy makers. Polling was used in the 1960s in the preparation of the East Central Florida Regional Planning Council (Kennedy Space Center area) planning process and the Columbia, Maryland, new town planning process.

The polling method identifies experts (typically from outside the planning area) on a wide range of community development issues. These are generally the steps that are followed:

Background information is sent to the experts to familiarize them with issues.

The experts, staff, and policy makers gather to discuss and sharpen the definitions of the issues.

The staff or experts prepare issue papers that are distributed to the group.

The group reassembles to determine tentative priorities and solutions.

The staff or the experts prepare draft recommendations to be incorporated into the plan.

The group reassembles to review the experts' draft plan and implementation priorities.

Further refinement of the materials may proceed from this point.

A key element of the polling method is the interaction among the experts, staff, and policy makers. Maintaining careful records of communication among them increases the utility of the priority-setting process and the speed with which an implementation plan can be prepared.

Nominal group technique

The nominal group technique (NGT) structures small group meetings in a way that will ensure a systematic outcome. It is most effective when the group consists of fewer than fourteen persons and the meeting lasts less than three hours. NGT has three essential elements:

1. A carefully thought-out question that will elicit very specific responses from the participants in the group
2. A group of participants who are task oriented and who possess expertise in the subject matter to be discussed
3. A leader for the group who is thoroughly familiar with NGT. This individual must play the role of NGT process facilitator, without offering substantive input or expertise on the topic to be discussed.[17]

Because NGT is a single-question technique, the phrasing of the question is particularly important. Several people should participate so that the wording is closely related to the objective. The basic steps of the NGT process are: silent generation of written ideas, recording of ideas, and voting on the ideas discussed.

Ideas may be ranked or weighted. The ranking technique prioritizes each idea and may leave more than one idea with the same ranking. The rating approach lists the ideas in order of importance from one through n.

Because only one question can be evaluated at a time, NGT does not lend itself to generating ideas on complex questions such as: What is your preferred distribution of development in the community in five years? This is a multifaceted policy issue that needs to be broken down into component questions if NGT is to be workable.[18] NGT is especially useful for resolving simpler questions such as: What density should site A accommodate?

Delphi

This technique uses a carefully designed sequence of questionnaires to seek opinions and reasons for those opinions from participants. Each successive response from the group generates new information as opinion feedback. This process is reiterated until the marginal increase in opinions and their justifications becomes negligible. Unresolved, conflicting views are then documented by the group leader.

The Delphi technique lends itself to quantitative forecasting of such factors as the number of jobs or budget limits. Responses from participants are arranged in order of magnitude by quartiles. Each quartile (one-fourth) of a forecast is grouped together and shared with respondents. Each respondent then reconsiders his or her previous forecast and restates the reasons for it. When responses are no longer solicited, the median of results and the summary of reasons for them are recorded. Because the Delphi technique can estimate the consequences of alternative actions and is quantitative, it is particularly well suited to the types of issues often faced by planners.

In 1977 the city of Norman, Oklahoma, revised its comprehensive plan, in part, by the Delphi method: For the first round of questionnaires, the staff developed a series of 18 questions under the five basic issue headings. . . . Ample space was allowed for respondents to write in comments about each statement, and additional statements, or even add other general topics not included. Following the first response, a total of 22 statements were incorporated into the exercise.[19]

These issue statements were ranked during four successive iterations. None of the twenty-two issue statements were ranked the same during each of the four iterations. The process permitted sixty-three respondents to think through the relative importance of issues facing the community and enabled the staff to use this information to influence plan recommendations.

Interpretive structural modeling

Relations within a set of issue statements can be delineated through interpretive structural modeling (ISM). A five-step process is used:

1. An issue is stated.
2. Relevant data variables are described.
3. A relational statement is constructed such as the contrast between two variables.
4. A digraph—a graphic representation of the rankings of relational statements—is prepared.
5. A structural model is drafted expressing preferred relationships among elements.

This process may be repeated as participants reconsider and refine their contributions. It can be especially useful in ranking community development goals. Because ISM is so subjective, it is important to structure the process carefully and define terms so that participants understand what is meant by another participant's description of elements. ISM has been used for ranking and structuring regional goals by areawide planning districts in Louisiana and as a teaching aid in the Urban Studies Institute of the University of New Orleans.

Conclusion

To manage is to communicate. So it is with planning. Even in the earliest days of urban planning, planners depended on written reports, maps, diagrams, speeches, and other means of communication. But today the organizational environment has changed: more people are involved; more people depend on information; information is more complex, subtle, and subliminal; and communication depends far more on technological devices.

Any planner who has worked with neighborhood groups knows that everybody wants a piece of the action—and action depends on communication. This chapter has pointed out several ways that planners employ communication—through feedback, writing, oral communication, telecommunications, working with the media, and working with small groups. Communication has its own setting in local government planning because planning is future-oriented, speculative, uncertain, and afflicted with more variables than even the largest computer can handle. Communication in planning and management, therefore, aims at demystifying the facts, showing what is uncertain and speculative, recognizing the exogenous variables that are largely uncontrollable, and producing a framework for achieving community and economic development objectives.

As a spokesperson for the local government interest, the planner is often at odds with those supporting personal gain from community development at the expense of the public at large. The result is that planners are deeply involved technically in political issues with both short- and long-term consequences. This calls for special attention to facts, consideration of all sides of issues, and clear communication of reasons for recommendations. Persons aspiring to planning careers and to influencing management are those whose communications skills can be developed.

Communication demands placed on planners are changing. Availability and more widespread use of cable television permits information on community development issues to be shared with more people, since they can absorb it in the comfort of their homes. CATV also is effective in presenting graphic information that planners commonly work with. The data and meeting information so important to the planning process can be more widely disseminated through videotex transmission.

Planners can effectively use several small-group techniques to solicit and share information, set priorities, quantify forecasts, interpret the relationships of an issue, and recommend solutions. In essence, communication is a social affair, a means of sharing.

1   See: Ladislas Segoe, *Local Planning Administration* (Chicago: International City Managers' Association, 1941).

2   See: F. Stuart Chapin, Jr., *Urban Land Use Planning* (New York: Harper & Brothers, 1957).

3   Based on interviews conducted by the author in 1982 and 1983 and on observations of the twelve-member advisory committee for this book.

4   Laurence Rutter, *The Essential Community: Local Government in the Year 2000* (Washington, D.C.: International City Management Association, 1980), 126–28.

5   Elizabeth K. Kellar, "Communicating with Elected Officials," in *Effective Communication: Getting the Message Across*, ed. David S. Arnold, Christine S. Becker, and Elizabeth K. Kellar (Washington, D.C.: International City Management Association, 1983), 49.

6   Based on interviews conducted by the author in 1982 and 1983.

7   David S. Arnold, "Publications Planning, Development, and Production," in *Effective Communication*, ed. Arnold, Becker, and Kellar, 149.

8   Calvin D. Linton, *Effective Revenue Writing* (Washington, D.C.: Government Printing Office, 1973), 3.

9   Ibid., 2.

10 Interview with James M. Davis, Planning Director, Rockville, Maryland, 13 October 1982.

11 Christine S. Becker, "Interpersonal communication," in *Effective Communication*, ed. Arnold, Becker, and Kellar, 181–82.

12 Camille Cates Barnett, "The Art of Listening," *Public Management* 62 (September 1980): 2–4.

13 Interview with Robert S. Noe, Jr., County Executive, Prince William County, Virginia, 7 January 1983.

14 Telephone conversation with John Hansman, Office of Management and Budget, Montgomery County, Maryland, 11 February 1983.

15 Clyde Forest and Serge Sevard, *Municipal Use of Telecommunications Technology*, Management Information Service Reports, vol. 14, no. 6 (Washington, D.C.: International City Management Association, 1982): 9.

16 Sue McCauley Patterson, "Working with the Media," in *Effective Communication*, ed. Arnold, Becker, and Kellar, 102.

17 James L. Mercer and Susan Woolston, *Setting Priorities: Three Techniques for Better Decision Making*, Management Information Service Reports, vol. 12, no. 9 (Washington, D.C.: International City Management Association, 1980): 2.

18 Mercer and Woolston, *Setting Priorities*, 7.

19 David R. Morgan, John P. Pelissero, and Robert E. England, "Urban Planning: Using a Delphi as a Decision-making Aid," *Public Administration Review* 39 (July/August 1979), 382.

10 Values and ethics

Planners are sometimes thought of as a breed apart. Who else spends time thinking about the long-range future and what communities could be like, when the problems of getting through the day are the real problems for many people? Who else believes you can understand the interrelatedness of the social, physical, economic, and transportation aspects of communities enough to influence public policy? Who else is convinced that technical development standards and political decisions can be mutually supportive and can achieve short- and long-term public purposes? People who think this way—and many planners do—are probably more convinced than the public at large that community development decisions can be improved and that better decisions will lead to a higher quality of life for most people.

A firm definition of the public interest is probably the most recognizable attribute of persons who enter the planning profession compared with persons who enter the management profession. Many inexperienced planners believe they know what an acceptable definition of their profession is while many inexperienced managers believe one of their roles is to find it. Furthermore, many managers frequently amend their perception of the public interest, whereas many planners are convinced that the public interest has many irrefutable standards. As a result, planners often find themselves defending their perception of the public interest against attacks from people they work with and for. More than one planner has been "run out of town" or has had his or her "wings clipped" because of disagreements with developers, citizens, elected officials, or staff members.

In order to thrive in this setting, both the planning director and the planning staff need to evaluate continuously their professional and personal values, and their ethics, which by definition are personal. The balance of this chapter will review values and ethics for planners and make a few comparisons with city and county managers.

Values of planners

In broad measure, planners work with competing professional and political values and try to strike a balance between what elected officials think the community wants and what the planner thinks the community ought to have. Happy is the planner where these perceptions are the same, but of course this seldom happens in the real world. Some planning values that have been identified are health, conservation of resources, efficiency, beauty, equity, pluralism and individuality, democratic participation and democratic responsibility, and rational management.[1] It is the last value, rational management, that may be the most difficult to observe. *Rational*, which is often used as a pejorative term by humanists, means characterized by seasoned judgment, logic, information, citizen input, data analysis, and other elements discussed throughout this book. But rational planning does not exist without the *irrational* elements—political upsets, compromises, outside forces (the exogenous variables), and decisions that are reevaluated and changed.

Career and job cycles

Planners—just like city managers, county managers, librarians, and civil engineers—come into the profession laden with values. Their education and experience in planning blend with the socialization that occurs both in school and in the early years of planning practice. As planners move through their careers (usually from their midtwenties to their midsixties), they are initially concerned with gaining acceptance in their profession and in their first jobs.

Figure 10–1 shows the stages in a career from preentry training to retirement.[2] Note that these stages, in the career sense, are much more likely to apply to professions and technical occupations than to quasi-professional, semiskilled, and unskilled jobs. The planner typically enters the first stage with training in one of the graduate planning programs in the United States or Canada, where he or she first comes into contact with the values of public service, community betterment, impartial analysis of information, and the physical environment. The first professional job involves job hunting, recruitment procedures, formal and informal testing, job acceptance, and job orientation. On-the-job values are likely to be acquired during the stages of the first and second regular assignments and the acquisition of "legitimacy" as a regular member of the work group, the planning agency, and the city or county government. Stage 5, "Granting of tenure," is not likely to occur for the planner who moves to several jobs, perhaps in several locations, during the first ten to fifteen years of his or her career.

The thirties and forties are the years when careers are established. For most planners, these are likely to be the most creative years, and for some, the most exciting. The years from the late forties to the midsixties are generally likely to follow patterns set in earlier jobs. The early sixties to the midsixties are a period of winding down for most planners, but some keep active on an emeritus status with special assignments.

Keep in mind that these are generalizations. Most of us know firsthand a few exceptions: the young fogey who stops growing professionally in the early thirties, the burnout who begins to tread water in the midforties, the young firebrand who never ages and is creative for decades, the steadily productive planner who continues into his or her seventies, and the whiz kid who stops growing in the thirties and then is reborn and generates a new period of creativity in the forties.

In most cases the job cycle will probably be limited (after the first professional appointment) to steps 3, 4, and possibly 5 in the seven steps shown in Figure 10–1. Both job changes and outside forces can modify a planner's values over a long period of time. Some might flippantly say that this means the planner becomes more practical, more in tune with the real world, as he or she grows older. It is more likely, however, that some values will be added while earlier values are retained. The strong influence of youth, exposure to mentors, and professional training is not to be denied.

Thus the planner's earlier background (social, economic, and psychological) is the base underlying his or her education and experience in planning and the socialization that occurs in higher education and in the early years of planning practice. Planners gradually assume the responsibilities for conducting objective work while providing technically neutral advice to clients. Planners, like members of other professions, also advocate what they think is the "right thing to do."

Working in the "fishbowl" of public meetings, negotiations, idea exchanges, and citizen complaints forces the planner to express value judgments instantaneously. These values are assessed by the persons the planner works with and thus are a factor in determining the planner's network for information exchange. Values may also tend to "box" the planner into positions that people expect him or her to take.

Like nearly everyone else, the planner will find that experience has a way of altering one's values. A balance is struck among competing values that may

Figure 10–1 Stages, positions, processes, and transactions in a career.

Basic stage or transition	Status or position	Psychological and organizational processes: transactions between individual and organization
1. Preentry	Aspirant, applicant, rushee	Preparation, education, anticipatory socialization
Entry (transition)	Entrant, postulant, recruit	Recruitment, rushing, testing, screening, selection, acceptance ("hiring"); passage through external inclusion boundary; rites of entry; induction and orientation
2. Basic training, novitiate	Trainee, novice, pledge	Training, indoctrination, socialization, testing of the man by the organization, tentative acceptance into group
Initiation, first vows (transition)	Initiate, graduate	Passage through first inner inclusion boundary, acceptance as member and conferring of organizational status, rite of passage and acceptance
3. First regular assignment	New member	First testing by the man of his own capacity to function; granting of real responsibility (playing for keeps); passage through functional boundary with assignment to specific job or department
Substages		
3a. Learning the job 3b. Maximum performance 3c. Becoming obsolete 3d. Learning new skills, et cetera		Indoctrination and testing of man by immediate workgroup leading to acceptance or rejection; if accepted, further education and socialization (learning the ropes); preparation for higher status through coaching, seeking visibility, finding sponsors
Promotion or leveling off (transition)		Preparation, testing, passage through hierarchical boundary, rite of passage; may involve passage through functional boundary as well (rotation)
4. Second assignment	Legitimate member (fully accepted)	Processes under no. 3 repeat
Substages		
5. Granting of tenure	Permanent member	Passage through another inner inclusion boundary
6. Termination and exit (transition)	Old-timer, senior citizen	Preparation for exit, cooling the mark out, rites of exit (testimonial dinners, and so on)
7. Postexit	Alumnus, emeritus, retired	Granting of peripheral status, consultant or senior advisor

change with the personalities involved, or with prevailing circumstances. Land development negotiations provide an example. The planner must assess the power of each negotiating party, the costs and benefits to each party, and the values of each party. The city council or county board sees the strong possibility of more jobs (or more housing or more property tax revenue); the developer sees the opportunity for profit and personal gratification; the planner sees historic buildings or a low-income but economically viable neighborhood, or an irreplaceable wildlife refuge.

Planners may thus be distinguished from other public professionals by the values many of them bring to the job. Widespread among planners is the belief that the individual planner can apply his or her values to (1) influence investments to improve society, (2) influence political decisions with information, and (3) convince others of the rightness of recommendations.

Improve society

Most planners believe that planning can improve the quality of life. They believe that by working on physical, social, and economic problems they will contribute to resolving them. Further, resolving these problems is considered a high personal and public priority. Many planners would consider the following statements to be axiomatic:

1. The way that some public investment decisions are made and their priorities are set is inconsistent with the improvement of the physical, social, and economic status of society.
2. The planning process can improve the quality of the political process by which these public investment decisions are made.
3. Greater priority should be given to investment in human services and in communities where people live.
4. If greater emphasis could be placed on the future consequences of current decisions, the quality of life would be improved.

Information for decision makers

Many planners think that improving the quality and increasing the amount of information available to decision makers will increase the likelihood that their decisions will reflect the political will of a community, rather than the political will of special interests. Many planners believe that neither special interest groups nor the cumulative interests of those groups are comparable to or represent the public interest. Planners believe that a technical approximation of the public interest can be determined by applying the scientific method: recognition of a problem; factual description of the problem; collection of data through observation and experimentation; and formulation and testing of hypotheses to resolve the problem. Resolving continuing conflicts between application of the scientific method and the local political process is the essence of planning.

Obvious truths

Many planners believe that if others are exposed to the same information, they will draw the same conclusions planners do. By collecting and analyzing data, the planner expects to readily identify the course of action that should be taken. Many planners assume that like himself or herself, others will respond to facts with unvarnished conclusions.

Many local government employees besides planners bring to their assignments their definitions of the public interest, which may or may not revolve around improving the physical, social, and economic condition. Their perspectives may

Figure 10–2 Planners' values as reflected in Columbia, Maryland.
The top photo was taken in 1966 and shows an architect's
model of the Columbia town center as projected for 1980. Photo
by Ezra Stoller © ESTO. The bottom photo, taken in 1983, shows the
actual development of the Columbia town center.

not be as long range as those of the planner. The task of systematically gathering and analyzing facts may not be a high priority. The relative importance of technical analysis compared to political reality may be mixed in different proportions, and planners may be more willing to go out on a limb with their beliefs than other professionals.

Ethics of planners

Ethics are often confused with morals, but there is a difference. Ethics is both the science of morals and the prevailing code of morals. Morals is the practice of ethics. This may seem like theological hairsplitting, but the point is that the person who violates an ethical standard or prescription acts immorally.[3] The ethical codes for members of professional societies are guides or standards for behavior. Sometimes the standards are quite clear; at other times the standards blend into professional values. The following example of nine ethical prescriptions for planners shows this range from the specific to the ambiguously professional:

1. Concern for the public interest. Although planners may have a more systematic approach to defining the public interest than the average citizen, this does not give them the right to actually make decisions in public matters.
2. Statutory responsibilities to enforce public policies.
3. Advancement of knowledge for its own sake. This means complete exploration of all facts before arriving at conclusions, and full disclosure of methods and results.
4. Dissent. If the planner believes his or her agency is not acting in the best interests of the public—in spite of the obligation of loyalty to his or her employer—dissent may be required. The more responsible the position of the employee (for example, planning director) and the more venal or egregious the issue, the more likely are ethics to demand the expression of dissent.
5. Loyalty, including obedience to instructions within the scope of responsibilities, service, the employer's interest, and confidentiality.
6. Guild loyalty to assist those entering the profession, support education and research in the field, and protect the good name of planning.
7. Knowledge and competence to understand the processes required for making public decisions, weighing costs and benefits, comparing long-term against short-term results, considering all aspects of a single proposal, separating public from private interests, and understanding consequences.
8. Autonomy to provide independent advice and to refuse to follow circumscribed instructions that will have a deleterious effect on the end product.
9. Allegiance to the client with respect to maintaining confidentiality, avoiding conflicts of interest, abstaining from personal involvement in the client's affairs, and uniformly representing the client's interests in dealing with others.[4]

Ethical standards

Managing the planning office includes paying attention to opportunities for unethical staff performance. The ethical prescriptions listed above can help planners respond to these situations. Yet, prescriptions such as these and the codes of ethics such as those adopted and administered by the American Planning

Association and the International City Management Association are of greatest value in circumstances when ethical decisions are the least obvious. Professionals know you should not lie, cheat, or steal. Their individual values and judgment have greatest bearing, however, on the gray areas of ethical choice.

Behavioral norms comprise professional ethics and represent guidelines for planners and others to follow. The political and economic importance of the planner's work increases the likelihood that he or she will face ethical choices. Election to public office can hinge on a citizen's position on a land use issue being addressed by the planner. Economic windfalls to developers can hinge on a zoning map amendment recommended by the planner. The planner brings the long-range and issue-related perspective to public decisions. Others therefore try to influence his or her opinions and recommendations. These types of pressures on the planner to come up with predetermined answers, or answers that are "right" only for selected persons or groups, are responsible for the typical ethical dilemmas faced by planners.

Other ethical pressures develop during job hunting, report writing, and activities off the job. Here are five examples provided by two city managers and a county manager that apply equally well to planners.

1. Be truthful in preparing a professional résumé. Although it is a temptation to fudge on the facts, several members of the International City Management Association have been penalized for falsifying their résumés.
2. Do not skew a staff report to your point of view. With the complexities of data and analysis, this temptation is especially strong since there is less chance of getting caught. But your planning staff peers will not be fooled.
3. Restrict real property ownership to your own house. The temptations and opportunities in land development are almost unlimited in some cities and counties, but nothing undermines public confidence as much as conflict of interest.
4. Devote your working time to your employer. If you moonlight as a planning consultant, restrict those activities to evenings and weekends. Obviously you do not work for a consulting firm that is doing work for the city or county government that employs you.
5. Do not make a development permission recommendation that is obviously contrary to your professional standards or judgment. When the threat of dismissal accompanies pressure to make a recommendation contrary to your judgment, remember your reputation is part of the communications networks.[5]

Planners have special ethical obligations because they have access to more information—some of which is very sensitive—than almost anyone else in local government. Questions constantly arise with respect to (1) the right of the citizen to expect confidentiality of information; (2) the right of the public to have access to information; and (3) the professional obligation of the planner to present information that does not conceal essential facts and that is not distorted.

In surveys of what planners think is ethical, and why, several types of behavior by planners in the gray area of ethics have been identified:

1. Releasing draft recommendations on request from an unpublished plan
2. Distorting information to show personal opinion in a more favorable light
3. Leaking information without authorization
4. Threatening negative project recommendations if political support on another issue is not forthcoming
5. Organizing a coalition of citizen support to change public policy
6. Changing technical judgment due to pressure from a superior
7. Dramatizing an issue through the media to overcome public apathy.[6]

Political activity

Planners who are both employees and citizens of the jurisdiction(s) in which they work are expected to be nonpartisan in their jobs while participating in the political process as citizens. The American Society for Public Administration (ASPA) has prepared some self-diagnostic questions for persons in this position:

1. Do I allow my recommendations regarding policy, programs or personnel to be influenced by partisan political considerations? Are there instances in which I feel that this would be justified?
2. Am I fully aware of the laws governing my political activity? Is my citizenship compromised by these laws? Do I feel that they should be changed in any way?
3. Is it possible for me to act as a responsible professional administrator and also be active in partisan politics?
4. How do I view politically appointed administrators in my organization? Should expectations concerning their behavior and performance differ from those applied to me?
5. Has the potential risk of jeopardizing my career and professional standing caused me to withdraw from political activity? Am I satisfied with the situation? If not, what ought I to do about it?
6. How do I view the "playing of politics?" Is my most appropriate role one of participation, withdrawal, or something else?[7]

By answering these questions in advance of making personal decisions, the planner can prepare himself or herself for responding extemporaneously to these types of questions.

Policing ethics

Several state and local legislative bodies have adopted codes of ethics in recent years. They provide standards and guidelines for evaluating actions in the gray area between obviously ethical behavior and what is widely acknowledged as unethical behavior. Here are two examples.

New York In 1969 the New York state legislature required the governing body of every city, county, school district, town, and village to adopt a code of ethics. All municipal officials and employees receive a copy of the code, which stresses that "office-holding is a public trust and standards of political morality are higher than those of the marketplace."[8]

St. Mary's County, Maryland In 1982 the St. Mary's County, Maryland, Board of County Commissioners adopted a public ethics ordinance to assure that "the impartiality and the independent judgment of public officials and employees will be maintained."[9] All elected and appointed officials and employees are required to identify their interests in property, corporations, and noncorporate business entities doing business with the county. Gifts from them must also be identified and valued. A three-member ethics commission provides advisory opinions on ethical issues. Lobbyists spending over $100 annually must file registration statements with the commission.

Professional codes

Many professional associations have adopted codes of ethics. As might be expected, these codes vary widely in their coverage. Some are little more than pious statements of good intentions. A few seem to be self-serving statements of vocational objectives. Some are intended as public proclamations to encourage trust on the part of the public and clients. Still others are used for guidance and enforcement. The last group includes the well-known codes for the practice of law and medicine as well as two more modest efforts to guide the conduct of local government planners and managers.

American Institute of Certified Planners (AICP)   The AICP, an institute of the American Planning Association, is concerned with qualifications and standards for professional planners and for the development of the profession. The AICP makes up about one-fourth of the twenty thousand APA members. The three major requirements for AICP membership are that the individual must be engaged in professional planning (this is thoroughly defined in the membership criteria), must have completed specified combinations of education and experience, and must pass an AICP written examination that is administered by the Educational Testing Service.

AICP members are obligated to observe the AICP Code of Ethics and Professional Conduct. The origins of this code can be traced to a code adopted by the American Institute of Planners in 1948. (The American Institute of Planners merged with the American Society of Planning Officials in 1978 to form the American Planning Association.)

In 1959 the code was revised to include more tenets and tighten administrative procedures. In 1970 a Code of Professional Responsibility was adopted to correct two principal flaws of its predecessor by (1) reducing the preoccupation with regulation of intraprofessional economic issues, and (2) increasing the clarity of the language to aid in enforcement. Further improvements were made with the 1981 adoption of the Code of Ethics and Professional Conduct. Among these improvements were the removal of language protecting consultant members from unfair competition and a broadening of the responsibility for code administration to chapters representing AICP members in most states.

The substance and administration of the code have been sensitive to member interests. Restrictive trade practices, antitrust measures, and fee competition were concerns after Section 701 greatly increased the funding of planning in 1954. Social concerns became ethical issues after the urban riots and Great Society programs of the 1960s. Free competition and discreet advertising became acceptable in the 1980s. The two codes in effect from 1978 to 1984 had two cases brought against members.

Members are obligated to observe the AICP Code of Ethics and Professional Conduct. The code has twenty-eight provisions grouped into four subjects: responsibilities to the public, to clients and employers, to the profession, and to oneself. These provisions are an unusual combination of prohibitions (conflict of interest, for example); maxims ("strive for excellence of environmental design"); and positive and negative admonitions relative to the professional practice of planning. Among the latter are provisions governing confidentiality of information from clients and employers, the obligation to provide full and accurate information on planning issues, the responsibility to obtain citizen input both from groups and from individuals, and the obligation to contribute time and information to the training and professional development of others.

The introduction to the code points out that the basic values of society "are often in competition with each other," and that the "principles of this code sometimes compete. For example, the need to provide full public information may compete with the need to respect confidences." Other sections of the code strive for a balance between the political and social (that is, public) side of planning and the professional, technical, interrelated, and long-range side of planning. It is not an easy marriage!

The present version of the code has written procedures involving the APA executive director, the professional committees of APA chapters, and the AICP Ethics Committee. Any person, member or nonmember, can obtain informal advice and advisory rulings upon request. The sanctions, progressively, are private reprimand, public censure, and suspension and expulsion from membership.

Figure 10–3   Code of
Ethics and Professional
Conduct, American
Institute of Certified
Planners.

The Planner's Responsibility to the Public

A. A planner's primary obligation is to serve the public interest. While the definition of the public interest is formulated through continuous debate, a planner owes allegiance to a conscientiously attained concept of the public interest, which requires these special obligations:

1) A planner must have special concern for the long range consequences of present actions.

2) A planner must pay special attention to the interrelatedness of decisions.

3) A planner must strive to provide full, clear and accurate information on planning issues to citizens and governmental decision-makers.

4) A planner must strive to give citizens the opportunity to have a meaningful impact on the development of plans and programs. Participation should be broad enough to include people who lack formal organization or influence.

5) A planner must strive to expand choice and opportunity for all persons, recognizing a special responsibility to plan for the needs of disadvantaged groups and persons, and must urge the alteration of policies, institutions and decisions which oppose such needs.

6) A planner must strive to protect the integrity of the natural environment.

7) A planner must strive for excellence of environmental design and endeavor to conserve the heritage of the built environment.

The Planner's Responsibility to Clients and Employers

B. A planner owes diligent, creative, independent and competent performance of work in pursuit of the client's or employer's interest. Such performance should be consistent with the planner's faithful service to the public interest.

1) A planner must exercise independent professional judgment on behalf of clients and employers.

2) A planner must accept the decisions of a client or employer concerning the objectives and nature of the professional services to be performed unless the course of action to be pursued involves conduct which is illegal or inconsistent with the planner's primary obligation to the public interest.

3) A planner must not, without the consent of the client or employer, and only after full disclosure, accept or continue to perform work if there is an actual, apparent, or reasonably foreseeable conflict between the interests of the client or employer and the personal or financial interest of the planner or of another past or present client or employer of the planner.

4) A planner must not solicit prospective clients or employment through use of false or misleading claims, harassment or duress.

5) A planner must not sell or offer to sell services by stating or implying an ability to influence decisions by improper means.

6) A planner must not use the power of any office to seek or obtain a special advantage that is not in the public interest nor any special advantage that is not a matter of public knowledge.

7) A planner must not accept or continue to perform work beyond the planner's professional competence or accept work which cannot be performed with the promptness required by the prospective client or employer, or which is required by the circumstances of the assignment.

8) A planner must not reveal information gained in a professional relationship which the client or employer has requested be held inviolate. Exceptions to this requirement of non-disclosure may be made only when (a) required by process of law, or (b) required to prevent a clear violation of law, or (c) required to prevent a substantial injury to the public. Disclosure pursuant to (b) and (c) must not be made until after the planner has verified the facts and issues involved and, when practicable, has exhausted efforts to obtain reconsideration of the matter and has sought separate opinions on the issue from other qualified professionals employed by the client or employer.

The Planner's Responsibility to the Profession and to Colleagues

C. A planner should contribute to the development of the profession by improving knowledge and techniques, making work relevant to solutions of community problems, and increasing public understanding of planning activities. A planner should treat fairly the professional views of qualified colleagues and members of other professions.

1) A planner must protect and enhance the integrity of the profession and must be responsible in criticism of the profession.

2) A planner must accurately represent the qualifications, views and findings of colleagues.

3) A planner, who has responsibility for reviewing the work of other professionals, must fulfill this responsibility in a fair, considerate, professional and equitable manner.

4) A planner must share the results of experience and research which contribute to the body of planning knowledge.

5) A planner must examine the applicability of planning theories, methods and standards to the facts and analysis of each particular situation and must not accept the applicability

of a customary solution without first establishing its appropriateness to the situation.

6) A planner must contribute time and information to the professional development of students, interns, beginning professionals and other colleagues.

7) A planner must strive to increase the opportunities for women and members of recognized minorities to become professional planners.

The Planner's Self-Responsibility

D. A planner should strive for high standards of professional integrity, proficiency and knowledge.

1) A planner must not commit a deliberately wrongful act which reflects adversely on the planner's professional fitness.

2) A planner must respect the rights of others and, in particular, must not improperly discriminate against persons.

3) A planner must strive to continue professional education.

4) A planner must accurately represent professional qualifications, education and affiliations.

5) A planner must systematically and critically analyze ethical issues in the practice of planning.

6) A planner must strive to contribute time and effort to groups lacking in adequate planning resources and to voluntary professional activities.

Figure 10–4
City Management
Code of Ethics.

THE PURPOSE of the International City Management Association is to increase the proficiency of city managers, county managers, and other municipal administrators and to strengthen the quality of urban government through professional management. To further these objectives, certain ethical principles shall govern the conduct of every member of the International City Management Association, who shall:

1 Be dedicated to the concepts of effective and democratic local government by responsible elected officials and believe that professional general management is essential to the achievement of this objective.

2 Affirm the dignity and worth of the services rendered by government and maintain a constructive, creative, and practical attitude toward urban affairs and a deep sense of social responsibility as a trusted public servant.

3 Be dedicated to the highest ideals of honor and integrity in all public and personal relationships in order that the member may merit the respect and confidence of the elected officials, of other officials and employees, and of the public.

4 Recognize that the chief function of local government at all times is to serve the best interests of all of the people.

5 Submit policy proposals to elected officials, provide them with facts and advice on matters of policy as a basis for making decisions and setting community goals, and uphold and implement municipal policies adopted by elected officials.

6 Recognize that elected representatives of the people are entitled to the credit for the establishment of municipal policies; responsibility for policy execution rests with the members.

7 Refrain from participation in the election of the members of the employing legislative body, and from all partisan political activities which would impair performance as a professional administrator.

8 Make it a duty continually to improve the member's professional ability and to develop the competence of associates in the use of management techniques.

9 Keep the community informed on municipal affairs; encourage communication between the citizens and all municipal officers; emphasize friendly and courteous service to the public; and seek to improve the quality and image of public service.

10 Resist any encroachment on professional responsibilities, believing the member should be free to carry out official policies without interference, and handle each problem without discrimination on the basis of principle and justice.

11 Handle all matters of personnel on the basis of merit so that fairness and impartiality govern a member's decisions, pertaining to appointments, pay adjustments, promotions, and discipline.

12 Seek no favor; believe that personal aggrandizement or profit secured by confidential information or by misuse of public time is dishonest.

International City Management Association

International City Management Association (ICMA)   The International City Managers' Association adopted the City Manager's Code of Ethics in 1924 by a membership vote at its annual conference in Montreal. The code was amended and revised in 1938, 1952, 1969, 1972, and 1976. The major changes made in these years were instituted to clarify the prohibition on partisan political activity, emphasize the community and policy responsibilities of the city manager, and broaden membership eligibility to cover all chief appointed management executives in local government. In addition, in 1969 the name of the association was changed to the International City Management Association, and the name of the code was changed to the City Management Code of Ethics.

The code includes standards and principles for professional conduct and is buttressed by interpretive guidelines for each of the twelve provisions in the code, and by rules of procedures to be followed by the executive director, the Committee on Professional Conduct, and the Executive Board in handling cases of alleged violations of the code. The ICMA constitution provides for enforcement through censure, suspension, or expulsion of members.

Since the late 1960s the code has been strengthened by the adoption of guidelines and procedures, with the following positive results:

1. The code has symbolic as well as substantive value for members. It is a frequent reminder of membership obligations.
2. The Committee on Professional Conduct provides positive guidance as well as discipline. In recent years the committee has issued advisory opinions to members upon request.
3. Guidelines for interpreting code provisions, adopted in 1972, have provided practical suggestions for membership conduct in relation to the code.
4. The code has been used several times to reaffirm the ethical conduct of a member who was under attack locally.[10]

ICMA ethics cases   The ICMA Committee on Professional Conduct is a standing committee that investigates all alleged violations of the City Management Code of Ethics with the help of state associations of managers and administrators. Some of the cases involve clear-cut felonies and conflicts of interest that lead to expulsion from membership. Others, however, involve professional areas of job hunting and management practices. Here are examples of the variety of such issues that the committee deals with:

A job applicant omitted references on his résumé to two cities where he had served as city manager and extended his employment dates in another city to reduce the appearance of being a job hopper.

A manager falsified his age and education on his résumé.

A manager left his job and the city without notice to accept a job elsewhere.

A manager amended the budget without consulting the department head.

A manager solicited a job as manager in another city before the job was open.

A manager accepted a job but failed to report to take up his duties.

Conclusion

This chapter opens with the statement, "Planners are sometimes thought of as a breed apart." This view reflects a difference in values as well as in other characteristics compared with other groups. Planners are well educated, intellectually inclined, and imbued with a strong sense of social consciousness. A planner's values and actions will be noticed and judged in a local government, especially the smaller city or county government. The wise planner holds to his or her values, recognizes that others may have quite different values, and adjusts actions accordingly.

Most planners believe that their values will enable them to improve society, influence political decisions, and convince others that their recommendations are correct. In applying these values, planners must recognize but not judge the values of others. The developer who is out to maximize profit by all legal means is not unethical. The neighborhood spokesperson who is out to protect property values is not necessarily narrow and selfish. If you and the other person or group can agree on the facts underlying a problem or issue, and acknowledge the differences in values, the discussions, hearings, and negotiations will be much more effective.

Codes of ethics for professional associations help bring group values into focus by providing standards, guidelines, procedures, opinions, and sanctions. They are not statutory codes with criminal and civil penalties, but they can be powerful tools, especially in that a person who violates them can be denied the right to practice or engage in his or her profession. But codes cannot do it all, of course. The Committee on Professional Standards of the American Society for Public Administration concluded that higher public service standards lie not so much in standards of behavior as in organizational processes that insist that the individual "consciously confront his values and take responsibility for consequent behavior."[11]

One way to build value consciousness into your daily work is to consider these three questions:

To what extent do you consciously consider the value premises of your recommendations, decisions, and actions?

To what extent have value assumptions been an articulated part of the policy development dialogue with legislators, citizens, and subordinates?

To what extent have you accepted the definition of public interest values as a desirable and needed dimension of training and development for yourself and others?[12]

Ethics has been defined as a code of morals, but that code pertains to the behavior of individuals who are trying to resolve problems that often can only be resolved by personal decisions. Guidelines, advisory opinions, and procedures—such as those outlined by the City Management Code of Ethics—are helpful. In addition, several tests can be applied to make ethics an integral part of your daily work.

In handling an incident are you willing to talk about it with family and friends? In extreme cases, are you willing to testify in administrative or judicial hearings?

Can you maintain the integrity of the planning process? Can you sustain your professional effectiveness without compromising your values? Can you balance the ideal and the expedient without losing your self-respect?

Can you maintain the respect of your professional peers and your associates where you work?

Can you handle information equitably, in terms of both disclosure and of privacy?

Can you evaluate every proposal, issue, and decision on the basis of your *public* responsibility?

1 Israel Stollman, "The Values of the City Planner," in *The Practice of Local Government Planning*, Frank S. So et al., eds. (Washington, D.C.: International City Management Association, 1979), 8–14.

2 The following paragraphs on career and job cycles are based on: Wayne F. Anderson et al., *The Effective Local Government Manager* (Washington, D.C.: International City Management Association, 1983), 213–14.

3 H. W. Fowler, *A Dictionary of Modern English Usage*, 2d ed., revised by Sir Ernest Gowers (New York: Oxford University Press, 1965), 170–71. Fowler draws this distinction between ethics and morals, but many would turn this distinction around and define ethics as the practice or application of morals.

4 Abstracted from: Peter Marcuse, "Professional Ethics and Beyond: Values and Planning," *Journal of the American Institute of Planners* 42 (July 1976): 268–71.

5 Information abstracted from: Buford M. Watson, Jr., "Gray Areas for Professional Conduct"; Robert D. McEvoy, "Ethical Challenges in Local Government"; and Jack B. Arnold, "Ethical Dilemmas," in *Public Management* 63 (March 1981): 12–13, 20.

6 Elizabeth Howe and Jerome Kaufman, "The Ethics of Contemporary American Planners," *The Journal of the American Planning Association* 45 (July 1979): 244–45.

7 Herman Mertins, Jr., and Patrick J. Hennigan, eds., *Applying Professional Standards and Ethics in the '80s: A Workbook and Study Guide for Public Administrators* (Washington, D.C.: American Society for Public Administration, 1982), 16.

8 Joseph F. Zimmerman, "A Code of Ethics and Town Government," presented at the annual meeting of the Association of Towns of the State of New York, New York City, 16 February 1976.

9 St. Mary's County, Maryland, Public Ethics Ordinance, 1982, unpaginated.

10 These points have been abstracted from: William E. Besuden, "The Profession's Heritage: The ICMA Code of Ethics," *Public Management* 63 (March 1981): 4–5. For further background on the ICMA Code of Ethics, see three issues of *Public Management*: vol. 66 (February 1984) with the theme, "Ethics"; vol. 63 (March 1981) with the theme, "Ethics: Dictates and Dilemmas"; and vol. 57 (June 1975) with the theme, "Ethics in Local Government."

11 Frank P. Sherwood, "Professional Ethics," *Public Management* 57 (June 1975): 14.

12 Ibid.

Annotated bibliography

This bibliography is highly selective and is limited to references that augment the text. Many additional books, articles, and other references are cited in the endnotes to the individual chapters. The American Planning Association and the International City Management Association provide much of the current information on planning and management trends, developments, and applications for local governments through their extensive publications programs. The major periodical publications of each association will serve as basic reference points for users of this book. These references are shown in the following paragraphs.

Baseline Data Reports. Monthly. International City Management Association. Previously titled *Urban Data Service Reports* (1969–82), these reports provide data on current local government activities. Published in chart and tabular form with explanatory text. Data for most reports are gathered through year-round questionnaire surveys of local governments and other organizations.

Journal of the American Planning Association. Quarterly. American Planning Association. Professional and scholarly coverage of planning and urban affairs through articles, commentary, and extensive book reviews.

Management Information Service Reports. Monthly. International City Management Association. Published since 1946, many of these reports are topical case studies of planning and management techniques that have been successfully implemented.

The Municipal Year Book. Annual. International City Management Association. Published since 1934 with articles and data on local government issues of the year. Most data cover cities with populations over 10,000. In recent years, substantial attention has been given to transportation, local government planning, alternative services, local resources, and financial management.

Planning. Monthly. American Planning Association. Wide coverage of city and county planning, including articles on current developments, news reports and analyses, question-and-answer section, and book reviews and book notes.

Planning Advisory Service Reports. Monthly. American Planning Association. Reports are based on extensive research and analysis and cover almost every conceivable subject in urban and regional planning.

Public Management. Monthly. International City Management Association. Published since 1919, the magazine has evolved over the years in accordance with the changing interests of managers and the issues confronting local government. Each issue covers a specific subject. In recent years much of the coverage has dealt with urban economic issues, professional development, and the personal side of management.

1 The Context of Public Planning

Anderson, Wayne F., et al. *The Effective Local Government Manager.* Washington, D.C.: International City Management Association, 1983. For local government managers and assistants as well as students of public administration. Looks at the manager as a planner, budgeter, community relations expert, organizational leader, council facilitator, liaison with other governments, and family member.

Mosher, Frederick C., ed. *American Public Administration: Past, Present, Future.* University, Alabama: University of Alabama Press, 1975. Essays on teaching public administration in American universities.

Newland, Chester A., ed., *Professional Public Executives.* Washington, D.C.: American Society for Public Administration, 1980. A collection of articles from *Public Administration Review* that appeared between 1945 and 1977. The opening article by Chester A. Newland, written for this book, is a good overview of the changing roles of public managers.

Rabinovitz, Francine F. *City Politics and Planning*. New York: Atherton Press, 1969. Analyzes relation between city politics and city planning. Suggests problem-solving strategies.

Rutter, Laurence. *The Essential Community: Local Government in the Year 2000*. Washington, D.C.: International City Management Association, 1980. By using examples of local governments' failure to anticipate trends, such as the need for light rail transit, the contributors demonstrate the need for urbanists to be futurists also. They identify social, economic, and technological forces that will shape local government and propose strategies municipalities can use to cope with change. Projections about the local management profession are provided.

2 The Blending of Planning and Management

Crane, Donald P., and William A. Jones, Jr. *The Public Manager's Guide*. Washington, D.C.: Bureau of National Affairs, 1982. Introduction for graduate and undergraduate students to environment of the public manager. Describes the various roles of the public manager: policy maker, planner, personnel manager, labor relations negotiator, financial manager, and member of the management profession. Includes case studies.

Frieden, Bernard J. *The Environmental Protection Hustle*. Cambridge, Mass.: MIT Press, 1979. Two trends make it clear that there is, and will continue to be, a housing crisis: an unprecedented number of families looking for homes, and a slump in home building. Reasons that so few houses are being put on the market partly because of overly strict zoning regulations that are based on false notions of environmental protection. Postulates that home building has little to do with serious environmental issues

Godschalk, David R., ed. *Planning in America: Learning from Turbulence*. Washington, D.C.: American Institute of Planners, 1974. Papers presented at a symposium on urban planning: theory, method, practice, and education. In each section one paper discusses the state of the art while another looks at the future of informational needs, roles of the planner, land location forecasting, and the use of practices from real estate and business planning.

Johnson, M. Bruce, ed. *Resolving the Housing Crisis: Government Policy, Decontrol, and the Public Interest*. San Francisco: Pa-

cific Institute for Public Policy Research, 1982. Worsening housing crisis has resulted from current property owners' exploitation of land use regulations to prevent newcomers from buying in their neighborhoods. This collection of essays covers a wide range of topics: rent controls, building codes, exclusionary zoning, water policy, housing search costs, and constitutional property rights.

Judd, Dennis R. "Trickle-down Theory as Urban Policy." Paper presented at the 1982 annual meeting of the Association of Collegiate Schools of Planning, Chicago, 22 October 1982. The urban impact of the Reagan administration's "New Federalism" is described. Includes tables that rate individual states' abilities to assume formerly federal program funding and administration.

McLean, Mary, ed. *Local Planning Administration*. Chicago: International City Managers' Association, 1959. Describes the functions of local government planning. It is the third edition of five books on planning prepared by ICMA.

Miller, Gary J. *Cities by Contract: The Politics of Municipal Incorporation*. Cambridge, Mass.: MIT Press, 1981. A political analysis of the trend-setting Lakewood (California) Plan of city incorporation. Describes land use and tax burden political rationales for creating new municipalities in Los Angeles and Orange counties after World War II.

Moore, Barbara H., ed. *The Entrepreneur in Local Government*. Washington, D.C.: International City Management Association, 1983. Twenty-five articles on municipal enterprises, user fees and charges, local government marketing, pricing policies, and strategic planning. Several of the articles are case studies of specific enterprises launched in individual cities.

Nenno, Mary K., and Paul C. Brophy. *Housing and Local Government*. Washington, D.C.: International City Management Association, 1982. Topics include conservation, rehabilitation, assisted housing management, conversion, and gentrification. Case studies of creative finance and provision of units are provided.

Regional Municipality of Ontario, Canada. "Briefing on Past Work on the Corporate Plan to the Task Force Leaders' Steering Committee on the Corporate Plan." C. E. Babb. 1982. Mimeograph. Describes the steps used to assist department heads to set in order of priority tasks required to provide public services. Describes new programs needed in the next five years.

Ridley, Clarence E., and Herbert A. Simon. *Measuring Municipal Activities: A Survey of Suggested Criteria and Reporting Forms for Appraising Administration*. Chicago: International City Managers' Association, 1938. Discusses productivity measurement techniques, statistical measures, and criteria for measuring efficiency. Analyzes a wide range of municipal services, discussing measurement practices for each. A classic that is out of print but available in many research libraries.

Scott, Mel. *American City Planning Since 1890: A History Commemorating the Fiftieth Anniversary of the American Institute of Planners*. Berkeley, Calif.: University of California Press, 1969. A history of the growth of city planning and the planning profession in modern government. Shows the interplay of political, social, and economic forces that made up the environment in which planners made the decisions that influenced the growth and development of American cities in each of eight time periods since 1890.

So, Frank S., et al., eds. *The Practice of Local Government Planning*. Washington, D.C.: International City Management Association, 1979. A comprehensive introductory text for college-level students of planning, planners without extensive education in planning, and urban administrators from other fields. Responds to the growing complexity of city planning by focusing on issues rather than techniques. Covers subjects such as urban renewal, recreational services, and transportation planning for the nongrowing municipality.

———. *The Practice of State and Regional Planning*. Chicago: American Planning Association. Forthcoming. Companion volume to *The Practice of Local Government Planning*.

U.S. Advisory Commission on Intergovernmental Relations. *An Agenda for American Federalism: Restoring Confidence and Competence*. A-86. Washington, D.C.: ACIR, 1981. Conclusions and recommendations on what the federal role should be.

U.S. General Accounting Office. *Housing and Community Development: National Problems*. Gaithersburg, Md.: GAO, 1982. Major issues related to federal involvement in housing and community development: mortgage credit and finance, community and economic development, aid to small businesses and farmers, and other topics.

Weiner, Edward. *Evolution of Urban Transportation Planning*. Washington, D.C.: Urban Analysis Program, Office of Transportation Systems Analysis and Information, 1976. Photocopy. This report traces the evolution of transportation planning, including such factors as citizen participation, environmental regulations, land development, and social issues.

Wikstrom, Gunnar, Jr., and Nelson Wikstrom, eds. *Municipal Government, Politics, and Policy: A Reader*. Washington, D.C.: University Press of America. 1982. Readings on urban politics. Topics include the role of local government within the federal system, community power, organization of city government, and urban planning.

3 Organizing for Comprehensive Planning

Baily, R. Lance, and Cortus T. Koehler. "Citizens in the Planning Process: How Sacramento County Does It." *National Civic Review* 71 (September 1982): 415–24. Sacramento County, California, has institutionalized citizen participation. Local planning councils advise the county planning commission but have no legal authority.

Burke, Edmund M. *A Participatory Approach to Urban Planning*. New York: Human Sciences Press, 1979. Planning is part of a social change process that depends on public participation for its effectiveness. Part I defines planning and explains the principles for successful public participation. Part II divides the planning process into six phases and shows how these principles can be applied to each phase.

Catanese, Anthony James. *Planners and Local Politics: Impossible Dreams*. Sage Library of Social Research, vol. 7. Beverly Hills, Calif.: Sage Publications, 1974. Proposes changes in training state and local government planners. To best function in our society of special interest groups, planners should be skilled in mediation, negotiation, and bargaining so that they can help solve policy questions, resolve group disputes, and effectively intervene in the political process.

City of Charlottesville, Virginia. Department of Community Development. *Comprehensive Plan*. 1979. Outlines community needs and potential in physical environment, social needs, and economic programs. Special considerations include the community's relations with the University of Virginia, the need for distinct neighborhoods, and the need for community participation.

City of Charlottesville, Virginia. Department
of Planning and Community Development.
"Department of Community Development."
Prepared by Satyendra Singh Huja. [1981?]
Four-page public information statement describing the task force approach to planning
with involvement from governmental agencies and community groups. Includes goals
and future roles for the department.

City of Eugene, Oregon. Eugene Economic
Development Committee. *Eugene's Economic Development Strategies*. 1980. Describes the process used by the city to
identify four economic development goals:
(1) expansion of local firms; (2) provision of
land for firms wishing to locate in the city;
(3) training for unemployed workers, particularly youth and women; and (4) expansion of
tourist industries. Specific strategies are
proposed for each goal.

City of Modesto, California. Department of
Planning and Community Development. *Urban Growth Policy Review, 1981*. Describes
Modesto's urban policy: containing growth
within the city's current service area as long
as economically reasonable and restricting
annexations to areas contiguous to the city.

City of Modesto, California. Planning Commission. *Modesto Urban Area General Plan*.
1981. A compilation of separate, state-man-
dated plans for land use, housing, open
space and recreation, conservation, noise,
safety, scenic highways, and seismic safety.

City of Phoenix, Arizona. *Phoenix Concept
Plan 2000: A Program for Planning*. 1979.
This plan is based on the "urban village"
concept of areas that have a dense core
and thin out toward the periphery.

City of Phoenix, Arizona. Planning Department. *Issue Papers: The Best of '81*. May
1982. Part of an annual series published by
the city. The 1981 reports cover the concentration of high-rise buildings in the downtown core, the development of the "urban
village" for multifamily housing, the city's af-
fordable housing plan, commercial office
development, zoning, and current housing
conditions.

Corporation of the District of West Vancouver, British Columbia. *Official West Vancouver Community Plan*. 1980. Documents objective to preserve the city's park-like,
neighborhood-oriented character by excluding industrial development and allowing only
slow, controlled growth.

King County, Washington. Department of
Planning and Community Development.

Planning Division. *King County General Development Guide*. Seattle, 1981. This plan
includes findings on population and employment, energy use, public improvement
costs, energy-efficient land use, diversity of
housing and employment opportunities, and
aesthetic and recreational use of natural resources.

————. *Shoreline Community Plan and Area
Zoning*. Seattle, 1980. Findings and recommendations on land use, transportation,
parks and recreation, and comprehensive
zoning for Shoreline area of King County.

Lexington–Fayette Urban County Planning
Commission. *1980 Comprehensive Plan,
Growth Planning System*. Lexington, Kentucky, 1980. Covers growth management
and public service objectives: promoting vocational education, increasing citizen involvement, improving the appearance of the
downtown area, and encouraging employment locations near residential areas and
mass transportation.

Maryland–National Capital Park and Planning Commission. *Functional Master Plan for
the Preservation of Agriculture and Rural
Open Space in Montgomery County*. Silver
Spring, Md.: The Commission, 1980. Documents the use of such techniques as rural
open space zones, greenbelts, open space
inventories, and growth management systems.

Montgomery County Planning Board of the
Maryland–National Capital Park and Planning Commission. *1981 Report on Comprehensive Planning Policies*. Silver Spring,
Md., 1982. Major staging guidelines and
forecasts for population, housing, and employment by planning area. Land inventory
and adequacy of transportation facilities are
described.

————. *Planning, Staging, and Regulating:
Fifth Growth Policy Report of the Montgomery County Planning Board*. Silver Spring,
Md., 1979. Describes the concepts and
techniques used to forecast population and
economic growth and incorporate these
findings into the capital improvement plan.
Adequacy of public facilities and their fiscal
impact are highlighted.

National Council for Urban Economic Development. *Coordinated Urban Economic Development: A Case Study Analysis*. Washington, D.C., 1978. Shows city governments
how to coordinate an economic development planning process. Case studies illustrate alternative techniques.

Powers, Stanley Piazza, F. Gerald Brown, and David S. Arnold, eds. *Developing the Municipal Organization.* Washington, D.C.: International City Management Association, 1974. Useful chapters on organization, human relations, management styles, motivation, decision making, administrative communication, management by objectives, and citizen participation.

Regional Municipality of Halton, Ontario, Canada. *The Next Five Years: Corporate Plan 1982–1986.* 1982. Priorities for allocating resources. Relates economic conditions (businesses seeking to escape the high costs of the Toronto area) to continued growth in population, employment, and housing.

Reigeluth, George A., and Harold Wolman. *The Determinants and Implications of Communities' Changing Competitive Advantages: A Literature Review.* Washington, D.C.: Urban Institute, 1981. Many studies make the mistake of assuming that national demand, federal regulations, and technology trends will remain the same. This report identifies tax levels, transportation, raw materials, and other factors that determine competitive advantages of cities.

Sayles, Leonard R. *Leadership: What Effective Managers Really Do . . . and How They Do It.* New York: McGraw-Hill, 1979. A definitive assessment of executive-level roles and competencies, focusing on responsibilities to keep uncertainty to a minimum and to manage contingencies.

Steil, Kenneth M. *Strategic Planning in Local Government: Background Paper.* Washington, D.C.: Department of Housing and Urban Development, 1982. Compares "strategic planning" in public and private sector projects and describes the components of a strategic planning process.

Topping, Kenneth C. "Thinking Big in California." *Planning* 48 (October 1982): 16–20. San Bernardino County's use of the "specific plan" technique as a cost-saving alternative to zoning. Under state law California localities can use specific implementation of a general plan that is more flexible than zoning. Using this approach the county developed an environmentally sensitive area for 90,000 residents, channeling development away from the most fragile areas.

Triangle J Council of Governments. *Focus on Tomorrow.* Research Triangle Park, N.C., 1982. Plan to provide training and investment for residents of a six-county area, as an alternative to bringing in large numbers of skilled workers from outside the area, which would result in urban sprawl and strained public services. Plan proposes to attract high growth industries that pay wages above the national average.

Wagner, Kenneth C. *Economic Development Manual.* Jackson, Miss.: University of Mississippi Press, 1978. This is an easy-to-read guide for chambers of commerce, industrial foundations, city and county officials, development organizations, and private developers.

Walter, Susan M. *Proceedings of the White House Conference on Strategic Planning, February 10–12, 1980; Baltimore, Maryland.* Washington, D.C.: Council of State Planning Agencies, 1980. Many corporations use "strategic planning" to develop a consistent long-term plan of action and to adapt to environmental change. This conference was called to discuss the possibility of applying this concept to government. Executives from several companies reviewed their use of strategic planning.

Wildavsky, Aaron. *Leadership in a Small Town.* Totowa, N.J.: Bedminster Press, 1964. Case study of the way community decisions are made in a small town (Oberlin, Ohio). Shows how information gets around.

Wolman, Harold. *Making Local Economic Development Decisions: A Framework for Local Officials.* Washington, D.C.: Urban Institute, 1981. How to renew local economies. A series of questions is proposed to produce creative thinking on identifying problems, choosing policies and techniques, assessing resources, and projecting the impact of present and proposed policies.

4 Organizing for Project Planning

Branch, Melville C. *Continuous City Planning: Integrating Municipal Management and City Planning.* New York: John Wiley & Sons, 1981. Proposes both the ideas and direct methods and tools for continuous city planning. Plans of different departments and agencies would be correlated through information, analysis, and projection. Tools would include maps, charts, sophisticated graphics, computer models, and representation-simulation—all controlled through a "city planning center."

Branston, Ann, Charles J. Schwabe, and Nancy Shamberg. *Thirty-Nine Program Ideas.* Washington, D.C.: International City Management Association, 1977. Descriptions of innovative projects for policy planning and evaluation, housing, budget planning, land use studies, growth management, natural resources management, land use planning, and other topics.

Charles F. Kettering Foundation. "Negotiating the City's Future: A Report on an Experimental Plan for Pooling Urban Investments and Bargaining to Coordinate Policy Goals." A supplement to *Nation's Cities Weekly*, 26 November 1979. Negotiated Investment Strategy (NIS) is a method federal, state, and local officials use for agreeing on priorites and committing money and time to improve a community's physical and human capital. Describes NIS in Columbus, Ohio; Gary, Indiana; and St. Paul, Minnesota.

City of Eugene, Oregon. Planning Department. *Private Reinvestment and Neighborhood Revitalization in Eugene*. 1980. Summarizes the private sector's reinvestment in downtown neighborhoods and Eugene's three-pronged attack on neighborhood blight: neighborhood plans, publicly funded projects, and private reinvestment. Data for reinvestment are drawn from legal documents of twenty-two financial institutions.

City of Phoenix, Arizona. Office of Development Services. Development Coordination Office. *Policy and Procedures Manual*. [1981?] Compiles site plan and subdivision information into a single document that highlights development policies and procedures for urban growth. Procedures for obtaining permits are described on a step-by-step basis: presubmittal conference, filing, review, appeals, final plan approval, and fast tracking. Special sections are included for residential, commercial and industrial development.

Committee for Economic Development. Research and Policy Committee. *Public-Private Partnership: An Opportunity for Urban Communities:* New York and Washington, D.C.: CED, 1982. Examines how urban communities can organize government, business, and community resources to meet varied needs, covering topics ranging from the civic foundations of public-private partnership to economic development, neighborhood improvement, and community services.

Creighton, James L. *The Public Involvement Manual*. Cambridge, Mass.: Abt Books, 1981. Guide to citizen participation for public and corporate officials: general principles, program design, organization for public involvement, conduct of meetings, and public relations methods.

Cullinan, Terrence. *In Good Company: Corporate Community Action and How to Do It in Your Community*. Menlo Park, Calif.: SRI International, 1982. Extensive public/private collaboration will grow further because local governments must assume more services. Studies have shown, however, that local problems hurt corporate profits. Therefore, a neutral third party often can successfully arrange public/private ventures.

Dotson, A. Bruce. "Notes on Political Feasibility: Getting Around 'No.'" Paper presented at national convention of the American Planning Association, Dallas, Texas, 8–12 May 1982. The success of planning proposals often depends upon trust and communication, yet little has been written for planners on this topic. This paper surveys the literature available to help planners avoid "no win" situations. A list of nine possible obstacles to acceptance is included.

Fosler, R. Scott, and Renee A. Berger. *Public-Private Partnerships in American Cities*. Lexington, Mass.: Lexington Books, 1982. Seven case studies of public-private partnerships in Atlanta, Baltimore, Chicago, Dallas, Minneapolis-St. Paul, Pittsburgh, and Portland.

Meshenberg, Michael J. *The Administration of Flexible Zoning Techniques*. Planning Advisory Service Report No. 313. Chicago: American Society of Planning Officials, June 1976. Covers nine techniques for flexible zoning and the negotiation process, standards, and the role of comprehensive planning.

Miller, Donald. "Project Location Analysis Using the Goals Achievement Method of Evaluation." *Journal of the American Planning Association* 46 (April 1980): 195–208. Method for determining neighborhoods for rehabilitation loan assistance in Everett, Washington. Uses indicators to measure a neighborhood's need and potential for successful rehabilitation. Both the city council and a citizens advisory committee endorsed this method for its logic and simplicity.

Murphy, Michael J. *Reforming Local Development Regulations: Approaches in Five Cities*. Municipal Management Innovation Series, no. 35. Washington, D.C.: International City Management Association, Spring 1982. Methods used in five cities to cut down the paper work and processing time for land development applications and other procedures. The cities are Salinas, California; Cleveland Heights, Ohio; Phoenix, Arizona; Brattleboro, Vermont; and Fort Collins, Colorado.

Porter, Douglas. "Helping Your Community Streamline the Development Process." *Urban Land* 41 (May 1982): 18–25. Suggests streamlining local land development permission application process by bringing government administrators together to diagnose problems and quicken each stage of the process: preapplication, staff review, and citizen review.

SRI International. *Developing Public/Private Approaches to Community Problem Solving.* Management Information Service Report, vol. 14, no. 7 (Washington, D.C.: International City Management Association, 1982). Pinpoints ways a government can reap maximum benefit from community's resources. Shows ways public and private sectors can identify areas of mutual interest.

————. *Rediscovering Local Governance: Public-Private Community Initiatives.* Menlo Park, Calif.: SRI International, 1982. Discusses public-private community problem solving trends. New developments are examined from the state government, local government, business, and community perspectives with applications to housing, employment, business development, health care, and human services.

Vranicar, John. *Setting Zoning and Subdivision Fees: Making Ends Meet.* Planning Advisory Service Report No. 357. Chicago: American Planning Association, January 1981. Examines questions to be considered in redesigning fee structures for processing development applications to compensate for inflation and diminished tax revenue.

Vranicar, John, Welford Sanders, and David Mosena. *Streamlining Land Use Regulation: A Guidebook for Local Governments.* American Planning Association and Urban Land Institute for the U.S. Department of Housing and Urban Development, Office of Policy Development and Research, no. H 2996. Washington, D.C.: Government Printing Office, 1980. GPO no. 0–723–106/581. A manual for planning officials that offers advice on streamlining development permission application review. Explains why streamlining is so appealing to local officials by describing a typical review process and highlighting factors that have complicated local regulation and driven up the cost of housing. The regulatory process is examined: preapplication, technical staff review, and lay review to determine ways of streamlining.

Warren, Charles R. *National Implications of a Negotiated Approach to Federalism.* Dayton, Ohio: Charles F. Kettering Foundation, 1981. As the federal government turns over more social programs to the states there will be an increased need for negotiated solutions to urban problems. The three levels of government and the private sector will need to cooperate since the current fiscal environment has increased their need to rely on each other. Negotiated Investment Strategy problems are listed.

Wilentz, C. J. *Syllabus: So. Burlington NAACP et al. v. Township of Mount Laurel (A-35/36/172) and others.* New Jersey Superior Court, 1983. A summary of six housing discrimination law suits. In each case the plaintiff is suing a township under the "Mount Laurel Doctrine," which requires a locality to make all reasonable efforts to provide low-cost housing in proportion to its share of the region's low-income families.

5 Managing Financial Planning

Aronson, J. Richard, and Eli Schwartz, eds. *Management Policies in Local Government Finance.* 2d ed. Washington, D.C.: International City Management Association, 1981. Thorough coverage of revenues, budgeting, debt, intergovernmental finance, risk management, accounting, capital budgeting, and other aspects of local government finance. Chapters on revenues and revenue forecasting are especially useful.

Association of Bay Area Governments. *Development Fees in the San Francisco Bay Area: An Update.* Berkeley, Calif., 1982. A survey assessing development fees for new residential, commercial and light industrial construction. Four hypothetical structures are used to compare fees in various jurisdictions: a single-family home, a multifamily dwelling of seven units, a restaurant seating forty-eight people, and a print shop.

Bahl, Roy. *The Impact of Local Tax Policy on Urban Economic Development.* Washington, D.C.: Economic Development Administration, U.S. Department of Commerce, 1980. This report is practitioner oriented and deals with how local officials might adjust local taxes to stimulate job creation. Coverage includes (1) evaluating costs and benefits of proposed tax policy changes, (2) tax policy reforms to influence urban economic change, (3) existing literature on taxation and industrial location, and (4) a research agenda on use of tax policy to enhance city economies.

City of Baltimore, Maryland. Department of Planning and Department of Public Works. *A Summary Description of the Project Data*

Display System and the Project Scheduling and Tracking System. 1979. In order to control cost and time overruns, automated systems have been developed to monitor capital project schedules. By using cathode ray tubes (CRTs) the city is able to display project data four different ways and to perform eleven checks for delays. The "critical path" method of tracking projects is used to predict delays.

City of Baltimore, Maryland. Planning Commission. *Baltimore's Development Program*. 1981. Annual six-year capital improvement program.

City of Davis, California. *Preliminary Budget: 1982–83*. Recommends fiscal year 1982–83 operating budget.

City of Kansas City, Missouri. *Five-Year Financial Forecast: 1982–83 to 1986–87*. 1981. Predicts budget deficits based on econometric studies and on Congressional Budget Office figures on the national economy. Shows a need for further cost containment strategies.

City of Modesto, California. *Four Year Operating Revenue and Expenditure Forecast: 1981–82 to 1984–85*. 1981. Prepared for the city council and staff as a means of extending reaction time to financial trends. Forecasts population and inflation and projects financial condition by fund and department.

City of Walnut Creek, California. *Administrative Policy: City Four-Year Capital Improvement Program*. 1980. Forecasts equipment and personnel requirements, helps relate capital improvement planning to the city operating budget, and allows better coordination between capital improvement projects. Criteria for inclusion of projects within the plan are described.

Council for Northeast Economic Action. *How Banks Participate in Local Economic Development: Five Models*. U.S. Department of Housing and Urban Development, 1982. Summarizes how banks organize for local economic development and compares five models. The models vary according to the degree of initiative taken by higher bank executives and the level of government involved.

———. *Local Economic Development: Public Leveraging of Private Capital*. U.S. Department of Housing and Urban Development, 1980. This handbook provides an understanding of the local economic process and the need for public-private partner-

ships. Five case studies show the variety of ways public and private participants work together and how leveraging can be used.

Grindley, W. C., et al. *Forming Urban Partnerships*. Menlo Park, Calif.: SRI International, 1982. Explains how outside parties can foster public/private relationships for urban development through brokers who can encourage local leaders yet remain neutral, experts who have built these partnerships before, and documentation from similar projects.

Groves, Sanford M., and W. Maureen Godsey. *Evaluating Local Government Financial Condition*. Washington, D.C.: International City Management Association, 1980. Five handbooks: 1. *Evaluating Financial Condition*, by Sanford M. Groves. Defines financial condition factors used in financial trend monitoring system. 2. *Financial Trend Monitoring System*, by Sanford M. Groves. Detailed workbook with descriptions of financial indicators and how to use them. 3. *Financial Jeopardy!*, by W. Maureen Godsey. Summarizes hazardous financial practices, including short-term borrowing, internal borrowing, deferring current costs, drawing down reserves, ignoring full, long-term costs of employee fringe benefits, and ignoring full-life costs of capital assets. 4. *Financial Performance Goals*, by W. Maureen Godsey. How to set financial policies for prudent financial management. 5. *Tools for Making Financial Decisions*, by W. Maureen Godsey. Covers forecasting revenues, adjusting for inflation, discounting to present value, and other methods.

Hatry, Harry P. *Alternative Service Delivery Approaches Involving Increased Use of the Private Sector*. Washington, D.C.: Urban Institute, 1982. A report for the Greater Washington Research Center on contracting out, franchises, voucher systems, volunteerism, and other alternative local government service delivery approaches.

Hayes, Frederick O'R., et al. *Linkages: Improving Financial Management in Local Government*. Washington, D.C.: Urban Institute Press, 1982. Shows how to develop linkages between budgeting, accounting, performance management, and auditing for better financial management. Includes many examples and exhibits that draw on experience in cities.

International City Management Association. *Current Approaches to Financial Management: A Directory of Practices*. Washington, D.C.: Department of Housing and Urban Development, n.d. A collection of forty-four case studies on forecasting, evaluating financial condition, policy analysis, capital improvement programming, budgeting, and performance measurement. Among the studies' topics are the integrated comprehensive plan, the five-year forecast, and the capital improvement project tracking system.

Kellar, Elizabeth K., ed. *Managing with Less: A Book of Readings*, Washington, D.C.: International City Management Association, 1979. Strategies for coping with the cost/revenue crisis facing local government managers and planners: public services, trends, organization, tax revolts, and financial management.

Kohlwes, S. Wayne. "The Capital Improvements Program: An Implementation Technique for the Comprehensive Plan." Master's thesis, The Graduate School, Pennsylvania State University, 1982. Describes the interrelationships between comprehensive planning and the capital improvements programming process. Provides the theoretical basis for each and ten case studies.

Lewis, Charles R., IV, Stanley R. Hoffman, and Jay Bodutch. "The CRIS Model: A Cost/Revenue Impact System for Local Jurisdictions." Paper available from Diametrics, Hotel Claremont, Berkeley, California 94705. Describes computer model for analyzing current and future costs for a wide range of municipal services and revenue yields from property taxes, sales taxes, grants, and service charges. The model has been tested by Fairfield and several other Bay Area cities.

Manchester, Lydia, and Carl Valente. *Rethinking Local Services: Examining Alternative Delivery Approaches*. Washington, D.C.: International City Management Association, 1984. A comprehensive catalog focusing on alternative systems for delivering services to the public.

Matzer, John, Jr., ed. *Capital Financing Strategies for Local Governments*. Washington, D.C.: International City Management Association, 1983. Nineteen articles on municipal borrowing, innovative financing techniques, leasing, industrial revenue bonds, and marketing bonds. Many of the articles show how cities have met capital needs in unusual and creative ways.

Moak, Lennox L. *Municipal Bonds: Planning, Sale, and Administration*. Chicago: Municipal Finance Officers Association, 1982. Comprehensive reference covering policy questions, how to issue bonds, types of local government securities, true interest costs, and debt management. Written by and for public administrators.

Musgrave, John C. "Government Owned Fixed Capital in the United States, 1925–79." *Survey of Current Business* 60 (March 1980), 33–43. Discusses the gross and net values of federal, state, and local government fixed capital and analyzes reasons for historical fluctuations in values over those years.

Regional Municipality of Peel, Brampton, Ontario. *Financial and Economic Review, 1981*. Sixth in a series of annual reports on the local economy. Includes text and data on finance, economic indicators, major construction projects, commercial and industrial employers, capital budgets and forecasts, and current and projected long-term debt.

Shulman, Martha A. *Alternative Approaches for Delivering Public Services*. Urban Data Service Report, vol. 14, no. 10. Washington D.C.: International City Management Association, 1982. Analyzes range of services local governments provide, methods of provision, and frequency of alternatives such as contracting, volunteers, self-help, and tax incentives.

Snyder, James C. *Fiscal Management and Planning in Local Government*. Lexington, Mass.: D.C. Heath and Company, 1977. An introductory fiscal management text for planners and managers.

Ukeles, Jacob B. *Doing More with Less: Turning Public Management Around*. New York: AMACOM, 1982. Demonstrates for public officials and administrators that state and local governments can become more productive by applying planning concepts from the private sector.

Wacht, Richard F. *A New Approach to Capital Budgeting for City and County Governments*. Research Monograph No. 87, College of Business Administration. Atlanta: Georgia State University, 1980. Reviews need for a more formal approach to capital expenditure analysis, consequences of public investment, and their effect on a locality's ability to grow. Includes a mathematical model that will test proposed projects for financial viability.

6 Working with Councils, Boards, and Commissions

Anderson, Wayne F. et al. "Relating to the Community." In *The Effective Local Govern-*

ment Manager. Washington, D.C.: International City Management Association, 1983. How the manager can assess his or her community relations style, evaluate community needs and resources, and foster effective relations with community groups.

Banovetz, James M., ed. *Small Cities and Counties: A Guide to Managing Services*. Washington, D.C.: International City Management Association, 1984. For local government managers, assistants, and department heads. Covers overall management, intergovernmental relations, and major functions of police and fire services, planning, economic development, finance, public works, etc.

Bradshaw, Chris. "Beyond Public Participation: A Networking Approach to Planning." Planning Department. Regional Municipality of Ottawa-Carleton. Background paper prepared for annual conference of the Canadian Institute of Planners, Hull, Quebec, 22 June 1982. Decribes how citizen participation in the planning process was changed from formal meetings to one-to-one "networking." This enabled the city to avoid high costs and adversarial relationships with the public.

Bromage, Arthur W. *Urban Policy Making: The Council-Manager Partnership*. Chicago: Public Administration Service, 1970. Distributed by the International City Management Association. Clear and concise discussion of the teamwork required for effective work with city councils and county boards.

Burke, Edmund M. *A Participatory Approach to Urban Planning*. New York: Human Sciences Press, 1979. This book notes three specific changes which have influenced modern planning practices: multiple planning centers, citizen participation, and changed decision environments. The book is divided into two parts: (1) an explanation of planning as a social and political process, and (2) an application of the social and political processes of planning to a strategy of community planning.

Corey, Canapary & Galanis. "Walnut Creek Citizens Survey: Wave III, October 21–November 23, 1981." Summary prepared for City of Walnut Creek, California, Office of City Manager, 7 December 1981. Reports citizen attitudes toward using city services, reducing services, and charging higher fees to keep them. Compares service usage with previous years by area, age, and presence of children. Describes budget-cutting preferences by specific service.

Crosby, Philip B. *The Art of Getting Your Own Sweet Way*. New York: McGraw-Hill, 1972. Presents laws of behavior that can be applied to any organization. A manager can cope by preparing strategies in advance to achieve goals.

Cullinan, Terrence. *In Good Company: Corporate Community Action and How to Do It in Your Community*. Menlo Park, Calif.: SRI International, 1982. Concise report on how businesses and local governments can work together for mutually beneficial community improvement. SRI has many other reports available on public-private partnerships, small business, and social services.

Glendening, Parris N., and Mavis Mann Reeves. *Pragmatic Federalism: An Intergovernmental View of American Government*. Pacific Palisades, Calif.: Palisades Publishers, 1977. Relations between levels of government are the by-product of governmental programs pragmatically seeking support at first one, then another level as they are implemented. Intergovernmental relations are forged by people voting, administering, pressuring, and negotiating.

Gottdiener, Mark. *Planned Sprawl: Private and Public Interests in Suburbia*. Sage Library of Social Research, vol. 38. Beverly Hills: Sage Publications, 1977. Shows the importance of planners being leaders who are sensitive to the political tensions in their communities.

Hentzell, S. W., et al. *Exploring Urban Action Options for Local Firms*. Menlo Park, Calif.: SRI International, 1982. Social responsibilities of company managers and local firms in mitigating factors that threaten profits. Discusses problems of mutual public-private interest such as school improvement, modernization of public services, housing, community development, health, and recreation.

Institute for Participatory Planning. *Citizen Participation Handbook for Public Officials and Other Professionals Serving the Public*. 3d ed. Laramie, Wyo., 1978. Training handbook covering program design, citizen participation techniques, and program administration. Includes case studies.

Jacobs, Allan B. *Making City Planning Work*. Chicago: American Society of Planning Officials, 1978. Case studies of six San Francisco city planning department topics with a personal discussion of the political, administrative, and professional aspects of being a city planner.

Kellar, Elizabeth K. "Communicating with Elected Officials." In *Effective Communication: Getting the Message Across*, edited by David S. Arnold, Christine S. Becker, and Elizabeth K. Kellar. Washington, D.C.: International City Management Association, 1983. Communication, information flow, and the leadership team vis-à-vis the local government body.

Lutzin, Sidney G., ed. *Managing Municipal Leisure Services*. Washington, D.C.: International City Management Association, 1980. A comprehensive look at leisure services. Emphasis is on management in the 1980s, an era when strong leadership is required to meet the challenge of increased demand for leisure services and decreased support from tax sources. This revised edition contains new chapters on community setting, recent service trends, working with agency boards and volunteers, serving the handicapped and elderly, and comprehensive planning.

Meehan, Edward T. *The Meehan Plan for Mansfield*. Mansfield, Ohio, 1979. This is the four-point plan of a mayoral candidate to improve life in Mansfield: it covers industrial growth, services, finances, and the quality of community life.

Oner, Caner. "Factors Influencing the Effectiveness of Planning in Central Cities." Paper presented at the annual meeting of the Urban Affairs Association, Flint, Michigan, March 1983. Survey of city planners and academics to find what issues are most important in their decision making. Each of seven factors are ranked against each other to find a quantifiable consensus.

Scheffler, Peter Knox. "The Conners Island Experience: A Case Study of Collaborative Resolution of Environmental Conflict." Master's thesis, University of Tennessee, Knoxville, 1982. Describes the use of a nine-step joint problem-solving process to resolve an environmental dispute. Nine parties engaged in conflict arbitration by forming a local citizen planning team led by a process guide hired by the Tennessee Valley Authority.

Solnit, Albert. *The Job of the Planning Commissioner*. 3d ed. Belmont, Calif.: Wadsworth Publishing Company, 1982. Procedural and substantive guide for commissioners and staff on what a good plan includes, how to conduct meetings and hearings, standards of fairness, development reviews, and other responsibilities.

Webb, Kenneth, and Harry P. Hatry. *Obtaining Citizen Feedback: The Application of Citizen Surveys to Local Governments*. Washington, D.C.: Urban Institute, 1973. Concise and easy-to-use guide.

Wright, Deil S. *Understanding Intergovernmental Relations*. 2d ed. Monterey, Calif.: Brooks/Cole, 1982. Basic text on the intertwined politics and management of intergovernmental relations. Concentrates on how the shared decision-making process really works.

7 Personnel Management

Becker, Christine. *So Now You're a Trainer: A Practical Guide for Practical Trainers*. Washington, D.C.: International City Management Association, 1979. Handbook for someone who is not a training specialist but whose job demands communication and leadership skills to "help others learn."

Godsey, W. Maureen. *Employee Involvement: A Local Government Approach to Quality Circles*. Training package : handbook and user's guide. Washington, D.C.: International City Management Association, 1982. Examines the uses of quality circles in local government.

————. *Productivity Improvement in Local Governments*. Urban Data Service Report, vol. 14, no. 10. Washington, D.C.: International City Management Association, 1982. Survey of methods local governments use to increase productivity, including new technology.

Hays, Steven W., and Richard C. Kearney, eds. *Public Personnel Administration: Problems and Prospects*. Englewood Cliffs, N.J.: Prentice-Hall, 1983. An up-to-date reader covering technical and theoretical issues. The book covers four main areas: environment of public personnel administration, techniques, policies and issues, and merit system reform and the future.

Hersey, Paul, and Kenneth H. Blanchard. *Management of Organizational Behavior: Utilizing Human Resources*. 4th ed. Englewood Cliffs, N.J.: Prentice-Hall, 1982. Discusses behavioral approach to management theory; provides individual and group perspectives on management; and identifies leadership and employee motivation techniques.

Kirkpatrick, Donald L. *How to Improve Performance through Appraisal and Coaching*. New York: AMACOM, 1982. Logical steps for the manager to improve productivity through effective appraisal and coaching of employees. Includes case studies.

Klingner, Donald E. *Public Personnel Management.* Englewood Cliffs, N.J.: Prentice-Hall, 1980. A basic personnel text, written from an MBO perspective, with balanced orientation to local, state, and national governments.

Matzer, John, Jr., ed. *Creative Personnel Practices: New Ideas for Local Government.* Washington, D.C.: International City Management Association, 1984. Readings to help managers evaluate personnel activities, create a sound performance appraisal system, improve employee motivation through innovative incentives, and respond to emerging issues.

Patton, Bobby R., and Kim Griffin. *Decision-Making in Group Interaction.* New York: Harper & Row, 1978. A good overview of group dynamics, group processes, group decision making, and group communications.

8 Information Management

City of Louisville, Kentucky, and Jefferson County, Kentucky. Louisville and Jefferson County Planning Commission. *Work Program and Budget.* Louisville, Kentucky, 1982. Budget proposal, which includes a work measure study for each activity, a description of functions and methods, and ongoing and proposed projects.

Commonwealth of Massachusetts, Executive Office of Communities and Development. *Municipal Electronic Data Processing: A Primer for Local Government Officials.* Boston, 1980. A resource guide and checklist for officials considering buying or contracting for data processing equipment and services. Includes planning applications.

Davis, Barbara, and Harold Wolman. *Local Economic Development Data Inventory.* Washington, D.C.: Urban Institute, 1981. Identifies key economic concepts and their sources of data. Practical aspects of local economic development planning are identified.

Fairfax County, Virginia. Office of Research and Statistics. *Computer Systems Plan: FY 1983–FY 1987.* 1982. Describes policy of upgrading equipment and programs that are demonstrably cost-justified. Departments estimated staff hours and money that would be saved through their proposed upgrade.

Hatry, Harry P., et al. *How Effective Are Your Community Services? Procedures for Monitoring the Effectiveness of Municipal Serv-*

ices. Washington, D.C.: Urban Institute and International City Management Association, 1977. Handbook on effectiveness measures for solid waste, recreation, crime control, and six other local government services; survey and rating procedures; and appendices with survey questionnaires for various services.

Hoover, Paul. *Microcomputers: Tools for Local Government.* Management Information Service Report, vol. 14, no. 10. Washington, D.C.: International City Management Association, 1982. Case study of successful applications in two cities. Discusses integration with existing data processing system, possible pitfalls, and proven advantages.

Kraemer, Kenneth L., and John Leslie King, eds. *Computers and Local Government.* Vol. 1, *A Manager's Guide.* Vol. 2, *A Review of the Research.* New York: Praeger, 1977–78. Definitive papers that summarize extensive research financed by the National Science Foundation. Coverage includes procurement; planning and operations; systems development; impact of computers on personnel policy, organizational structure, jobs, and job tasks; data base management; geoprocessing; and privacy and disclosure.

———. *Computers in Local Government: Urban and Regional Planning.* Pennsauken, N.J.: Auerbach, 1980. Loose-leaf publication covering applications, systems management, and hardware and software selection and evaluation. Includes case studies and applications software directory.

Lexington–Fayette Urban County Government. Division of Planning. Department of Community Development. *Division of Planning FY 82 Work Program.* Lexington, Ky., 1981. States program objectives in relation to specific activities and schedules.

McLaren, Robert I. *Organizational Dilemmas.* New York: John Wiley & Sons, 1982. Every organization must decide how to divide its resources among conflicting goals. This book discusses the various types of dilemmas a decision maker may face in such activities as planning, budgeting, and controlling.

Mundt, Barry M., Raymond T. Olsen, and Harold I. Steinberg. *Managing Public Resources.* New York: Peat Marwick International, 1982. The current demand for increased local government services in the midst of diminishing resources has made public resource management more important. The authors outline a process of needs assessment, goal identification, program development and evaluation, and productivity improvement. They discuss the various techniques that local governments use, such as performance budgeting, interlocal agreements, and contracting with the private sector.

Schmitt, Rolf R., and Harlan J. Smolin, eds. *Practical Applications of Computers in Government: Papers from the Annual Conference of the Urban and Regional Information Systems Association, August 22–25, 1982.* Washington, D.C.: International Science and Technology Institute for the Urban and Regional Information Systems Association, 1982. This association seeks to enhance communication between users and providers of information for public decision making. Papers were presented on the following themes: (1) planning and policy analysis, (2) technology, (3) geoprocessing and graphics, (4) land records systems, (5) data processing, (6) improving public works through computers, and (7) natural resources.

Stockman, Robert. "Microcomputers Stretch the Limits of Planning." *Government Data Systems* 11 (November/December 1982): 28–30. Discusses the potential of the microcomputer to meet the information needs of local planners. Promising new applications are transportation planning and fiscal impact analysis.

9 Communication Management

Aleshire, Fran, and Frank Aleshire. *Spreading the Word in Public Places.* Tempe, Ariz.: Center for Public Affairs, Arizona State University, 1981. Useful guide for government employees who are writing memos and reports, making speeches, and designing simple reports and manuals.

Armstrong, Ann. *Public Relations for Local Government.* Management Information Service Report, vol. 13, no. 10. Washington, D.C.: International City Management Association, 1981. Introduction to media relations, reports, photography, community relations, and other aspects of public relations. Especially useful for small communities.

Arnold, David S., Christine S. Becker, and Elizabeth K. Kellar, eds. *Effective Communication: Getting the Message Across.* Washington, D.C.: International City Management Association, 1983. Covers the communication responsibilities of local government managers, supervisors and employees. Discusses community relations, communication with elected officials, publicity, the media, expository writing, publications development

and production, interpersonal communication, and communication and management.

Cutlip, Scott M., and Allen H. Center. *Effective Public Relations.* 5th ed. Englewood Cliffs, N.J.: Prentice-Hall, 1978. A comprehensive, highly useful bible for people who work in public relations or who must deal with the media. Includes information on legal aspects of public relations.

Knight, Fred S., Harold E. Horn, and Nancy J. Jesuale, eds. *Telecommunications for Local Government.* Washington, D.C.: International City Management Association, 1982. Describes how cable systems, automated office equipment, and new telephone systems are changing the ways local governments are using information. Includes case studies and examples.

Mercer, James L., Susan W. Woolston, and William V. Donaldson. *Managing Urban Government Services: Strategies, Tools, and Techniques for the Eighties.* New York: AMACOM, 1981. A collection of pragmatic solutions for overcoming the continuing cost/revenue squeeze facing local governments. Alternative sources of revenue, enhanced sharing of ideas, and cost-cutting systems are discussed.

Morgan, David R., John P. Pelissero, and Robert E. England. "Public Management Forum: Urban Planning: Using a Delphi as a Decision-Making Aid." *Public Administration Review* 39 (July/August 1979): 380–84. Use of the Delphi method for eliciting citizen participation in the goal-setting stage of preparing the Norman, Oklahoma, comprehensive plan. Its advantages and disadvantages are discussed.

10 Values and Ethics

American Institute of Certified Planners. Ethics Committee. *Introduction to Ethics Awareness.* AICP Publication Series, no. 4. Washington, D.C., 1983. Offers definitions and examples of ethical and unethical behavior and differentiates between technical planners and those more politically oriented.

Cherniss, Cary. *Staff Burnout: Job Stress in the Human Services.* Sage Studies in Community Mental Health, vol. 2. Beverly Hills, Calif.: Sage Publications, 1980. Burnout is the defensive withdrawal from a situation in which a worker is regularly subjected to emotional stress. Looks at the factors of personality, culture, and work environment. Four guidelines for supervisor intervention are suggested: change of personal life, change of job expectations, increased worker resources, and coping methods.

Commonwealth of Virginia. General Assembly. Senate. *S.B. No. 23: Comprehensive Conflict of Interest Act.* 20 December 1982. This bill would establish standards to apply to conflicts of interest of state and local employees. Covers bribery, personal interests in public contracts and purchasing, and mandatory personal financial disclosure by high officials.

Derr, C. Brooklyn, ed. *Work, Family, and the Career.* New York: Praeger, 1980. A pioneering collection of articles by scholars and management consultants on the interrelationship between work and personal life.

Howe, Elizabeth, and Jerome Kaufman. "The Ethics of Contemporary American Planners." *Journal of the American Planning Association* 45 (July 1979): 243–55. A survey of planners about ethical behavior. While there was broad agreement that bribery and threats are wrong, there was lack of agreement on the use of political tactics.

———. "The Values of Contemporary American Planners." *Journal of the American Planning Association* 47 (July 1981): 266–78. Attitudes toward five issues were recorded: the environment, mass transit, development and developers, minority and low-income groups, and citizen participation. Responses differed according to role identification and politics.

Marcuse, Peter. "Professional Ethics and Beyond: Values in Planning." *Journal of the American Institute of Planners* 42 (July 1976): 264–73. Asserts that professional planners must go beyond professional ethics to determine their conduct. Presents five cases in which professional ethics conflict with planners' obligations to the public they serve. Identifies attributes of public and professional ethics and discusses each, showing sources and means of enforcement.

Miller, Donald. *Plans and Publics: Assessing Distribution Effects.* Planning memorandum. Delft, Netherlands: Institute of City and Regional Planning, Technical University of Delft. Describes a formula called "multidimensional assessment" for assessing the equity of planning decisions and determining the extent to which various population groups receive equal satisfaction from public services.

Schwarz, Christine. *Time Management.* Management Information Service Reports, vol. 8, no. 9. Washington, D.C.: International City Management Association, 1976. A short, well-organized, and pragmatic essay on what managers can do about the time problem.

Zimmerman, Joseph F. "A Code of Ethics in Town Government." Paper presented at the annual meeting of the Association of Towns of the State of New York, New York City, 16 February 1976. Discusses the state law requiring local governments to have a code of ethics. Identifies realistic expectations of citizens for the conduct of public business.

Acknowledgments

The author of *Management of Local Planning*, David C. Slater, is Vice President of Hammer, Siler, George Associates, consultants in planning and development economics. He has been with HSG since 1972 and has worked with city, county, regional, and state planning agencies in more than one hundred jurisdictions in the United States and Canada. His extensive experience in planning includes service with the staff of the American Institute of Planners, the Metropolitan Washington Council of Governments, the Atlanta Regional Commission, and the Knoxville–Knox County Metropolitan Planning Commission. Mr. Slater holds a bachelor's degree in urban planning from Michigan State University and a master's in regional planning from the University of North Carolina at Chapel Hill. He has been a teacher and lecturer at the University of Virginia, American University, and several other schools.

In an undertaking of this scope, the support, advice, and information shared by many people were invaluable. The key person was David S. Arnold, who has had a hand in all of the "Green Books" published by the International City Management Association since 1959. His conceptual review, advice, and editor's hand were important determinants in shaping this book.

Many planners, managers, teachers, and consultants who helped at several stages in development of the book should be recognized. These persons are shown below with their affiliations at the time of their involvement.

An advisory committee was established by ICMA to respond to the draft outline of the book and to make suggestions regarding coverage. The committee members, with their affiliations at the time, were Wilbur K. Avera, City Manager, Thomaston, Georgia; William A. Bassett, City Manager, Mankato, Minnesota; Kathleen Jenks, Town Manager, Windham, Maine; Donald L. Kinney, Planning Director, Arvada, Colorado; John S. Lamb, Executive Director, Municipal Research and Service Center of Washington, Seattle, Washington; Jerry S. McGuire, Executive Director, Panhandle Regional Planning Commission, Amarillo, Texas; Barton R. Meays, Executive Director, Southern California Association of Governments, Los Angeles, California; Thomas J. Mikulecky, City Manager, Bartlesville, Oklahoma; Kenneth C. Needham, Town Manager, Oakville, Ontario; J. Louis Yates, Assistant City Manager for Planning and Budgeting, Raleigh, North Carolina; Dale B. Thoma, Director, Department of Community Development, Division of Planning, Lexington–Fayette Urban County Government, Lexington, Kentucky; and Wylie L. Williams, Jr., City Manager, Inkster, Michigan.

Especially important to the final development of content were the managers, planners, and educators who shared their diverse experiences with the author in interviews. These persons, listed alphabetically with their affiliations at the time, are as follows: Franklin D. Aleshire, City Manager, Carlsbad, California; Andrea W. Beatty, City Manager, Bellevue, Washington; Dale F. Bertsch, Associate Professor, Department of City and Regional Planning, Ohio State University, Columbus, Ohio; Terrell Blodgett, Lyndon Baines Johnson School of Public Affairs, University of Texas, Austin, Texas; Daniel Boggan, Jr., City Manager, Berkeley, California; Del D. Borgsdorf, City Administrator, Southfield, Michigan; James D. Braman, Consultant, Bellevue, Washington; Melville C. Branch, Department of Urban and Regional Planning, University of Southern California, Los Angeles, California; Karl Brendle, Planning Director, Laurel, Maryland; Gilbert H. Castle, III, Vice President, Comarc Systems, San Francisco, California; James A. Clapp, Chairman, School of Public Administration and Urban Studies, San Diego State University, San Diego, California; Robert W. Collier, Deputy Municipal Manager, West Vancouver, British Columbia; John B. Collins, Deputy Mayor, Seattle, Washington; Richard F. Counts, Planning Director, Phoenix, Arizona; John B. Czarnecki, Council Member, East Lansing, Michigan; James M. Davis, Director of Planning, Rockville, Maryland; John E. Dever, City Manager, Long

Beach, California; Malcolm C. Drummond, Senior Vice President, Harland Bartholomew & Associates, St. Louis, Missouri; Tim Dugan, Planning Director, Garrett County (Oakland), Maryland.

Thomas G. Dunne, City Manager, Walnut Creek, California; Bernard W. Dworski, Attorney, Washington, D.C.; John H. Eckenroad, III, Village Manager, Northbrook, Illinois; Thomas W. Fletcher, Consultant, SRI International, Menlo Park, California; Frank B. Friedman, Vice President, Occidental Petroleum Corporation, Los Angeles, California; Frank Gerred, Director, Department of Planning and Community Development, St. Mary's County, Maryland; Frank Gerstenecker, City Manager, Troy, Michigan; Michael D. Gleason, City Manager, Eugene, Oregon; Carl Goldschmidt, Director, School of Urban Planning and Landscape Architecture, Michigan State University, East Lansing, Michigan; Charles M. Graves, Director, Office of Planning, Urban Mass Transportation Administration, U.S. Department of Transportation, Washington, D.C.; A. J. "Flash" Gray, Consultant, Knoxville, Tennessee; Randy H. Hamilton, Dean, Graduate School of Public Administration, Golden Gate University, San Francisco, California; Philip Hammer, Consultant, Palm Harbor, Florida; Irving Hand, Director, Institute of State and Regional Affairs, and Chairman, Urban and Regional Planning Program, Pennsylvania State University, Harrisburg, Pennsylvania; David K. Hartley, Consultant, Washington, D.C.; Donald B. Hayman, Institute of Government, University of North Carolina at Chapel Hill; Cole Hendrix, City Manager, Charlottesville, Virginia; Charles T. Henry, CTH Associates, Eugene, Oregon; John V. Highfill, Director of Human Services Planning, Mecklenburg County (Charlotte), North Carolina; Henry C. Hightower, Professor, University of British Columbia, Vancouver, British Columbia.

Kenneth Howard, Executive Director, U.S. Advisory Commission on Intergovernmental Relations, Washington, D.C.; Frederick A. Howell, Community Development Director, Davis, California; Johnathan B. Howes, Director, Center for Urban and Regional Studies, University of North Carolina at Chapel Hill; Satyendra Singh Huja, Director, Department of Community Development, Charlottesville, Virginia; Kurt J. Jenne, Institute of Government, University of North Carolina at Chapel Hill; Michael Jennings, Planning Director, Chapel Hill, North Carolina; Mark E. Keane, Executive Director, International City Management Association, Washington, D.C.; Don L. Kinney, Director of Planning, Arvada, Colorado; Kenneth A. Knight, Consultant,

Brawley, California; James M. Kunde, Director, Urban Affairs Program, Charles F. Kettering Foundation, Dayton, Ohio; Bruce C. Laing, Council Member, King County (Seattle), Washington; Garth Lipsky, City Manager, Modesto, California; Sonna M. Lowenthal, Assistant Town Manager for Development, Chapel Hill, North Carolina; William Lucy, Head, Department of Urban and Environmental Planning, Charlottesville, Virginia; Ron McConnell, Consultant, Mercer Island, Washington; Dave A. McRill, Director, Department of Planning and Community Development, Genessee County, Michigan; Lawrence P. Malone, Director of Research, Council of State Community Affairs Agencies, Washington, D.C.; David Mars, Professor of Public Administration, University of Southern California, Los Angeles, California; Edward T. Meehan, Mayor, Mansfield, Ohio; Thomas J. Mikulecky, City Manager, Bartlesville, Oklahoma.

Donald H. Miller, Consultant, Seattle, Washington; Gary J. Miller, Assistant Professor, Political Science, Michigan State University, East Lansing, Michigan; Gretchen Miller, Council Member, Eugene, Oregon; Chester A. Newland, Professor of Government and Politics, George Mason University, Fairfax, Virginia; William S. Nichols, Director, Department of Planning and Community Development, Modesto, California; Robert S. Noe, Jr., County Executive, Prince William County (Manassas), Virginia; Emerson B. Ohl, Executive Director, Economic Development Corporation and Downtown Development Authority, Lansing, Michigan; Raymond T. Olsen, Developer, Reston, Virginia; Art O'Neal, Planning Director, Thurston Regional Planning Council, Olympia, Washington; Steven Orlick, Chairman, School of Environmental Studies in Planning, Sonoma State University, Rohnert Park, California; Robert J. Paternoster, Planning Director, Long Beach, California; Robert L. Plavnick, Consultant, Arlington, Virginia; M. John Porter, Planning Director, Eugene, Oregon; Bradford L. Price, Planning Director, East Lansing, Michigan; Howard L. Reese, City Manager, Davis, California; Roscoe E. Reeve, Land Records Manager, Orange County (Hillsborough), North Carolina; Larry Reich, Director, Department of Planning, Baltimore, Maryland; David A. Ripple, Assistant Planning Director, Louisville and Jefferson County Planning Commission, Louisville, Kentucky; Orlando A. Riutort, Planning Director, James City County, Virginia; John C. Robison, City Administrator, Fredericton, New Brunswick.

T. Duncan Rose, III, County Manager, Seminole County, Sanford, Florida; Dean Runyan,

Consultant, Richard L. Ragatz Associates, Eugene, Oregon; Peter K. Scheffler, Office of Economic and Community Development, Tennessee Valley Authority, Knoxville, Tennessee; Lee A. Schoenecker, Community Impact Coordinator, U.S. Air Force, Arlington, Virginia; James M. Selvaggi, Deputy Director, Office of Program Policy Development, Community Planning and Development, U.S. Department of Housing and Urban Development, Washington, D.C.; John W. Shore, III, Assistant Manager for Operations, Guilford County (Greensboro), North Carolina; George M. Siler, Executive Vice President, The 1982 World's Fair, Knoxville, Tennessee; John M. Simmons, U.S. Department of Housing and Urban Development, Washington, D.C.; Walter Slipe, City Manager, Sacramento, California; Frank S. So, Deputy Executive Director, American Planning Association, Chicago, Illinois; Albert S. Solnit, Consultant, Portland, Oregon; James R. Spackman, Deputy Planning Director, Lansing, Michigan; James A. Spencer, Professor, Graduate School of Planning, University of Tennessee, Knoxville, Tennessee; Raymond E. Straffon, Jr., Planning Director, Port Huron, Michigan; Kenneth E. Sulzer, Deputy Executive Director, San Diego Association of Governments, San Diego, California; Robert B. Teska, Consultant, Evanston, Illinois; Kyle C. Testerman, Mayor, Knoxville, Tennessee; Dale B. Thoma, Director, Department of Community Development, Division of Planning, Lexington–Fayette Urban County Government, Lexington, Kentucky; Revan A. F. Tranter, Executive Director, Association of Bay Area Governments, Berkeley, California; Martin Wachs, Head, Urban Planning Program, University of California at Los Angeles.

Charles W. Washington, Associate Professor, School of Government and Business Administration, George Washington University, Washington, D.C.; Theodore J. Wessel, Director, Office of Comprehensive Planning, Fairfax County (Fairfax), Virginia; Sharon Wilbert, Director, Human Resources Cabinet, Louisville, Kentucky; James E. Williams, Executive Director, Sacramento Area Council of Governments, Sacramento, California; B. Gayle Wilson, City Manager, Fairfield, California; Frank P. Wise, City Manager, East Cleveland, Ohio; Edward A. Wyatt, City Manager, Fairfax, Virginia; Sally N. Yankee, Community Development Cabinet, Louisville, Kentucky; April L. Young, Executive Director, Fairfax County Economic Development Authority, Vienna, Virginia; and Paul C. Zucker, Consultant, San Diego, California.

The following persons reviewed the manuscript at various stages: Dale F. Bertsch, Professor, Department of City and Regional Planning, Ohio State University, Columbus, Ohio; William I. Goodman, Professor, Department of Urban and Regional Planning, University of Illinois at Urbana–Champaign, Urbana, Illinois; Kathleen Jenks, Town Manager, Windham, Maine; Thomas J. Mikulecky, City Manager, Bartlesville, Oklahoma; and Dale B. Thoma, Director, Department of Community Development, Division of Planning, Lexington–Fayette Urban County Government, Lexington, Kentucky.

Management of Local Planning is a visually oriented book with 64 figures and 32 sidebars. Herbert Slobin worked closely with David S. Arnold and David C. Slater in developing ideas for the figures and sidebars, and Mr. Slobin prepared many of the figures in final form. David S. Arnold wrote the figure captions.

Harriett E. Page keyboarded the manuscript from initial draft to final diskettes; Venka V. Macintyre handled final editing of the manuscript; and Diana Regenthal prepared the index.

Figure
credits

Chapter 1 Figure 1–1: Photo courtesy of the Public Information Office, City of Scottsdale, Arizona; Figure 1–2: Early office (top), National Archives, neg. no. 121–BA, 303–C; office in 1984 (bottom) courtesy of NBI, Inc.

Chapter 2 Figure 2–1: Wholesale market (top), National Archives, neg. no. 83–G, Box 12, 546; Woodfield Mall (bottom) from "Case Studies" in *Shopping Center Development Handbook* (Washington, D.C.: ULI—Urban Land Institute, 1977), 240; Figure 2–2: Photo on left-hand page courtesy of the Frances Loeb Library, Graduate School of Design, Harvard University; facsimile on right-hand page courtesy of the Maxwell Library, Maxwell School of Citizenship and Public Affairs, Syracuse University; Figure 2–3: Photostats selected from the files of Harland Bartholomew & Associates, Inc., by Malcolm C. Drummond, Senior Vice President, and HBA staff; Figure 2–4: Richard Hedman and Fred Bair, Jr., *And on the Eighth Day. . . .*, 2d ed. (Chicago: American Society of Planning Officials, © 1967); Sidney G. Lutzin, ed. *Managing Municipal Leisure Services* (Washington, D.C.: International City Management Association, 1979), 157.

Chapter 3 Figure 3–3: Charles O. Jones and Dieter Matthes, "Policy Formation," in *Encyclopedia of Social Studies*, ed. Stuart S. Nagel (New York: Marcel Dekker, 1983), 118.

Chapter 4 Figure 4–1: Laurence Conway Gerckens, "Historical Development of American City Planning," in *The Practice of Local Government Planning*, ed. Frank S. So et al. (Washington, D.C.: International City Management Association, 1979), 24–25; Figures 4–2 and 4–6: Drawn by Herbert Slobin; Figure 4–5: Adapted from Arlington County (Virginia) Planning Division, *Development Process: A General Description* (1978).

Chapter 5 Figure 5–1: James C. Snyder, *Fiscal Management and Planning for Local Government* (Lexington, Mass.: Lexington Books, 1977), 77–78; Figures 5–2, 5–7, 5–8, and 5–9: Lewis Friedman, "Budgeting," in

Management Policies in Local Government Finance, 2d ed., ed. J. Richard Aronson and Eli Schwartz (Washington, D.C.: International City Management Association, 1981), 97, 106, 108, and 110–11; Figure 5–4: Drawn by Herbert Slobin; Figure 5–6: Fairfax County, Virginia, Budget Office, *Fiscal Year 1984 Budget, Fairfax County, Virginia* (1983); Figure 5–11: Sanford M. Groves and W. Maureen Godsey, *Evaluating Financial Condition*, handbook 1 of *Evaluating Local Government Financial Condition* (Washington, D.C.: International City Management Association, 1980), 8; Figures 5–12, 5–13, and 5–14: City of Modesto, California, *Four Year Operating Budget: Revenue and Expenditure Forecast, 1981–82 to 1984–85* (1981), 3, 10, and 21; Figure 5–15: City of Modesto, California, *Capital Improvement Program, 1982–83 to 1985–86* (1982), B-1; Figure 5–16: City of Kansas City, Missouri, Office of the City Manager, *Five-Year Financial Forecast, 1982–83 to 1986–87* (1981), 9–10.

Chapter 6 Figure 6–1: From William Hamilton, *Money Should Be Fun*. Copyright © 1980 by William Hamilton. Reprinted by permission of Houghton Mifflin Company; Figures 6–2 and 6–3: Wayne F. Anderson et al., *The Effective Local Government Manager* (Washington, D.C.: International City Management Association, 1983), 17 and 22; Figure 6–5: Ronald M. Caines, "Advocacy for the Seventies Will Aim at Public Policies," *AIP Newsletter* (January 1970), 10. Copyright © 1970 by the American Institute of Planners (now the American Planning Association).

Chapter 7 Figure 7–1: Wayne F. Anderson et al., *The Effective Local Government Manager* (Washington, D.C.: International City Management Association, 1983), 110; Figure 7–2: *Washington Post*, 15 May 1983, H33; Figures 7–5 and 7–6: Drawn by Herbert Slobin.

Chapter 8 Figures 8–1, 8–5, and 8–6: Drawn by Herbert Slobin; Figure 8–7: Fairfax County, Virginia, Office of Research and Statistics, *Computer Systems Plan, FY 1983–FY 1987* (1982), 62.

Index

Municipal Management Series

**Management of
Local Planning**

Text type
Times Roman, Helvetica

Composition
EPS Group Inc.
Baltimore, Maryland

Printing and binding
Kingsport Press
Kingsport, Tennessee

Design
Herbert Slobin

Cover illustration, softbound edition
David S. Arnold